Lecture Notes in Computer Science   14696

Founding Editors

Gerhard Goos
Juris Hartmanis

The series Lecture Notes in Computer Science (LNCS), including its subseries Lecture Notes in Artificial Intelligence (LNAI) and Lecture Notes in Bioinformatics (LNBI), has established itself as a medium for the publication of new developments in computer science and information technology research, teaching, and education.

LNCS enjoys close cooperation with the computer science R & D community, the series counts many renowned academics among its volume editors and paper authors, and collaborates with prestigious societies. Its mission is to serve this international community by providing an invaluable service, mainly focused on the publication of conference and workshop proceedings and postproceedings. LNCS commenced publication in 1973.

Margherita Antona · Constantine Stephanidis
Editors

Universal Access in Human-Computer Interaction

18th International Conference, UAHCI 2024
Held as Part of the 26th HCI International Conference, HCII 2024
Washington, DC, USA, June 29 – July 4, 2024
Proceedings, Part I

 Springer

Editors
Margherita Antona
Foundation for Research and Technology - Hellas (FORTH)
Heraklion, Crete, Greece

Constantine Stephanidis
University of Crete, and Foundation for Research and Technology - Hellas (FORTH)
Heraklion, Crete, Greece

ISSN 0302-9743 ISSN 1611-3349 (electronic)
Lecture Notes in Computer Science
ISBN 978-3-031-60874-2 ISBN 978-3-031-60875-9 (eBook)
https://doi.org/10.1007/978-3-031-60875-9

This Springer imprint is published by the registered company Springer Nature Switzerland AG
The registered company address is: Gewerbestrasse 11, 6330 Cham, Switzerland

If disposing of this product, please recycle the paper.

Foreword

This year we celebrate 40 years since the establishment of the HCI International (HCII) Conference, which has been a hub for presenting groundbreaking research and novel ideas and collaboration for people from all over the world.

The HCII conference was founded in 1984 by Prof. Gavriel Salvendy (Purdue University, USA, Tsinghua University, P.R. China, and University of Central Florida, USA) and the first event of the series, "1st USA-Japan Conference on Human-Computer Interaction", was held in Honolulu, Hawaii, USA, 18–20 August. Since then, HCI International is held jointly with several Thematic Areas and Affiliated Conferences, with each one under the auspices of a distinguished international Program Board and under one management and one registration. Twenty-six HCI International Conferences have been organized so far (every two years until 2013, and annually thereafter).

Over the years, this conference has served as a platform for scholars, researchers, industry experts and students to exchange ideas, connect, and address challenges in the ever-evolving HCI field. Throughout these 40 years, the conference has evolved itself, adapting to new technologies and emerging trends, while staying committed to its core mission of advancing knowledge and driving change.

As we celebrate this milestone anniversary, we reflect on the contributions of its founding members and appreciate the commitment of its current and past Affiliated Conference Program Board Chairs and members. We are also thankful to all past conference attendees who have shaped this community into what it is today.

The 26th International Conference on Human-Computer Interaction, HCI International 2024 (HCII 2024), was held as a 'hybrid' event at the Washington Hilton Hotel, Washington, DC, USA, during 29 June – 4 July 2024. It incorporated the 21 thematic areas and affiliated conferences listed below.

A total of 5108 individuals from academia, research institutes, industry, and government agencies from 85 countries submitted contributions, and 1271 papers and 309 posters were included in the volumes of the proceedings that were published just before the start of the conference, these are listed below. The contributions thoroughly cover the entire field of human-computer interaction, addressing major advances in knowledge and effective use of computers in a variety of application areas. These papers provide academics, researchers, engineers, scientists, practitioners and students with state-of-the-art information on the most recent advances in HCI.

The HCI International (HCII) conference also offers the option of presenting 'Late Breaking Work', and this applies both for papers and posters, with corresponding volumes of proceedings that will be published after the conference. Full papers will be included in the 'HCII 2024 - Late Breaking Papers' volumes of the proceedings to be published in the Springer LNCS series, while 'Poster Extended Abstracts' will be included as short research papers in the 'HCII 2024 - Late Breaking Posters' volumes to be published in the Springer CCIS series.

I would like to thank the Program Board Chairs and the members of the Program Boards of all thematic areas and affiliated conferences for their contribution towards the high scientific quality and overall success of the HCI International 2024 conference. Their manifold support in terms of paper reviewing (single-blind review process, with a minimum of two reviews per submission), session organization and their willingness to act as goodwill ambassadors for the conference is most highly appreciated.

This conference would not have been possible without the continuous and unwavering support and advice of Gavriel Salvendy, founder, General Chair Emeritus, and Scientific Advisor. For his outstanding efforts, I would like to express my sincere appreciation to Abbas Moallem, Communications Chair and Editor of HCI International News.

July 2024   Constantine Stephanidis

HCI International 2024 Thematic Areas
and Affiliated Conferences

- HCI: Human-Computer Interaction Thematic Area
- HIMI: Human Interface and the Management of Information Thematic Area
- EPCE: 21st International Conference on Engineering Psychology and Cognitive Ergonomics
- AC: 18th International Conference on Augmented Cognition
- UAHCI: 18th International Conference on Universal Access in Human-Computer Interaction
- CCD: 16th International Conference on Cross-Cultural Design
- SCSM: 16th International Conference on Social Computing and Social Media
- VAMR: 16th International Conference on Virtual, Augmented and Mixed Reality
- DHM: 15th International Conference on Digital Human Modeling & Applications in Health, Safety, Ergonomics & Risk Management
- DUXU: 13th International Conference on Design, User Experience and Usability
- C&C: 12th International Conference on Culture and Computing
- DAPI: 12th International Conference on Distributed, Ambient and Pervasive Interactions
- HCIBGO: 11th International Conference on HCI in Business, Government and Organizations
- LCT: 11th International Conference on Learning and Collaboration Technologies
- ITAP: 10th International Conference on Human Aspects of IT for the Aged Population
- AIS: 6th International Conference on Adaptive Instructional Systems
- HCI-CPT: 6th International Conference on HCI for Cybersecurity, Privacy and Trust
- HCI-Games: 6th International Conference on HCI in Games
- MobiTAS: 6th International Conference on HCI in Mobility, Transport and Automotive Systems
- AI-HCI: 5th International Conference on Artificial Intelligence in HCI
- MOBILE: 5th International Conference on Human-Centered Design, Operation and Evaluation of Mobile Communications

List of Conference Proceedings Volumes Appearing Before the Conference

23. LNCS 14706, Virtual, Augmented and Mixed Reality: Part I, edited by Jessie Y. C. Chen and Gino Fragomeni
24. LNCS 14707, Virtual, Augmented and Mixed Reality: Part II, edited by Jessie Y. C. Chen and Gino Fragomeni
25. LNCS 14708, Virtual, Augmented and Mixed Reality: Part III, edited by Jessie Y. C. Chen and Gino Fragomeni
26. LNCS 14709, Digital Human Modeling and Applications in Health, Safety, Ergonomics and Risk Management: Part I, edited by Vincent G. Duffy
27. LNCS 14710, Digital Human Modeling and Applications in Health, Safety, Ergonomics and Risk Management: Part II, edited by Vincent G. Duffy
28. LNCS 14711, Digital Human Modeling and Applications in Health, Safety, Ergonomics and Risk Management: Part III, edited by Vincent G. Duffy
29. LNCS 14712, Design, User Experience, and Usability: Part I, edited by Aaron Marcus, Elizabeth Rosenzweig and Marcelo M. Soares
30. LNCS 14713, Design, User Experience, and Usability: Part II, edited by Aaron Marcus, Elizabeth Rosenzweig and Marcelo M. Soares
31. LNCS 14714, Design, User Experience, and Usability: Part III, edited by Aaron Marcus, Elizabeth Rosenzweig and Marcelo M. Soares
32. LNCS 14715, Design, User Experience, and Usability: Part IV, edited by Aaron Marcus, Elizabeth Rosenzweig and Marcelo M. Soares
33. LNCS 14716, Design, User Experience, and Usability: Part V, edited by Aaron Marcus, Elizabeth Rosenzweig and Marcelo M. Soares
34. LNCS 14717, Culture and Computing, edited by Matthias Rauterberg
35. LNCS 14718, Distributed, Ambient and Pervasive Interactions: Part I, edited by Norbert A. Streitz and Shin'ichi Konomi
36. LNCS 14719, Distributed, Ambient and Pervasive Interactions: Part II, edited by Norbert A. Streitz and Shin'ichi Konomi
37. LNCS 14720, HCI in Business, Government and Organizations: Part I, edited by Fiona Fui-Hoon Nah and Keng Leng Siau
38. LNCS 14721, HCI in Business, Government and Organizations: Part II, edited by Fiona Fui-Hoon Nah and Keng Leng Siau
39. LNCS 14722, Learning and Collaboration Technologies: Part I, edited by Panayiotis Zaphiris and Andri Ioannou
40. LNCS 14723, Learning and Collaboration Technologies: Part II, edited by Panayiotis Zaphiris and Andri Ioannou
41. LNCS 14724, Learning and Collaboration Technologies: Part III, edited by Panayiotis Zaphiris and Andri Ioannou
42. LNCS 14725, Human Aspects of IT for the Aged Population: Part I, edited by Qin Gao and Jia Zhou
43. LNCS 14726, Human Aspects of IT for the Aged Population: Part II, edited by Qin Gao and Jia Zhou
44. LNCS 14727, Adaptive Instructional System, edited by Robert A. Sottilare and Jessica Schwarz
45. LNCS 14728, HCI for Cybersecurity, Privacy and Trust: Part I, edited by Abbas Moallem
46. LNCS 14729, HCI for Cybersecurity, Privacy and Trust: Part II, edited by Abbas Moallem

https://2024.hci.international/proceedings

Preface

The 18th International Conference on Universal Access in Human-Computer Interaction (UAHCI 2024), an affiliated conference of the HCI International (HCII) conference, provided an established international forum for the exchange and dissemination of scientific information on theoretical, methodological, and empirical research that addresses all issues related to the attainment of universal access in the development of interactive software. It comprehensively addressed accessibility and quality of interaction in the user interface development life-cycle from a multidisciplinary perspective, taking into account dimensions of diversity, such as functional limitations, age, culture, background knowledge, etc., in the target user population, as well as various dimensions of diversity which affect the context of use and the technological platform and arise from the emergence of mobile, wearable, ubiquitous, and intelligent devices and technologies.

UAHCI 2024 aimed to help, promote, and encourage research by providing a forum for interaction and exchanges among researchers, academics, and practitioners in the field. The conference welcomed papers on the design, development, evaluation, use, and impact of user interfaces, as well as standardization, policy, and other non-technological issues that facilitate and promote universal access.

Universal access is not a new topic in the field of human-computer interaction and information technology. Yet, in the new interaction environment shaped by current technological advancements, it becomes of prominent importance to ensure that individuals have access to interactive products and services that span a wide variety of everyday life domains and are used in fundamental human activities. The papers accepted to this year's UAHCI conference present research, methods, and practices addressing universal access issues related to user experience and interaction, and approaches targeted to provide appropriate interaction means to individuals with specific disabilities, but also issues related to extended reality – a prominent technological medium presenting novel accessibility challenges, as well as advancements in learning and education.

Three volumes of the HCII 2024 proceedings are dedicated to this year's edition of the UAHCI conference. The first focuses on topics related to User Experience Design and Evaluation for Universal Access, and AI for Universal Access. The second focuses on topics related to Universal Access to Digital Services, Design for Cognitive Disabilities, and Universal Access to Virtual and Augmented Reality, while the third focuses on topics related to Universal Access to Learning and Education, Universal Access to Health and Wellbeing, and Universal Access to Information and Media.

Papers of these volumes were accepted for publication after a minimum of two single-blind reviews from the members of the UAHCI Program Board or, in some cases, from members of the Program Boards of other affiliated conferences. We would like to thank all of them for their invaluable contribution, support and efforts.

July 2024

Margherita Antona
Constantine Stephanidis

18th International Conference on Universal Access in Human-Computer Interaction (UAHCI 2024)

Program Board Chairs: **Margherita Antona**, *Foundation for Research and Technology - Hellas (FORTH), Greece*, and **Constantine Stephanidis**, *University of Crete and Foundation for Research and Technology - Hellas (FORTH), Greece*

- Basel Barakat, *University of Sunderland, UK*
- Joao Barroso, *INESC TEC and UTAD, Portugal*
- Ingo Bosse, *University of Teacher Education in Special Needs, Switzerland*
- Laura Burzagli, *National Research Council of Italy (CNR), Italy*
- Pedro J.S. Cardoso, *Universidade do Algarve, Portugal*
- Silvia Ceccacci, *University of Macerata, Italy*
- Nicole Darmawaskita, *Arizona State University, USA*
- Carlos Duarte, *Universidade de Lisboa, Portugal*
- Pier Luigi Emiliani, *National Research Council of Italy (CNR), Italy*
- Andrina Granic, *University of Split, Croatia*
- Gian Maria Greco, *Università di Macerata, Italy*
- Francesco Ermanno Guida, *Politecnico di Milano, Italy*
- Simeon Keates, *University of Chichester, UK*
- Georgios Kouroupetroglou, *National and Kapodistrian University of Athens, Greece*
- Monica Landoni, *Università della Svizzera Italiana, Switzerland*
- Barbara Leporini, *CNR-ISTI, Italy*
- John Magee, *Clark University, USA*
- Daniela Marghitu, *Auburn University, USA*
- Jorge Martin-Gutierrez, *Universidad de La Laguna, Spain*
- Maura Mengoni, *Università Politecnica delle Marche, Italy*
- Silvia Mirri, *University of Bologna, Italy*
- Federica Pallavicini, *Università degli Studi di Milano-Bicocca, Italy*
- João M. F. Rodrigues, *University of the Algarve, Portugal*
- Frode Eika Sandnes, *Oslo Metropolitan University, Norway*
- J. Andres Sandoval-Bringas, *Universidad Autónoma de Baja California Sur, Mexico*
- Muhammad Shoaib, *University College Cork, Ireland*
- Hiroki Takada, *University of Fukui, Japan*
- Philippe Truillet, *Université de Toulouse, France*
- Kevin C. Tseng, *National Taipei University of Technology, Taiwan*
- Gerhard Weber, *TU Dresden, Germany*

The full list with the Program Board Chairs and the members of the Program Boards of all thematic areas and affiliated conferences of HCII 2024 is available online at:

http://www.hci.international/board-members-2024.php

HCI International 2025 Conference

The 27th International Conference on Human-Computer Interaction, HCI International 2025, will be held jointly with the affiliated conferences at the Swedish Exhibition & Congress Centre and Gothia Towers Hotel, Gothenburg, Sweden, June 22–27, 2025. It will cover a broad spectrum of themes related to Human-Computer Interaction, including theoretical issues, methods, tools, processes, and case studies in HCI design, as well as novel interaction techniques, interfaces, and applications. The proceedings will be published by Springer. More information will become available on the conference website: https://2025.hci.international/.

General Chair
Prof. Constantine Stephanidis
University of Crete and ICS-FORTH
Heraklion, Crete, Greece
Email: general_chair@2025.hci.international

https://2025.hci.international/

Contents – Part I

AI for Universal Access

Contents – Part II

Design for Cognitive Disabilities

Universal Access to Virtual and Augmented Reality

Contents – Part III

Universal Access to Health and Wellbeing

Universal Access to Information and Media

User Experience Design and Evaluation
for Universal Access

Exploring the Need of Assistive Technologies for People with Olfactory Disorders

Palavi V. Bhole[✉], Kripa K. Kundaliya, Garreth W. Tigwell,
and Roshan L. Peiris

School of Information, Rochester Institute of Technology, Rochester, NY 14623, USA
{pb7169,kk2712,garreth.w.tigwell,roshan.peiris}@rit.edu

Abstract. Olfactory disorders can significantly affect a human's quality of life. We sought to investigate whether there are opportunities for assistive technologies to support people with olfactory disorders in day-to-day life. To achieve this goal, we surveyed 70 people with olfactory disorders to understand their behaviors, experiences, technologies used, and challenges with olfaction. We then conducted 10 follow-up interviews to further discuss views on current technology for people with olfactory disorders and the design opportunities for assistive technologies for olfaction from their point of view. Our results illustrated participants' varied views on current technology, behaviors/technologies adopted when presented with particular scenarios, and potential solutions for designing assistive technologies for olfactory disorders. Through these findings, we discuss design considerations for assistive technology for olfaction.

Keywords: Olfactory Disorder · Human-centered computing · Assistive Technology Design

1 Introduction

Sense of smell–also known as olfaction—is an important mode of perception that enhances our engagement with daily experiences and understanding of tasks [33]. Olfaction plays a key role in enjoyable situations such as when forming memories [21], enjoying food [29] and cooking [12,27], as well as in more critical situations such as when identifying gas leaks, burning food or detecting fires. 19% of the population over the age of 20 and 25% of the population over the age of 53 have olfactory disorders, which is defined as the reduced or the loss of the sense of smell [15]. The most common categories of olfactory disorders are: Anosmia (complete loss of sense of smell), Hyposmia (partial loss of sense of smell) [18], Parosmia (change in normal perception of smell), and Phantosmia (sensing smell that is not there) [7]. People with olfactory disorders may face hazardous situations due to failing to sense odors in situations such as from a fire, spoiled food, or gas leaks. Olfactory disorders can occur based on a variety of factors, including genetics, injuries, and, more recently, as a key symptom of the COVID-19 virus.

An emerging area of research has explored the concept of digital olfaction [16,25] and digitizing smells for new immersive experiences [6,30], enhancing memories [5], etc. However, research has yet to sufficiently explore from a Human-Computer Interaction (HCI) perspective how to address accessibility issues due to olfactory disorders. We investigated the challenges faced by people with olfactory disorders to understand how they use current technologies for assistance and examine potential opportunities for assistive technologies through two main research questions: (1) RQ1: What are the behaviors, experiences, challenges faced by people with olfactory disorders in regards to the technologies they currently use? (2) RQ2: Is there a desire for new assistive technology for people with olfactory disorders?

We conducted a two-part study to answer our research questions. For the first part, a pre-study survey was conducted with 70 people with olfactory disorders. The second part (main study) conducted follow-up interviews with 10 participants. Both studies found interesting behaviors and usage of technologies they had adopted, as well as design approaches they had suggested for assistive devices. Our main research contribution is the exploration of assistive technology/design that has been found through two studies. This will potentially address olfactory disorders in the future.

2   Background

Nearly 12.4% of the population in the United States over the age of 40 has measurable olfactory disorders [14]. Furthermore, a study reported between 70,000 and 1.6 million people in the United States who had contracted COVID experienced loss of olfactory senses. Although a temporary impairment for some, since it was reported that 72% of the population who had COVID had recovered from the loss of sense of smell [9], other people may not recover so quickly and have a longer-term loss of olfactory senses. Prior research has shown that some of the people who have lost their sense of smell show signs of depression and decreased quality of life [10]. People with olfactory disorders can also find themselves in dangerous situations by not detecting gas leaks, smoke, fires, etc. [17]. Although previous research [10] discusses the impact of olfactory disorders on the quality of life and various coping mechanisms adopted by people with olfactory disorders, there is limited focus on the technologies used currently to address the issues and possible future designs of assistive technologies.

In the broader field of human-computer interaction, sense of smell has been explored through 'digital olfaction' through the use of 'olfactory devices' [16,25]. Olfactory devices have been discussed focusing on improving immersive characteristics in virtual reality application [11,28,30], to influence behaviors (e.g., help with stress, work) [5,36], and enhance communication features such as notifications [1,26,39,40]. Furthermore, much work has used the olfactory sense as a part of multi-sensory experiences [28–30]. For example, in Season Traveller [30], the authors used the olfactory sense (using several scents emitted from an olfactory device) together with the wind feedback and thermal feedback to improve the sense of realism in virtual reality. The olfactory sense has also been used in cross-modal applications as well—i.e., an interaction between two different senses. For example, Brooks et al. [6] created illusions of temperature using smells produced by olfactory devices. However, in these studies, the olfactory sense has been used in an enhancing or complementary capacity, that is, the sense of smell is *required* for such experiences, and, thus, there was a lack of discussion on the accessibility issues that might be faced in the absence of the sense of smell.

As observed through prior work, further investigations are required to explore how people with olfactory disorders face challenges in terms of HCI and any design opportunities for this space. Reflexivity in research practice establishes the researcher's standpoint through which research is conducted [3]. The lead researcher is a 23-year-old female who cannot smell due to an olfactory disorder that is likely congenital.

3   Study 1 Methods: Online Survey

We conducted an online survey to understand barriers faced by people with olfactory disorders in their day-to-day life and the ways they have been typically dealing with those issues (RQ1).

3.1   Materials

Our online questionnaire included 30 questions (15 open-ended) covering three areas. We collected demographic information, focusing on age, gender, field of work, condition, cause, and period of olfactory disorders. Then, the questionnaire asked about treatments and effectiveness, current technology/devices used by people with olfactory disorders and their effectiveness, effects of olfactory disorders on day-to-day life, dangerous situations and ways of dealing with it, effects on other senses, and frustrations or pain points.

3.2   Procedure

Our 10–15 min questionnaire was posted online during a one-month period to collect responses from a wide participant pool. We utilized social media and online community groups (e.g., Facebook groups, Twitter, and Reddit) to share the questionnaire, with the intention of increasing reach beyond where we were advertising and asking people to also share more widely. All 30 questions were optional and there was no reimbursement offered for completing the study.

3.3   Participants

We had useful responses from 70 participants (Male = 24, Female = 44, Non-binary = 1, Unknown = 1) were aged between 18–66 years old (Mean: 34, SD: 12.21).

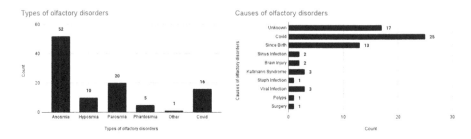

Fig. 1. Participant distributions of the (left) Type of olfactory disorders (right) Causes of olfactory disorders

Condition. Fifty-two participants had anosmia, 10 had hyposmia, 20 had parosmia, five had phantosmia, 16 had COVID-related conditions, and one responded 'other' but did not specify further (Fig. 1-left). Seventeen participants were unsure of the caused, 25 participants had mentioned COVID, while 13 participants lost their sense of smell since birth or were born without it. Two participants each indicated sinus infection and brain injury; three each indicated Kallmann syndrome [2] and viral infection; one each indicated Staph infection, polyps, and surgical as the main causes.

Duration. Forty-two participants had olfactory disorder for more than five years, six responded 1–5 years, 14 responded 1–12 months, five responded less than a month, two participants a few days and one participant unknown (Fig. 1-right).

Treatment. Fifty-seven participants indicated that they did not receive/seek any treatment, while 13 indicated treatments such as surgery, steroids, smell training, nasal sprays, etc.

3.4   Analysis

The lead author analyzed the open-ended responses using an open coding approach [34]. They started by first familiarizing themselves with the data by reading the responses thoroughly. They then assigned initial codes to each of the responses from the open-ended questions. They grouped the codes in an iterative process to create high-level categories that provide a summary understanding of the data.

3.5   Findings

Behaviors Changed and Adopted: Here, we discuss behaviors changed or adopted by the participants. Overall, we found several sub-themes in the participants' feedback.

Eating Habits. In total, 30% (21 participants) indicated that their condition had a main effect on their eating, such as increases or decreases in eating. For example, P6 mentioned *"Not Eating enough. Decrease in certain vitamins/minerals due to lack of food"* while P31 indicated *"I over eat constantly because I cannot get the satisfaction of tasting my food."* As a result, participants adopted interesting behaviors, especially to avoid spoilt food, with P64 indicating *"I taste the air and use visual and temperature inputs to decide if something smell"* whereas P21 stated looking for signs of spoilage in food: *"I check my bread for signs of spoilage like a hawk when it's near its expiration date/been open awhile".*

Conscious About Body Odor. Five participants indicated that they shower frequently to avoid body odor, *"I also shower very frequently because I can't detect my own body odor"* (P12). Furthermore, five participants discussed frequently washing or sorting clothes to avoid such situations. P34 said *"I always wash all clothes (even jeans) after wearing them once, even if only for a couple of hours"* and P39 said *"I keep a pile of "half clean" clothes - clothing I've worn once or just briefly - to remind myself that they're not completely clean, but they're probably not dirty yet either. I guess this is because I can't just sniff my clothes to see if they're clean/dirty?"*

Daily Activities. When it came to daily activities, 7 participants indicated that they did not have any issues. From the rest, two participants discussed having to pay more attention to food preparation. Comments included *"Sometimes the food gets burnt if I am not continuously in the kitchen focusing on it."* (P39) and *"I pay attention to colours of the food that I cook"* (P44). Interestingly, four participants indicated about having to frequently and visually check baby-diapers, *"Since I can't smell my kids dirty diapers, I've had to visually check pretty often until they were old enough to help tell me"* (P21).

Asking for Help. Seven participants mentioned informing others about the condition so other people can help when in need. P19 mentioned *"Normally, I also make it extra clear to my peers about my anosmia and that they should point out when bad/different smells come from me or my bedroom."* Several others also mentioned asking for help during some activities, where P17 indicated *"asking my mum to smell my clothes to determine whether I smell"* and P36 saying *"I had other people help me to determine whether or not something smells off or spoiled."*

Technology Adoptions. Only eight participants indicated the use of technology to specifically assist with their tasks, such as gas detectors, smoke detectors, etc. Although the majority of modern homes and spaces are equipped with such sensors, here, however, we believe most other participants did not specifically purchase these types of equipment due to their condition. Two of the other participants stressed the importance of such devices, saying *"As someone with anosmia, gas leak detectors are useful to avoid potentially dangerous situations involving gas leaks"* (P35) and *"Could save my life since I live alone. I'm still vulnerable to food poisoning."* (P47).

Experiences: We found several sub-themes of participant experiences specifically due to their condition.

Hazardous Situations. Participants reported that they faced different types of hazards due to their condition: gas leaks (10), fire/smoke (12), consumptional hazards-eating rotten food unsuitable items (19), cooking hazards (21), and overuse of cleaning chemicals (2). There were several comments that detailed the seriousness of the situation that would have been avoidable if not for olfactory disorders: Participant P64 shared an experience with a gas leak at school: *"When I got to class, no one was there so I sat down. 5 mins later a maintenance man walked in and said I had to leave due to their being a gas leak in the lab that I was currently setting in. Apparently they had evacuated that wing of the building to outside until they could shut it off"* (P64); P41 about consumptional hazard: *"drinking isopropyl alcohol thinking it was water....";* "*currently pregnant, almost ate applesauce that went bad."* (P13); *"Cant smell bleach and some cleaners so I often get dizzy while cleaning because I can't smell them so I continue cleaning without rinsing."* (P52). Due to such situations, participants often had to rely on others to notify them or, as P22 mentioned, *"NEVER own a gas stove".*

Effect on Workplace/Career. Ten participants identified that due to their condition, their workplaces related to chemicals, cooking, medicine, healthcare, and electrical were sometimes found to be dangerous to work in. P52, who is in the healthcare industry, mentioned *"Sometimes need smell to assess a patient, missed that patients were drunk a few times."* Furthermore, six participants indicated that their career choices were affected by their condition. While three indicated that they had to give up the idea of becoming a chef, one changed their field from medicine. However, there were positive impacts as well such as when P39 went into the pet care industry since *"I have no problem scooping litterboxes, picking up stools, etc."*

Effect on Taste. Olfactory disorders have effects on other senses as well. Fifty-three participants discussed the effect of the condition on their taste. Among the comments were *"Can only taste if something is sweet/sour/salty/bitter/spicy. Can't taste if something is "sweet bc there's strawberries in it" or "this is spicy bc there's paprika"* (P48), *"...I tend to choose a lot of foods based on texture, like crunchy crumbed fish etc..."* (P45).

Other Concerns. Due to their conditions, participants also had other concerns. P37 discusses paranoia for body odor and house smell: *"I'm paranoid that I stink or my home stinks. So I usually have air fresheners around a lot".* P24 talks about the difficulty in connecting with people and intimate scents: *"I worry I can't make lasting connections without understanding pheromones and intimate scents".* P36 shares their views on olfactory disorders: *"To me, there are no positive effects of smell loss, all negative. The only overall silver lining from the prevalence of smell loss due to covid is increase in awareness and research to help solve and cure smell disorders. But for me personally, its nothing but a big reduction in quality of life."*

3.6 Summary

The results from our survey illustrate data under two particular themes: 1) Behaviors changed and adopted by people with olfactory condition and 2) Experiences of people with olfactory disorder. In the first theme, we discovered various behavioral changes and technological adoptions the participants had to make due to the condition. The findings demonstrate various areas or ways in which these adoptions were made: eating habits, getting conscious about body odor, changes in day-to-day activities, asking for help from other people, and use of technology like gas detectors, smoke detectors, etc. The second theme illustrates the participants' experiences in various areas like hazardous situations, effects on workplace/career paths, effects on sense of taste, and other concerns that the participants had due to the condition.

4 Study 2 Methods: Interview Study

Our survey provided an overview of the habits and experiences of people with olfactory disorders. We conducted follow-up interviews to gain deeper insights and identify potential design considerations (to answer RQ2).

4.1 Materials and Procedure

We used Zoom to conduct the interviews remotely. The interviews were semi-structured and supported by a three-part interview guide. We used the guide to support the discussion, but since these were semi-structured interviews, we allowed our interviewees flexibility in sharing their views, and we would ask follow-up questions where necessary to continue discussing interesting points.

The interview was structured as follows. Part 1: We aimed to make the interviewees comfortable through introductions and by asking general questions about their condition and the information submitted through the survey study (e.g., can you tell me about your condition?). Part 2: We directed the conversation toward asking interviewees regarding current technology or behaviors used by people with olfactory disorders. Part 3: We provided a few scenarios to determine whether the participants have experienced exact or similar situations. Once we had this information, we asked the participants to imagine a device that could help in that situation and whether they would like an assistive technology for that particular situation. Finally, we discussed their frustrations and pain points.

It should be noted that the interviews were an opportunity to gain insights on possible design solutions for assistive technology for people with olfactory disorders, and we wanted to investigate those specific design possibilities to take the opportunity to explore with our interviewees the areas where an assistive technology could be helpful.

The interviews were scheduled for 45 min. The average recording time from the interviews was 22 min (min = 11, max = 36). The interviewees were reimbursed with $15 for their time.

4.2 Participants

We recruited 10 participants (5 females, 4 males, 1 non-binary) aged 18–59 (M:34 SD:12.29) from our initial survey sample who had olfactory disorders. The olfactory disorder conditions were anosmia (9) and unsure (1). Five participants had anosmia by birth, or for most of their lives, four experienced acquired olfactory disorders, and one participant was unsure of duration. One participant had anosmia due to COVID, two participants experienced olfactory disorder due to Kallmann's syndrome, one participant each due to brain injury, polyps, viral infection and congenital, and three participants were unsure of the cause.

4.3 Analysis

The lead researcher analyzed the interview transcripts using Braun and Clarke's thematic analysis [4]. The lead researcher generated initial codes from the data, reviewed the codes, and grouped them as required while looking for themes.

5 Findings

Our findings from the interview focus mainly on the participants' views on current technologies, behaviors/technologies adopted during presented scenarios, and potential solutions for assistive technologies for olfactory disorders.

5.1 Exploring Views on Current Technology

Based on the previous discussions from the survey, devices such as gas/smoke detectors were mostly mentioned in this context. All participants in this study had used or owned devices such as gas detectors, smoke alarms, etc. Although these technologies and devices are not developed explicitly as assistive technologies for people with olfactory disorders, participants had mixed feelings about them. Overall, participants commented on their reliability and usability in different scenarios.

Reliability: In terms of reliability, participants were concerned about the devices' need for batteries. For example, in case a battery dies, the risk is increased for people with olfactory disorders. I2 mentioned *"...But just relying on something that requires batteries, or like plugins, you just never quite know...When it's just like my life at stake, you know?"* Another participant, I9, indicated that in some cases, the devices' sensitivity is unreliable: *"maybe they should be a little bit more sensitive. You know, like, we have a fairly high-powered sensor. But like this, the frying pan [accidentally on for an hour] didn't set it off."*

Usability Outdoors: Another common concern was the absence or the usability of such devices in different scenarios, such as outdoors. During outdoor activities such as camping, such devices may be unavailable, which could potentially mean a dangerous situation for people with olfactory disorders. I8 indicated "*Well, just like camping, or [outdoors], and they have gas, and you don't have your detectors with you, or whatever*".

5.2 Understanding Behaviors and Tools Adopted by People with Olfactory Disorder in Various Scenarios

We presented the interviewees with three different scenarios: smelling baby/animal feces (scenario 1), eating spoiled food (scenario 2), overcooking, and causing smoke in the microwave in the break room/public areas (scenario 3). We asked the interviewees whether they had experienced such situations and what they did to deal with them. If they did not experience such situations, what would they do if they were to experience it in the future. Some participants shared their behavioral tactics. Overall, participants had mixed experiences with the above scenarios. Most had experienced the second scenario. How the participants responded to the above scenarios was mainly themed around adopting behavioral tactics and the use of technologies/tools.

Adopting Behavioral Tactics: Similar to some of the survey responses, participants indicated behaviors they would adopt in the presented scenarios. Mostly, such behaviors were centered around using other senses, such as vision, hearing, or intuition. For example, I1 discussed using other senses in scenario 1, "*I suppose when you can't smell, you have to use your other senses. And in that case, I wouldn't want to do a touch test. So, I think I would have to visualize each time.*" Similarly, I7 explained "*[baby] will give some kind of a signal they start crying he or she will start crying or something*", thus, adopting to understanding the baby's signals when using smell is not possible. In the second scenario, participants discussed visually examining the food. For example, I2 said "*I would probably just like pour a little bit and see if it's like curdles you know, or if it's like chunky because then obviously I would throw it or if it's like a little discolored*".

Use of Technology/Tools: Participants discussed a few interesting ways they have resorted to using tools. Interestingly, again, these tools are not specifically developed for people with olfactory disorders. Here, participants had reported simple uses of tools: a few participants used temperature sensors when cooking to prevent overcooking (scenario 3), I4 used the flashlight on a phone to shine through an egg to ensure it was not spoiled (scenario 1), I1 indicated the use of timers to avoid any overcooking scenarios, "*because of my brain injury, I'm pretty obsessive about setting timers for things. So probably would have set a timer for myself on my phone when I put the food in the oven*". I7 described a more sophisticated approach, "*the cartons will have a barcode, right and barcodes.*

If we now everyone has Google lens, they can just scan the barcode and they know what they expire is even if it's somehow blanked out on the milk pack. I think that should be sufficient for that".

5.3 Exploring Design Solutions for Assistive Technology in Olfaction in Various Scenarios

We also asked the participants to discuss what, if any, technologies they might like to use in the above scenarios and, in addition, any other thoughts they would have for assistive technologies for people with olfactory disorders. Overall, the responses were themed around non-technological solutions, wearable/mobile technologies, and other devices.

Non-technological: Here participants imagined solutions such as the use of service dogs and color changing diapers, etc., "*I just think, well, a dog if I could, if you could somehow teach it to [smell]*", I10. While many such products and services already exist, interestingly, such have not been thought from an olfactory disorder point of view.

Wearable/Mobile: Several participants described the importance of the assistive technologies being available. Responding to the 2nd scenario, I4 described "*something handheld which could be poked into the food to check if it's spoiled*". I2 discussed "*If it was just already on my wrist or already, like, hooked up to my phone somehow*". Similarly, inspired by previous discussions, I8 suggested portable smoke and gas detectors that can be carried outdoors, and P48 emphasized that they are never without a phone or a watch, so a wearable device could be really useful.

Other-Devices: In addition to suggesting the use of existing sensors, such as gas sensors, participants also described other devices such as smart fridges. Inspired by Scenarios 2, participants discussed having smart fridges, which could determine the expiry for food in it: "*just like those smart fridges. It would say, Oh, this, this product has been here for so many days. And normally, it just goes bad in that many days. So be careful. Don't get*" (I4).

5.4 Summary

Although participants were not very enthusiastic about *assistive* technologies for people with olfactory disorders initially, we identified that they had actually adopted interesting alternative/new behaviors or resorted to using existing technologies in useful ways. Furthermore, through the presented scenarios, participants also brainstormed approaches based on non-technological, wearable/mobile, and equipment-like devices as assistive devices. Inspired by this feedback, next, we discuss potential design considerations for assistive technologies for people with olfactory disorders.

6   Discussion

We conducted an online survey and interview study to answer two research questions. In answering RQ1, our survey indicated that the participants had many adoptions or changes in behaviors in daily activities, eating habits, being more conscious about body odor, etc., due to olfactory disorders. In addition, participants reported concerns about facing hazardous situations and their conditions affecting their careers and choices. As a result, participants resorted to asking others for help, while very few reported technological adoptions to overcome challenges.

In answering RQ2, our interview findings indicated that the participants were not very enthusiastic about current technologies or assistive technologies for olfactory disorders. However, we found that participants had adapted to interesting behaviors and/or interesting ways to use existing technologies and tools to assist their daily activities. Furthermore, we also found that the participants were motivated to discuss future assistive technologies and three approaches were suggested for assistive methods/technologies for olfactory disorder: non-technological, wearable/mobile technologies, and device/equipment.

Based on these findings, we propose a set of preliminary design solutions when designing assistive technologies and methods for people with olfactory disorders. According to most participants, having a handheld or wearable device would be an ideal design for assistive technologies for olfactory disorders. Wearable technology continues to grow in popularity [19], and there is increasing acceptance for wearable devices that monitor us throughout the day, such as health and fitness trackers so long as they are perceived as useful [23] and meet individual needs [31]. Chatchawal et al. [38] discuss armpit odor detection using an electronic nose, which is composed of a set of metal oxide gas sensors. While the presence of relevant sensor technology for olfactory disorders is in its infancy in terms of consumer products, research indicates potential for adopting such technologies for this scope.

Furthermore, through the interviews, we also found the participants discussing how, in some situations, the surroundings play an essential role in informing them about some dangerous happening. Thus, with the existing technologies such as IoT devices in our living spaces [20,22,32], this space opens up opportunities to focus on more such devices as olfactory assistive devices. These devices can also be made portable to resolve the participants' concerns about not having detectors outdoors.

6.1   Design Considerations

Based on these findings, we propose a set of preliminary design considerations when designing assistive technologies and methods for people with olfactory disorders. Here, we propose that designing future 'olfactory assistive technologies' should primarily consider the space: personal, intermediate, environmental/external. (as illustrated in Fig. 2).

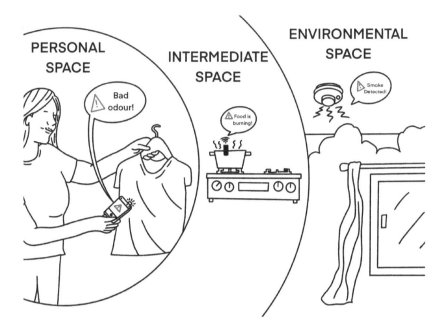

Fig. 2. Design considerations for olfactory disorder assistive devices.

Personal Space. Many participants raised concerns about being unable to detect their body odor or the odor of their clothes. As such, this space is defined as the space around the person and those things that can be considered as the person's frequently used belongings (clothes, etc.). We identify that technologies such as wearable devices and mobile devices (plugins for smartphones) would be suitable here. Consideration should be given that such assistive technologies would be used frequently. Example technology: a smart watch-like device that frequently or on-demand checks the odor of the person's clothes. While the presence of relevant sensor technology for olfactory disorders is in its infancy in terms of consumer products, research as above indicates potential for adopting such technologies for this scope.

Intermediate Space. This is a space where the person would interact with other objects or people in the immediate space (e.g., cooking or talking to another person). This space is inspired by the concerns and habits that participants described around cooking, changing diapers, etc. Thus, here we identify technologies such as mobile devices or other devices to be useful, and these might be used semi-frequently. Example technology: sensors for cooking that might be used only when cooking, devices for detecting spoiled food that might be used only when eating, etc. Technologies such as methods for interactive cooking [37], wearable technologies for baby monitoring [13], etc. demonstrate the potential of embedding sensors and, in turn, integrating new olfactory assistive technologies.

External/Environmental Space. The external space is the user's surrounding area and the space where the user usually lives, for example, the home or workplace. As such, we identify devices such as gas or smoke detectors that would fall under this space that would suffice the requirement. Furthermore, through the interviews, we also found participants discussing how, in some situations, the surroundings play an essential role in informing them about some dangerous happening. For instance, if there is a gas leak in a closed public space, the people around would react in a certain way that would enable the person to know about the happening and take steps accordingly.

6.2   Limitations and Future Work

As a major limitation, although most of the interviewees had anosmia (one was unsure), there are different types of olfactory disorders that we did not observe in the demographics of our interview participants. It would be interesting to see how the concerns due to the condition, views, and opinions on future assistive technologies for olfaction, etc., vary based on different olfactory disorders. We will aim to have focus groups with people who have different types of olfactory disorders to understand how to design future systems for different needs in the best way.

   As for our future work, our work was useful in identifying the *personal, intermediate*, and *environmental/external* spaces, and it provides three directions for future work as we continue to explore new assistive technology for each level that will support people with olfactory disorders. Particularly, based on our previous experiences and work on mobile and wearable assistive technologies [8, 24, 35] we identify the future research space for exploring the design considerations towards developing wearable and mobile sensors such as olfactory sensors and multisensory displays for presenting notifications at varying levels of priorities, urgencies, etc. of olfactory events.

7   Conclusion

In this research, we explored the accessibility issues of olfaction disorders. Through an online survey with 70 people, we presented concerns and behaviors changed or adopted by people with olfaction disorders. Next, through an interview with 10 participants, we presented findings on preferences, adoptions, and expectations of assistive technologies (for olfactory disorders). Finally, we presented three preliminary design considerations for developing olfactory assistive devices focusing on the space of the user.

References

1. Amores, J., Maes, P., Paradiso, J.: Binary: detecting the state of organic trash to prevent insalubrity. In: Adjunct Proceedings of the 2015 ACM International Joint Conference on Pervasive and Ubiquitous Computing and Proceedings of the 2015 ACM International Symposium on Wearable Computers, pp. 313–316 (2015)
2. Anık, A., et al.: Olfactory dysfunction in children with Kallmann syndrome: relation of smell tests with brain magnetic resonance imaging. Hormones **14**(2), 293–299 (2015)
3. Attia, M., Edge, J.: Be(com)ing a reflexive researcher: a developmental approach to research methodology. Open Rev. Educ. Res. **4**(1), 33–45 (2017). https://doi.org/10.1080/23265507.2017.1300068
4. Braun, V., Clarke, V.: Using thematic analysis in psychology. Qual. Res. Psychol. **3**(2), 77–101 (2006). https://doi.org/10.1191/1478088706qp063oa
5. Brooks, J., et al.: Smell, Taste, and Temperature Interfaces. Association for Computing Machinery, New York (2021). https://doi.org/10.1145/3411763.3441317
6. Brooks, J., Nagels, S., Lopes, P.: Trigeminal-Based Temperature Illusions, pp. 1–12. Association for Computing Machinery, New York (2020). https://doi.org/10.1145/3313831.3376806
7. Burges Watson, D.L., Campbell, M., Hopkins, C., Smith, B., Kelly, C., Deary, V.: Altered smell and taste: anosmia, parosmia and the impact of long covid-19. PLoS ONE **16**(9), e0256998 (2021). https://doi.org/10.1371/journal.pone.0256998
8. Chen, Z., Peng, W., Peiris, R., Minamizawa, K.: Thermoreality: thermally enriched head mounted displays for virtual reality. In: ACM SIGGRAPH 2017 Posters (SIGGRAPH 2017). Association for Computing Machinery, New York (2017). https://doi.org/10.1145/3102163.3102222
9. Christensen, J.: More than a million people in the us may not have regained sense of smell months after covid-19 infection, study estimates (2021). https://www.cnn.com/2021/11/18/health/covid-loss-of-smell-wellness/index.htm. Accessed 14 Apr 2022
10. Croy, I., Nordin, S., Hummel, T.: Olfactory disorders and quality of life-an updated review. Chem. Senses **39**(3), 185–194 (2014). https://doi.org/10.1093/chemse/bjt072
11. Dinh, H.Q., Walker, N., Hodges, L.F., Song, C., Kobayashi, A.: Evaluating the importance of multi-sensory input on memory and the sense of presence in virtual environments. In: Proceedings IEEE Virtual Reality (Cat. No. 99CB36316), pp. 222–228. IEEE (1999)
12. Fjaeldstad, A.W., Smith, B.: The effects of olfactory loss and parosmia on food and cooking habits, sensory awareness, and quality of life—a possible avenue for regaining enjoyment of food. Foods **11**(12), 1686 (2022). https://doi.org/10.3390/foods11121686
13. Hasan, M., Negulescu, I.: Wearable technology for baby monitoring: a review. J. Text. Eng. Fash. Technol. **6**(112.10), 15406 (2020)
14. Hoffman, H.J., Rawal, S., Li, C.M., Duffy, V.B.: New chemosensory component in the us national health and nutrition examination survey (nhanes): first-year results for measured olfactory dysfunction. Rev. Endocr. Metab. Disord. **17**(2), 221–240 (2016). https://doi.org/10.1007/s11154-016-9364-1
15. Holbrook, E.: Smell disorders: when your sense of smell goes astray (2021). https://www.health.harvard.edu/blog/smell-disorders-when-your-sense-of-smell-goes-astray-2018121215539. Accessed 14 Apr 2022

16. Holloman, A.K., Crawford, C.S.: Defining scents: a systematic literature review of olfactory-based computing systems. ACM Trans. Multimedia Comput. Commun. Appl. **18**(1), 1–22 (2022). https://doi.org/10.1145/3470975
17. Hüttenbrink, K.B., Hummel, T., Berg, D., Gasser, T., Hähner, A.: Olfactory dysfunction: common in later life and early warning of neurodegenerative disease. Dtsch. Arztebl. Int. **110**(1–2), 1 (2013). https://doi.org/10.3238/arztebl.2013.0001
18. Huynh, P.P., Ishii, L.E., Ishii, M.: What Is Anosmia? JAMA **324**(2), 206–206 (2020). https://doi.org/10.1001/jama.2020.10966
19. IDC. Smaller companies fuel growth in worldwide wearables market in 1q21, says idc (2021). https://www.idc.com/getdoc.jsp?containerId=prUS47794121 Accessed 14 Apr 2022
20. Irawan, Y., Novrianto, A.W., Sallam, H.: Cigarette smoke detection and cleaner based on internet of things (IoT) using arduino microcontroller and mq-2 sensor. J. Appl. Eng. Technol. Sci. **2**(2), 85-93 (2021). https://doi.org/10.37385/jaets.v2i2.218
21. Lai, M.K., Cao, Y.Y.: Designing interactive olfactory experience in real context and applications. In: Proceedings of the Thirteenth International Conference on Tangible, Embedded, and Embodied Interaction (TEI 2019), pp. 703–706. Association for Computing Machinery, New York (2019). https://doi.org/10.1145/3294109.3295659
22. Leonidis, A., et al.: Ambient intelligence in the living room. Sensors **19**(22) (2019). https://doi.org/10.3390/s19225011
23. Lunney, A., Cunningham, N.R., Eastin, M.S.: Wearable fitness technology: a structural investigation into acceptance and perceived fitness outcomes. Comput. Hum. Behav. **65**, 114–120 (2016). https://doi.org/10.1016/j.chb.2016.08.007
24. Maeda, T., Peiris, R., Nakatani, M., Tanaka, Y., Minamizawa, K.: Wearable haptic augmentation system using skin vibration sensor. In: Proceedings of the 2016 Virtual Reality International Conference (VRIC 2016). Association for Computing Machinery, New York (2016). https://doi.org/10.1145/2927929.2927946
25. Maggioni, E., Cobden, R., Dmitrenko, D., Hornbæk, K., Obrist, M.: Smell space: mapping out the olfactory design space for novel interactions. ACM Trans. Comput.-Hum. Interact. **27**(5), 1–26 (2020). https://doi.org/10.1145/3402449
26. Maggioni, E., Cobden, R., Dmitrenko, D., Obrist, M.: Smell-o-message: integration of olfactory notifications into a messaging application to improve users' performance. In: Proceedings of the 20th ACM International Conference on Multimodal Interaction, pp. 45–54 (2018)
27. Nakamoto, T., Otaguro, S., Kinoshita, M., Nagahama, M., Ohinishi, K., Ishida, T.: Cooking up an interactive olfactory game display. IEEE Comput. Graph. Appl. **28**(1), 75–78 (2008). https://doi.org/10.1109/MCG.2008.3
28. Narumi, T., Kajinami, T., Tanikawa, T., Hirose, M.: Meta cookie. In: ACM SIGGRAPH 2010 Posters (SIGGRAPH 2010). Association for Computing Machinery, New York (2010). https://doi.org/10.1145/1836845.1836998
29. Ranasinghe, N., Jain, P., Karwita, S., Do, E.Y.L.: Virtual lemonade: let's teleport your lemonade! In: Proceedings of the Eleventh International Conference on Tangible, Embedded, and Embodied Interaction (TEI 2017), pp. 183–190. Association for Computing Machinery, New York (2017). https://doi.org/10.1145/3024969.3024977
30. Ranasinghe, N., et al.: Season traveller: multisensory narration for enhancing the virtual reality experience. In: Proceedings of the 2018 CHI Conference on Human Factors in Computing Systems (CHI 2018), pp. 1–13. Association for Computing Machinery, New York (2018). https://doi.org/10.1145/3173574.3174151

31. Shin, G., et al.: Wearable activity trackers, accuracy, adoption, acceptance and health impact: a systematic literature review. J. Biomed. Inform. **93**, 103153 (2019). https://doi.org/10.1016/j.jbi.2019.103153

32. Statista: Smart Home (2022). https://www.statista.com/outlook/dmo/smart-home/united-states. Accessed 14 Apr 2022

33. Stevenson, R.J.: An initial evaluation of the functions of human olfaction. Chem. Senses **35**(1), 3–20 (2009). https://doi.org/10.1093/chemse/bjp083

34. Tracy, S.J.: Qualitative Research Methods: Collecting Evidence, Crafting Analysis, Communicating Impact. Wiley (2019)

35. Wang, Y., Li, Z., Chelladurai, P.K., Dannels, W., Oh, T., Peiris, R.L.: Haptic-captioning: using audio-haptic interfaces to enhance speaker indication in real-time captions for deaf and hard-of-hearing viewers. In: Proceedings of the 2023 CHI Conference on Human Factors in Computing Systems (CHI 2023). Association for Computing Machinery, New York (2023). https://doi.org/10.1145/3544548.3581076

36. Warrenburg, S.: Effects of fragrance on emotions: moods and physiology. Chem. Sens. **30**(suppl_1), i248–i249 (2005)

37. Wei, J., et al.: Food media: exploring interactive entertainment over telepresent dinner. In: Proceedings of the 8th International Conference on Advances in Computer Entertainment Technology (ACE 2011). Association for Computing Machinery, New York (2011). https://doi.org/10.1145/2071423.2071455

38. Wongchoosuk, C., Lutz, M., Kerdcharoen, T.: Detection and classification of human body odor using an electronic nose. Sensors **9**(9), 7234–7249 (2009). https://doi.org/10.3390/s90907234

39. Xiang, W., Chen, S., Sun, L., Cheng, S., Bove, Jr., V.M.: Odor emoticon: an olfactory application that conveys emotions. Int. J. Hum. Comput. Stud. **91**, 52–61 (2016)

40. Yamada, T., Yokoyama, S., Tanikawa, T., Hirota, K., Hirose, M.: Wearable olfactory display: using odor in outdoor environment. In: IEEE Virtual Reality Conference (VR 2006), pp. 199–206. IEEE (2006)

Enhancing Accessibility for Collectible Card Games: Adopting Guidelines, Applying AI, and Creating New Guidelines

Cooper Biancur[✉] and Christopher Martinez

University of New Haven, 300 Boston Post Road, West Haven, CT 06516, USA
cooperbiancur@gmail.com, cmartinez@newhaven.edu
https://www.newhaven.edu/faculty-staff-profiles/christopher-martinez.php

Abstract. The development of accessible digital games has been discussed through multiple publications in the 21st century; however, little to no attention has been given to analog gaming. Like video games, Collectible Card Games (CCG) have also gained massive popularity, but no accessible guidelines have been created to assist their base. With the aging of gamers that started playing thirty years ago and the strain the card's text places on the player's vision, accessibility work is needed in this area. The need for inclusion in gaming is critical because it can act as a medium for social interaction and a learning tool for teaching. In addition, technologies that can help those with disabilities, such as microcomputers and Artificial Intelligence, can be used to help those disabilities. In this paper, we adopt guidelines from video game accessibility and create a proof of concept that applies Artificial Intelligence and affordable microcomputers to assist those with low vision. After evaluating 53 evaluators, we found that the text-to-speech and volume of information caused significant issues; however, most ratings and responses showed that the proof of concepts functioned as an assistive technology and was successful.

Keywords: Accessible Games · Accessible Technology · Accessibility Design And Evaluation Methods · Applied AI · Guidelines · HCI · Human Factors · Visual Impairment

1 Introduction

Making the world accessible is important, as 12.4% of people worldwide have some impairment. Where disability positively correlates with age as cell production goes down [2]. With over 600 million people over 60, providing aid for the impaired plays an important role today [3]. Thankfully, numerous technologies have been incorporated towards accessibility, usually replacing the impaired sense with another [28,32]. Furthermore, breakthroughs in software such as Optical Character Recognition (OCR), Text-to-speech (TTS), Language Correction,

M. Antona and C. Stephanidis (Eds.): HCII 2024, LNCS 14696, pp. 19–34, 2024.
https://doi.org/10.1007/978-3-031-60875-9_2

and Predictive Text Suggestion are readily available and can help assist the impaired [14,17,24,30,32,35,37].

A large area of today's accessibility research is accessible game research. Games are part of everyday life; many watch and play them for fun and competition. Where humans have played dice, variations of Chess, and card games dating back to before the medieval era [18]. Furthermore, games can serve as a teaching mechanism, language games serve as a motivational drive for improvement, and in the case of math, it serves as a repetitive drill [5,13].

Digital gaming (DG) is one genre of games that has gained tremendous interest in this century, where several academic researchers and organizations have developed guidelines [1,15,34]. Even though much work has been done on accessible DG (ADG), analog gaming (AG), games that require no digital interface, have received little attention. While there is some work done on this topic, [7,11,20], these efforts are recent, and all, except [11], only address the lack of accessibility and suggest high-level techniques to fix the lack of accessibility. Furthermore, this research is on a large staple of tabletop games where the actual play style between games can differ by extremes. Tabletop gaming can provide numerous challenges to impairments ranging from vision, cognitive, motor, hearing, and more.

Collectible Card Games (CCG), a sub-genre of tabletop gaming, require strategy, cooperation, and negotiation skills to achieve victory [4]. Notably, CCG relays information through visual instructions such as text, color, and symbols, where the area of the card's text space, the size of the font, and reliance on color coordination heavily affect low-vision players. [11]. The most popular CCG 'Magic The Gathering' has over 10 million players and has been in production since the 1990s [22], where long-term game fans have aged by 30 years, and their vision has started to degrade.

With low vision being a concern of CCG players, we developed an Accessible Technology (AT) to assist impaired players. Our work on Accessible AG (AAG) had three goals: adopting ADG vision guidelines from previous research, creating an AT using ADG guidelines by applying Artificial Intelligence (AI) tools, and evaluating the AT in a series of evaluations where the objective is to create new guidelines from the evaluation data. This work is essential in human-computer interaction as it goes over strategies used in previous ADG and aims to build an AT that serves as an accessible interface for the vision impaired. Therefore, we are assisting the impaired and elderly in playing games and creating guidelines to further this field of research. Section 2 goes over related work to our research, where Sect. 2.1 goes over work on ADG, and Sect. 2.2 goes over work on AAG. Section 3 goes over the application of our research, where Sect. 3.1 covers the guidelines we incorporated from previous work, Sect. 3.2 presents the work done on constructing our AT and applying AI, Sect. 3.3 discusses the procedure of the evaluations and the questions in the survey. Section 4 goes over the survey's results, and Sect. 5 goes over a complete discussion of the results and concludes this work. This endeavor aims to be a leap in research targeting interfaces and

AT towards the elderly and disabled people so they can participate in the CCG community.

2   Related Work

This section covers Accessible Gaming research for DG and AG. The first subsection covers ADG, discussing the importance of flow and the segregation disability can cause. The second subsection covers the recent work on AAG, specifically in the genre of tabletop gaming.

2.1   Accessible Digital Games

When creating accessible games, the point should be to make them accessible to a large demographic and make all parts of the game playable. An accessible game must remain with all the challenges and mastering of skills of non-accessible games, [16, 29]. To this end, researchers try to balance between in-game challenges and abilities to engage a player's sense of flow and presence with the game [6]. To do this, designers need to consider what is creating the barrier for players [21], where a methodology can be defined to assist with play by applying an interaction model. This model ascertains what stage of interaction can not be performed, and then from there, the researcher can diagnose the sense that is causing the loss [9, 40]. The idea of flow versus presence and the state of user activity are shown in Fig. 1.

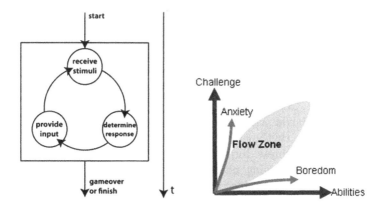

Fig. 1. The image on the left shows how a player will evaluate their next move. Where they first receive stimuli, determine a response, and then provide input. The Figure on the right shows the relationship between challenge and skill and how a balance creates a flow state. © 2011, 2007 [6, 40]

Companies and researchers have two standard methods for incorporating accessible guidelines: create an accessible game from scratch or add AT to assist the player. The former suffers from forming segregation within a group of gamers, and companies usually will not invest in a top-to-bottom solution for a small market. The latter has numerous compatibility issues amongst peripherals, and some games might not be adaptable to an AT approach [16]. Even with these practices being deployed, the gaming world is still segregated by impairments, where a survey conducted by [34] reports that most disabled players enjoy PC games over consoles and mobile games and that most prefer to play single or cooperative versus competitive. Meanwhile, [40] observes that these are the focused games due to the open-use gaming engine of First-person Shooters.

Two approaches have been taken to reduce segregation in video games, the first being the creation of Guidelines by a group of developers and studios [1], and the second the attempt at creating Universally Accessible Video Games (UAVG) [15,16]. The first has created a list of possible guidelines for general disabilities that are spread out based on the difficulty of employing them. The latter focuses on the work done in UA-Chess and Access Invaders, where both are fully or mostly UAVG. Furthermore, [15] discusses using an inclusive model where steps are taken to ensure accessible practices are followed and lead to the creation of a UAVG. The model uses professional reviews in each step, breaking down basic game interaction and dissecting the player's reaction to game mechanics. From there, the mapped-out interactions are placed in a matrix, guidelines versus impairments, where analysis is performed to see if that interaction is impaired. Compatibility and appropriateness are checked similarly before developing a prototype to test the applied guidelines.

Many accessible games have come out where the primary approach seems to be split into two areas: replacement and enhancement, where these same approaches are used in other accessibility fields [12,40]. The former replaces the impaired sense with another, and the latter enhances the interface's features in the domain of that impaired sense. As previously mentioned in [16], UA-Chess replaces sight with audio queues and enhances the brightness and size of pieces on the screen. Similarly, another genre of DG includes Audio Games and Tactile Games, in which visual components in video games are replaced with sound and touch (Archambault, 2007). Another replacement example was done by [39], where they replaced sight with haptic responses from a glove. The glove was used to play the classic rhythm game "Guitar Hero", where the glove would alert the player which key to press during the game.

Focusing on the enhancing portion of the problem, [23] created a list of questions they gave Japanese video game developers where they highlighted the accessibility features they implemented in their games. The features concerning visual impairment included color changing, zooming, high construction, and large font. Furthermore, [1], and [16] also mention the above enhancement features, where others include speed change for in-game play and instructions and adaptable controls as beneficial accessible features. [40] names numerous examples of ADG low-level solutions (guidelines) that can be deployed. The most common solutions for visual replacement were to provide speech, audio cues, or sonification, and the most common enhancement solutions were to increase the size of fonts, zoom in features, and use highly contrasting color schemes.

2.2 Acessible Analog Gaming

The previous work discusses digital gaming accessibility, whereas little to no work has been performed on analog gaming. In this paper, analog gaming refers to non-electronic and can include card games, board games, and other genres. The MEEPLE Project aims to create accessible guidelines and apply them to tabletop gaming. Where [19] evaluates general categories of creating AAG. Specifically on visual accessibility, we see a large percentage of players not recommending tabletop games with this disability, where these evaluations examined over 30 different tabletop games over many sub-genres. The same group of researchers go on in [20] to address the problems of each generalized disability category. The main drivers for visual disabilities for CCG would be color, contrast, and font type. Furthermore, there are overlapping game issues from other disabilities and sight, such as reading level requirements and game flow, that are listed as cognitively impaired problems.

More recently, [7] has come out with an article that reviews interviews conducted on blind and low-vision tabletop players and their relationship with their impairment and how it relates to tabletop gaming. The central part of the findings separates what makes an analog game inaccessible and how to make it accessible using the participants' suggestions. The sound, text, contrast, and color were once again presented as limiting factors, while essential suggestions to fix were using AI/OCR and adding sound for directions and mechanics. Another paper focusing on the inaccessibility of analog gaming towards visually impaired players is [11], where researchers found generic issues with tabletop games, applied them to the games Pandemic and Carcassonne, and then developed an AT that utilized a headset that could enhance and give auditory feedback when necessary. The majority of these papers, while an excellent start to solving this problem, deal with addressing the issue but still need to adopt solutions fully. Also, these papers deal with tabletop, which could mean their studies do not consider the CCG genre, where many visual issues are apparent, as mentioned in paragraph four, Sect. 1.

3 Methodology

This section presents the overall methodology for assembling our initial guidelines, creating a Proof Of Concept (POC) for our AT, and the evaluation to test the POC. The first subsection covers the guidelines and why we included them in our POC. The second subsection goes over the application of the guidelines and the construction of our POC. The third subsection covers the survey questions, the evaluation procedure, and the changes to the CCG game we use for our evaluations.

3.1 Guidelines

These guidelines were considered the simplest to incorporate into our AT and are not the only ones that can be applied to this problem. We break our guidelines into developmental, replacement, and enhancement guidelines.

1. Developmental
   - D1:Retain the quality of a game
   - D2:Create from scratch or adapt technology
   - D3:Apply Universal Model
2. Replace
   - R1:Focus on other senses for feedback
   - R2:Replace common sense with technology
   - R3:Control Output Speed
3. Enhancement
   - E1:Large and simple font
   - E2:Large interface input devises
   - E3:Contrasting foreground with background

Our Developmental guidelines look at high-level approaches that provide a framework for moving forward in the accessibility process. Guideline D1 expresses that a game should have its natural qualities, whereas a game should still be fun and competitive, as discussed in the first paragraph of Sect. 2.1. Guideline D2 aims to apply one of the two methods discussed in the second paragraph of Sect. 2.1. While both strategies have merit, we go with the latter due to the former being unrealistic on a large scale. Creating a new CCG from scratch would cause the segregation of more popular CCG from disabled players, and the amount of money to reprint already established cards would be an expensive endeavor for both companies and players. An example of this method being used is in [39], where the glove is a good instance of AT being developed to support play. Guideline D3 applies the Universal model discussed in the third paragraph of Sect. 2.1. While this model is usually used to create UAG and our AT aims to assist only one impairment, the model is an excellent first step at creating a list of issues the player may run into, so we apply steps 1 to 3 of the model.

The replacement guidelines aspire to replace the impaired sense with another sense or with machinery, where the majority of these are discussed in paragraph four Sect. 2.1. Applying both the unifying and interaction models, we see that sight is needed to review cards in all game planes [15,40]. Guideline R1 aims to replace the impaired sense with another. We chose to replace sight with hearing, where the other sense was touch, but we decided on the former due to the amount of information and the low number of people who know Braille. Guideline R2 focuses on the need to use technology to replace the impaired senses' role, where this can be indirect, for example, using a screen reader to read text, as done in games such as UA-chess. To accomplish R1 and R2, we decided on using AI tools, where OCR will do the work of the eye to interpret characters, and TST will read the text to the player. Guideline R3 is a secondary guideline to ensure R1 is deployed effectively, where the speed of information can impede recognition.

Enhancement guidelines strive to make a user interface as visually accessible as possible, where these are mentioned in paragraph five of Sect. 2.1 and paragraph two of Sect. 2.2. Guidelines E1 and E2 ensure the player can determine what is on the interface's screen. Therefore, we ensure that any font has simple characteristics and is large and bold. Guideline E3 is to create a high contrast between the foreground and the background so that visibility is as straightforward as possible. In our case, we have three layers: the background, buttons and instructions, and labels on the buttons. Therefore, we chose the first and last items to be white and the second to be black to provide the highest visibility grade.

3.2 Proof of Concept

To test our guidelines, we designed a proof of concept where our AT reads the card information to the player. The complete algorithm of our AT is shown in Fig. 2, where we utilize AI tools to complete actions two, four, and six.

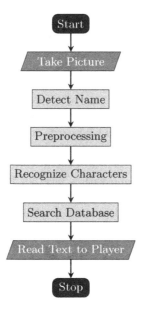

Fig. 2. This flowchart shows the algorithm that processes our card picture. The procedure follows: take the picture, then detect the name, preprocess the image, recognize the text, use the name as a query, and read the information found in our database to the player. The pink blocks are outside our algorithm, the purple parallelograms are the input and outputs of our AT, and the yellow blocks are operations our AT performs. (Color figure online)

The use of AI for accessible gaming is still a new topic, and there is little mention of guidelines for using AI in this area of research. This lack of representation could be due to AI, such as speech recognition, in the past giving inconsistent results, and the development of analog gaming guidelines being a new topic in the accessible gaming field, where the benefit of AI in an analog domain is tremendous. In the past, the most common technologies utilized to assist the visually impaired in playing DG have been screen readers and magnifying readers. Screen readers have difficulty reading alternative text and images where symbols are used in CCG to specify card type or faction [8,25,31]. This flaw and the fact that symbols differ between CCG makes applying Screen Readers challenging. Magnifying readers with small displays have shown to be problematic in application, and the constant physical interaction with the interface would cause many difficulties [26]. The dissertation [11] has performed similar work to ours using a headset to apply visual enhancement and visual replacement with audio. While this work was promising, it showed problems using markers to enhance inaccessible game pieces. We attempt to use AI to detect a vital game element and then read the whole of a card's information to the player, thus removing the need to enhance game pieces. While there are no direct guidelines on applying AI toward accessibility, we are excited to touch new ground as AI, in recent years, has shown much progress and interest.

Our AT can be split into four elements: input, capture, retrieving data, and output, where item three contains most of the algorithm. The first item is controlled by our interface, which uses a Raspberry Pi 8-inch monitor with a stand as the main body. The GUI was made using the T-kinter Python library, encompassing the digital buttons, instructions, and scroll-down menu. The scroll-down menu is used to switch between CCG, and the digital button begins the algorithm in Fig. 2, where both of these follow guidelines E1 to E3. Multiple modems, such as a mouse, touch screen, and keyboard, are available to use as controls for our interface. Capturing is done by a digital camera, where we decided that the Raspberry Pi HD camera offered the best in terms of quality and price [27]. The camera acts as a microscope with a base for the player to place the CCG card. After the digital button is pressed, the camera will take a picture of the respective CCG card, which will proceed to item 3, discussed in the following paragraph. This framework offers limited interaction with the camera, and the player has a consistent area for card placement. The process is quick and easy, where the player needs limited sight to act. The final stage of our algorithm takes the information retrieved from the database and reads it to the, as suggested in guideline R2. This action is performed through TTS, where we use a Python wrapper called PYtssx3 with numerous synthesizers available; we use Espeak, a TTS engine. Espeak allows us to alter the speed of our TTS voice and is free to use. We apply guideline R3 here, where the output speed is essential to the player's recognition of words. The device is outfitted with a headset to keep the card information for its owner only. This technique follows guideline D1, where part of the genre is the secrecy of cards not in play.

After the picture is taken, it is fed into our Raspberry Pi 4B (RP4B) micro-computer, where this microcontroller has been used in multiple computer vision projects. This element of our AT contains parts three to five of our algorithm in Fig. 2, making it the most complex process. The card information is stored in a digital database, where, after capturing the card's name, it is compared to the names in the database until it finds the closest match. After the previous step, the AT retrieves all the information in the record, which is used as the output in the final stage. The name is the most common feature amongst CCG cards as it is one-to-one with a card, where the image on the card is not necessarily unique. To detect the name of the card, we use OCD software, which is known as EAST (Efficient and Accuracy Scene Text Detector) [41]. EAST is a two-stage-pipeline FCN that is faster and more accurate than other free-use Scene Detection software. The OCD is trained to locate the boldest characters in an image, making it ideal for CCG. However, after we detect the card name, the RP4B still does not understand the characters in the image. Therefore, we apply OCR to read the card information into the database query using the Pytesseract software. Pytesseract is a Python wrapper of Tesseract, a multi-stage AI-powered algorithm that applies blobbing and segmentation [33]. We must apply preprocessing to the image to utilize OCR to remove artifacts or noise effectively. We used an Open-CV python wrapper for this stage, where this library was the most common library used in our readings [10,36,38]. The preprocessing stages are shown in Fig. 3, where the final result read to the player is shown in Fig. 4. Due to not training the Tesseract software with common words used in CCG, depending on the lighting in the room, the software may return symbols not found or come out with an incorrect guess. Due to this, we incorporated a checking software, shown in Fig. 4.

Fig. 3. These images are our preprocessing steps-the sequence takes. From left to right, we show that the first image is the CCG card we capture, the second is the detected words, the third is the denoised name, the fourth is the grayscaled image, and the final image is the threshold image.

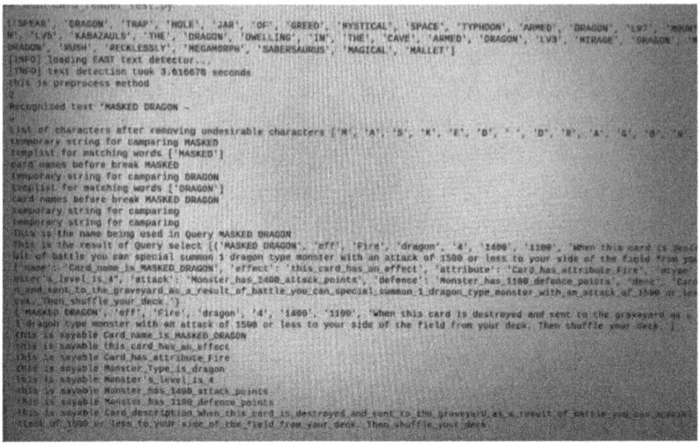

Fig. 4. Shows the device process recognizing the card name and then pulling the card information from the database. At the top are the names in the database that eliminate words that do not match. Following the acceptable words are the characters being recognized from Tesseract, where the correct name is shown. The acceptable characters are then put together into words, and finally, the name is used as a query. At the bottom of the figure is the correct information read to the player.

3.3   Evaluations

To test our proof of concept, we conducted a series of evaluations, where participants played a game of Yugioh against one of the authors of this paper. The evaluations showed that the AT was easy to use and enabled the player to play the game without interrupting their state of presence and flow. The evaluations proceeded with brief demonstrations of how the AT worked; the participant would get to try the device a few times to get used to its operation. This author then explained the game's rules, where we focused on card mechanics, field mechanics, and order of play. After the explanation, we further explained the changes to the game's rules. Some changes included a time limit, using the AT at least once per turn, reduced life points (a metric to show who wins and when the game ends), and simulator glasses giving the user the impression of impaired vision.

After completing a game, the participant would be asked to take an 11-question survey with ten multiple-choice and one open-ended question. The multiple-choice questions were divided into three groups that addressed the enhancement and replacement guidelines, the developmental guidelines, and the player's experience towards CCG. The final question would be used so the participant could voice any improvements, problems, or suggestions they had with the AT.

1. Enhancement and Replacement Guidelines
    - Question 1: How was the Simplicity of the device?
    - Question 2: How easy is the system to use?
    - Question 3: How comfortable was the interface of the device?

- Question 4: How difficult was the device to learn?
- Question 5: Could you recover quickly when a mistake was made?
2. Developmental guidelines
   - Question 6: How helpful was the device in playing the CCG?
   - Question 7: Did the device take away from the enjoyment of playing a CCG?
   - Question 8: Were you aware of the different cards in your hand?
3. Experience
   - Question 9: What is your familiarity with a CCG?
   - Question 10: Would you suggest a device like this for playing CCG?

The last question asked what suggestion the participants thought could improve the AT's performance. We use a five-point system for each question in the previous section, where one is the lowest and five is the highest rating. In total, there were 53 participants in the evaluation.

4   Results

The full results of our evaluations can be found in Table 1, where this section is broken up among the different types of questions. For the first set of questions, the following was found. Question 1 got an average of 4.039 with a standard deviation of 0.747; 70% of participants found the AT simple. Question 2 had an average of 4.039 with a standard deviation of 0.662; over 60% of participants thought the AT was easy to use. Question 3 had an average of 3.078 with a standard deviation of 1.246; 50% of participants thought the AT was slightly uncomfortable or moderately comfortable. Question 4 had an average of 4.180 with a standard deviation of 0.523; 90% of participants thought the device was slightly easy to learn. Question 5 had an average of 4.041 with a standard deviation of 0.706; 70% thought it was easy to recover when they made a mistake. These results suggest that our interface was accessible to the participants overall, and sensory replacement steps were incorporated well.

In our second set of guidelines, we found that question 6 had an average of 3.882 with a standard deviation of 0.816; 70% thought the AT helped them play the game. Question 7 had an average of 4.196 with a standard deviation of 1.020; over 70% of participants thought the device did not interfere with the game's flow. Question 8 averages 3.706 with a standard deviation of 1.082; 60% of participants said they could differentiate between the cards in their hands. However, the high number of twos and standard deviation suggest many had difficulty. From these results, our developmental guidelines served the AT's primary function: allowing the player to enjoy the game as it should.

The following two questions checked the player's experience with CCG and whether the device had a good impression on the player. Question 9 had an average of 2.667 with a standard deviation of 0.931; 80% of participants had little to no experience playing a CCG, whereas the majority had only heard of a CCG but never played one. Question 10 had an average of 4.118 with a standard deviation of 0.816; over 70% of the players said they would suggest a similar AT to someone they knew. These results give the impression that most participants thought the AT was visually friendly and helpful, allowing even a novice to enjoy the game. Further extrapolation of these results is provided in Sect. 5.

Table 1. These are the results of the ten multiple choice questions asked in our evaluations questionnaire. The first column is the number of question, the 2nd to 6th column are the number of participants that rated the question, and the final two columns are the average and standard deviation of the question ratings.

Questions	Rating1	Rating2	Rating3	Rating4	Rating5	Average	Standard Deviation
1	0	1	10	25	14	4.039	0.747
2	0	1	7	31	11	4.039	0.662
3	4	13	18	4	11	3.078	1.246
4	0	0	3	34	12	4.180	0.523
5	0	2	4	31	11	4.041	0.706
6	0	3	10	26	11	3.882	0.816
7	1	2	9	11	27	4.196	1.020
8	1	9	6	22	12	3.706	1.082
9	3	21	19	4	3	2.667	0.931
10	0	1	10	20	19	4.118	0.816

5   Discussion and Conclusion

When reviewing the results of our evaluations overall, we see a positive outcome, where the majority of our questions received greater than an average of four with standard deviations below one. However, a few questions showed mixed results, such as questions three and eight. Both had high standard deviations, with three also having a low average. Using question 11, we asked our evaluators what suggestions they have for the AT to gain insight into what problems occurred during their evaluations. Their responses showed that the results of question 3 were due to card placement and the robotic-sounding TTS causing discomfort. The length of the card information led to the result of question eight, which contributed to participants' confusing cards in their hands. We created new guidelines to fix the prior issues to compensate for this lack of foresight.

For future work, we encourage these new guidelines to be followed:

- N1: Secure placement area for CCG card that fixes the card in place and allows for stable capturing
- N2: TTS voice must be clear and with analog quality; as human as possible
- N3: Split card information into categories and read independently
- N4: Save more than one card at a time, depending on the allowed cards in hand; if the max is six, save up to six.

For guideline N1, we want to ensure a precise location for the card. During evaluations, we noticed the participant having trouble finding a precise location to place their card, whereas adding a slot will give such a location for placement. Another issue was that the card could be easily moved due to its light weight; therefore, slots with a holding capability would assist with this issue. Guideline N2 addresses the poor TTS quality. TTS is important as it is how we replace sight with audio, so more significant investments should be made. Where in today's market, there are numerous speech recognition software that can be applied. Amazon Polly and Dragon both offer TTS engines that have human-sounding voices.

Guideline N3 addresses the information fed to the player per card capture, where a large amount of information can confuse the user. Therefore, card information should be requested for each area by the player's request, where information on the card should be broken up into different categories of computer memory. Each area on a CCG card relates a different piece of information, which can be separated into pieces of memory and then read to the player upon demand. Furthermore, guideline N4 aims at the number of cards in the player's hands, whereas, in a game of Yugioh, a player is generally allowed to hold up to six cards. Therefore, the AT should simultaneously hold up to six cards worth of information. This idea can then be broken down further in later work. Speech recognition can be applied here where the different cards would be given a number to be called out by the user, and following this, the piece of card information can be read.

Future work will be aimed in two directions: first, to further these current practices by applying the new guidelines and making further improvements using the Universal model format; second, by adapting guidelines targeting other disabilities; cognitive, auditory, and motor are generalized examples. The former continues this work, where further evaluations in larger groups can find more issues with the current device. Furthermore, where this work showed how OCD and OCR could be applied, more AI solutions, such as speech recognition with auditory commands, can be applied in later work. With the guidelines adopted from video game accessibility proving successful in this work, we can move other guidelines, such as adjustable zooming being one idea among many. The latter approach will focus on similar work but apply to other disabilities, where auditory, cognitive, and motor impairments can impede the player significantly. Communication is crucial in CCG, for being aware of the phase of their turn an opponent is in can be critical, making auditory important. The player must hold their cards in a position to conceal them from their opponent, making a motor impairment challenging to play around, and cognitive problems can slow down the game and sometimes prevent players from playing altogether. The main goal here would be to create an AT that makes the CCG genre UAG.

In the latter half of the last century and this current century, there has been a large wave of accessible research aimed at digital games, more specifically, video games, where research in analog gaming has been recent, and most are not providing a POC. A big field of research in Human-Computer Interaction is aimed at assisting the impaired and elderly, and our research is a considerable contribution to this area. Therefore, we adopted some of the currently available guidelines for digital gaming and applied them to an analog game genre such as CCG. Another goal was to test how well AI software, for example, OCD, OCR, and TTS, could be used to solve this problem. In this research, we have successfully adopted guidelines to develop a framework, replace vision with audio using AI, and enhance visuals. To prove our guidelines could work, we created a POC that followed the algorithm in Fig. 2, where the AT would capture the card name, locate the name in a database, and read the card information to the player. To test our POC and gain data, we held a series of evaluations where participants played a game of Yugioh against an evaluator. After the game, they would answer a survey so we could gather data, which showed that our AT successfully gave proper auditory replacement and visual enhancement. Even more critically, the players could perform correct functions, showing that the AT could render information successfully to a novice. In this work, we showed that digital gaming accessibility guidelines could be brought over to analog gaming and that AI could be used as the primary mechanism in an AT.

References

1. Game Accessibility Guidelines (June 2016). http://gameaccessibilityguidelines. com/full-list/
2. Un Disability Statistics (2016). https://unstats.un.org/unsd/demographic-social/ sconcerns/disability/statistics/#!/activities
3. Ageing and Health (Feb 2018). https://www.who.int/news-room/fact-sheets/ detail/ageing-and-health
4. Adinolf, S., Turkay, S.: Collection, creation and community: a discussion on collectible card games. In: Proceedings of the 7th International Conference on Games+ Learning+ Society Conference, pp. 3–11 (2011)
5. Ageenko, N., Rybkina, A., Startseva, N.: Motivation fostering through gaming technologies. In: SHS Web of Conferences, vol. 113. EDP Sciences (2021)
6. Archambault, D., Ossmann, R., Gaudy, T., Miesenberger, K.: Computer games and visually impaired people. Upgrade **8**(2), 43–53 (2007)
7. Bolesnikov, A., Kang, J., Girouard, A.: Understanding tabletop games accessibility: exploring board and card gaming experiences of people who are blind and low vision. In: Sixteenth International Conference on Tangible, Embedded, and Embodied Interaction, pp. 1–17 (2022)
8. Borodin, Y., Bigham, J.P., Dausch, G., Ramakrishnan, I.: More than meets the eye: a survey of screen-reader browsing strategies. In: Proceedings of the 2010 International Cross Disciplinary Conference on Web Accessibility (W4A), pp. 1–10 (2010)
9. Cavender, A., Trewin, S., Hanson, V.: General writing guidelines for technology and people with disabilities. ACM SIGACCESS Access. Comput. **92**, 17–22 (2008)
10. Chadha, A., Kashyap, S., Gupta, M., Kumar, V.: License plate recognition system using opencv and pytesseract. CSI J. 31 (2020)
11. Da Rocha Tomé Filho, F.: Board game accessibility for persons with visual impairment. Ph.D. thesis (2018)

12. Elmannai, W., Elleithy, K.: Sensor-based assistive devices for visually-impaired people: current status, challenges, and future directions. Sensors **17**(3), 565 (2017)
13. Eriksson, K., Gavel, H.: Exploring the educational possibilities of computer games for 7th grade math (2010)
14. Goldenthal, E., Park, J., Liu, S.X., Mieczkowski, H., Hancock, J.T.: Not all AI are equal: exploring the accessibility of AI-mediated communication technology. Comput. Hum. Behav. **125**, 106975 (2021)
15. Grammenos, D., Savidis, A., Stephanidis, C.: Unified design of universally accessible games. In: International Conference on Universal Access in Human-Computer Interaction. LNCS, vol. 4556, pp. 607–616. Springer, Heidelberg (2007). https://doi.org/10.1007/978-3-540-73283-9_67
16. Grammenos, D., Savidis, A., Stephanidis, C.: Designing universally accessible games. Comput. Entertain. **7**(1), 1–29 (2009)
17. Hamad, K., Mehmet, K.: A detailed analysis of optical character recognition technology. Int. J. Appl. Math. Electron. Comput. (Special Issue-1), 244–249 (2016)
18. Hargrave, C.P.: A history of playing cards and a bibliography of cards and gaming. Courier Corporation (2000)
19. Heron, M.J., Belford, P.H., Reid, H., Crabb, M.: Eighteen months of meeple like us: an exploration into the state of board game accessibility. Comput. Games J. **7**(2), 75–95 (2018)
20. Heron, M.J., Belford, P.H., Reid, H., Crabb, M.: Meeple centred design: a heuristic toolkit for evaluating the accessibility of tabletop games. Comput. Games J. **7**, 97–114 (2018)
21. Jackson, M.A.: Models of disability and human rights: informing the improvement of built environment accessibility for people with disability at neighborhood scale? Laws **7**(1), 10 (2018)
22. Johansson, S.J.: What makes online collectible card games fun to play? In: DiGRA Conference, p. 34 (2009)
23. Kaigo, M., Okura, S.: Game accessibility and advocacy for participation of the Japanese disability community. Information **11**(3), 162 (2020)
24. Karmel, A., Sharma, A., Garg, D., et al.: Iot based assistive device for deaf, dumb and blind people. Procedia Comput. Sci. **165**, 259–269 (2019)
25. Lazar, J., Allen, A., Kleinman, J., Malarkey, C.: What frustrates screen reader users on the web: a study of 100 blind users. Int. J. Hum.-Comput. Interact. **22**(3), 247–269 (2007)
26. Legge, G.E.: Reading digital with low vision. Visible Lang. **50**(2), 102 (2016)
27. Ltd., R.P.T.: Raspberry pi high-quality camera. WWW-dokumentti. Saatavilla: https://www.raspberrypi.org/documentation/hardware/raspberrypi/README.md [viitattu 12.4. 2021] (2020)
28. Lucía, M.J., et al.: Vibrotactile captioning of musical effects in audio-visual media as an alternative for deaf and hard of hearing people: an EEG study. IEEE Access **8**, 190873–190881 (2020)
29. Miesenberger, K., Ossmann, R., Archambault, D., Searle, G., Holzinger, A.: More than just a game: accessibility in computer games. In: Symposium of the Austrian HCI and Usability Engineering Group. LNCS, vol. 5298, pp. 247–260. Springer, Heidelberg (2008). https://doi.org/10.1007/978-3-540-89350-9_18
30. Mithe, R., Indalkar, S., Divekar, N.: Optical character recognition. Int. J. Recent Technol. Eng. **2**(1), 72–75 (2013)
31. Morris, M.R., Johnson, J., Bennett, C.L., Cutrell, E.: Rich representations of visual content for screen reader users. In: Proceedings of the 2018 CHI Conference on Human Factors in Computing Systems, pp. 1–11 (2018)

32. Nazemi, A., Murray, I., Fernaando, C., McMeekin, D.A.: Converting optically scanned regular or irregular tables to a standardised markup format to be accessible to vision-impaired. World J. Educ. **6**(5), 9–19 (2016)

33. Patel, C., Patel, A., Patel, D.: Optical character recognition by open source OCR tool tesseract: a case study. Int. J. Comput. Appl. **55**(10), 50–56 (2012)

34. Porter, J.R., Kientz, J.A.: An empirical study of issues and barriers to mainstream video game accessibility. In: Proceedings of the 15th International ACM SIGACCESS Conference on Computers and Accessibility, pp. 1–8 (2013)

35. Raskind, M.: Assistive technology and adults with learning disabilities: a blueprint for exploration and advancement. Learn. Disabil. Q. **16**(3), 185–196 (1993)

36. Sajjad, K.: Automatic license plate recognition using python and opencv. Department of Computer Science and Engineering MES College of Engineering (2010)

37. Schlünz, G.I., et al.: Applications in accessibility of text-to-speech synthesis for south African languages: initial system integration and user engagement. In: Proceedings of the South African Institute of Computer Scientists and Information Technologists, pp. 1–10 (2017)

38. Xie, G., Lu, W.: Image edge detection based on opencv. Int. J. Electron. Electric. Eng. **1**(2), 104–106 (2013)

39. Yuan, B., Folmer, E.: Blind hero: enabling guitar hero for the visually impaired. In: Proceedings of the 10th International ACM SIGACCESS Conference on Computers and Accessibility, pp. 169–176 (2008)

40. Yuan, B., Folmer, E., Harris, F.C.: Game accessibility: a survey. Univ. Access Inf. Soc. **10**(1), 81–100 (2011)

41. Zhou, X., et al.: East: an efficient and accurate scene text detector. In: Proceedings of the IEEE Conference on Computer Vision and Pattern Recognition, pp. 5551–5560 (2017)

Embarking on Inclusive Voice User Interfaces: Initial Steps in Exploring Technology Integration Within the Seminar 'AI and Educational Sciences'

Matthias Busch[✉], Robin Ibs, and Ingo Siegert

Mobile Dialog Systems, Otto von Guericke University, Magdeburg, Germany
`matthias.busch@ovgu.de`

Abstract. Voice assistants, widely integrated into daily life, demonstrate vast potential across various applications, primarily catering to typical users with occasional focus on children, the elderly (specifically those with dementia), but not yet extending to those with mental disabilities. This paper explores the underutilization of Voice User Interfaces (VUIs) among individuals with disabilities, particularly those with mental disabilities. Drawing from Smith and Smith's [40] emphasis on inclusive co-design, we advocate for involving individuals with disabilities as well as including domain experts in the development of VUIs from the outset. The "AI and Educational Sciences Seminar" at the Otto-von-Guericke-Universität Magdeburg (OVGU) serves as a practical exploration ground, engaging educational sciences students in developing an inclusive Alexa Skill for a diverse user group. Establishing a true co-design process is a complex endeavour, and as Dirks argues in [6], overcoming social challenges is as crucial as addressing technical ones. This work presents an initial step towards 'Developing a Co-Design Process for digital Speech Assistant (DSA) Systems', focusing on the presentation of the concept and the introduction of a local focus group.

Our approach aligns with existing literature on involving domain experts, technicians, and individuals with disabilities in complex software development. To meet the diverse expertise needed for effective VUI development, we advocate for a comprehensive curriculum covering technical skills, domain knowledge, and human-computer interaction. The paper concludes by introducing a prototype tool, a Dialog-Content Management Systems (Dialog-CMSs) for Alexa Skills, enabling non-programming educational sciences students to contribute to inclusive VUI development.

Keywords: human computer interaction · co-design · inclusive development · voice user interfaces

© The Author(s), under exclusive license to Springer Nature Switzerland AG 2024
M. Antona and C. Stephanidis (Eds.): HCII 2024, LNCS 14696, pp. 35–50, 2024.
https://doi.org/10.1007/978-3-031-60875-9_3

Motivation

Technologies for developing digital Speech Assistants (DSAs) or Voice User Interfaces (VUIs) have reached an advanced stage [19,42]. Furthermore, VUI and DSA technology is commercially available for a wide range of users, enabling applications as home automation, web search, and music control [2]. Additionally, the market for commercial voice assistants has rapidly grown in recent years. This growth can be attributed to the inherent naturalness and simplicity of spoken communication, which contrasts with the need for additional external peripherals. VUIs are thus on the one hand seen as easy to use assistants, but on the other hand still require an adaptation of the human to the technical system, cf. [36,38].

However, within the community of individuals with disabilities, these systems are infrequently used and are particularly uncommon among those with mental disabilities, although those systems are considered beneficial. Speech input is favoured in comparison to textual input for humans with intellectual disabilities [1,7,18]. Several studies address various approaches to speech assistance systems that specifically aim to support individuals with mental disabilities [13,21].

The full potential of these technologies for people with disabilities remains unrealized by currently available products on the market. In their work, Smith and Smith [40] showcase how they utilize currently available 'Artificial Intelligence (AI)' systems to support their daily lives. In their conclusion, the authors underscore the significance of involving individuals with disabilities in the design of 'AI' software and technology intended for use by those with disabilities. They advocate for true co-design, where individuals with disabilities actively contribute to the design process.

VUI Technology Potential and Terminology

The term AI is commonly used across the media, industry, and academia to describe computer technologies capable of solving complicated problems or possessing 'intelligent' behaviour [20,24,35,45]. It frequently refers to technologies underpinned by Machine Learning (ML) algorithms. In the field of Speech Technology, the terminology is often ambiguous, covering a broad spectrum of related technologies known by similar names, including Voice User Interfaces (VUI), digital/smart speech or voice assistants, virtual personal assistants, (spoken) dialogue systems, conversational interfaces, and conversational agents, to name a few. This is especially true for digital Speech Assistant (DSA), which are at times collectively referred to as 'AI assistants', adding to the confusion by merging distinct concepts under one umbrella. In this paper, the term Voice User Interface (VUI) will be used for all types of technical interfaces that allow users to operate technical systems via speech. Within this paper, DSA are understood primarily as examples of *VUI-Level 2* and *VUI-Level 3*, according to the subsequent VUI classification.

Siegert et al. and Busch et al. differentiate between three different VUI levels [3,38]. This categorization is based on the required capabilities for a successful interaction and reflects the necessary technical complexity for implementation of said VUI systems. This classification aims to highlight the potential for the use of speech technology and to support categorizing individual terms and concepts. However, this overview remains broad and not exhaustive.

VUI-Level 1—*Voice Commands*[1]
Focusing on straightforward interactions, this level is characterized by basic voice commands for immediate tasks. In the context of smart homes, it enables users to control devices—such as turning lights on/off, adjusting thermostats, setting timers, or playing music—using voice commands. The system's responses are typically limited to confirmations. For interpreting user requests, Automatic Speech Recognition (ASR) and Natural Language Understanding (NLU) systems are generally sufficient. Additionally, a 'Slot-Filling' technique, facilitated by the NLU, can be used to gather any missing information [33]

VUI-Level 2—*Voice as Intelligent Process Support* (see footnote 1)
Enhancing user support, VUIs at this level process complex user queries and apply domain knowledge using a Dialogue Manager (DM) component supplemented by knowledge graphs or external databases when necessary. Both rule-based, for precise dialogue flow and easy integration of external sources, and statistical approaches, for adaptable and robust dialogues, are used in DM implementation. Rule-based methods demand manual development of dialogue states, while statistical models learn from existing conversations, making them scalable but challenging to develop without extensive annotated dialogue data [11,23]. In practice, *VUI-Level 2* functionalities can be developed as 'Alexa Skills' [17], exemplified by skills for purchasing train tickets or delivering interactive audio plays for entertainment.

VUI-Level 3—*Voice as Personalized Digital Assistant* (see footnote 1)
Characterized by advanced personalization, this level sees Voice Assistants (VAs) adapting dialogues and responses according to users' needs, preferences, and expertise. Rooted in the concept of *Companion Systems*, it encompasses proactive information provision, suggestion of alternative actions, error notification, and the alignment with users' overarching goals. Currently, VUI Level 3 is mainly in the research stage, focusing on developing capabilities for negotiating complex solutions and offering highly personalized user support [32,44].

Reflecting on the systems discussed by Smith and Smith [40], many of the mentioned commercial systems can be categorized under *VUI-Level 1*. Furthermore, it's important to note that interactions with speech technology (particularly at Level 2 and with DSA) involve social effects such as anthropomorphisation, which significantly influences users' expectations and perceptions of the system's capabilities. If a DSA fails to meet these expectations, the interaction is often perceived as confusing, complicated, or unfriendly [16].

This highlights that the successful development of speech technology assistance projects require more than just technical competencies; understanding and

---

[1] as described in [3,38].

addressing the social dynamics at play are crucial for enhancing user experience and acceptance. In the realm of GUIs, some existing design guidelines also consider the needs and abilities of people with disabilities (mostly visual). Especially, the HTML Accessibility Standards, which, to some extent, also consider individuals with mental disabilities [9]. Unfortunately, such guidelines or development tools do not exist for VUI design. In the area of traditional voice dialogue systems, i.e. call centre services, there is a uniform standard with VXML[2], but it does not take into account the special needs of users (whether with or without disabilities).

Similarly, to the best of our knowledge, there is no research available on how VUIs, especially in the design of *VUI-Level 2* interactions, should be developed to meet the special needs of users with mental disabilities. Currently, existing research is mostly in an explorative stage, where current available VUIs and DSAs are analysed, for different forms of treatment, cf. [1,18,21,43]. Therefore, this paper presents the first steps in the direction of developing a co-design approach for VUIs with a focus on people with mental disabilities.

'AI' and Educational Sciences Seminar at OVGU

In the seminar 'AI and Educational Sciences' initial experiences are gathered to foster a more diverse development process of VUIs. Students majoring in educational sciences serve as domain experts and develop an Alexa Skill for a diverse user group with various limitations. The development process is iterative, and the progress is reflected regularly with users from the target group.

In the following, the seminar concept and initial findings regarding the interaction of the target group with VUIs will be presented.

Emphasizing previous studies highlighting the challenges and benefits of involving domain experts, technicians, and individuals with disabilities in the development process of complex software solutions [31,39], we argue that these efforts need to be intensified, particularly for the development of VUIs. Developing successful interactions with voice assistants is a challenging task that requires expertise in various domains [5,15]. In addition to technical skills (spoken language understanding, software development), having an understanding of Human-Computer-Interaction and human interaction in general (formulating system responses, usability analysis, defining system behaviour) is crucial for VUI development. Additionally, VUI projects require expertise about the target audience (prior knowledge of users, interaction behaviour of the user group as well as the individual needs and abilities of the users) and domain knowledge of the specific use case.

Murad and Munteanu [25] provide an overview of VUI designers' education, arguing that, "[...] more HCI designers will need the appropriate knowledge to design for these emerging interfaces. HCI curricula need to be adapted to account for voice as an emerging form of interaction[...]" [25]. Building upon

---

[2] Voice Extensible Markup Language: https://www.w3.org/TR/voicexml21/.

this foundation, our research seeks to broaden this perspective by emphasizing the value of diverse development teams. Specifically, we focus on the integration of educational science students into AI development processes, arguing that such involvement enriches the students' learning experience and enhances the development process by incorporating domain expertise and digital competencies. This, in turn, facilitates the provision of digital competencies and accessible knowledge for teaching and assisting individuals with disabilities

In [6], Dirks points out the multifaceted challenges of inclusive co-design, noting the lack of user inclusion with disabilities in development projects despite the recognized advantages of participatory approaches. It is also stated that addressing these challenges necessitates the creation of a fair and integrative environment that supports voluntary participation without conflicts and is mindful of communication to prevent false expectations.

Hence, the seminar 'AI and Educational Sciences Seminar' is embedded within the course 'Werkstatt Uni—Inclusive University Education' at Otto-von-Guericke-University Magdeburg. This workshop and seminar is offered in cooperation with the sheltered workshop of the'Pfeiffersche Stiftungen', providing a practical platform for mutual learning and development among students and participants. The course is inspired by the philosophy of "Encountering the World" [28] and aims to support individuals with disabilities in their personal development by offering learning opportunities within Vygotsky's "Zone of Proximal Development" [4,8].

Additionally, the workshop expands its educational scope through'learning corners' that address a wide array of life skills, ranging from foreign languages and basic math to practical technology applications in everyday life. This multifaceted approach creates an ideal setting for the'AI and Educational Sciences' seminar. The learning corners serve as an ideal starting point for the'AI and Educational Sciences' seminar, having established a trusting atmosphere where all participants can voluntarily engage and immerse themselves in new experiences and shared discussions. Alongside the learners, caregivers, students, and educators are also keen on exchanging ideas and engaging with voice assistants.

Looking forward, we plan to leverage this environment to collaboratively develop guidelines for co-designing VUI and DSA projects. This will enable early identification and discussion of challenges and opportunities from technical, professional, social, and ethical perspectives.

Both, seminar and workshop are part of the Project 'Labor inklusive Erwachsenenbildung(-sforschung)' that is conducted by the chair of Educational Science Specializing in Scientific Continuing Scientific Education and Continuing Education Research led by Prof. Dr. Olaf Dörner.

Scientific Objectives of the Current Iteration

In its first iteration, the "AI and Educational Sciences Seminar" aims to address the following issues:

1. Creating a technical platform that enables educational science students to take an active role in the development of VUI systems.
2. Gathering initial experiences of our local focus group to understand attitudes towards new technology.
3. Collecting first-hand experiences on how individuals with disabilities interact with DSA systems.

This work introduces a Dialog-CMS designed to assist students in adopting the role of a VUI designer. Utilizing this Dialog-CMS, students have implemented a prototype Alexa Skil—an interactive audio play. The interaction extends beyond single user commands and, because of its extended dialogue sequences, it is comparable to systems from *VUI-Level 2*. In our "AI and Educational Sciences Seminar", early iterations of the prototype, which is still in development, have been presented to individuals with mental disabilities. This allowed for initial observations of interactions between these individuals and DSA systems. Furthermore, a questionnaire by Spelter et al. [41], an adaptation from the technology commitment model by Neyer et al. [27], was used to inquire about the technical commitment of our local focus group.

Dialogue Systems and Alexa: Understanding VUI Design

Within the seminar, an Alexa Skill is developed as a practical example of a VUI. Alexa, a widely used DSA system, often operates within the Smart Home ecosystem is used offers the possibility to develop Alexa Skills through the Alexa Service Kit (ASK) [17] and the Alexa Service. The dialogue between the user and Alexa follows a turn-based structure, where interactions are divided into user and system turns without overlap-Alexa does not listen while speaking, preventing it from being interrupted. Each input from the user is mapped to a specific intention.

Figure 1 provides a general overview of the subtasks in a speech processing pipeline, corresponding to a commonly used architecture for VUI and DSA systems, where processing is understood as a'pipeline' of several subtasks [17,22]. The upper half processing pipeline depicts how the dialogue system evaluates the user's 'utterance'. The lower half illustrates how the system's responses are generated. The dialog manager orchestrates these two pipelines using the dialog context (history of the actual conversation) and external services to properly interpret the utterances and generate appropriate answers.

The acoustic signal captured by the device is first converted into text form by an Automatic Speech Recognition (ASR) component. Based on this text, the Natural Language Understanding (NLU) component attempts to assign one, and in some VUIs, multiple intents to the user's utterances'. An intent can be associated with additional information. In the case of Alexa, these additional pieces of information are referred to as slots'. They are used to recognizing variables in the user's statement.

For example, the utterance "I want to depart from Magdeburg" could be assigned the intent tellDeparture' with the slot (location = Magdeburg'). Based

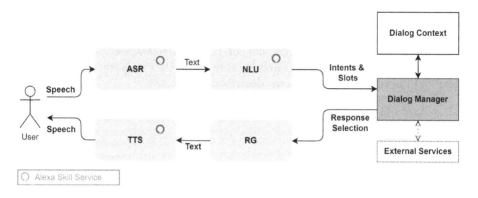

Fig. 1. Classical processing pipeline of dialog systems, as described in [22]

on the results of the NLU component, the DM of the VUI makes the decision on which action the system will perform next. This decision can be informed by context information that represents the state of the conversation or information about the user, as well as external information sources (databases, external interfaces). The system can also use program interfaces to initiate actions.

If the user is to be replied to, the Response Generation (RG) component must first generate a text response, which is then converted into audio signals by the Text to Speech (TTS) component. For Alexa Skills, several voices are available. The device will then play this audio stream, thus completing the conversation turn of the DSA / VUI.

Additionally, Fig. 1 also shows which subtasks are taken over by the Alexa Service. In the context of Alexa Skills, the NLU and, to some extent, the ASR components can be configured through the so-called interaction model. The interaction model includes the definition of intents, slots, and corresponding user utterances. The utterances are example statements of how users might express certain intents. The entire interaction model can be configured and tested without programming knowledge via the Alexa console of the Alexa Service[3]. Moreover, in our current development state, all responses of the system are predefined as text modules. It is possible to insert dynamic content through variables in text by using information from the dialogue context and external services. However, technologies such as Natural Language Generation (NLG) are not utilized. In future versions of the Dialog-CMS, the use of Large Language Models (LLMs) is to be tested to try out features such as personalization of the response texts, similar to *VUI-Level 3* features.

Rapid VUI Prototyping with Dialog-CMS

To enable students without programming experience to design interactions, a Dialog-CMS for rapid prototyping was developed. Figure 2 shows the connection

---

[3] see https://developer.amazon.com/alexa/console/ask.

between our Dialog-CMS and the DM of our system. As previously mentioned, the Amazon Alexa Service platform is responsible for ASR and NLU. Furthermore, the figure displays how the roles of *User*, *VUI-Designer*, and *Developer* interact with the overall system architecture. The *User*'s interaction with our Alexa Skill is similar to the process described in Fig. 1.

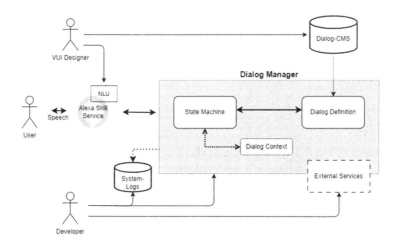

Fig. 2. Software Architecture Dialog-CMS and Alexa-Skill

First, the Alexa device transmits the spoken data to the Alexa Service, which then sends the NLU results and other metadata to our backend (represented as 'Dialogue Manager' in Fig. 2). Seminar instructors, in the role of *Developers*, oversee the software system's stability, fix errors, and develop links to external services like databases and web services, if necessary.

Students can modify the NLU through the Alexa Console[4] and can take on the role of *VUI-Designers*, defining the skill's behavior, training NLU, and analyzing the quality of the interaction model. Students, acting as *VUI-Designers*, configure the dialog definition in the Dialog-CMS. The dialog definition consists of two parts: the definition of text blocks (name and content of the text block) and the dialog states, which represent the behavior of the Alexa Skill. The dialog states are a rule-based approach to determine how the DM responds to user intents.

User statements can alter the state of the conversation, Fig. 3 shows an example dialog. The depicted dialog consists of three dialog states: *welcome*, *question*, and *end*. Furthermore, the initial start state is also defined in the dialog definition. Additionally, only two user intents (Yes' and No') are considered in this dialog; reactions to help intents are not shown. The Dialog State-Machine determines the handling of subsequent user intents, based on the present conversation state and the recognized user intent. This current state of the conversation is

---

[4] https://developer.amazon.com/alexa/console/ask.

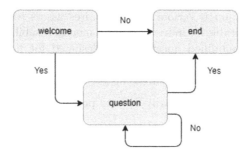

Fig. 3. Example Dialog State-Machine visualized as Graph

stored in the *Dialog Context* by the DM. According to the user intent, the Dialog-State Machine will perform a transition to the next suitable state and the DSA will utter the corresponding text.

Table 1. Example Dialog State-Machine visualized as Graph

State Name	Dialog-End	Prompt-Text	Help-Text	Yes	No
welcome	0	welcomeText	welcomeHelp	question	end
question	0	question	question	end	question
end	1	endText			

The current version of the Dialog-CMS utilizes Google Sheets[5] as a frontend for *VUI-Designers*. This allows non-programming experts to have an easy access to the states, intent definitions and systems responses on the one hand and also allows the ASK to access the data through an easy API. Students are only required to specify the conversation flow as a State-Transition Table. Table 1 presents the corresponding State-Transition Table for the state machine from Fig. 3. Each state is listed as a separate row. The columns *Yes* and *No* indicate how the system responds to the corresponding intent. Moreover, Table 1 displays which text block is used es respone when the State-Machine reaches that state. In addition, the *VUI-Designer* can define what help text is pronounced if the user uttered no valid intent. *VUI-Designers* can also configure whether this state concludes the conversation.

Experimental Design

This study primarily provides an initial general overview of a local focus group comprising individuals with mental disabilities and their interaction with technology, particularly voice assistants. Technological affinity indicates how comfortable people feel with technology and whether they are open to its use or

---

[5] https://docs.google.com/spreadsheets.

tend to avoid it. Although various questionnaires assess technological affinity [14, 26, 29], few are suitable for individuals with mental disabilities. Consequently, this work utilizes a modified questionnaire designed for people with aphasia [27, 41].

The survey adopted the same three categories from [27]:

Technology Acceptance primarily reflects personal interest in technological innovations.

Technology Competence Beliefs represent both biographically accumulated experiences with familiar technologies and the subjective expected adaptability to as yet unknown technological innovations.

Technology Control Beliefs subjective perceptions of influence and control expectations over technical processes and their consequences in the personal environment and for one's own life.

The survey comprises 12 questions, four for each category. Participants can answer each item with either *stimmt gar nicht* (not true at all), *stimmt wenig* (little true), *stimmt teilweise* (partly true), *stimmt ziemlich* (quite true), *stimmt völlig* (completely true). For analysis of the results, these answers are mapped to -2 to 2 with 0 being the neutral answer (partly true). During answering the survey, participants were supported by students and educators.

No medical data was collected in this preliminary study. It is important to note that the abilities and limitations of individual participants vary greatly, and thus experiences and prerequisites are highly individualized and thus difficult to generalize. The findings of this study are therefore initial indicators and experiences; they are not intended for a reliable investigation and conclusive findings on interactions with VUI/DSA systems and individuals with mental disabilities in general.

The first prototype developed in the seminar was tested to identify difficulties encountered during use. Six volunteers were asked to interact with the Alexa Skill. The prototype was implemented as an audio play where Alexa guides the user through a story that aims to convey information on the "UN Convention on the Rights of Persons with Disabilities". The skill provided a brief introduction and then asked the user if they wanted to hear more information. Additionally, the information was thematically divided into different landscapes (Antarctica, Arctic, Desert, and Jungle). Each landscape was represented by an animal character that narrated its part in a different voice. The current iteration of the prototype supports the following additional intents alongside Amazon's default intents: *HelpIntent*, *YesIntent*, and *NoIntent*. During the interaction, observers assisted only in cases of repeated problems.

After the interaction with the Alexa Skill, semi-structured interviews were conducted individually with each participant.

Results

Figure 4 depicts the results of the survey on simplified technological affinity. The simplified Technology Affinity Questionnaire was completed by 20 participants

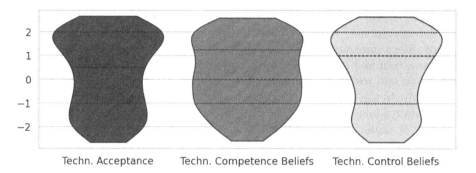

Fig. 4. Resulting ratings of the conducted survey on simplified technological affinity.

during the workshop. All participants were individuals with mental disabilities. For the dimensions of technology acceptance and technology beliefs, participants tend to lean towards the maximum poles. Thus, it seems that there are two distinct groups with varying degrees of acceptance and control belief. Regarding the dimension of competence beliefs, however, there is no clear maximum. Here, it seems that participants have a wide range of competence beliefs and can handle technology more or less effectively. It is important to mention in this analysis that the utilized survey is more focused on technology in general and not directly oriented towards the use and experience of VUIs. In comparison to other surveys, which have not specifically targeted individuals with mental disabilities but have focused on the use and acceptance of voice assistants, a similar distribution, especially for the dimension of acceptance, is observed [10]. Thus, it seems plausible to infer from this general technological affinity to the affinity regarding voice assistants.

The Alexa Skill was tested by 6 voluntary participants from the seminar. Two of these participants had prior experience with VUI technology (Alexa and Siri). The skill was launched by the investigators using the invocation word 'Meinungswerkstatt.' The investigators then observed the interaction and intervened only if the participants actively requested assistance or if the conversation was on the verge of termination. Overall, 3 participants were able to navigate the entire conversation without assistance. In the following, interesting observations of the three remaining participants and their interaction will be reported.

One individual reported difficulties understanding Alexa's statements approximately after 3 min into the conversation, prompting the experimenter to adjust the device's volume. It is noteworthy that this individual successfully interacted with the skill until that point, responding to the system's questions with yes or no. For the second participant who received assistance, the conversation was terminated by Alexa. Technologically, this can be explained as follows: during interactions with Alexa Skills, users have approximately 8 s to formulate a response; if the system does not detect speech within this time, a 'reprompt' can be issued. If this 'reprompt' is also not answered within 8 s, Alexa may terminate the conversation, assuming the user is no longer interested in the interaction. In the case described above, the second participant took longer to formulate a response, and when they did speak, the response was too quiet. As a result, Alexa interrupted the user with the 'reprompt'. Subsequently, the individual was confused and unable to respond to the 'reprompt'. However, after a short pause and restarting the interaction, the participant was able to navigate it smoothly. In the post-interaction discussion, this participant noted that they did not always understand why the system behaved accordingly.

These or similar situations highlight the problems that could arise in a VUI development project. The root cause here was an inadequate collection of all possible utterances for the corresponding intents. In VUI development projects, this is a common cause of errors, as VUI designers cannot always conceive of all possible statements and responses during the design phase. Therefore, user tests are so relevant for the development of speech technology. However, it also shows how difficult it can be to receive feedback from the target group of people with mental impairments. It is questionable whether the person could have described their problem in an automated feedback survey. Moreover, it demonstrates that systems intended to support this target group permanently require validation of the conversation to independently recognize exceptional situations and offer individualized assistance. However, these capabilities require complex implementations of *VUI-level 3*.

Discussion and Outlook

Our study aligns with the results of other studies in confirming the use of VUI technology as a positive experience [1,18,21]. Thereby, our paper comprises three parts, stated in the following research questions:

1. Creating a technical platform that enables educational science students to take an active role in the development of VUI systems.
2. Gathering initial experiences of our local focus group to understand attitudes towards new technology.
3. Collecting first-hand experiences on how individuals with disabilities interact with DSA systems.

Regarding the first research question, we introduced the Dialog-CMS, a tool that allows for the independent development and testing of an Alexa Skill within the 'AI and Educational Sciences Seminar'. In the future, the Dialog-CMS will be expanded with an editor that enables direct editing of the conversation flow according to the 'Visual-Programming' approach. This would mean that students no longer need to convert the state machine (as shown in Fig. 3) into a State-Transition Table (see Table 1).

Regarding the second research question, the simplified Technology Affinity Questionnaire proves to be a suitable initial step. However, it was noticed in our experiments with our group of participants that the questionnaire could not be answered by our participants without assistance. They encountered difficulties while completing it, as some questions are negated, the relation of questions to their own everyday lives was sometimes hard. A uniform format of questioning and perhaps more concrete connections to daily life would have been helpful for our user group. For the continuous development of the VUI application, repeated surveys measuring the attractiveness, e.g. AttrakDiff [12], user experience or usability, e.g. UEQ+ [34], of VUI-systems would be beneficial for comparing different iterations of development. But these other surveys would need to be adapted for the use by people with mental disabilities. Tools from usability research would be particularly relevant for targeted design decisions.

Through initial experiences, we are optimistic about the use of VUI. The current iteration of the 'AI and Educational Sciences Seminar' is a first step to answer to the third research question. Overall, our focus group reflects an interest in this technology. Many participants find the use of voice for controlling simpler systems to be sensible. However, it is shown that more complex dialogues (interactions with multiple turns) require examination to ensure the skill has knowledge of the dialogue flow and then needs dialogue strategies to early detect when the conversation is not functioning correctly, for example, running in a loop, and to offer adequate and individualized assistance. This requires implementations of *VUI level 2* or *VUI level 3*. How such interventions tailored to individual needs can look has been discussed in [30, 37] for people without mental disabilities.

Overall, it becomes clear that involving user groups at an early stage is beneficial, as user behaviour can vary significantly from one individual to another. Particularly, there is a notable limitation, as current and previous studies have limited experience in developing longer and more complex dialogues. These dialogues are essential for supporting people with mental impairments and involve extended user requests, system responses, and more complex interactions in general

Especially, different types of support must be offered to users, ideally by the system itself. For these challenges, there is a need for a 'Co-Design Guideline' for developing more complex inclusive VUI applications. This includes providing simple design tools for dialogue flows and developing adapted measurement methods, such as dialogue success, usability, and attractiveness. Additionally, it involves extending the research to longitudinal studies, enabling the examination of long-term usage and training effects. Therefore, a goal could be to collaboratively develop DSAs of *VUI level 3* that can offer ongoing support to users with mental impairments in their daily lives.

References

1. Balasuriya, S.S., Sitbon, L., Bayor, A.A., Hoogstrate, M., Brereton, M.: Use of voice activated interfaces by people with intellectual disability. In: Proceedings of the 30th Australian Conference on Computer-Human Interaction (OzCHI 2018), pp. 102–112. ACM, New York (2018). https://doi.org/10.1145/3292147.3292161

2. Bentley, F., Luvogt, C., Silverman, M., Wirasinghe, R., White, B., Lottridge, D.: Understanding the long-term use of smart speaker assistants. Proc. ACM Interact. Mob. Wearable Ubiquitous Technol. **2**(3), 1–24 (2018). https://doi.org/10.1145/3264901

3. Busch, M., Kania, M., Assmann, T., Siegert, I.: Radlogistik als Anwendungsgebiet für digitale Sprachassistenten – Ein Diskussionsbeitrag. In: Elektronische Sprachsignalverarbeitung 2023. Tagungsband der 34. Konferenz. Studientexte zur Sprachkommunikation, vol. 107, pp. 220–227. TUDpress, Munich (2023)

4. Chaiklin, S.: Die Zone der nächsten Entwicklung, pp. 78–87. Kohlhammer (2010)

5. Corbett, E., Weber, A.: What can i say? addressing user experience challenges of a mobile voice user interface for accessibility. In: Proceedings of the 18th International Conference on Human-Computer Interaction with Mobile Devices and Services (MobileHCI 2016), pp. 72–82. ACM, New York (2016). https://doi.org/10.1145/2935334.2935386

6. Dirks, S.: Ethical challenges in inclusive software development projects with people with cognitive disabilities: ethische herausforderungen in inklusiven softwareentwicklungsprojekten mit menschen mit kognitiven beeinträchtigungen. In: Proceedings of Mensch Und Computer 2022 (MuC 2022), pp. 556–560. ACM, New York (2022). https://doi.org/10.1145/3543758.3547575

7. Smith, E., Petroc Sumner, C.H., Powell, G.: Smart-speaker technology and intellectual disabilities: agency and wellbeing. Disab. Rehabilit.: Assist. Technol. **18**(4), 432–442 (2023). https://doi.org/10.1080/17483107.2020.1864670

8. Feuser, G.: Die "Kooperation am Gemeinsamen Gegenstand". behinderte menschen **3**, 16–35 (2013)

9. Friedman, M.G., Bryen, D.N.: Web accessibility design recommendations for people with cognitive disabilities. Technol. Disabil. **19**(4), 205–212 (2007)

10. Haase, M., Krüger, J., Siegert, I.: User Perspective on Anonymity in Voice Assistants. Springer, Cham (2023). https://doi.org/10.1007/978-3-031-35921-7_11

11. Haase, P., Nikolov, A., Trame, J., Kozlov, A., Herzig, D.: Alexa, Ask Wikidata! Voice interaction with knowledge graphs using Amazon Alexa. In: Proceedings of the ISWC 2017 (2017)

12. Hassenzahl, M., Burmester, M., Koller, F.: AttrakDiff: ein fragebogen zur messung wahrgenommener hedonischer und pragmatischer qualität. In: Szwillus, G., Ziegler, J. (eds.) Mensch & Computer 2003, Berichte des German Chapter of the ACM, vol. 57, pp. 187–196. Vieweg+Teubner, Wiesbaden (2003)

13. Huq, S.M., Maskeliūnas, R., Damaševičius, R.: Dialogue agents for artificial intelligence-based conversational systems for cognitively disabled: a systematic review. In: Disability and Rehabilitation: Assistive Technology, pp. 1–20 (2022)

14. Karrer, K., Glaser, C., Clemens, C., Bruder, C.: Technikaffinität erfassen-der fragebogen ta-eg. Der Mensch im Mittelpunkt technischer Systeme **8**(2009), 196–201 (2009)

15. Kim, Y., Reza, M., McGrenere, J., Yoon, D.: Designers characterize naturalness in voice user interfaces: their goals, practices, and challenges. In: Proceedings of the 2021 CHI Conference on Human Factors in Computing Systems (CHI 2021). ACM, New York (2021). https://doi.org/10.1145/3411764.3445579

16. Krüger. Siegert: das ist schon gruselig so dieses Belauschtwerden - subjektives Erleben von Interaktionen mit Sprachassistenzsystemen zum Zwecke der Individualisierung . In: Sprachassistenten - Anwendungen, Implikationen, Entwicklungen : ITG-Workshop: Magdeburg, 3. März, 2020, p. 29 (2020)

17. Kumar, A., et al.: Just ask: building an architecture for extensible self-service spoken language understanding. arXiv preprint arXiv:1711.00549 (2017)

18. Lewis, L., Vellino, A.: Helping persons with cognitive disabilities using voice-activated personal assistants. In: 2021 8th International Conference on ICT & Accessibility (ICTA), pp. 1–3 (2021). https://doi.org/10.1109/ICTA54582.2021.9809777
19. Liu, S.: Number of google assistant actions by language 2019 (2021). https://www.statista.com/statistics/1062722/worldwide-google-action-disappearance-by-language/
20. Lu, Y.: Artificial intelligence: a survey on evolution, models, applications and future trends. J. Manag. Analyt. **6**(1), 1–29 (2019)
21. Masina, F., et al.: Investigating the accessibility of voice assistants with impaired users: mixed methods study. J. Med. Internet Res. **22**(9), e18431 (2020). https://doi.org/10.2196/18431
22. McTear, M.: Conversation modelling for chatbots: current approaches and future directions. Studientexte zur Sprachkommunikation: Elektronische Sprachsignalverarbeitung **2018**, 175–185 (2018)
23. McTear, M., Callejas, Z., Griol, D.: The conversational interface: talking to smart devices. In: The Conversational Interface: Talking to Smart Devices, pp. 1–422 (2016). https://doi.org/10.1007/978-3-319-32967-3/COVER
24. Mühlroth, C., Grottke, M.: Artificial intelligence in innovation: how to spot emerging trends and technologies. IEEE Trans. Eng. Manage. **69**(2), 493–510 (2020)
25. Murad, C., Munteanu, C.: Designing voice interfaces: back to the (curriculum) basics. In: Proceedings of the 2020 CHI Conference on Human Factors in Computing Systems (CHI 2020), pp. 1–12. ACM, New York (2020). https://doi.org/10.1145/3313831.3376522
26. Murphy, C.: Assessment of computer self-efficacy: instrument development and validation. Educ. Psycholog. Measur. **49**(4), 893–899 (1988)
27. Neyer, F.J., Felber, J., Gebhardt, C.: Entwicklung und validierung einer kurzskala zur erfassung von technikbereitschaft. Diagnostica (2012)
28. Platte, A.: Alle Kinder lernen lesen...?! Inklusive Didaktik und Schriftspracherwerb, Zeitschrift für Inklusion (2007)
29. Popovich, P., Hyde, K., Zakrajsek, T., Blumer, C.: The development of the attitudes toward computer usage scale. Educ. Psychol. Measur. **47**, 261–269 (1987). https://doi.org/10.1177/0013164487471035
30. Prylipko, D., et al.: Analysis of significant dialog events in realistic human-computer interaction. J. Multim. User Interfaces **8**, 75–86 (2014)
31. Rajapakse, R., Brereton, M., Sitbon, L., Roe, P.: A collaborative approach to design individualized technologies with people with a disability. In: Proceedings of the Annual Meeting of the Australian Special Interest Group for Computer Human Interaction, pp. 29–33. ACM, New York (2015). https://doi.org/10.1145/2838739.2838824
32. Schmidt, M., Braunger, P.: A survey on different means of personalized dialog output for an adaptive personal assistant. In: Adjunct Publication of the 26th UMAP, pp. 75-81. ACM, New York (2018). https://doi.org/10.1145/3213586.3226198
33. Schnelle-Walka, D., Radomski, S., Milde, B., Biemann, C., Mühlhäuser, M.: Nlu vs. dialog management: to whom am i speaking? In: Joint Workshop on Smart Connected and Wearable Things (SCWT 2016), vol. 2 (2016). https://doi.org/10.13140/RG.2.1.1928.4247
34. Schrepp, M., Thomaschewski, J.: Design and validation of a framework for the creation of user experience questionnaires. Int. J. Interact. Multim. Artif. Intell. **7**(5), 88–95 (2019). https://doi.org/10.9781/ijimai.2019.06.006

35. Nemorin, S., Andreas Vlachidis, H.M.A., Andriotis, P.: Ai hyped? a horizon scan of discourse on artificial intelligence in education (AIED) and development. Learn. Media Technol. **48**(1), 38–51 (2023). https://doi.org/10.1080/17439884. 2022.2095568

36. Siegert, W.: Wendemuth: acoustic-based automatic addressee detection for technical systems: a review. Front. Comput. Sci. (2022). https://doi.org/10.3389/fcomp. 2022.831784

37. Siegert, I., Krüger, J.: How do we speak with alexa - subjective and objective assessments of changes in speaking style between HC and HH conversations. Kognitive Systeme **1** (2018)

38. Siegert, I., Busch, M., Metzner, S., Krüger, J.: Voice assistants for therapeutic support - a literature review. In: Salvendy, G., Wei, J. (eds.) Design, Operation and Evaluation of Mobile Communications, pp. 221–239. Springer, Cham (2023). https://doi.org/10.1007/978-3-031-35921-7_15

39. Sitbon, L.: Engaging it students in co-design with people with intellectual disability. In: Extended Abstracts of the 2018 CHI Conference on Human Factors in Computing Systems (CHI EA 2018), pp. 1–6. ACM, New York (2018). https://doi.org/10.1145/3170427.3188620

40. Smith, P., Smith, L.: Artificial intelligence and disability: too much promise, yet too little substance? AI Ethics **1**(1), 81–86 (2021)

41. Spelter, B., et al.: Modification of the brief measure of technology commitment for people with aphasia. In: Antona, M., Stephanidis, C. (eds.) Universal Access in Human-Computer Interaction, pp. 489–509. Springer, Cham (2023). https://doi.org/10.1007/978-3-031-35681-0_33

42. Vailshery, L.S.: Amazon Alexa: Skill Growth 2016–2019 (2021). https://www.statista.com/statistics/912856/amazon-alexa-skills-growth/

43. Vona, F., Torelli, E., Beccaluva, E., Garzotto, F.: Exploring the potential of speech-based virtual assistants in mixed reality applications for people with cognitive disabilities. In: Proceedings of the International Conference on Advanced Visual Interfaces (AVI 2020). ACM, New York (2020). https://doi.org/10.1145/3399715. 3399845

44. Wendemuth, A., Biundo, S.: A companion technology for cognitive technical systems. In: Esposito, A., Esposito, A., Vinciarelli, A., Hoffmann, R., Müller, V. (eds.) Cognitive Behavioural Systems, LNCS, vol. 7403, pp. 89–103. Springer, Heidelberg (2012). https://doi.org/10.1007/978-3-642-34584-5_7

45. Zhang, J., Tao, D.: Empowering things with intelligence: a survey of the progress, challenges, and opportunities in artificial intelligence of things. IEEE Internet Things J. **8**(10), 7789–7817 (2021). https://doi.org/10.1109/JIOT.2020.3039359

A Study on the Effect of Free-Viewing Eye Movement on Microsaccades

Fumiya Kinoshita[(⊠)] [iD]

Toyama Prefectural University, Toyama, Japan
f.kinoshita@pu-toyama.ac.jp

Abstract. Recently, several attempts have been made to quantitatively evaluate covert attention, using microsaccades. Simultaneously, the number of reports on microsaccade-detection algorithms has also increased. In particular, the EK method proposed by Engbert et al. in 2003 and the OM method proposed by Otero–Millan et al. in 2014 are still being utilized in many works. However, most of the microsaccade-detection algorithms proposed so far assume that the measured eye movement data do not include blinks or saccades, and there are very few reports on the detection of microsaccades using measurement data obtained during free viewing, which include such information. If microsaccades can be detected from the measurement data obtained during free viewing, in which blinks and saccades are mixed, it will be possible to evaluate potential attention without requiring fixation in experimental protocols. This can further the applied research on microsaccades. Therefore, in this study, we investigate an algorithm for detecting microsaccades in the measurement data obtained during free viewing, and conduct experiments on the effect of free-viewing eye movements on microsaccades. The results suggest that a combination of a microsaccade-detection algorithm using the EK method and an amplitude threshold may be able to detect microsaccades in free-viewing data as well as fixed-point viewing data.

Keywords: Covert Attention · Fixational Eye Movement · Microsaccades · Interval of Occurrence · Gaze Point

1 Introduction

Our eyes are constantly moving; even when we stare at a fixed point, minute eye movements are always occurring [1]. These involuntary eye movements are known as fixational eye movements, and their characteristic behavior is classified into three types: microsaccade, drift, and tremor. Previously, fixational eye movements were assumed to be nothing more than a spasm of the nervous system, simply correcting the deviation of the gaze from the gaze target. However, in 1804, Troxler discovered a phenomenon in which vision disappeared with a decrease in fixational eye movement [2]. Later, in 1860, Helmholtz Helmholz announced that moving the line of sight in small increments prevented vision loss for stationary objects [3]. In the 1950s, with the development of measuring equipment, it became possible to isolate microsaccades from eye movements; thus, experiments to directly measure the relationship between microsaccades and visual

© The Author(s), under exclusive license to Springer Nature Switzerland AG 2024
M. Antona and C. Stephanidis (Eds.): HCII 2024, LNCS 14696, pp. 51–62, 2024.
https://doi.org/10.1007/978-3-031-60875-9_4

ability increased [4–6]. In the 1990s, researchers began to study the types of neural activities produced in the eye and brain by fixational eye movements, and it became clear that fixational eye movements were closely related to higher brain functions [7, 8]. In 2003, Engbert and Kliegl reported the possibility of the orientation and frequency of microsaccades containing information on potential attention [9], and attempts began to quantitatively evaluate the potential attention from microsaccade information.

Previous studies have evaluated the level of arousal while driving a car, based on the information from microsaccades [10]; the performance during exercise [11]; and a group of patients with dementia [12]. Simultaneously, the number of reports on microsaccade-detection algorithms has increased. In particular, the EK method proposed by Engbert and Kliegl in 2003 [9] and the OM method proposed by Otero–Millan et al. in 2014 [13] are microsaccade-detection algorithms that can still be found in many works. However, most of the microsaccade-detection algorithms proposed so far assume that the measured eye movement data do not include blinks or saccades. There are very few reports on the detection of microsaccades using the measurement data during free viewing, which include such information. If microsaccades can be detected from the measurement data obtained during free gaze, in which blinks and saccades are mixed, it will be possible to evaluate the potential attention without requiring fixation in experimental protocols, which can lead to further applied research on microsaccades. Therefore, in this study, we investigate an algorithm for detecting microsaccades in the measurement data obtained during free viewing, and conduct experiments on the effect of free-viewing eye movements on microsaccades.

2 Method

The subjects of our experiments were 20 healthy young men and women (Mean $\pm$ SD: 21.8 ± 1.5 years old) with no history of nervous-system disease. The subjects were fully informed of the experiment in advance and consented to participate. This experiment was conducted after obtaining approval from the Toyama Prefectural University ethics committee (R3-3).

An eye-mark recorder EMR-9 (Nac Image Technology, Tokyo) with a temporal resolution of 240 Hz was used as the microsaccade measuring instrument. The measurement posture during the experiment was a resting sitting position, and EMR-9 was fixed to a chin table used in ophthalmology. In addition, before the measurement of microsaccades, calibration of nine points was always performed using EMR-9.

The microsaccade task in this experiment consisted of two types of tasks: a "single-point–gaze task" in which participants gazed at a fixed point 1 m away for 120 s, and a "free-gaze task" in which they searched a white wall 1 m away for 120 s. The microsaccade task was performed in the same way as the free-gaze task, with a single point of view at each point of view. In this experiment, we attempted to detect microsaccades in the data measured during free eye movement by comparing the results of each experiment on a single-point–gaze task and free-gaze task. The microsaccades detected were examined in terms of the microsaccade onset interval, amplitude, and maximum velocity. Considering the influence of the order, the measurement order of each measurement task was randomized. The subjects were not allowed to move their eyes extremely quickly or extremely far out of the measurement range of the eye-mark recorder.

3 Microsaccade Detection Methods

Various methods have been proposed for detecting microsaccades; there is no unified method. However, microsaccades must be outliers in the velocity space; thus, in this study, we used a detection algorithm modeled after the "EK method" proposed by Engbert and Kliegl in 2003. In the EK method, the blink-removal method and analysis interval are not strictly determined, and the detection algorithm using the EK method did not assume the detection of mixed saccades in the time-series data. Therefore, in this study, we attempted to separate the saccade component from the microsaccade time-series data by setting an amplitude threshold for the detected jumping eye movements. We also checked the effect of each amplitude threshold on the experimental results by comparing five different amplitude thresholds of 0.25, 0.5, 0.75, 1.0, and 1.25 deg. The microsaccade-detection algorithm used in this study is described below:

1. To exclude the effect of blinking, for each time-series data acquired from the left and right eyes, if there is a section that has been determined to be a blink even in one place in the same time zone, then all are replaced the value with 0 from 0.02 s (five points) before to 0.02 s (five points) after the blink occurrence time. The interval is treated as a missing-data interval from then on.
2. All time-series data in EMR-9 are displayed in pixel coordinates; thus, they are converted to angular coordinates using Eq. (1).

$$\theta_x = 44 * \frac{P_x}{639} - 22$$
$$\theta_y = -33 * \frac{P_y}{479} + 16.5 \tag{1}$$

3. The time-series data of the velocity component are obtained using Eq. (2). After that, the 120 s time-series data are simply divided into 5 s intervals (Fig. 1).

$$\vec{v}_{xn} = \frac{\vec{x}_{n+2} + \vec{x}_{n+1} - \vec{x}_{n-1} - \vec{x}_{n-2}}{6\Delta t}$$
$$\vec{v}_{yn} = \frac{\vec{y}_{n+2} + \vec{y}_{n+1} - \vec{y}_{n-1} - \vec{y}_{n-2}}{6\Delta t} \tag{2}$$

4 The detection threshold $\eta_{x,y}$ is derived for all divided time-series data according to Eq. (3) and Eq. (4), where $<\dots>$ denotes the median value. In this experiment, the value of λ was set to 4, and if the time series data contain missing data intervals, these intervals are excluded from the analysis.

$$\sigma_{x,y} = \sqrt{\langle v_{x,y}^2 \rangle - \langle v_{x,y} \rangle^2} \tag{3}$$

$$\eta_{x,y} = \lambda \sigma_{x,y} \tag{4}$$

5. The time-series data of the left and right eyes are transformed into the feature space $\left(\frac{v_x}{\eta_x}\right)^2 + \left(\frac{v_y}{\eta_y}\right)^2$ using the derived detection thresholds. In this case, jumping eye movements with a minimum duration of 0.08 s (2 points) or more, which exceed "1" in the feature space occurring at the same time in the left and right eyes, are selected as "microsaccade candidates" (Fig. 2).

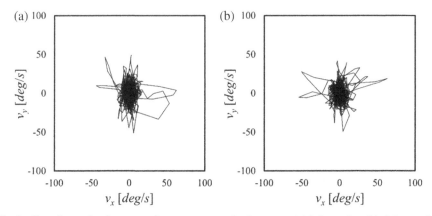

Fig. 1. Transformation from coordinate space to velocity space. (a) left eye 5-s, (b) right eye 5-s.

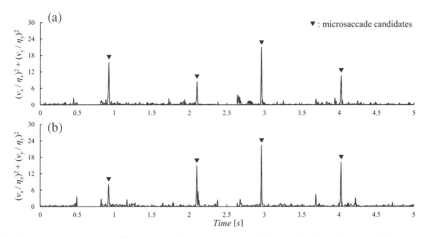

Fig. 2. Microsaccade candidates detection using binocularity. (a) left eye 5-s, (b) right eye 5-s.

6. The amplitude values of the selected microsaccade candidates for each eye are checked. If the amplitude value of either the left or right exceeds the preset amplitude threshold, this is identified as a saccade component, and the interval is considered a missing-data interval. Steps ④ through ⑥ are then repeated.

7. If the amplitude values of all the selected candidate microsaccades are below the set amplitude threshold, these candidates are selected as microsaccades.

8. Each 5 s time-series data converted to the feature space are concatenated into a single time-series data again (Fig. 3). The interval of occurrence of microsaccades is calculated from the concatenated 120 s time-series data. Here, referring to the refractory period of saccades, the normal range for the interval of occurrence of microsaccades is set in the range of 0.2–6 Hz, and values outside the normal range are excluded from the analysis. The microsaccades are identified as microsaccades when all the above conditions are met.

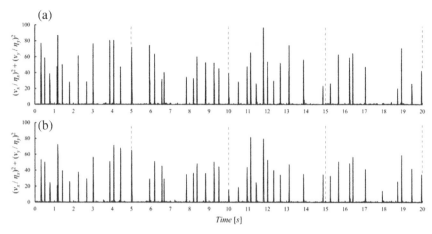

Fig. 3. Examples of concatenated time-series data. (a) left eye 0–20 s, (b) right eye 0–20 s.

9. In this study, three items are calculated for each microsaccade detected in the 120 s time-series data: interval of occurrence [Hz], amplitude [deg], and maximum velocity [deg/s], and the median value of each is considered representative of the subject (Fig. 4). As the amplitude and maximum velocity of the microsaccade are calculated for each eye, the average of the values calculated for the left and right eyes is defined

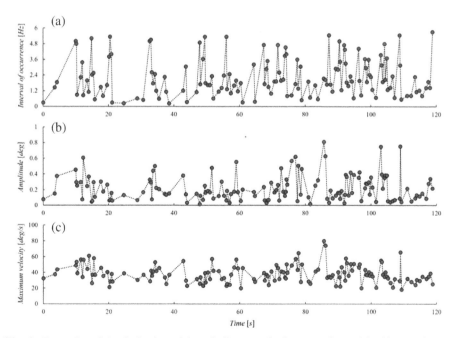

Fig. 4. Examples of the derivation of three indicators of microsaccade used in this experiment. (a) interval of occurrence, (b) amplitude, (c) maximum velocity.

as the amplitude and maximum velocity of the microsaccade in this experiment. The amplitude of the microsaccade is calculated by finding the Euclidean distance from the angular coordinates of the start and end times of the microsaccade, and the maximum velocity is calculated as the maximum velocity amplitude of the microsaccade, which occurs between the start and end times of the microsaccade.

4   Results

Figure 5 shows a typical example of the velocity space during a single-point–gaze task and the free-gaze task obtained from the same subject. During the single-point–gaze task, the gaze is directed to a fixed viewpoint; therefore, there is no significant variation in the time-series data. On the contrary, the saccade component is superimposed on the time-series data during the free-gaze task because the gaze is not fixed, and the velocity amplitude is larger than that during the single-point–gaze task. Next, Fig. 6 shows a typical example of the feature space during the single-point–gaze task and free-gaze task. Compared to the single-point–gaze task, the amplitude value of the vertical axis

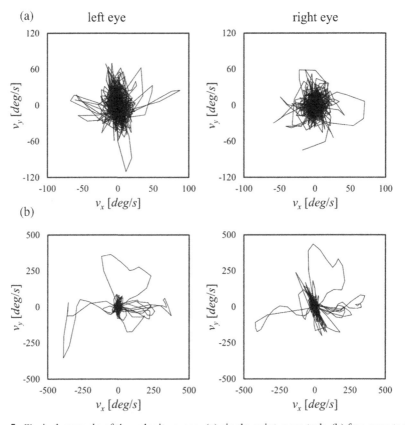

Fig. 5. Typical example of the velocity space. (a) single-point–gaze task, (b) free-gaze task.

is larger and the number of microsaccade candidates detected is higher in the free-gaze task.

Next, Fig. 7 shows the changes in the feature space and selected microsaccade candidates when an amplitude threshold is set for the selected microsaccade candidates, which is a feature of the detection algorithm developed in this experiment. In the free-viewing task, the vertical axis of the feature space shows larger values when no amplitude threshold is set. On the other hand, by setting an amplitude threshold for the selected microsaccade candidates and continuing to exclude candidates until the amplitude falls below the threshold, we can confirm that the vertical axis of the feature space becomes smaller, even during the free-viewing task.

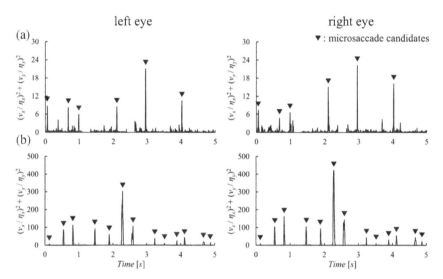

Fig. 6. Typical example of the feature space. (a) single-point–gaze task, (b) free-gaze task.

The mean interval of occurrence calculated from all subjects is presented in Fig. 8. The interval of occurrence during the single-point–gaze task is 1.11 ± 0.49 Hz. During the free-viewing task, the amplitude thresholds are 1.24 ± 0.45 Hz at 1.25 deg, 1.14 ± 0.41 Hz at 1.0 deg, 1.02 ± 0.47 Hz at 0.75 deg, 0.84 ± 0.4 Hz at 0.5 deg, and 0.69 ± 0.29 Hz at 0.25 deg. Statistical analysis is performed using a paired t-test for each value during the single-point–gaze task and free-gaze task. The results show that the values are significantly lower during the free-gaze task when the amplitude threshold is 0.25 and 0.5 deg, compared to the single-point–gaze task ($p < 0.05$).

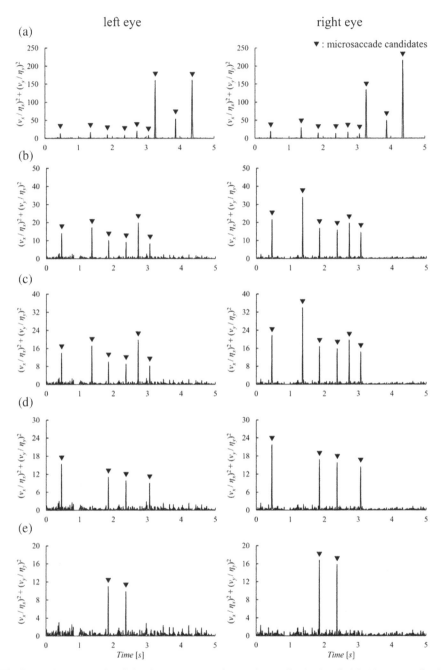

Fig. 7. Typical example of the feature space of at each amplitude threshold. (a) no amplitude threshold, (b) 1.25 deg, (c) 1.0 deg, (d) 0.75 deg, (e) 0.5 deg

The mean amplitude calculated from all subjects is presented in Fig. 9. The amplitude during the single-point–gaze task is 0.21 ± 0.1 deg. During the free-viewing task, the amplitude thresholds are 0.39 ± 0.19 deg at 1.25 deg, 0.3 ± 0.14 deg at 1.0 deg, 0.21 ± 0.09 deg at 0.75 deg, 0.15 ± 0.06 deg at 0.5 deg, and 0.1 ± 0.03 deg at 0.25 deg. Statistical analysis is performed using a paired t-test for each value during the single-point–gaze task and free-gaze task. The results show that the values significantly decrease ($p < 0.05$) during the free-gaze task when the amplitude threshold is 0.25 and 0.5 deg, and significantly increase ($p < 0.05$) during the free-gaze task when the amplitude threshold is 1.0 and 1.25 deg, compared to the single-point–gaze task.

The mean maximum velocity calculated from all subjects is presented in Fig. 10. The maximum velocity during the single-point–gaze task is 70.2 ± 42.7 deg/s. During the free-viewing task, the amplitude thresholds are 83.3 ± 24.7 deg/s at 1.25 deg, 77.6 ± 24.2 deg/s at 1.0 deg, 70.7 ± 24.2 deg/s at 0.75 deg, 65 ± 22.6 deg/s at 0.5 deg, and 60.4 ± 22.2 deg/s at 0.25 deg. Statistical analysis is performed using a paired t-test for each value during the single-point–gaze task and free-gaze task. The results show no significant difference in all comparisons.

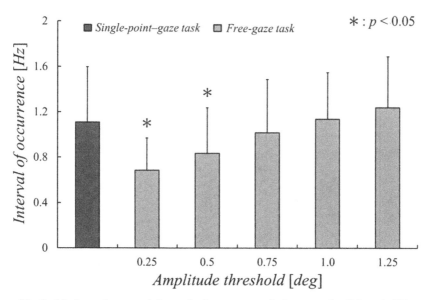

Fig. 8. Median value at each interval of occurrence of microsaccades (Mean ± SD).

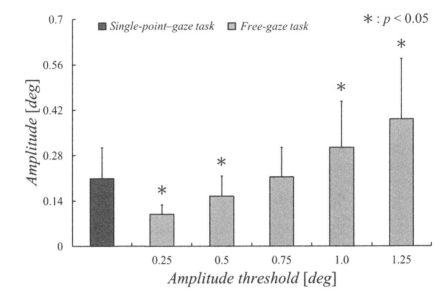

Fig. 9. Median value at each amplitude of microsaccades (Mean ± SD).

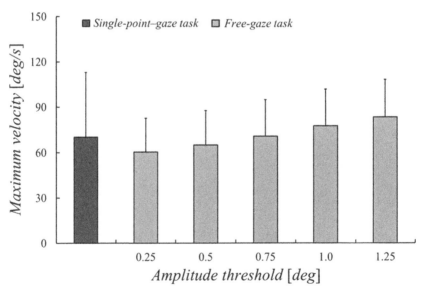

Fig. 10. Median value at each maximum velocity of microsaccades (Mean ± SD).

5 Discussion

Most of the microsaccade-detection algorithms proposed so far assume that the measured eye movement data do not include blinks or saccades, and there have been very few reports on the detection of microsaccades using measurement data during free viewing, which include such information. However, if microsaccades can be detected from the measurement data obtained during free gaze, in which blinks and saccades are mixed, it will be possible to evaluate the potential attention without requiring fixation in experimental protocols, and this is expected to lead to further applied research on microsaccades. Therefore, in this work, we investigated a detection algorithm for microsaccades in the measurement data obtained during free viewing.

In this study, we used a detection algorithm modeled after the "EK method" proposed by Engbert and Kliegl in 2003. In the EK method, the blink-removal method and analysis interval were not strictly determined. Here, the detection algorithm using the EK method did not assume the detection of mixed saccades in the time-series data. Therefore, in this study, we attempted to separate the saccade component from the microsaccade time-series data by setting an amplitude threshold for the detected jumping eye movements. First, the mean interval of occurrence during the single-point–gaze task was 1.11 Hz, the mean amplitude was 0.21 deg, and the mean maximum velocity was 70.2 deg/s. As this was consistent with the microsaccade features reported in previous studies [11, 14–17], we believe that the microsaccades were correctly detected during the single-point–gaze task performed in this experiment. Next, microsaccade detection was performed by setting an amplitude threshold for the microsaccade time-series measured during the free-viewing task. When comparing the values during the single-point–gaze task and free-gaze task, significant differences were found for the interval of occurrence when the amplitude threshold was 0.5 and 0.25 deg, and for the amplitude when the amplitude threshold was 1.25, 1.0, 0.5, and 0.25 deg. In particular, the increase/decrease trend in amplitude was reversed after the amplitude threshold value of 0.75. Therefore, it was considered possible that when the amplitude threshold was large, saccades with small amplitudes would remain, and when the amplitude threshold was small, microsaccades with large amplitudes would be identified as the saccade component. On the other hand, when the amplitude threshold was 0.75 deg, there was no significant difference in any of the analysis indices. The microsaccade indices for this case showed that the mean value of the interval of occurrence was 1.02 Hz, the mean value of the amplitude was 0.21 deg, and the mean value of the maximum velocity was 70.7 deg/s. As with the single-point–gaze task, these values were within the range of microsaccade features reported in the previous studies. These results suggest that the combination of the microsaccade-detection algorithm using the EK method and the amplitude threshold may be able to detect microsaccades in free-viewing data as well as fixed-point viewing data.

Acknowledgments. The authors have no competing interests to declare that are relevant to the content of this article.

References

1. Kaneko, H.: Fixational eye movements. J. Inst. Image Inf. Telev. Eng. **63**(11), 1538–1539 (2009)
2. Troxler, D.: Ueber das Verschwinden gegebener Gegenstande innerhalb unseres Gesichtskreises. Ophthalmologische Bibliothek **2**, 1–119 (1804)
3. Helmholtz, H.V.: Handbuch der physiologischen Optik. Leopold Voss, Leipzig (1867)

4. Cornsweet, T.N.: Determination of the stimuli for involuntary drifts and saccadic eye movements. J. Opt. Soc. Am. **46**(1), 987–993 (1956)
5. Bert, L.Z.: Models of Oculomotor Behavior & Control. CRC Press, Boca Raton (1981)
6. Westheimer, G.: The spatial sense of the eye. Proctor lecture. Invest. Ophthalmol. Vis. Sci. **18**(9), 893–912 (1979)
7. Snodderly, D., Kagan, I., Moshe, G.: Selective activation of visual cortex neurons by fixational eye movements: Implications for neural coding. Vis. Neurosci. **18**(2), 259–277 (2001)
8. Martinez-Conde, S., Macknik, S., Hubel, D.: The function of bursts of spikes during visual fixation in the awake primate lateral geniculate nucleus and primary visual cortex. Proc. Natl. Acad. Sci. U.S.A. **99**(21), 3920–13925 (2002)
9. Engbert, R., Kliegl, R.: Microsaccades uncover the orientation of covert attention. Vis. Res. **43**(9), 1035–1045 (2003)
10. Miki, S., Hirata, Y.: Microsaccades generated during car driving. In: 35th Annual International Conference of the IEEE Engineering in Medicine and Biology Society (EMBC), pp. 2148–2151 (2013)
11. Takahashi, M., Isogai, H., Raalte, J.L.V.: Atempts to detect microsaccades from eye movements in anticipatory response situation: Introducing anticipatory response tasks toward tennis serve. J. Jpn. Soc. Sports Ind. **28**(1), 13–29 (2018)
12. Kapoula, Z., et al.: Distinctive features of microsaccades in Alzheimer's disease and in mild cognitive impairment. J. Am. Aging Assoc. **362**, 535–543 (2014)
13. Otero-Millan, J., Castro, J.L.A., Macknik, S.L., Martinez-Conde, S.: Unsupervised clustering method to detect microsaccades. J. Vis. **14**(2), 1–17 (2014)
14. Lord, M.P.: Measurement of binocular eye movements of subjects in the sitting position. Br. J. Ophthalmol. **35**(1), 21–30 (1951)
15. Ditchburn, R.W., Ginsborg, B.L.: Involuntary eye movements during fixation. J. Physiol. **119**(1), 1–17 (1953)
16. Møller, F., Laursen, M., Tygesen, J., Sjølie, A.: Binocular quantification and characterization of microsaccades. Clin. Investig. **240**, 765–770 (2002)
17. Ohara, T., Kinoshita, F.: Effect of alcohol consumption on the frequency of microsaccades. J. Adv. Comput. Intell. Intell. Inform. **27**(2), 148–153 (2023)

The Participation of People with Disabilities in (Citizen) Science Projects. Best Practice Examples from a Toolbox to Support Inclusive Research

Daniel Krüger⬤, Bastian Pelka⬤, and Ann Christin Schulz[✉]⬤

Sozialforschungsstelle Dortmund, Department of Social Sciences, TU Dortmund University, Dortmund, Germany
{daniel2.krueger,bastian.pelka,
annchristin.schulz}@tu-dortmund.de

Abstract. People with disabilities encounter barriers and are thus restricted in their participation in social and societal areas, among that science. As a rising field of research, citizen science has lately been fostered to gain new insights in fields of research, especially application oriented research. As citizen science experiences strong expectations in research fields connected to civil life, the article argues that citizen science must enable full participation of people with disabilities. To grant people with disabilities' access to these areas of life, participatory approaches should be the state of the art. Due to this, the article will start with a discursive discussion of different participatory approaches of various contexts. Thereby the different theoretical references, as (Participatory) Action Research, (Community-Based) Participatory Research, Practice Research, are presented and located into the methodological frame. After this, the focus is on the Citizen Science project "IncluScience – Disability Mainstreaming in science and practice" in which participatory approaches are being prepared in a target strand and bundled into a so-called "Citizen Science Toolbox".

Keywords: Citizen Science · People with Disabilities · Participatory Approaches · Participation · Toolbox

1 Introduction

The ratification of the Convention on the Rights of Persons with Disabilities (UNCRPD) [29] and its incorporation into national law of the signatory states has established the right to full social participation of persons with disabilities as a legal norm. This places demands on all areas of society and all stakeholders to enable this social participation. Thus, the science system is also faced with the need of enabling more social participation of people with disabilities. This applies not only to research on people with disabilities and their living environment. It also includes the need to make scientific findings and knowledge accessible to people with disabilities. More importantly, fully opening up the scientific system to the participation of people with disabilities requires a further step: the creation of barrier-free access to participation in research.

© The Author(s), under exclusive license to Springer Nature Switzerland AG 2024
M. Antona and C. Stephanidis (Eds.): HCII 2024, LNCS 14696, pp. 63–74, 2024.
https://doi.org/10.1007/978-3-031-60875-9_5

In recent years, increasing efforts have been made to democratise the science system and open it up to citizens [8]. The framework model of Responsible Research and Innovation (RRI) as a result of policy agenda setting at the European level [22] plays an important role here, which, against the backdrop of emerging social challenges, calls for more participation of non-scientists, "with the aim to foster the design of inclusive and sustainable research and innovation" [9]. In this context, the idea of citizen science has also gained new momentum and has increasingly been taken into account in international research framework programmes such as the European Commission's research frameworks - for instance with the aim of supporting "relevance and effectiveness" of results of scientific research and innovation, "creativity and quality by enlarging the collective capabilities" or "transparency, science literacy and confidence of the public in research" [10]. This development was accompanied by an opening up of citizen science to other research disciplines than had previously been the case. The concept also increasingly gained a foothold in the humanities and social sciences, where it encountered a tradition of participatory research, such as participatory action research, community-based participatory research or practice research.

Opening up the science system to society, in the sense of citizen science, firstly brings with it existing pathways for more participation by people with disabilities who have not previously been part of the science system. Secondly, there is also the need to make the opening up of the science system barrier-free. The democratization of the science system must enable the social participation of people with disabilities. This means that citizen science offers not only an opportunity for more social participation but also a challenge if this opportunity is not used with consideration for the needs of people with disabilities.

A necessary prerequisite for citizen science is therefore the removal of barriers and the provision of assistance and aids. If an approach to a universal design [27] for citizen science projects is achieved in this respect, not only people with disabilities can benefit. If citizen science is fully accessible, one can also speak of a participatory approach to granting all people access to science, regardless of environmental factors they encounter in everyday life and personal factors.

With the IncluScience project, a consortium consisting of an activist NGO (Sozialhelden e.V.) and a social science-oriented research institute at a university (Social Research Centre at TU Dortmund University) is taking up this perspective on citizen science. The pivotal point is the guiding principle of disability mainstreaming in science. In this respect, science should not only be open to the participation of people with disabilities. Rather, inclusive citizen science is to serve as a model for the barrier-free design of science in general. In order to act as a prototype for inclusive citizen science, the IncluScience approach not only includes ways of participating in research. In fact, people with disabilities in the project team are actively involved in determining the project design, the research objects and all interventions. In the spirit of "citizen control" [3], they also decide on the progress of the project as project coordinators in the NGO team. In addition, citizens with and without disabilities are included in research activities and the selection of future research priorities using participatory formats like workshops for needs assessment, surveys for the co-selection of research objects (accessibility criteria) or the participative collection of data on the accessibility of places (mapping) (for more information about the project and its participate approach, see the contribution to HCII 2023 [15]). At the heart of IncluScience is the participatory further development of the wheelmap (www.wheelmap.org), an online service providing information on the accessibility of places on a world map. Accessibility is therefore also the main object of research and development in IncluScience.

To support the accessible design of research projects, thus disability mainstreaming in science, IncluScience is also creating a toolbox in which specific recommendations for action, information about counselling centres and recommendations for accessibility tools are collected. The article at hand provides initial insights into this toolbox and can thus be understand as a blueprint for a way to open up science to participation of people with disabilities. The toolbox is aiming at citizens that might (or might not) be experienced in specific fields of science and research, but are not familiar with working with people with disabilities or even the concept of inclusion. Therefore, the toolbox is designed as a scalable entry and support point for different target groups. The overall aim is to engrave the concept of inclusion at the roots of the emerging field of citizen science. Therefore, it must be informed on existing approaches, methods and policies that aim for similar purposes and could be used as stepping stones.

2 Participatory Approaches

Participatory approaches involve stakeholders as co-researchers in science and research. Measures are taken to conduct research in partnership with them as scientists. The aim is also to empower co-researchers. However, there is no such thing as "the" participatory approach. Rather, there is a variety of different approaches, depending on the research context, discipline and target group. In the following, we will therefore look at three that support the participation and empowerment of people with disabilities as co-researchers.

2.1 Participatory Action Research

The tradition of action research is characterised by [18]. Initially, the focus was on practice-relevant solutions for social and societal problems, which were developed together with communities, organisations and other institutions - primarily in the form of field experiments [2, 30]. In the 1970s, action research (in the German-speaking context) was then predominantly characterised by historical materialism and the Marxist critique of capitalism [2, 30]. From an international perspective, however, action research should rather be seen as a participatory process for generating knowledge [2, 30]. Furthermore, research is conducted into individual living and working environments, organisations and communities as well as social structures of the inter-subjective, organisational and communal sphere [28]. In this context, "Participatory Action Research" [6] as well as "Participatory Research Practices" [6] appears to be of particular interest. In participatory action research, (organisational) stakeholders are fundamentally involved in the knowledge process and the researchers only have an advisory function [6]. With regard to the IncluScience target group, participatory research practices are far more interesting. This is because not only (organisational) stakeholders are involved here. Rather, marginalised groups of people are the target group in the participation process.

This is therefore less about quality development in organisations, as in the first form of action research mentioned, and more about emancipation, empowerment and inclusion. The participation of people with different types of disabilities, which is being tested in IncluScience, therefore corresponds to the criterion of *involving marginalised groups of people in the research process* postulated in Participatory Research Practices.

2.2 Practice Research

Practice Research builds on Action Research, but does not differentiate itself from applied research [30]. The focus here is on cooperation between science and practice. Be it through consultation, cooperation or concrete participation formats. Practice Research thus corresponds to the interface between science and practice [19] but still considers both systems as separate. For example, Practice Research does not include necessarily the participation of practice partners. They serve a purely scientific purpose as data providers. The linking of Practice Research with Action Research criteria goes beyond this by striving for closer cooperation between science and practice. Practitioners are given expert knowledge of their skills and needs, which science uses for its research purposes. For example, people with disabilities can be seen as experts in their own needs and skills. Scientists can ultimately use this knowledge to make their research much more practical and target group-specific. The solutions also meet the needs of the target group to a greater extent and thus make a significant contribution to inclusion. A much closer collaboration, which we believe is desirable in science and research with the target group of people with disabilities, is ensured by the following participatory approach.

2.3 Community-Based Participatory Research

Community-based participatory research has its roots in North America, in the context of the health sector. Since the 1990s, a decisive role has been attributed not only to scientific partners and practitioners, but also to communities [12]. The role of the communities is so crucial that they are even a decisive or characterising feature of this participatory approach. In and with communities, the causes of problems - in the origin of the approach still health problems, but this can also be transferred to other social and societal problems, such as poverty, unemployment, discrimination, etc. - are researched and solutions are developed in the form of action strategies [30]. This is characterised by the fact that all stakeholders - for example, people with and without disabilities, as practised in IncluScience - work together on an equal footing and at eye level in all phases of the research process. The aim is also to empower them, strengthen their community and improve their living situation. Applied to the context as the central target group in this paper, this means that this participatory approach empowers people with different disabilities. In addition, the community of people with disabilities is strengthened by first listening to them - for example with regard to their problems and needs - and then working with them in partnership. As a result, they experience participation in science and research on the one hand, but also opportunities for development and design on the other. Furthermore, in the specific context of IncluScience, they can express their needs in relation to barriers and present possible solutions for other people from their community in the form of the online map Wheelmap. The expert knowledge of people with disabilities is particularly appreciated by the scientific partners. This is because they know their needs best and the concerns of people with disabilities can therefore be addressed in real terms.

2.4 Citizen Science

Citizen science developed partly in parallel with the development of the participatory research approaches described above. The Christmas Bird Count, which was first carried out in 1900 with the support of citizens in the USA, is often referenced as the starting point of citizen science [8, 13, 20, 25]. This initially resulted in a tradition of citizen science in the natural sciences and only in the last decade has there been an increasing transfer to the humanities and social sciences. At the same time, there is a long tradition of participatory research in the social sciences using the approaches described above. Citizen science is now conceptually coming closer to these approaches. The socio-scientific examination of citizen science leads to new localisations and classifications. [13] differentiate between different forms of citizen science with a focus on environmental research: (1) "instrumental citizen science" [13] in the sense of instrumentalisation to reach target groups or social spaces that are difficult to access; "communicative citizen science" [13] with the aim of dialogical or dialectical negotiation of research processes and research questions against the background of citizens' expert knowledge; (3) "transformative citizen science" [13] with the aim of mutual learning and the transformation of society and science [13]. The focus of citizen participation is no longer just on data collection, as in the Bird Count. Participation in science and co-determination are also becoming increasingly important. In Germany, for example, this is made clear by the Citizen Science Green Paper. It conceptualizes citizen science as the "active participation of citizens [...] in research processes in the humanities, natural and social sciences" [4]. At the same time, the German Federal Ministry of Education and Research explicitly calls for the involvement of citizens in terms of co-creation of a whole project (including its design), the collaboration in terms of the creation of a research question and support of data analysis or the involvement in data collection, with a recent funding scheme for citizen science projects [11].

Overall, citizen science is experiencing an upswing worldwide, not least due to new funding schemes aiming at more social responsibility, an opening up and a democratization of science. Despite the general goal of being inclusive, in citizen science projects full accessibility still seems to be the exception rather than the rule and is not anchored in the core project designs. [7] Disability mainstreaming in citizen science has therefore not yet been achieved and not all groups of citizens have the opportunity to participate. A desktop search in 2022 revealed only a few examples of projects that took accessibility into account or specifically targeted the participation of people with disabilities [16]. Among the international examples, there were mainly those that aimed to enable accessibility for specific target groups of the respective citizen science research - for example in the context of health research or research to create more accessibility, for example by focussing on the development of assistive devices. For instance, with the EU-funded research project Made4you, the Careables platform (careables.org) aims to provide freely accessible 3D-models for 3D-printing aids for people with disabilities. These aids are developed together with people with disabilities. Another example is provided by the EU-funded Action project and its pilot Sonic Kayaks [1]. Underwater sensors were developed here to collect environmental data in bodies of water. The reference to the needs of people with disabilities was the testing of the sensors for use by people with visual impairments. Both examples show that disability is an issue in the projects and that people with disabilities participate in the activities. However, people with disabilities are part of the target groups of the research and the artifacts developed. With reference to [13], one can mainly observe references to instrumental and communicative citizen science. Similar to IncluScience, these target groups are therefore in the foreground and the necessity of their participation in the research alone requires barrier-free approaches. However, universal designs for participation in citizen science in projects outside of these focal areas appear to be an exception [7].

The Citizen Science Toolbox, which is being developed in IncluScience, is intended to provide support against the background of a lack of approaches for full participation opportunities in citizen science. Therefore, it is also aimed at contributions to a transformation of science by the promotion of disability mainstreaming, which shows links to the idea of transformative citizen science as described for environmental research [13] - however, here the focus is not on contributions to ecological transformation but on social transformation.

2.5 Discussion

While participatory action research, practice research, community-based participatory research and, increasingly in recent years, citizen science has established themselves as participatory research approaches over the years, there is an overall lack of approaches to participation in science that put the participation of people with disabilities into focus. With the aim of collecting, processing and providing knowledge about aids and counselling services that can facilitate the inclusion of people with disabilities in scientific projects, the IncluScience toolbox aims to address a need that has so far received little attention. The overall lack of experience of scientific work in collaboration with people with disabilities across scientific disciplines and research fields also requires the toolbox to emphasise and explain the fundamental requirements of accessible research design and project design. Particularly in research projects that are not dedicated to the investigation of subjects that directly affect the lives of people with disabilities and are anchored, for example, in rehabilitation sciences or health research, it can happen that no experience has been gained in collaboration with people with disabilities. However, in order to help open up such projects to the participation of people with disabilities, it is therefore (1) essential for the toolbox to also impart basic knowledge. This can relate to the question of what disability actually is. It is also important to explain why the involvement of people with disabilities in participatory research is essential and how this can be made possible at an early stage in the project planning phase. (2) Existing experience from the tradition of participatory research can also enrich the accessible design of future research projects. Accordingly, the toolbox must build on this previous experience. At the same time, it is important to reflect on how previous practices of participation in research have helped or hindered the participation of people with disabilities and how this can be dealt with in the future.

2.6 Conclusion

After reflecting the history and recent developments of participatory research, three dimensions appear to be central to the accessible implementation of participatory research with people with disabilities:

- (I): The planning phase of a research project:

  If a research project is to be designed to be barrier-free, this requires ongoing efforts and detailed planning. It is therefore advisable to consider accessibility as an objective as early as the project planning phase and to anchor it accordingly [7]. In addition to the allocation of resources available to a research project, this also results in the need to apply for resources specifically for achieving accessibility from funding organisations. A barrier-free planning phase allows people with disabilities to actively participate in the planning phase which is a key ingredient for an inclusive project set-up. Against this background, IncluScience's toolbox will also provide concrete advice for incorporating accessibility into the project planning phase. Initial cornerstones are outlined below in Sect. 3.1.

- (II) Counselling:

  Over the decades, numerous counselling services for and by people with disabilities have been established, some of which have emerged from the context of self-help or self-advocacy and some of which are part of healthcare or the rehabilitation system. Such counselling services generally promise help in creating accessibility - even if they are not explicitly aimed at research projects. IncluScience initially focuses on the German-speaking countries, so various counselling services in Germany and German-speaking countries were researched for the toolbox and the work in IncluScience itself [7]. The focus of these counselling services is not explicitly on counselling for research projects. The IncluScience toolbox will therefore not only list existing advisory services, but also represent an advisory service itself that is explicitly aimed at research projects.

- (III) Tools:

  Traditionally, accessibility is supported by professionally provided aids and assistance systems, which in many countries can be obtained through the public healthcare system. In addition, the last decade in particular has seen the development, manufacture and provision of low-cost, decentralised tools as part of do-it-yourself activities [5]- structures that could then also be used during the Covid-19 pandemic to make healthcare solutions available quickly and cost-effectively to people with and without disabilities [14]. However, new mobile apps have also created a new type of aids that can cover a wide range of needs and are also accessible via mobile devices and therefore do not need to be individually produced as tangible artifacts for each individual. For the IncluScience toolbox, such low-cost or free-of-charge assistive apps will be collected and listed that can be supportive for accessible participation of people with disabilities in research projects. The toolbox will therefore also address remaining gaps in the provision of information on existing assistive mobile apps, for instance for people with motor disabilities [17] focusing on the needs of accessible and participative research projects.

3   The "Citizen Science Toolbox"

3.1   Planning Citizen Science in a Participative and Inclusive Manner

Participatory research can only be opened up to people with disabilities if barrier-free access is made possible. Ensuring accessibility requires resources, both human and financial. The provision of aids, for example, can help to enhance accessibility. However, such aids or human assistance can incur costs. It is therefore important to plan for such costs at an early stage to avoid later bottlenecks [7] and crucial to avoid a dilemma at an early stage that can arise in the case of scarce remaining resources during a project implementation: between the decision in favour of allocating remaining resources for the implementation of further necessary project activities or the decision in favour of allocating further resources in order to ensure accessibility. It can be helpful to establish milestones for accessibility at an early stage already in the activity plan, making it a necessary rather than an optional project activity. At the same time, the creation of accessibility requires continuous planning - for example, due to individual accessibility requirements, which can vary depending on the persons involved in each project activity. It is also important to identify barrier-free locations for events or to make places that are being researched as accessible as possible.

In order to fulfill the aforementioned requirements resulting from the planning of accessibility for a research project design (1) a work package or task addressing participation and accessibility is recommended, including specific milestones for the whole project duration and all phases. In order to ensure the suitability of measures and to support self-determination, (2) people with disabilities should be involved in the planning phase as experts on their own accessibility needs. With their help, (3) accessibility needs can also be identified and addressed at an early stage, for example due to the subject of the research requiring research in places that are difficult to access or making face-to-face events necessary. (4) Counselling services that can be used as early as the planning phase can provide support here. Resources for the procurement of aids or the recruitment of assistants, experts in their own right or other advisors should also be taken into account when applying for funding (5). (6) In addition, the procurement of aids and the employment of appropriate personnel can also be initiated at an early stage and should also be considered for a proposed project budget [7].

In view of the observation that the creation of accessibility requires a solid level of resources, there is another important note that is also linked to a demand: Project consortia can usually only apply for third-party funding within a limit defined by the funding organisations. Against this background, the mentioned dilemma between using funds for accessibility or using them to achieve research objectives is currently already occurring in the application phase of third-party funded projects. In order not to play off accessibility and the achievement of research goals against each other, it is necessary for funding bodies to provide funding pools that can be used exclusively for the creation of accessibility.

3.2   Counselling Services for Citizen Science

Counselling services explicitly aimed at inclusive and participatory citizen science do not yet exist. Nevertheless, existing advisory and information services can be used to organise such citizen science. For example, services dedicated to the topic of accessibility. The variety ranges from the professional participation and inclusion of people with disabilities to the dissemination of easy/simple language to public relations work and counselling services for companies and institutions with people with disabilities as a target group (ibid.).

The online platform REHADAT [24] is particularly prominent in German-speaking countries. With 14 portals as well as various publications, apps and seminars, it offers a comprehensive range of information on the professional participation of people with disabilities. The platform is not only aimed at the target group of those affected, but also at all people who are committed to their participation and inclusion. The "Assistive Technology Finder", which is available free of charge, is of particular interest for inclusive citizen science. This is because it can be used to identify aids for the barrier-free design of citizen science.

The "Netzwerk Leichte Sprache e.V." [21] is also important for the use of easy language. This is because they support (project) plans with regard to the implementation of easy language by offering training courses and presentations, but also by providing trained reviewers for the comprehensibility of texts already written in easy language.

Equally helpful is the Sozialhelden association [26], which advises companies and institutions that deal with the target group of people with disabilities on accessibility in a variety of projects. The range of focal points is diverse and extends from digital and spatial accessibility to sensitive language and barrier-free communication. In addition, an "Accessibility Cloud" provides accessibility data on locations.

This exemplary presentation of three information and advice services for inclusive citizen science shows that there are indeed services available. Nonetheless, the examples given here are not explicitly tailored to inclusive citizen science, meaning that there are still several services that need to be used to design inclusive citizen science (to date). Those who want to design inclusive citizen science must therefore identify those offers that are relevant to them.

3.3 Aids

It becomes obvious from the previous chapters that special tools are required for the accessible design of citizen science. On the one hand, this requires the above-mentioned information and advice services, but on the other hand also specific aids and assistance tools that create accessibility in different ways. The range of different lists of accessible tools is just as diverse as the information and advice services described in the previous chapter.

The toolbox is based on a list initiated by the team of authors that originated during the coronavirus pandemic. It is a padlet that is available free of charge [23] and initially focused on digital tools for educational and social work. Over time, other tools were added that focused more on communication with relatives or assistance with everyday issues, rather than more cost-effective and data protection-compliant platforms for employees of social institutions. Offers for different target groups can also be identified from this list. For instance, tools that are explicitly designed for people with visual, hearing or physical impairments, with limited or no spoken language and for people with learning difficulties. This is because the needs of people with a visual impairment are very different to those of people with a hearing impairment. As some digital tools are already listed in [7] according to the target group, only a few are given here as examples and otherwise reference is made to the article by [7]. People with visual impairments, for example, benefit from the free "Seeing AI" app, which describes environments audibly or allows visual content such as documents and texts etc. to be experienced audibly. People with a hearing impairment, on the other hand, do not have the need to experience something audibly. This target group is more concerned with communication without speech. This means that what is said is transcribed and what is written is spoken again. AVA is an app that can be used as an example.

The assistance and tools compiled in the padlet are exciting for the toolbox, but not comprehensive. One reason for this is that the padlet does not claim to be exhaustive. Secondly, because the padlet still focuses primarily on social work. It was therefore particularly important, in the workshops initiated by IncluScience, to also ask about aids and assistance tools used by the target group. In addition to a large number of the tools already listed in the padlet, other tools were also mentioned, which in turn fed into the toolbox.

It is clear from this that the toolbox is not really something "new" or inventive. Rather, it is a "rearrangement" of existing possibilities in the form of existing tools that can be used to make citizen science inclusive. Hereby, with a special focus on the needs of the target group.

4 Outlook

If we understand citizen science as a chance to open up science to civil society and set accessibility on the agenda of this new form of research, chances for inclusive research emerge. But a toolbox will not have huge impact on the raise of a new research paradigm. It is one building block that needs to be accompanied by others. The aforementioned challenge that inclusive research is more expensive than research done without empowering people with disabilities is implicitly setting the frame for researchers: Should I provide inclusive methodology, assistive aids and invest time in participation – or should I use scarce funding for employing scientific staff? As long as this dilemma works, science will rate inclusion as "nice to have". The answer to this challenge must be a change in the scientific funding system that is understanding inclusion either as "condition sine qua non" or as a bonus for researchers. If the additional costs for barrier-free research are not reductive on the research budget, but would be paid extra on the funding budget, researchers would find barrier-free research improving their budgets. Administratively, this could be organized by a parallel "barrier-free funding budget" that could be applied for by any research projects funded by that organization. By this budget every funded research project could cover the additional costs for making their research activities barrier free and inclusive. The projects doing this in a good way would receive the highest budgets. This is a call for scientific funding bodies to set pathways for inclusive research and by this foster the impact and applicability of research.

Acknowledgments. The authors are grateful to the German Federal Ministry of Education and Research for the funding. The project IncluScience has received funding from the Citizen Science area.

Disclosure of Interests. The authors have no competing interests to declare that are relevant to the content of this article.

References

1. Action. Sonic Kayaks. https://actionproject.eu/citizen-science-pilots/sonic-kayaks/. Accessed 13 Feb 2024
2. Adelman, C.: Kurt Lewin and the origins of action research. Educ. Action Res. **1**(1), 7–24 (1993)
3. Arnstein, S.R.: A ladder of citizen participation. J. Am. Inst. Plann. **35**(4), 216–224 (1969)
4. Bonn, A., et al.: Grünbuch Citizen Science Strategie 2020 für Deutschland (2016). https://www.buergerschaffenwissen.de/si-tes/default/files/assets/dokumente/gewiss-gruenbuch_cit izen_science_strategie.pdf
5. Bosse, I., Krüger, D., Linke, H., Pelka, B.: The maker movement's potential for an inclusive society. In: Howaldt, J., Kaletka, C., Schröder, A., Zirngiebl, M. (eds.) Atlas of Social Innovation, vol. 2, pp. 201–206. A World of New Practices, München (2019)
6. Cassell, C., Johnson, P.: Action research: explaining the diversity. Hum. Relat. **59**(6), 783–814 (2006)
7. Deister, J., et al.: Citizen Science für alle: Ansätze für inklusive Forschung (auch) mit Menschen mit Behinderungen (forthcoming)
8. Eckhardt, J., Krüger, D.: Teilhabe durch Co-Creation. In: Schröer, A., Blättel-Mink, B., Schröder, A., Späte, K. (eds.) Sozialwissenschaften und Berufspraxis. Soziale Innovationen in und von Organisationen, pp. 83–99. Springer, Wiesbaden (2023). https://doi.org/10. 1007/978-3-658-40695-0_6
9. European Commission: Horizon 2020: Details of the EU funding programme which ended in 2020 and links to further information (n. d.). https://ec.europa.eu. Accessed 14 Mar 2022
10. European Commission: Directorate General for Research and Innovation. Citizen Science: elevating research an innovation through societal engagement. Publications Office (2020)
11. Federal Ministry of Education and Research (BMBF): Richtlinie zur Förderung von bürgerwissenschaftlichen Vorhaben. https://www.bmbf.de. Accessed 17 Oct 2019
12. Israel, B.A., Schulz, A.J., Parker, E.A., Becker, A.B.: Review of community-based research: assessing partnership approaches to improve public health. Annu. Rev. Public Health **19**, 173–202 (1998)
13. Jaeger-Erben, M., Rigamonti, N.: Citizen Science. In: Sonnberger, M., Bleicher, A., Groß, M. (eds.) Handbuch Umweltsoziologie, pp. 1–17. Springer, Wiesbaden (2023)
14. Kieslinger, B., et al.: Covid-19 response from global makers: the careables cases of global design and local production. Front. Sociol. **6**, 629587 (2021)
15. Krüger, D., Krümpelmann, S., Pelka, B., Schulz, A.C.: Inclusiveness of citizen science. how people with disabilities can participate in citizen science approaches. In: Antona, M., Stephanidis, C (eds.) HCII 2023, Part I. LNCS, vol. 1402, pp. 88–98. Springer, Cham (2023). https://doi.org/10.1007/978-3-031-35681-0_6
16. Köster, M., Krüger, D., Schulz, A.C., Pelka, B.: Rechercheergebnisse zu Ansätzen für die Inklusion von Menschen mit Behinderung in Citizen Science Projekten (2022)
17. Larco, A., Peñafiel, P., Yanez, C., Luján-Mora, S.: Thinking about Inclusion: designing a digital app catalog for people with motor disability. Sustainability **13**(19), 10989 (2021)
18. Lewin, K.: Action research and minority problems. In: Lewin, K., Lewin, G.W. (eds.) Resolving Social Conflicts, pp. 201–216. Harper & Brothers, New York (1946)
19. Moser, H.: Grundlagen der Praxisforschung. Lambertus, Freiburg (1995)

20. Munke, M.: Citizen Science/Bürgerwissenschaft. In: Klingner, J., Lühr, M. (eds.) Forschungs-design 4.0: Datengenerierung und Wissenstransfer in interdisziplinärer Perspektive, pp. 107–124. ISGV digital (2019)
21. Netzwerk Leichte Sprache Website. https://www.leichte-sprache.org/. Accessed 7 July 2019
22. Owen, R., Macnaghten, P., Stilgoe, J.: Responsible research and innovation: from science in society to science for society, with society. Technol. Forecast. Soc. Chang. **39**(6), 751–760 (2012)
23. Pedlet. https://padlet.com. Accessed 13 Feb 2024
24. REHADAT Website. https://www.rehadat-forschung.de/. Accessed 13 Feb 2024
25. Silvertown, J.: A new dawn for citizen science. Trends Ecol. Evol. **24**(9), 467–471 (2009)
26. Sozialhelden Website. https://sozialhelden.de/. Accessed 13 Feb 2024
27. The Center for Universal Design (CUD): The Principles of Universal Design, Version 2.0. North Carolina State University, Raleigh, NC. https://projects.ncsu.edu/ncsu/design/cud/about_ud/udprinciplestext.htm. Accessed 07 July 2019
28. Torbert, W.R., Taylor, S.S.: Action inquiry: interweaving multiple qualities of attention for timely action. In: Reason, P., Bradbury, H. (eds.) The Sage Handbook of Action Research, pp. 239–251. Sage, Los Angeles (2008)
29. UN General Assembly. Convention on the Rights of Persons with Disabilities: resolution/adopted by the General Assembly. https://www.un.org/en/development/desa/population/migration/generalassembly/docs/globalcompact/A_RES_61_106.pdf. Accessed 14 Feb 2024
30. von Unger, H.: Partizipative Forschung. Einführung in die Forschungspraxis. Springer, Wiesbaden (2013). https://doi.org/10.1007/978-3-658-01290-8

Ergonomic Principles in Designing Assistive Systems

Karsten Nebe[1]([✉]) and Rüdiger Heimgärtner[2]

[1] Rhine-Waal University of Applied Sciences, Kamp-Lintfort, Germany
`karsten.nebe@hochschule-rhein-waal.de`
[2] Intercultural User Interface Consulting, Lindentraße 9, 93152 Undorf, Germany
`ruediger.heimgaertner@iuic.de`

Abstract. This investigation highlights the crucial application of ergonomic principles in the design of assistive systems, as outlined by the DIN EN 92419 Standard. Assistive systems are defined as technical components (hardware) in combination with logic (software) aiming to support the user in executing an action and to optimize the external load. Here, "external load" is defined as external conditions and demands in a system which influence a person's physical and/or mental internal load. It is important to note that while the external load is a constant presence, its perception varies significantly among individuals. This subjective experience underscores the need for ergonomically designed systems that can adapt to diverse user requirements.

The paper a) underscores the DIN Standard's guidelines for ergonomically designing assistive systems, advocating for development principles that transcend specific technical solutions or interaction methodologies. It introduces foundational concepts and their applicability in crafting assistive systems, alongside b) a novel classification aimed at elucidating the support type such systems offer. This classification not only highlights different functionalities and support mechanisms of assistive systems but also facilitates a more nuanced approach to catering to individual user needs. Through discussing the varying degrees of support that these systems can provide—conceptualized via a functional level model—the research offers insights into their capabilities and limitations, thereby enabling the creation of more customized, user-centric assistive technologies. This paper c) provides a thorough overview of ergonomic design principles within the context of assistive systems, incorporating new developments and experiences in the field, and presents a framework for classifying the type of support provided by these systems. It aims to d) serve as a guide for researchers, designers, and developers, encouraging the application of DIN Standard principles to forge assistive systems that are both more effective and user-friendly.

Keywords: Ergonomics · assistive systems · design principles · user experience · performance · DIN Standard

© The Author(s), under exclusive license to Springer Nature Switzerland AG 2024
M. Antona and C. Stephanidis (Eds.): HCII 2024, LNCS 14696, pp. 75–87, 2024.
https://doi.org/10.1007/978-3-031-60875-9_6

1   Introduction: Ergonomic Principles in Assistive System Design

Assistive systems aim to support individuals by compensating for their physical and mental limitations, assisting them as needed, and enhancing or facilitating the achievement of their goals. These systems are designed to optimize the user's load and strain, enhance their existing abilities, and provide new capabilities and skills, thereby broadening their range of actions. This includes offering support for activities that require innate or learned skills, which can be affected by life circumstances and can be improved through training. For example, assistive technologies like Braille displays can help compensate for the inability to see, thus enabling the skill of reading despite visual impairments. However, the optimization of external loads through assistive systems can inadvertently introduce new challenges or external loads. For instance, while an exoskeleton may enhance a user's ability to lift or carry heavy loads by reducing physical stress, its potential lack of adaptability could result in discomfort during wear. This highlights the importance of considering and addressing the balance between the benefits of assistive technologies and their potential downsides, such as comfort and usability issues.

The evolving landscape of assistive technology underscores the critical need for a robust ergonomic framework in system design. Central to this is the DIN EN 92419 [1] standard, a beacon guiding the integration of user-centric ergonomic principles into the design, development, and evaluation of assistive devices. Ergonomic design in assistive technology is pivotal in creating systems that are not only functional but also accessible to a broad spectrum of users, including but not exclusively those with diverse physical, cognitive, and sensory abilities. This inclusivity is paramount, as it ensures that assistive technologies can effectively serve their intended purpose without exacerbating existing challenges or creating new ones. The DIN EN 92419 standard advocates for designs that consider the entire spectrum of user interaction, from initial contact to prolonged use. This involves a careful analysis of how users engage with assistive systems, including the physical, cognitive, and emotional load these interactions place on them. Furthermore, this standard highlights the importance of adaptability in assistive systems. As user needs can vary greatly, systems must be flexible enough to accommodate these differences.

Systems must not only protect users from physical harm but also safeguard their personal data, especially as assistive technologies increasingly become interconnected, and data driven. The application of ergonomic principles as per the DIN EN 92419 standard is not merely about compliance; it is about enhancing the quality of life for users. Assistive technologies designed with these principles in mind can transform daily experiences, offering users a level of independence and functionality that may otherwise be unattainable.

DIN EN 92419 delineates six fundamental principles for the ergonomic design of Assistive Systems, aimed at improving the quality of interaction between humans and machines:

- **Acceptance:** Characterized by the user's positive decision to adopt a system, influenced by its perceived value and the quality of experience it offers. Strategies for enhancing acceptance include making the system enjoyable to use, offering significant added value, fostering trust, and ensuring the system is non-intrusive [1, pp. 3–4].

- **Safety, Security, and Privacy:** Concentrates on reducing risks and preventing unauthorized access, safeguarding user privacy, and handling personal data with transparency [1, pp. 4–5].
- **Optimization of Resultant Internal Load:** Seeks to optimize the user's external load by efficiently managing the internal load, thereby using it to motivate the user [1, p. 5].
- **Controllability:** Guarantees that the system operates in a predictable manner and can be influenced by the user, with clear communication regarding the extent of its support [1, pp. 6–7].
- **Adaptability:** Permits users to customize the system's functionality to suit their specific situation, including adjustments to privacy settings and the degree of assistance provided [1, p. 7].
- **Perceptibility and Identifiability:** Assures that all elements and information within the system are easy to understand and recognize by users, addressing various sensory modalities [1, p. 7].

In addition, the standard outlines a series of general design recommendations aligned with certain principles for creating assistive systems. However, it emphasizes that implementing just one recommendation does not suffice to fully meet the criteria of a principle. This implies that a comprehensive approach, incorporating multiple recommendations, is necessary to ensure that the design effectively embodies the intended principle. This approach ensures a holistic satisfaction of design principles, enhancing the functionality, usability, and effectiveness of assistive technologies.

In sum, the integration of ergonomic principles in the design of assistive systems is a multidimensional endeavor. It requires a deep understanding of user needs, a commitment to safety and privacy, and a willingness to embrace adaptability and inclusivity. By aligning with the DIN EN 92419 standard, designers and developers can create assistive systems that are not only effective but also empathetic to the real-world experiences of their users.

The integration of ergonomic principles in assistive system design, particularly in accordance with the DIN EN 92419 standard, is a critical aspect of developing effective and user-friendly assistive technologies. In this context, the work of [2] is particularly relevant. In addition, [3] developed a metric for the quantitative evaluation of the ergonomic principles defined in DIN 92419 for assistive systems. Their work involved a systematic literature review to identify dimensions relevant to these principles, leading to the creation of a questionnaire and a checklist for evaluating assistive systems. This approach provides a comprehensive framework for assessing the effectiveness of assistive technologies in adhering to ergonomic principles, thereby ensuring their suitability and user-friendliness.

2 Classifying Assistive Systems Based on Ergonomic Principles

The classification of assistive systems is a fundamental step in adapting technology to the different needs of users to consider differences in the context of use. A classification based on ergonomic principles divides assistive technologies into different categories: physical, cognitive, sensory, health, emotional, social, and environmental interaction systems. In addition, classification of assistive technologies from an ergonomic design perspective emphasizes the potential of these systems to improve the daily lives of all people. By categorizing these technologies according to their functional benefits rather than the specific needs they meet, we can highlight their universal value:

- **Mobility and Physical Enhancement Systems**: Includes not only traditional mobility aids like prosthetics and wheelchairs but also wearable technology that enhances physical performance and comfort for everyone. These systems improve mobility, physical endurance, and general comfort, catering to a wide audience including athletes, elderly individuals, and anyone seeking physical support.
- **Cognitive and Organizational Tools**: Encompassing memory aids, organizational applications, and decision-support systems, this category benefits anyone looking to optimize their cognitive abilities. From professionals managing complex schedules to students organizing study materials, these tools enhance cognitive efficiency and personal productivity.
- **Sensory Augmentation and Accessibility Devices**: Technologies such as augmented reality glasses and advanced hearing systems are designed to enhance sensory experiences for all users. These devices make environments more accessible and engaging, whether for experiencing art in a more vivid manner or navigating urban spaces more effectively.
- **Health and Wellness Monitors**: Ranging from fitness trackers to advanced health monitoring devices, this category supports proactive health management for individuals at all levels of health. These technologies encourage a healthy lifestyle, aid in disease prevention, and support those with specific health conditions in managing their well-being.
- **Emotional Well-being and Social Connectivity Applications**: Applications designed to support mental health, stress management, and social interaction cater to the universal need for emotional balance and social connections. From meditation apps to platforms that foster community engagement, these technologies enhance emotional resilience and social well-being.
- **Environmental Control and Interaction Systems**: Smart home technologies and environmental control devices offer everyone the ability to customize and interact with their living spaces for convenience, efficiency, and safety. These systems are valuable for creating adaptable and comfortable environments for work, leisure, and everyday activities.

This inclusive classification shows that assistive technologies are of significant benefit to the entire spectrum of society. By highlighting the universal applications of these systems, we emphasize the importance of developing technologies that improve the quality of life for all users and promote an environment of inclusion and accessibility. This classification of assistive systems based on ergonomic principles is well-supported by the existing literature in the field such as [1] and [2]. The emphasis on user-centered design and the categorization of assistive technologies according to their functional benefits align with the ergonomic design principles and the broader objectives of assistive technology development. Ergonomic design in assistive systems prioritizes user safety, comfort, and efficiency, ensuring the technology enhances rather than impedes the user's lifestyle. Moreover, these principles advocate for the inclusion of users in the design process, ensuring that their needs and feedback directly influence the development of the technology. This approach leads to the creation of assistive systems that are not only functional but also deeply aligned with the real-world experiences and challenges faced by users. To cover plenty of possibilities to design the adequate assistive system due to the relevant contexts of use, the classification of application areas for assistive systems above helps to reduce complexity and to relate the design principles for assistive systems.

3   Degrees of Support and Functional Level Model in Assistive Systems

Several established models emphasize the integration of the person, the activity, and the assistive technology within a specific context. These models offer a comprehensive view of how assistive technologies can be adapted to meet the varying needs of individuals.

One such model is the Human Activity Assistive Technology (HAAT) model (cf. [4]). This framework considers four primary components: the human (including physical, cognitive, and emotional elements), the activity (such as self-care, productivity, and leisure), the assistive technology (both intrinsic and extrinsic enablers), and the context (encompassing physical, social, cultural, and institutional contexts). The HAAT model emphasizes the dynamic interaction between these components, highlighting the need to consider all aspects for the effective design, selection, implementation, and evaluation of assistive technologies.

Another model that aligns with the concept of functional levels in assistive technologies is the Comprehensive Assistive Technology (CAT) model (cf. [5]). This model also focuses on the complex interaction of components like the person, activity, context, and assistive technology. It is designed to identify opportunities for assistive technology to support persons with disabilities, ensuring that the technology acts as an external enabler for the person to perform an activity in a relevant context. This model emphasizes the need for a dynamic framework that can adapt to the specific needs and situations of individuals with disabilities.

These models provide a comprehensive framework for understanding and developing assistive technologies that cater to the varying needs and contexts of users and embody the principles of categorizing assistive systems based on their complexity and adaptability. They underscore the importance of considering a range of factors—from personal abilities and activities to environmental contexts—in the development and application of assistive technologies. This aligns with the concept of tailoring technology to diverse user needs through a gradation of basic, intermediate, and advanced levels.

Hence, the concept of varying degrees of support in assistive systems is crucial for tailoring technology to diverse user needs. This can be conceptualized through the functional level model, which categorizes assistive systems based on their complexity and adaptability across three primary levels: basic, intermediate, and advanced.

- At the basic level, assistive systems focus on singular, straightforward tasks. These systems, such as basic hearing aids, are designed for ease of use and specific functionalities, offering direct and uncomplicated assistance.

- Intermediate level systems integrate multiple functions, offering broader support. Smartphones with accessibility features, for instance, fall into this category. These systems balance complexity with user-friendliness, catering to a range of needs while maintaining usability.
- Advanced level systems exemplify the highest degree of support, characterized by their adaptability and intelligent features. Smart home systems that learn and anticipate user needs and advanced prosthetics that adjust to the user's movements are examples of this level. Nowadays, these systems are often embedded with AI and machine learning, enabling them to adapt and evolve with the user's changing requirements (cf. RIA-Systems in ISO WD 9241-810 (not published yet)).

Understanding these degrees of support is essential in designing assistive systems that align with user needs because of reducing the design complexity within the context of use by dividing the functionality into levels. Hence, the functional level model serves as a guide for developers and designers, helping them assess and categorize systems based on intended functionality and user requirements. By acknowledging the diversity in functional levels, assistive technologies can be more effectively tailored to individual needs, enhancing their utility and impact. Hence, the functional level model underscores the importance of a user-centric approach in assistive technology design, ensuring systems are not only functional but also adaptable and responsive to the unique challenges faced by users.

4 Stage Model to Identify the Level of Assistance

In the realm of assistive technology, the development and implementation of systems that enhance human capabilities have become increasingly sophisticated. To effectively categorize and understand the progression of these technologies in terms of autonomy, support, and user comfort, we propose a Stage Model. This model delineates the gradual escalation of an assistive system's capabilities, from basic data interpretation to fully autonomous action execution and self-adjustment. The model is designed to provide a clear framework for the development, evaluation, and enhancement of assistive systems, ensuring they meet the evolving needs of users while maintaining a focus on ergonomics and user-friendly design. By identifying distinct stages of assistance, the model facilitates a structured approach to the innovation of assistive technologies, enabling more targeted research, development, and implementation strategies.

The Stage Model is meticulously structured into four major levels, each with its sublevels, designed to delineate the progression of assistance provided by assistive systems. This hierarchical arrangement facilitates a clear understanding of the increasing complexity and sophistication of the systems as they advance from one level to the next.

- LEVEL 1 serves as the foundational stage, where assistive systems begin by interpreting data to generate instructions or recommendations, focusing primarily on workload optimization. This level sets the baseline for applying ergonomic principles in assistive technology, emphasizing data analysis over simple data recording, or displaying. [6] examines the role of self-efficacy and self-confidence in the adoption of assistive technologies, which aligns with this stage of the model where users begin to interact with these technologies.

- LEVEL 2 marks the introduction of active support, with the system performing actions based on its interpretation of data. These actions are supportive, enhancing the user's capabilities without fully automating the process.
- LEVEL 2b introduces a feedback mechanism, where the system evaluates the effectiveness of its actions, ensuring they meet the intended objectives. [7] is an example for Level 2 and Level 2b, where assistive technology not only interprets data but also provides active support and feedback. The research demonstrates the use of a gamified, brain-computer interface-based program for children with ADHD, showing how technology can enhance cognitive functions.
- LEVEL 3 represents a significant leap in autonomy, with the system capable of fully taking over the execution of actions. This level signifies a closer move towards complete system independence in task management. In [8], it is discussed how assistive technology, like vision aids, can significantly impact educational outcomes exemplifying level 3, where technology begins to take over more autonomous roles (such as conducting vision screenings in schools).
- LEVEL 3b adds an evaluative component, with the system assessing the success of its actions, further refining its approach to ensure optimal outcomes.
- LEVEL 4 encapsulates the pinnacle of system autonomy and sophistication. Here, the system not only autonomously executes actions but also continually assesses and readjusts based on effectiveness. This level is indicative of highly intelligent assistive technologies capable of operating with minimal to no human intervention. [9] covers the development of assistive technologies for individuals with deafblindness, particularly emphasizing the need to move beyond prototype phases, resonating with Level 4 where systems are highly autonomous and sophisticate.

As the levels progress, there is a notable increase in autonomy, support, and comfort provided by the system. Importantly, the process of data input does not necessarily require automation; indeed, manual input might be regarded as an added convenience. It is crucial for an assistive system to engage in data analysis that goes beyond mere recording or display—actions that would categorize a system as LEVEL 0, indicating it does not offer actual assistance. The model encourages the consideration of long-term objectives alongside the optimization of immediate tasks. At its foundation, LEVEL 1 sets a standard for the application of these principles, while LEVEL 4 contemplates the deployment of actions by "relatively intelligent" robots, which could operate independently of human interaction.

This thorough introduction and subsequent detailed breakdown of the Stage Model underscore its relevance and utility in the creation of assistive technologies. These technologies are designed to be dynamic, evolving alongside the user's shifting needs. This ensures not only those current requirements are met but also that there is a forward-looking approach to future developments and potential challenges.

The following model shows the levels of assistive system and the type of support. The more specific support criteria are used to categorize or classify the corresponding systems and are intended to help differentiate between them. Level 0 is not relevant as there is no support from the system. Level 4 is already an autonomous system. Although this can generally also be supportive for the user, it does not fall within the scope of consideration of the referenced standard (Table 1).

Table 1. The Stage Model to Identify the Level of Assistance classifies assistive systems by their support levels, from Level 0 (no support) to Level 4 (autonomous), using specific criteria. Level 4, though possibly supportive, is beyond the standard's focus.

Levels of Assistive Systems	0	1	2	3	4
Type of support	None ac-cording to the defini-tion	Instruction or recom-mendation	Supporting action (sub-tasks if applicable)	Largely autonomous (complete task if necessary)	No assistance, since autonomous
Data is collected and analyzed, interpreted and a recommendation for action is communicated		X	X	X	X
The system carries out the handling independently[a]			X	X	X
The system checks whether the goal of the action has been achieved, communicates the status			X	X	X
The system adjusts automatically to complete the action (if necessary, according to specifications)				X	X

(*continued*)

Table 1. (*continued*)

Levels of Assistive Systems	0	1	2	3	4
Type of support	None ac-cording to the defini-tion	Instruction or recom-mendation	Supporting action (sub-tasks if applicable)	Largely autonomous (complete task if necessary)	No assistance, since autonomous
The system acts automatically and completes the action without the user having to do anything				X	X
Both the initiation and the execution of the action are carried out by the system (fully automatically) and the user does not need to actively participate in the action					X

[a]This implies that there is an action/deed that (would otherwise) be performed by a human.

[10–12] explores how assistive products contribute to the Sustainable Development Goals, highlighting the broader impacts of such technologies, which are essential considerations across all levels of the stage model above.

5 Discussion

Assistive systems are designed to help individuals by offsetting their physical and mental challenges, enhancing their abilities, and facilitating their goal achievement. These systems aim to reduce the user's overall burden while providing new skills, thereby expanding their action range [cf. 13]. They support activities that demand both innate and acquired skills, which can be honed through training. However, when optimizing for internal and external loads through these systems, it's important to recognize that while they can reduce stress, they might also introduce new forms of load, such as those associated with training and goal transfer, leading to further questions.

Is it important to distinguish between compensation and enhancement in the tasks or actions performed by assistive systems [cf. 14]? An assistive system extends the abilities and skills of an individual (and may include the compensation of a disability). However, it is conceivable that this general overarching view is not accepted, especially in the current phase of the desired differentiation of society and the exact designation of individual groups. In relation to the external load (objectively and "measurably" existing task), an assistive system will change this - ideally always with the aim of optimizing the load for the individual [cf. 15], whereby optimization can be a trivial relief on the one hand or targeted (development) training on the other. In this respect, a fundamental reduction of the load, which is typically the intention, is not always expedient. As part of the task analysis, it can be useful to differentiate the overall load into the individual partial loads (dimensions) to work out and prioritize the starting points for optimization (e.g. according to effectiveness (benefit) and feasibility (effort)). Regarding the internal load (individual reaction), it seems particularly important to emphasize that for an optimal assistive system, the performance requirements (long-term and short-term abilities and skills) of the respective individual or target group must be precisely determined, described, and analyzed against the background of the (intended) context of use (task, environment, framework conditions, etc.). Only then can the optimal change to the load be identified and implemented.

The presented approach is a first step that serves as the basis for further elaboration to answer e.g. further questions such as "Does an assistive system have to have a direct coupling/connection to the human to produce training effects (movement sequences, muscle development, etc.)?" or "Otherwise, I would have a substitution of the human rather than an assistance, wouldn't I?" We need to consider where exactly the boundary is.

In any case, to be an assistive system, humans should always be involved, even without active participation: they are and remain part of the scenario/context of use (whether in the autonomously driving vehicle or connected to the insulin pump without any intervention).

6   New Developments in Ergonomic Design of Assistive Systems

The integration of cutting-edge technologies in the ergonomic design of assistive systems represents a significant leap forward in this field [cf. 16–18]. Advances in artificial intelligence (AI) and machine learning have led to the development of highly adaptive assistive technologies that can learn from and respond to user interactions, offering a more personalized experience. This adaptability is particularly beneficial for all users as the systems can adjust to changing needs over time.

New technologies have emerged as powerful tools in assistive system design, such as Virtual and augmented reality (VR and AR). They offer immersive environments for rehabilitation and skill development, providing engaging and effective therapeutic and learning experiences [cf. 19]. The user interface design in assistive technologies has undergone substantial improvements, focusing on intuitive, user-friendly interfaces. This reduces cognitive load and makes the technology more accessible [cf. 20, 21].

These advancements not only enhance the functionality of assistive systems but also significantly improve their usability, making a profound impact on users' independence and quality of life.

7 Conclusion and Outlook

This paper delves into the integration of ergonomic design principles with assistive systems, emphasizing adherence to DIN Standard guidelines to improve these technologies' effectiveness and user-friendliness. We outlined essential ergonomic principles for developing intuitive assistive technologies and introduced a comprehensive classification system. This system categorizes assistive technologies into physical, cognitive, sensory, health, emotional, social, and environmental interaction systems based on their functional benefits, showcasing their universal value in enhancing daily life. While the exact term 'functional level model' is not yet commonly used in academic literature, the principles it represents are well-reflected in established models underscore the importance of a user-centric approach in assistive technology design, ensuring systems are not only functional but also adaptable and responsive to the unique challenges faced by users. Furthermore, we presented a novel framework, so called Stage Model to Identify the Level of Assistance, to understand the types of support provided by assistive systems, enabling the creation of customized, user-centric solutions. The proposed model offers a structured methodology for innovating assistive technologies by identifying specific stages of assistance and levels of functionality, which allows for more focused research, development, and deployment strategies.

In conclusion, our research offers a roadmap for leveraging ergonomic design principles and cutting-edge technology to develop more effective and universally accessible assistive systems, promising significant enhancements in the quality of life for users with diverse needs.

The outlook for this paper focuses on the ongoing evolution and future direction in the design of assistive systems. As technology advances, we anticipate further integration of AI and machine learning, enhancing adaptability and personalization. The potential of emerging technologies like brain-computer interfaces and nanotechnology could revolutionize how assistive devices interact with users. Additionally, a growing emphasis on inclusive design will likely lead to systems that are more universally accessible. Finally, the evolving landscape of ethical considerations, particularly regarding data privacy and user autonomy, will play a critical role in shaping the future of assistive technology design.

Acknowledgments. We thank Azadeh Rahimi Farahani and Flávia Xavier Macedo de Azevedo for supporting these reflections for the DIN AAL working group by elaborating their theses as well as all members of the DIN committee NA 023-00-04-09 AK Ergonomic aspects of AAL (ambient assisted living) and assistive systems.

Disclosure of Interests. The authors have no competing interests to declare that are relevant to the content of this article. The authors are members of the DIN committee NA 023-00-04-09 AK Ergonomic aspects of AAL (ambient assisted living) and assistive systems.

References

1. DIN 92419: Principles of the ergonomic design of assistive systems (Standard). Beuth (2020). https://doi.org/10.31030/3106725
2. Farahani, A.R.: Reliability of the metric to evaluate the ergonomic principles of assistive systems, based on the DIN 92419. Master's thesis. Rhine-Waal University of Applied Sciences (2022)
3. Xavier Macedo de Azevedo, F., Heimgärtner, R., Nebe, K.: Development of a metric to evaluate the ergonomic principles of assistive systems, based on the DIN 92419. Ergonomics **66**(6), 821–848 (2023). https://doi.org/10.1080/00140139.2022.2127920
4. Cook, A.M., Polgar, J.M.: Cook and Hussey's Assistive Technologies: Principles and Practice, 4th edn. Elsevier Health Sciences, Amsterdam (2015)
5. Debeuf, R., et al.:. Healthcare professionals' perspectives on development of assistive technology using the comprehensive assistive technology model. Assist. Technol. **36**(1), 51–59 (2024). https://doi.org/10.1080/10400435.2023.2202713
6. Shinohara, K., Wobbrock, J.O.: Self-efficacy and self-confidence as predictors of assistive technology adoption. In: Proceedings of the 18th International ACM SIGACCESS Conference on Computers and Accessibility, pp. 81–88. ACM (2016)
7. Lim, C.G., Poh, X.W., Fung, D.S., Gupta, B., En, H.: The effectiveness of a brain-computer interface-based attention training program for children with ADHD. Atten. Disord. **23**(5), 473–483 (2019)
8. Smith, S.T., Bastawrous, A.: Impact of assistive technology on educational achievement: insights from a school-based eye health program. J. Educ. Health Prom. **8**, 56.1 (2019)
9. Ozioko, O., Hersh, M.: Assistive technology for people with deafblindness: from prototypes to user-driven solutions. Assist. Technol. Res. Ser. **36**, 123–130 (2015)
10. Tebbutt, E., Brodmann, R., Borg, J., MacLachlan, M., Khasnabis, C., Horvath, R.: Assistive products and the sustainable development goals (SDGs). Glob. Health **12**(1), 79 (2016)
11. World Health Organization: Global report on assistive technology. WHO (2021)
12. World Health Organization & World Bank: World report on disability. WHO (2011)
13. Alharbi, M., Bauman, A., Neubeck, L., Gallagher, R.: The use of wearable technology in providing assistive solutions for mental well-being. Sensors **21**(7), 2350 (2021). https://www.mdpi.com/1424-8220/21/7/2350
14. Körtner, T.: Ambient Assistive Technologies (AAT): socio-technology as a powerful tool for facing the inevitable sociodemographic challenges? Philos. Ethics Hum. Med. **11**, 5 (2016). https://peh-med.biomedcentral.com/articles/10.1186/s13010-016-0036-6
15. Papadopoulos, C., Goudas, M.: The upcoming role for nursing and assistive robotics: opportunities and challenges ahead. Front. Robot. AI **8**, 687716 (2021). https://www.frontiersin.org/articles/10.3389/frobt.2021.687716/full
16. Da Silva, M.F., Xavier, A.A., Spolaôr, N., Rodrigues, J.J.P.C.: Artificial intelligence of things applied to assistive technology: a systematic literature review. Sensors **22**(21), 8531 (2022). https://doi.org/10.3390/s22218531
17. Pereira, F., Gomes, J., Oliveira, M.: Artificial intelligence of things applied to assistive technology: a systematic literature review. Sensors **22**(21), 8531 (2022). https://doi.org/10.3390/s22218531
18. Qiu, S., Hu, J., Han, T., Osawa, H., Rauterberg, M.: An evaluation of a wearable assistive device for augmenting social interactions. IEEE Access **2020**(8), 164661–164677 (2020)
19. Geiser, M.: Perspectives on assistive systems for manual assembly tasks in industry. Technologies **7**(12), 4–10 (2019). https://www.researchgate.net/publication/335074208_Perspectives_on_Assistive_Systems_for_Manual_Assembly_Tasks_in_Industry

20. Görner, M., Wiesbeck, M., Reisinger, J., Schulleri, K., Franke, J.: Perspectives on assistive systems for manual assembly tasks in industry. Technologies **7**(1), 12 (2019). https://doi.org/10.3390/technologies7010012
21. Pai, A., Goulart, C., Li, F., et al.: Cutting-edge communication and learning assistive technologies for disabled children: an artificial intelligence perspective. Front. Psychol. (2020). https://doi.org/10.3389/fpsyg.2020.01928

Effects of Electrical Muscle Stimulation on Memorability of Hand Gestures: A Preliminary Study

Yoshiki Nishikawa$^{(\boxtimes)}$, Yui Atarashi, Shogo Sekiguchi, and Buntarou Shizuki

University of Tsukuba, Tsukuba, Ibaraki 305-8573, Japan
{nisihkawa,atarashi,sekiguchi,shizuki}@iplab.cs.tsukuba.ac.jp

Abstract. While images and videos can be used to self-learn hand gestures, it can be difficult to learn gestures accurately in terms of the fingers one has to move and when in order to perform gestures by simply observing images or videos, especially with regard to gestures requiring the movement of multiple fingers. We focus on applying tactile sensation to the muscles of the fingers that should be moved to improve the learnability of hand gestures during self-learning. Specifically, we use electrical muscle stimulation (EMS). We consider EMS may decrease the tendency to move the wrong finger at the wrong time. We first developed a video and an EMS-based hand-gesture-learning support system. Our system applies EMS in synchronization with the movements shown in the videos. Then, we compared the memorability of hand-gesture learning with an existing video-based hand-gesture learning-support system. The results showed an increased number of errors when using EMS, which could be attributed to several factors, such as discomfort from the EMS and a decrease in active engagement and attention. Based on the discussion, we presented a new design for a hand-gesture-learning support system using EMS in response to user errors.

Keywords: Electrical Muscle Stimulation · Motor learning · Hand gestures

1 Introduction

While images and videos can be used to self-learn hand gestures (e.g., sign language), it can be difficult to learn gestures accurately in terms of the fingers one has to move and when in order to perform gestures by simply observing images or videos, especially with regard to gestures requiring the movement of multiple fingers. In addition, since self-learning is done without feedback from an instructor, there is also a risk of learning gestures incorrectly.

To mitigate this problem, research on assisting self-learning of hand gestures by using visual feedback has been conducted [16]. In this research, the system senses the hand motion and records and evaluates it providing real-time visual feedback that notifies the users of correct hand movements. Users can understand

© The Author(s), under exclusive license to Springer Nature Switzerland AG 2024
M. Antona and C. Stephanidis (Eds.): HCII 2024, LNCS 14696, pp. 88–105, 2024.
https://doi.org/10.1007/978-3-031-60875-9_7

the hand gestures of the sign language by referring to the visual feedback. The challenge in learning with visual feedback is that it would still be difficult to understand when and which users should move their fingers to form correct gestures by using only video or images.

In contrast to the above research, we focus on applying tactile sensation to the muscles of the fingers that should be moved to improve the learnability of hand gestures during self-learning. Specifically, we use electrical muscle stimulation (EMS). EMS is a technology that induces muscle contractions by directly applying electrical stimulation to the muscles through electrodes attached to the skin. The use of EMS is diverse; it is used in rehabilitation, exercise training, and muscle strengthening. Recently, EMS has been used for extending interactions based on tactile feedback (e.g., [2,4,8,9,15,18]). Furthermore, EMS has been used for assisting in motor learning [4,8,15], since humans can perceive that their body parts, such as fingers and arms, extend and bend through electrical stimulation [8]. Specifically, EMS is used in activities such as playing musical instruments [4], learning how to operate unfamiliar tools [8], and guiding the direction of pedestrians [15].

Similarly, the ability to move the fingers using EMS can assist in self-learning hand gestures. It allows users to understand which fingers they should move and when they should start to move their fingers, through stimulation. We consider that this functionality, which we call tactile instruction, may decrease the tendency to move the wrong finger at the wrong time. As a result, the ease of remembering hand gestures accurately and recalling them (hereafter referred to as "memorability") would increase. However, how EMS affects the memorability of hand gestures has yet to be explored.

In this study, we investigated how EMS-based tactile instruction improves memorability in hand gesture learning, particularly by indicating which finger should be moved and when through applying EMS to the muscle. For this investigation, we first developed a video and an EMS-based hand-gesture-learning support system. Our system applies EMS in synchronization with the movements shown in the videos, so that users can learn hand gestures by referring to visual cues and experiencing tactile sensations. Then, we compared the memorability of hand-gesture learning with an existing video-based hand-gesture learning-support system.

The contributions of this paper are as follows:

- We developed a hand-gesture-learning support system that uses EMS synchronized with a hand gesture video for each finger.
- We investigated the effects of EMS-based tactile instruction on memorability in hand-gesture learning. Our results showed that while EMS-assisted methods might decrease overall learning performance, they potentially reduce cognitive load for learners. Furthermore, our results showed that participants more easily perceive EMS when it is applied to a single location rather than multiple locations concurrently.
- We presented a system design that uses hand-gesture recognition based on our user study results. In this design, the system applies EMS only when

the user performs an incorrect hand gesture, effectively preventing incorrect movements. By providing feedback only for incorrect movements, learners could study at their own pace and reduce the discomfort associated with EMS.

2   Related Work

This study uses EMS as a tactile instruction for motor-learning support, specifically for improving memorability in hand-gesture learning. In this section, we describe research using EMS and research related to motor-learning support.

2.1   Electrical Muscle Stimulation

EMS is a technology developed in the 1960s for medical rehabilitation [7]. EMS provides electrical stimulation of continuous high-voltage pulse waveforms to muscles beneath the skin through electrodes attached to the skin. This induces involuntary muscle contractions, leading to movements in areas such as the arm or fingers. Recently, due to the size of the device being smaller compared to mechanical devices using motors, EMS has been gaining attention as a promising technology for tactile feedback and tactile actuation [4,8,9,15,18].

Research on finger control using EMS has included using it to provide force feedback in VR and AR [10,11] and movement assistance [4,9,10]. These studies use electrodes attached to the forearm. However, because the forearm is densely packed with muscles, it is difficult to move specific fingers when the forearm is stimulated electrically [19], therefore, research has been conducted that involves controlling each finger independently using EMS [14,18,19]. Takahashi et al. [18] demonstrated that by attaching electrodes to the back of the hand, the joints at the base of the fingers can be moved independently. Watanabe et al. [20] attached electrodes to the finger flexors and extensors and used feedback control to stop the finger at a desired angle; however, there was an issue with the finger vibrating when it was stopped. Nith et al. [14] improved on Watanabe et al.'s method [20] by adding mechanical stoppers.

In our study, we used the method of attaching electrodes to the back of the hand [18] to move each finger independently.

2.2   Research on Motor Learning Support

Numerous studies have been conducted to support motor learning. In this section, we discuss research related to motor learning using EMS and research related to hand-gesture-learning support.

Research on Motor Learning Assistance Using EMS. Research has been conducted to assist learners using EMS in learning human movements [1,4,8, 12,13]. Ebisu et al. [4] used EMS to assist in the playing of percussion instruments by presenting the timing for playing the instrument. Some studies used

EMS to assist with learning the piano, employing it to move the player's fingers [12,13]. Niishima et al. [13] enhanced the synergistic effect of the multiple muscles required to play the piano using EMS. Also, they improved efficiency and reduced fatigue in people practicing piano conventions such as octave tremolos and C major scales by applying EMS to the forearm and shoulder muscles [12]. Furthermore, Lopes et al. [8] presented a system that instructed people how to operate tools they had never used before using EMS. Chen et al. [1] developed a master-slave gesture learning system based on EMS to assist beginners by imitating a teacher's hand movements.

These studies did not investigate memorability of learning with EMS, whereas our research aims to explore the impact of EMS on the memorability of hand gestures.

Hand Gesture Learning Support. There already exists a study that aids in learning American Sign Language (ASL) within mixed reality environments [16]. This research provided visual feedback alone to assist learning; it did not explore tactile sensation. By contrast, we provide tactile sensation to the fingers required for hand gestures using EMS.

One major method for self-learning sign language is watching TV programs or videos, or looking at 2D images in books [6]. In our study, we employed a learning method based on videos as the baseline in our preliminary study.

3   System Design and Implementation

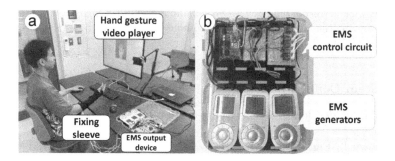

Fig. 1. Our hand-gesture-learning support system. (a) Overview of the system. (b) It is an EMS output device.

We developed a system that uses EMS to move the fingers in synchronization with hand-gesture videos. In this section, we first explain the overall system configuration. We then describe the system's calibration method.

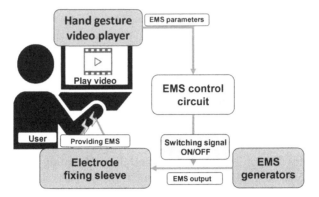

Fig. 2. System configuration.

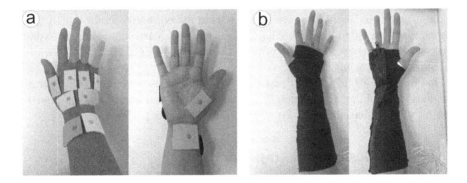

Fig. 3. Electrodes and electrode fixing sleeve. (a) The electrode positions for moving each finger with corresponding colors. For example, the index finger and the two electrodes for moving the index finger are colored blue. (b) The electrode fixing sleeve worn on the hand. (Color figure online)

3.1   System Configuration

The system we developed and its configuration are shown in Fig. 1 and Fig. 2, respectively.

As shown in Fig. 1a, the user wears an electrode fixing sleeve and watches videos that the hand-gesture video player shows in hand-gesture learning. The player shows the video and provides EMS parameters to the EMS output device to apply EMS in synchronization with the movements shown in the video. Beneath the sleeve, there are electrode pads for EMS attached to the skin, to which the electrical stimulation generated by the EMS output device is provided. The EMS output device consists of the electrical stimulation generator and electrical stimulation control circuit shown in Fig. 1b. We used a commercially available EMS device as the electrical stimulation generator.[1] This device

---

[1] Beurer Sanitas, SEM 43 Digital EMS/TENS.

can adjust the electrical stimulation's pulse width, frequency, and output intensity. After conducting author experiments in this study, we determined the values at a pulse width of 200 ms and a frequency of 70 Hz, where the fingers and wrists moved significantly. The output time of the electrical stimulation was adjusted to appropriate values for each hand gesture. The output intensity for each electrode was determined individually for each user through calibration before using the system.

Electrodes and an electrode fixing sleeve are shown in Fig. 3. As shown in Fig. 3a, we used four electrode pads for the back of the hand, one for the palm, four for the inside of the wrist, and one for the outside. We used wet-type electrode pads.[2] As shown in the figure, each finger receives electrical stimulation using two electrode pads. By providing electrical stimulation from 10 electrode pads, our system can induce muscle contractions that bend all five fingers. In addition, we used a sleeve, as shown in Fig. 3b, to ensure the electrodes did not detach after we secured the electrode pads and wired them.

3.2 Calibration Method

The position of these electrode pads (hereafter referred to as application points) was adjusted for each user until the appropriate muscle contraction occurred. To ensure the safe use of the system by users, we performed calibration for each user beforehand. The calibration procedure was as follows:

- Attach the electrode pads to the application points.
- Increase the output intensity of the EMS generators by one step. Continue this until the finger flexion due to electrical stimulation is sufficient.
- If muscle contraction does not occur, reduce the output intensity, adjust the position of the electrode pad, and apply electrical stimulation again.
- Once the fingers flex independently to a certain extent, the calibration is considered complete.

The above steps are performed for all five fingers of one hand. If the user indicates pain or discomfort, the process is immediately stopped.

4 Preliminary Study

We conducted a preliminary study to compare how EMS-based tactile instruction improves memorability in hand-gesture learning against an existing video-based hand-gesture-learning support system.

4.1 Participants

The participants were twelve students (two females) in our laboratory. Among them, eight had experience of EMS; none used it regularly. Eleven were right-handed, while one was left-handed. The average age was 22.6 (SD=0.86). Informed consent was obtained before the study.

---

[2] Omron Healthcare, HV-LLPAD.

4.2   Learning Methods

Neuroscience research has shown that active engagement and attention are fundamentals for effective learning [3]. We also thought that it was crucial to ensure that participants maintained active engagement, even when using external aids such as EMS. Therefore, we compared the following two methods in this user study:

- **Existing Method:** In this method, participants are encouraged to actively move their hands using only hand-gesture videos.
- **Our Method:** In this method, participants are encouraged to actively move their hands while watching the hand-gesture videos and simultaneously receive electrical stimulation through EMS.

4.3   Hand Gesture Set

For this user study, we constructed a gesture set, which is a multiset because it contains two instances for some elements (i.e., some gestures). Each gesture in this set consisted of the bending movements of the thumb, index finger, middle finger, ring finger, and little finger, and each was classified into nine types based on the combination of the following two conditions:

- Condition 1: Number of fingers bending simultaneously (one, two, or three fingers).
- Condition 2: Number of consecutive bending movements (once, twice, or three times).

Based on these conditions, we randomly created 30 gestures for bending a single finger (10 for bending one finger once, 10 for bending one finger twice, and 10 for bending one finger three times). Similarly, we created 30 gestures each for hand gestures involving two and three fingers, resulting in a set of 90 gestures.

Note that, for the conditions of bending one finger once, two fingers once, and three fingers once, we replicated some gestures to achieve ten gestures due to the absence of ten unique gestures. In addition, gestures that were difficult for humans to perform, such as bending the middle and little fingers without bending the ring finger, were excluded. Moreover, we constructed hand gestures involving two or three movements by connecting one-movement gestures. In total, the number of times each finger was bent was 75 for the thumb, 72 for the index finger, 67 for the middle finger, 83 for the ring finger, and 63 for the little finger in this set.

4.4   Task

We used a within-subject design; participants learned the same gesture set using the two methods. The order of methods was counterbalanced. The flow of the task performed by the participants is shown in Fig. 4 and described below:

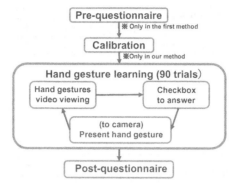

Fig. 4. Task of the study.

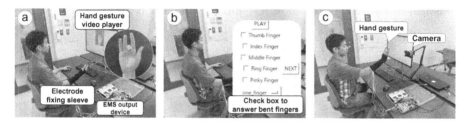

Fig. 5. Setup and procedure of the preliminary study. Participants learn hand gestures (a). After learning, they answer which finger is bent using checkboxes for each gesture (b) and then present it to the camera (c).

1. **Pre-questionnaire (only in the first method):** Participants were asked about their attributes and experience with EMS.
2. **Calibration (only in our method):** Calibration was performed to determine the output intensity of the electrical stimulation given to each electrode and the electrode position on to the user's right hand.
3. **Hand gesture learning (in both methods):** Figure 5 shows the hand-gesture-learning task performed by the participants. First, participants watched a hand-gesture video (Fig. 5a) while memorizing the fingers to bend and the timing. Then, they answered, using checkboxes, which fingers bent (Fig. 5b). Finally, they presented the remembered hand gesture to the camera, including the fingers to bend and the timing, as accurately as possible using the right hand (Fig. 5c). This series of flows is considered one trial, with 180 trials (90 trials × 2 methods) in the entire study. The order of hand gestures started with the gestures of bending one finger once, followed by one finger twice, one finger three times, two fingers once, ..., and ended with gestures bending three fingers three times.
4. **Post-questionnaire (in both methods):** Participants were asked about tasks they found easy (rated from 1–3), tasks they found difficult (rated from 1–3) among the nine types of gestures, what they paid attention to during

memorization, their overall impressions of the user study, and the NASA-TLX [5] scores for workload assessment.

4.5   Metrics for Evaluation

The metrics used for evaluating the methods were the number of incorrect answers in the checkbox-based test, discrepancies between checkbox responses and the actual hand gestures presented by the participants, the NASA-TLX [5] scores for workload assessment, and the answer to the post-questionnaire.

5   Results

In this section, we discuss the metrics used for evaluating the methods. All statistical tests were performed at a significance level of $\alpha = 0.05$.

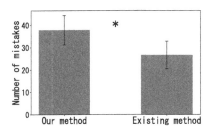

Fig. 6. Number of incorrect answers.

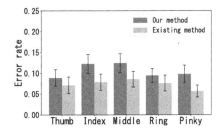

Fig. 7. Error rate by fingers.

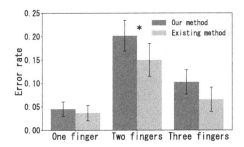

Fig. 8. Error rate by the number of fingers.

5.1 Number of Incorrect Answers

The overall number of incorrect answers in each method during the test is shown in Fig. 6. Additionally, the error rate by finger is shown in Fig. 7, and the error rate by the number of fingers is shown in Fig. 8. The results of incorrect answers in each method were analyzed using the Shapiro-Wilk test. If there was normality, paired t-tests were used, and if there was no normality, the Wilcoxon signed-rank test was used. The test methods used and the results of the p-values are shown in Table 1. As shown in Table 1, two p-values were less than 0.05, indicating that there was a significant difference in the overall number of incorrect answers and the error rate for two fingers. In addition, while no significant differences were observed in other items, the index finger, middle finger, and three fingers approached the significance level (the p-value was between 0.10 and 0.05), suggesting differences in these items.

5.2 Discrepancies Between Checkbox Responses and Actual Hand Gestures

Figure 9 shows the discrepancies between checkbox responses and the actual hand gestures performed by participants in front of the camera. Data from one participant was excluded because the entire hand was not visible in the video, thus we used the data from 11 participants.

The left of the figure shows the average number of times participants answered correctly in the checkbox but performed the gesture incorrectly (Checkbox ✓ Camera×). The right side shows the average number of times participants answered incorrectly in the checkbox but performed the gesture correctly (Checkbox× Camera ✓).

After conducting the Shapiro-Wilk test, which indicated a lack of normality in our data, we used the Wilcoxon signed-rank test for our statistical analysis of

Table 1. Test methods and the results of the p-values.

Item	Test method	p-value
Total	Paired t-test	0.036
Thumb	Paired t-test	0.054
Index	Paired t-test	0.092
Middle	Paired t-test	0.054
Ring	Paired t-test	0.28
Pinky	Paired t-test	0.065
One finger	Wilcoxon signed-rank test	0.46
Two fingers	Paired t-test	0.013
Three fingers	Wilcoxon signed-rank test	0.12
Checkbox✓ Camera×	Wilcoxon signed-rank test	0.83
Checkbox× Camera✓	Wilcoxon signed-rank test	0.072

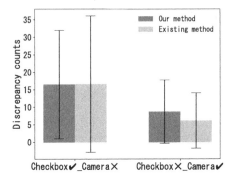

Fig. 9. The number of discrepancies between checkbox responses and actual hand gestures.

the discrepancies. The results showed that for the discrepancies where participants answered correctly in the checkbox but performed the gesture incorrectly, the p-value was 0.76, indicating no significant difference. Conversely, for discrepancies where participants answered incorrectly in the checkbox but performed the gesture correctly, the p-value was 0.072, which approached the significance level (the p-value was between 0.10 and 0.05), suggesting a difference.

5.3 NASA-TLX

The results of the NASA-TLX are shown in Fig. 10. The data for each item of the NASA-TLX were analyzed using the Shapiro-Wilk test. Then, items with normality were analyzed using paired t-tests, and items without normality were analyzed using the Wilcoxon signed-rank test. The results are shown in Table 2. As shown in Table 2, all items had p-values greater than 0.05, indicating no significant difference.

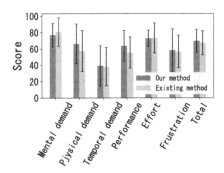

Fig. 10. Results of the NASA-TLX.

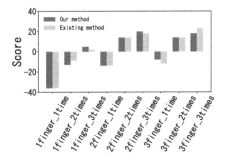

Fig. 11. Participants' ratings of difficulty of tasks.

Table 2. Results of tests for each item in NASA-TLX.

Item	Test method	p-value
Mental demand	Wilcoxon signed-rank test	0.37
Physical demand	Paired t-test	0.31
Temporal demand	Paired t-test	0.84
Performance	Paired t-test	0.39
Effort	Paired t-test	0.93
Frustration	Paired t-test	0.81
Total	Paired t-test	0.51

5.4 Questionnaire Results

The participants were asked about the ways in which they memorized the gestures and their impressions of the user study. The results are shown in Table 3 and Table 4.

Additionally, to quantitatively assess the perceived difficulty of the gestures task, participants were asked to rate the tasks related to the nine types of gestures from most difficult to easiest. Points were allocated as follows: 3 points for the most difficult task, 2 points for the second most difficult, and 1 point for the third most difficult. Conversely, negative points were allocated for the tasks perceived as easiest: -3 points for the easiest task, -2 points for the second easiest, and -1 points for the third easiest.

A composite score for each type was then calculated based on the summation of these points from all participants. The results are shown in Fig. 11.

6 Discussion

In this section, we discuss the results of our experiments. The discussion is broken into several subsections, each focusing on a distinct aspect. First, we explore the possible reasons for the increased error rate when using EMS. Next, the discussion delves into why gestures involving two fingers had the most errors. The section also looks into the observed lack of significant differences in both

Table 3. The ways in which gestures were memorized by participants.

No.	Responses	Participants	Method
1	I named the gesture shapes to help with memorizing them	P1–3, P7, P8, P11, P12	Both method
2	I repeated the names of the bent fingers in my mind	P2, P5, P6	Our method
3	I physically imitated the gesture	P6	Existing method
4	I remembered the sensation after feeling the stimulus	P8	Our method
5	I used both hands for memorization	P9	Our method Existing method
6	I tried to remember by shape.	P10	Exiting method

methods one-finger gestures and NASA-TLX scores. Finally, we describe a new design for a hand-gesture-learning support system that we have devised based on the above discussions.

6.1 Reasons for Increased Error Rates When Using EMS

Memory Inhibition Due to Discomfort. The post-questionnaire (Table 4, No. 6), suggests that the discomfort caused by EMS could impair memory retention and increase the likelihood of errors.

Diminishing Effects of EMS. The post-questionnaire (Table 4, No. 5) suggests that the effects of EMS may have diminished as participants became accustomed to the electrical stimulation of EMS.

Active Engagement and Attention. The movement of the fingers induced by EMS may have led to a decrease in users' conscious efforts to move their fingers actively, resulting in scattered attention and potentially an increase in errors. This observation aligns with neuroscience research that emphasizes the importance of active engagement and attention as fundamentals for effective learning [3].

Table 4. Overall impressions of the user study from participants.

No.	Comments	Participants	Method
1	I found it easier to remember when the fingers to be moved were adjacent or when the same finger was moved multiple times	P2	Existing method
2	By feeling the stimulus, I remembered the sensation, which made recalling easier and reduced cognitive load compared to the existing method	P2, P6, P5, P10, P12	Our method
3	Because EMS didn't move the fingers, I could practice moving my hand in my own time, making it easier to remember in the short term	P3	Existing method
4	Even if I remembered it during the checkbox input, I tended to forget it during the camera input	P4	Existing method
5	I felt that the effectiveness of EMS decreased as I got used to it	P4	Our method
6	The discomfort from EMS made it difficult to remember	P4	Our method
7	I felt a difference in how easily each finger bent	P5	Our method
8	For single fingers, I remembered the time the finger was bent due to the sensation from EMS	P7	Our method
9	I felt a change in the position of the electrical stimulation when bending multiple fingers	P8	Our method
10	Two fingers were more difficult to name	P1, P3, P7	Both methods

6.2   Why Two-Finger Gestures Tend to Cause Errors

The post-questionnaire (Table 3, No. 1) suggests that gestures involving three fingers were more easily named (such as "fox" and "peace"), and, therefore, more memorable. In contrast, two-finger gestures were found to be harder to name, according to the post-questionnaire (Table 4, No. 10), which could explain why they tend to cause errors.

6.3   Reason for Lack of Significant Difference in One-Finger Gestures

The lack of significant differences in one-finger gestures can be attributed to several factors. Firstly, fewer errors were observed in these gestures because the total number of finger bends for one-finger hand gestures was 30 for each method. Given this limited number, it is plausible that significant differences were less likely to emerge. Additionally, one-finger hand gestures involve electrical stimulation at only a single point, which likely reduces perceptual confusion because of the minimized discomfort. This notion is supported by feedback from the post-questionnaire (Table 4, No. 9), where P8 noted that he felt a shifting sensation when multiple fingers received electrical stimulation simultaneously. Therefore, limiting the number of points stimulated simultaneously might be beneficial.

6.4   Lack of Significant Differences in NASA-TLX Scores

The NASA-TLX scores suggest that while EMS did not significantly alleviate the task load, EMS did not amplify the task load due to discomfort. Moreover, feedback from the post-questionnaire (Table 4, No. 2) indicated that many participants felt the tasks of memorization and recall were intensified by EMS. It is conceivable that significant differences in mental demand scores might emerge with a larger sample of participants.

6.5   Discrepancy Between the Checkbox Response and the Hand Gesture Presented

Based on Fig. 9 and the p–value in Table 1, it was observed that for instances where participants answered incorrectly in the checkbox but performed the gesture correctly, that our method yielded a higher number of correct gestures and approached the significance level (the p-value was between 0.10 and 0.05), suggesting a difference. A plausible explanation for this could be that, while participants might not have been able to remember during the memory task, the sensation from EMS might have supported them in performing the correct gesture more frequently than the conventional method, when they performed the hand gesture.

6.6   Design of the Hand Gesture Learning Support System Using EMS

Based on the insights gathered from the previous discussion, we delve into the design for a hand-gesture-learning support system using EMS. In our current study, EMS was applied to all the fingers involved when users were learning the hand gestures. However, this frequent application of EMS might have led to increased discomfort. Moreover, the actuation of fingers by EMS could have diminished active user engagement, potentially reducing learning effectiveness. Considering these factors, we plan to implement tactile feedback Considering these factors, we plan to implement tactile feedback, which moves the incorrect fingers of an incorrect gesture in the opposite direction. This would act as a corrective mechanism, stopping the user making the wrong finger movement. In addition, such an approach ensures that active engagement is not compromised. Furthermore, by not applying EMS extensively, we anticipate reduced user discomfort.

7   Limitations

In this preliminary study, participants were recruited from within the laboratory. Moreover, there was a bias in attributes such as gender and age. Therefore, it is necessary to conduct further investigations with participants with a wider range of ages and attributes, including experience with sign language. Additionally, our method uses electrical stimulation, which may cause discomfort. The extent to which this discomfort affects learning has not been sufficiently investigated. It has also been suggested that the decrease in active engagement may have led to diminished attention. This could be measured and evaluated using biometric data such as brain waves and eye tracking during the experimental tasks.

Furthermore, in the preliminary study, participants were instructed to move their fingers along with the electrical stimulation to maintain a sense of agency. However, the timing of these movements depended on the participants, and due to individual differences, the electrical stimulation might have caused a loss of agency. Therefore, it is necessary to present electrical stimulation that aligns with the participants' movements, independent of their subjective timing, to maintain their sense of agency. Additionally, Tajima et al. [17] have investigated user agency trade-offs between user-initiated touch and computer-controlled touch timing with electrical stimulation. However, the impact of this trade-off on the effectiveness of motor learning with electrical stimulation has not been studied. Thus, it is necessary to adjust the timing of electrical stimulation in response to user movements and investigate its impact on learning effectiveness.

8   Conclusion

This study aimed to investigate the effectiveness of EMS on memorability in supporting the learning of hand gestures. While EMS is viewed as a promising technology for helping motor learning, its effects on memorability have not been thoroughly examined. In this study, we compared the performance and subjective workloads between the video-based hand-gesture-learning method and a hand-gesture-learning method using both EMS and video.

The results showed an increased number of errors when using EMS, which could be attributed to several factors, such as discomfort from the EMS and a decrease in active engagement and attention. Moreover, while no significant differences were observed in the NASA-TLX scores, the questionnaire provided insights into the user experience. Many participants found EMS helpful for memorization, despite the increase in errors, suggesting that EMS might reduce the cognitive load of the task at the expense of performance accuracy.

While this user study provides various insights, it also raises questions that warrant further investigation. In future research, we intend to consider a broader and more diverse participant pool and explore the long-term effects of learning with EMS. Additionally, we have not investigated how well users can remember the flexion time of the hand gestures presented by EMS. Furthermore, there is a need to examine the potential of a feedback system using EMS to guide users toward the correct hand gesture in response to their hand gestures.

In conclusion, while EMS is a complex technology, it is attractive for hand-gesture-learning support. However, incorrect utilization might diminish its learning efficacy. Moving forward, we will further explore the effects of EMS on memorability in hand gesture learning and seek optimal methods to harness its potential efficiently.

References

1. Chen, K., Zhang, B., Zhang, D.: Master-slave gesture learning system based on functional electrical stimulation. In: Intelligent Robotics and Applications (ICIRA 2014), pp. 214–223. Springer, Cham (2014)
2. Chen, Y., Yang, Z., Abbou, R., Lopes, P., Zhao, B.Y., Zheng, H.: User authentication via electrical muscle stimulation. In: Proceedings of the 2021 CHI Conference on Human Factors in Computing Systems (CHI 2021), pp. 6:1–6:15. Association for Computing Machinery, New York (2021)
3. Dehaene, S.: How We Learn: The New Science of Education and the Brain. Penguin, UK (2020)
4. Ebisu, A., Hashizume, S., Suzuki, K., Ishii, A., Sakashita, M., Ochiai, Y.: Stimulated percussions: techniques for controlling human as percussive musical instrument by using electrical muscle stimulation. In: SIGGRAPH ASIA 2016 Posters (SA 2016), pp. 37:1–37:2. Association for Computing Machinery, New York (2016)
5. Hart, S.G., Staveland, L.E.: Development of NASA-TLX (task load index): results of empirical and theoretical research. Hum. Mental Workload 1(3), 139–183 (1988)
6. Information, Center, C.: Information and Culture Center for the Deaf, Inc. (ICCD). http://www.jyoubun-center.or.jp/english/. Accessed 01 Sept 2024
7. Knapp, M.E.: Practical physical medicine and rehabilitation. Postgrad. Med. Taylor & Francis 41(3), A–113–A–116 (1967)

8. Lopes, P., Ion, A., Mueller, W., Hoffmann, D., Jonell, P., Baudisch, P.: Propriocep-tive interaction. In: Proceedings of the 2015 CHI Conference on Human Factors in Computing Systems (CHI 2015), pp. 939–948. Association for Computing Machin-ery, New York (2015)
9. Lopes, P., Jonell, P., Baudisch, P.: Affordance++: allowing objects to communicate dynamic use. In: Proceedings of the 33rd Annual ACM Conference on Human Fac-tors in Computing Systems (CHI 2015), pp. 2515–2524. Association for Computing Machinery, New York (2015)
10. Lopes, P., You, S., Cheng, L.P., Marwecki, S., Baudisch, P.: Providing haptics to walls & heavy objects in virtual reality by means of electrical muscle stimulation. In: Proceedings of the 2017 CHI Conference on Human Factors in Computing Systems (CHI 2017), pp. 1471–1482. Association for Computing Machinery, New York (2017)
11. Lopes, P., You, S., Ion, A., Baudisch, P.: Adding force feedback to mixed reality experiences and games using electrical muscle stimulation. In: Proceedings of the 2018 CHI Conference on Human Factors in Computing Systems (CHI 2018), pp. 1–13. Association for Computing Machinery, New York (2018)
12. Niijima, A., Aoki, R., Koike, Y., Miyahara, S.: Motor-skill-transfer technology for piano playing with electrical muscle stimulation. In: SIGGRAPH Asia 2023 Emerg-ing Technologies (SA 2023), pp. 14:1–14:2. Association for Computing Machinery, New York (2023)
13. Niijima, A., Takeda, T., Aoki, R., Miyahara, S.: Muscle synergies learning with electrical muscle stimulation for playing the Piano. In: Proceedings of the 35th Annual ACM Symposium on User Interface Software and Technology (UIST 2022). Association for Computing Machinery, New York (2022)
14. Nith, R., Teng, S.Y., Li, P., Tao, Y., Lopes, P.: DextrEMS: increasing dexterity in electrical muscle stimulation by combining it with brakes. In: Proceedings of the 34rd Annual ACM Symposium on User Interface Software and Technology (UIST 2021), pp. 414–430. Association for Computing Machinery, New York (2021)
15. Pfeiffer, M., Dünte, T., Schneegass, S., Alt, F., Rohs, M.: Cruise control for pedes-trians: controlling walking direction using electrical muscle stimulation. In: Pro-ceedings of the 2015 CHI Conference on Human Factors in Computing Systems (CHI 2015), pp. 2505–2514. Association for Computing Machinery, New York (2015)
16. Shao, Q., et al.: Teaching American sign language in mixed reality. In: Proceed-ings of the ACM on Interactive, Mobile, Wearable and Ubiquitous Technologies (IMWUT 2020). Association for Computing Machinery, New York (2020)
17. Tajima, D., Nishida, J., Lopes, P., Kasahara, S.: Whose touch is this?: understand-ing the agency trade-off between user-driven touch vs. computer-driven touch. ACM Trans. Comput.-Hum. Interact. 29(3) (2022)
18. Takahashi, A., Brooks, J., Kajimoto, H., Lopes, P.: Increasing electrical muscle stimulation's dexterity by means of back of the hand actuation. In: Proceedings of the 2021 CHI Conference on Human Factors in Computing Systems (CHI 2021). Association for Computing Machinery, New York (2021)

19. Tamaki, E., Miyaki, T., Rekimoto, J.: PossessedHand: techniques for controlling human hands using electrical muscles stimuli. In: Proceedings of the 2011 CHI Conference on Human Factors in Computing Systems (CHI 2011), pp. 543–552. Association for Computing Machinery, New York (2011)
20. Watanabe, K., Oka, M., Mori, H.: Feedback control to target joints angle in middle finger PIP and MP joint using functional electrical stimulation. In: Human Interface and the Management of Information. Information in Intelligent Systems, pp. 440–454. Springer, Cham (2019)

Converging Affective Computing and Ethical Challenges: The Quest for Universal Access in Human-Machine Cooperation

Joana Sousa(✉) ⓘ, Salvador Santos ⓘ, Luis André ⓘ, and João Ferreira

NOS Inovação, Lisbon, Portugal
joana.sousa@nos.pt

Abstract. Universal access in human-machine cooperation has gained significant attention with the emergence of affective computing technologies. This paper presents a comprehensive review of the current state of the field, focusing on how affective computing is shaping the landscape of universal access. We explore the key concepts, challenges, and opportunities at the intersection of affective computing and universal access, emphasizing its impact on individuals with disabilities and diverse cultural backgrounds. Additionally, we delve into ethical considerations and potential future directions for research and development. The paper delves into the realm of accessibility and affective computing, illuminating the potential of affective computing technologies to ameliorate accessibility barriers faced by individuals with disabilities. Through a comprehensive investigation, the paper assesses how emotion recognition and response systems can augment the user experience for individuals with diverse physical and cognitive impairments, thereby facilitating universal access to cutting-edge technology. Also, the European Union (EU) is currently developing an AI Act, which would establish a comprehensive regulatory framework for AI products and services within the bloc. This legislation would classify AI systems based on their risk level and impose specific requirements for each category. For example, high-risk AI systems would require mandatory conformity assessments and transparency reports. During the paper, a critical analysis about the implications of the new EU AI regulation (Act AI) will be performed, particularly in the affective computing applied to accessibility.

Keywords: Affective Computing · Applications · Ethic · Privacy

1 Introduction

Affective computing technologies have revolutionized accessibility by providing innovative solutions for individuals with disabilities. Emotion recognition systems, often integrated into assistive technologies, allow individuals with physical or cognitive impairments to interact with devices more intuitively. For example, emotion-aware interfaces can facilitate hands-free communication, enabling individuals with mobility impairments to control devices and access information effortlessly. Furthermore, emotion-aware technologies contribute to sensory substitution, enhancing the sensory experiences of those with sensory impairments. For instance, auditory feedback systems can convey emotional information through sound, allowing individuals with visual impairments to perceive and respond to emotions in their environment.

In the ever-changing world of technological innovation, the convergence of affective computing and universal access is reshaping the way humans interact with machines, opening new doors to empathy and inclusivity. Affective computing focuses on developing technologies that can recognize, interpret, express, and respond to human emotions and sensations to ameliorate human-machine interactions [1].

The emergence of emotion recognition systems has ushered in revolutionary solutions for individuals with physical and cognitive impairments. These technologies, integrated into assistive devices, are setting the path to more effective communication and interaction. Moreover, emotion-aware interfaces contribute to sensory substitution, enriching the experiences of those with sensory impairments. This paper delves into the potential of these technologies to dismantle barriers faced by individuals with disabilities, nourishing universal access.

However, in an era where emotional data is increasingly prominent in our daily lives, ethical considerations surrounding privacy, consent, and data security emerge as critical focal points. The paper recognizes the importance of ensuring users have control over their emotional data, aligning with global initiatives such as the OECD's AI Principles [2]. Amidst these worries, the European Union is taking a proactive stance by developing the AI Act [3], a comprehensive regulatory framework for AI products and services within its jurisdiction. The paper critically analyses the implications of the EU AI Act, particularly in the context of affective computing applied to accessibility.

Through this multidimensional exploration, the paper aims to contribute to the advancement of technology that promotes inclusivity, but also respects the right to safe and private human experiences. By addressing the intricacies of affective computing, universal access, and ethical considerations, the challenge is set for a future where human-machine cooperation is not only technologically advanced but also ethically grounded and universally accessible.

This paper is organized as following: Sect. 2 presents a brief description of the affective computing state-of-the-art; Sect. 3 highlights the main applications of affective computing; Sect. 4 goes to the ethical considerations in affective computing; Sect. 5 a brief analyze of how EU Act AI may impact affective computing; Sect. 6 future research directions for exploring the potential of affective computing; and finally Sect. 7 the main conclusions.

2 State-of-the-Art

2.1 Affective Computing

Affective computing is the field that seeks to imbue machines with the ability to recognize, interpret, process, and simulate human emotions [1]. This multidisciplinary field encompasses areas of knowledge as distant as psychology, physiology, engineering, sociology and computer science, in a search for more natural, intuitive, and empathetic interactions between humans and technology.

The term "affective computing" itself was only coined in 1995 by Rosalind Picard, a professor at MIT Media Lab, in his book "Affective Computing" [4], although affective computing could be traced back as a concept to early works on emotion recognition systems in the 1960's [5]. Since then, advancements in machine learning, computer vision, and signal processing have propelled affective computing into practical applications that will be later explored in this paper.

Addressing this subject requires a grasp of several fundamental concepts. The initial stage in developing a machine with affective intelligence is the recognition and process of human emotions. Consequently, the machine needs to possess affective sensing capabilities. This entails the ability to discern emotions by processing data conveyed through signals and patterns [1]. Moving forward in the development of such an affective intelligent machine involves emotion generation. In this next phase, the machine gains the capacity to express either innate emotional responses or convincingly simulate a range of emotions [6].

2.2 Universal Access

The Universal Declaration of Human Rights asserts in its initial article that "all human beings are born free and equal in dignity and rights" [7]. To fulfil this goal, the attainment of universal access is fundamentally crucial. Universal access is the principle that all individuals should have equal access to technology regardless of their abilities [8]. This inclusivity is crucial in ensuring that the benefits of technological advancements are extended to diverse populations. Hence, the primary objective is to avoid the marginalization of users from society, all the while enhancing the quality and usability of products and services.

Affective computing plays a significant role in advancing universal access by providing innovative solutions for individuals with disabilities. By incorporating emotion recognition systems into assistive technologies, universal access becomes a reality as these technologies empower individuals with physical or cognitive impairments to interact with devices more intuitively.

Every technological progress in computing platforms and environments, along with innovations in computing that introduce new possibilities for interaction, holds potential relevance to universal access. However, the essence of universal access goes beyond specific technological forms, given the dynamic evolution of interaction over time. This evolution is evident in the history of computing, beginning with command-line interfaces and undergoing various transformations, including graphical user interfaces, mobile computing, virtual reality, ubiquitous computing, and ambient intelligence. As a result, universal access must anticipate forthcoming evolutions by formulating innovative and more fundamental approaches to interaction [8].

2.3 Ethical Considerations

The development and deployment of affective computing technologies pose ethical considerations that demand careful attention. Core principles such as privacy, consent, and data security are essential to ensure responsible use. As noted by Picard (1997) [1], the prospect of a computer expressing itself emotionally raises concerns about potential tragic consequences when certain behaviors are involved. Human oversight and transparency in decision-making processes, as advocated by the OECD's AI Principles [2], become crucial ethical considerations.

Affective computing developers must adhere to ethical data practices, actively addressing concerns related to bias and fairness to prevent discriminatory outcomes. Establishing accountability mechanisms for both developers and users is imperative to uphold the responsible use of these technologies. Therefore, it is crucial to define a set of ethical principles that will function as a framework guiding the development and deployment of affective computing technologies. This framework aims to ensure alignment with societal values and, at the same time, respect individuals' rights and privacy. A more in-depth examination of these ethical considerations will be undertaken later in this paper.

3 Affective Computing Applications

A crucial dimension of affective computing lies in its applications to enhance accessibility, particularly for individuals facing disabilities. This section examines the transformative impact of affective computing technologies on addressing challenges encountered by diverse user groups. The subsequent list of real-world applications does not encompass the entirety of solutions devised by researchers and developers, given the massive number of innovations in this field. However, it endeavours to provide a comprehensive glimpse into the vast realm of affective computing, showcasing notable achievements that contribute to advancing universal access. By integrating emotion recognition systems and other innovations, these applications aim to foster a more inclusive and intuitive interaction paradigm for users with varying disabilities.

3.1 Mobility Disabilities

Individuals with mobility disabilities often encounter challenges in physical movement, impeding their ability to fully engage with the world. Traditional physical environments, such as public buildings and transportation systems, are frequently designed without adequate consideration for those with limited mobility. Moreover, digital interfaces, integral to modern life, may not be optimized for users facing mobility impairments, creating obstacles in accessing information, communication, and services.

Navigating physical spaces becomes particularly daunting due to architectural barriers like stairs, narrow doorways, and uneven surfaces, hindering the movement of individuals with mobility disabilities. Additionally, digital interfaces, encompassing websites and applications, may lack thoughtful design for users with mobility impairments, restricting their effective interaction with technology.

Considering these challenges, affective computing emerges as a potential solution to address certain issues. An illustrative example is "The Wheelie" [9], a collaboration between Intel and HOOBOX Robotics. This innovative solution involves a wheelchair kit leveraging facial recognition technology to capture, process, and translate facial expressions into real-time wheelchair commands. The result is enhanced autonomy for individuals, irrespective of the physical limitations they may be facing.

Other general applications of affective computing could involve facilitating hands-free communication through emotion-aware interfaces, interpreting gestures, facial expressions, or voice commands. This empowerment extends to smart homes where emotion-aware interfaces enable device control without the need for physical touch. Affective computing, thus, has the potential to significantly enhance the accessibility and quality of life for individuals with mobility disabilities.

3.2 Visual Impairments

Visual impairments cover a spectrum of conditions, ranging from partial sight to complete blindness, significantly impacting individuals' ability to perceive and interact with visual information. Traditional digital interfaces heavily rely on visual cues, making them less accessible to those with visual impairments. Websites, applications, and various digital platforms often lack accessibility features such as screen readers, magnification tools, and other assistive technologies, thereby creating barriers that limit information access and usability.

The challenges posed by visual impairments extend beyond mere inconveniences. They can profoundly impact educational opportunities, employment prospects, and social inclusion. As society becomes increasingly digitized, addressing these challenges becomes imperative, calling for innovative solutions to bridge the accessibility gap and ensure equal participation for individuals with visual impairments.

Recognizing these challenges, affective computing emerges as a transformative approach to enhance accessibility for individuals with visual impairments. An illustrative example of this transformative approach is Microsoft's Seeing AI solution [10]. This innovative application leverages the capabilities of artificial intelligence to describe people, text, currency, colour, and objects, providing an intelligent tool to assist users in navigating their daily lives. Seeing AI not only transforms the visual world into an audible experience but also has the ability to recognize and locate faces, facial characteristics, approximate age, and even emotions of the people around.

Furthermore, general solutions within affective computing may involve enhancing existing assistive technologies by incorporating emotional cues or utilizing sensory substitution. For instance, translating facial expressions into sound through auditory feedback systems can significantly benefit individuals with visual impairments, enhancing accessibility in diverse social environments. Affective computing thus holds the potential to offer meaningful solutions that go beyond traditional accessibility measures for those with visual impairments.

3.3 Hearing Impairments

Hearing impairments present a significant barrier to accessibility, impacting individuals in communication, information access, and overall societal engagement. These impairments create formidable challenges in interpersonal interactions, contributing to social isolation. Verbal communication, a fundamental aspect of social engagement, becomes intricate, influencing personal relationships and professional collaborations.

The prevalence of digital information further exacerbates the challenges faced by individuals with hearing impairments. Accessing audio-based content, from online lectures to podcasts, becomes a formidable task, potentially hindering educational and professional advancement. The need for inclusive solutions that address these challenges becomes increasingly crucial in ensuring equal opportunities and participation for individuals with hearing impairments.

In addressing these challenges, affective computing has been applied in various forms, and one notable application is the Ava software [11]. Ava aims to empower deaf and hard-of-hearing individuals by providing an innovative solution that breaks down communication barriers. The software utilizes multiple smartphones or computers strategically placed near participants to capture clear audio. Employing a sophisticated AI engine, Ava converts spoken words into text and presents captions in a readily accessible format on each device's screen, facilitating seamless participation and enhancing communication for individuals with hearing impairments.

Additionally, other general applications may involve the implementation of adaptive interfaces and inclusive design practices which ensure that visual and haptic feedback complements or substitutes auditory cues, thereby creating a more inclusive digital landscape. This way, affective computing provides tools and technologies that go beyond addressing communication challenges, ultimately contributing to a more accessible and inclusive digital environment for individuals with hearing impairments.

3.4 Autism Spectrum Disorder (ASD)

One of the primary challenges for individuals with autism spectrum disorder (ASD) lies in the domain of social communication. Many individuals with ASD find it challenging to comprehend and respond appropriately to both verbal and non-verbal cues, leading to difficulties in forming and sustaining relationships. Sensory sensitivities are also common among individuals with ASD, often causing them to become overwhelmed by sensory stimuli in their surroundings. Moreover, in educational and professional settings, individuals with ASD may face hurdles related to task engagement, attention, and organization. These factors collectively contribute to the unique set of challenges that individuals with ASD navigate in their daily lives.

In recent years, there has been a growing interest in harnessing affective computing technologies to tackle challenges and improve accessibility for individuals with ASD. An example of a solution introduced by affective computing is the Emotional Hearing Aid [12]. This technology has proven to be beneficial for individuals diagnosed with a mild form of autism, such as Asperger's Syndrome, aiming to assist in reading and responding to the facial expressions of individuals they interact with. The Emotional Hearing Aid incorporates two essential elements crucial for empathetic interactions: the ability to identify a person's mental state and the capacity to respond appropriately to it. This application showcases how affective computing can be applied to enhance social communication skills for individuals with ASD.

3.5 Psychiatric Disabilities

Psychiatric disabilities can significantly impact an individual's daily functioning, affecting their ability to navigate and interact with the world around them. Accessibility challenges faced by individuals with psychiatric disabilities often extend beyond physical barriers, encompassing social and cognitive dimensions.

Affective computing presents innovative solutions to tackle challenges and improve accessibility for individuals with psychiatric disabilities. Affective computing systems have the potential to provide personalized feedback and support based on an individual's emotional state. For instance, a mental health application could dynamically adapt its interface, offering encouraging messages or relaxation techniques when heighten stress levels are detected. One example of such an application is the headband Muse. Muse, a research-grade EEG headband, serves as a personal meditation coach. Advanced sensors precisely measure user biosignals, and gentle audio cues provide real-time feedback to redirect the user's focus to the present, showcasing how affective computing can contribute to mental health and well-being.

Further applications may include virtual reality applications powered by affective computing, contributing to the creation of immersive and inclusive environments. These virtual environments are designed to facilitate social interactions, enabling individuals with psychiatric disabilities to engage with others within a controlled and supportive space. Such applications have the potential to reduce the impact of social isolation, providing a novel and beneficial avenue for individuals with psychiatric disabilities to interact, communicate, and participate in social activities.

3.6 Learning Disabilities

Learning disabilities present significant challenges to individuals, impacting their ability to acquire, process, and retain information. Consequently, traditional methods of communication and interaction can be particularly challenging for those with learning disabilities, impeding their access to various resources and opportunities.

Affective computing, by incorporating emotional intelligence into technological systems, aims to create more intuitive and adaptive interfaces that cater to the diverse needs of users. For instance, a system could detect frustration in a user through the use of biosignals such as electrodermal activity (EDA) [13, 14]. Based on this information, the system could provide educators with valuable feedback, leading to alternative methods of explanation or additional resources tailored to the individual's learning style. This approach may no longer be viable due to the regulations introduced by the EU AI Act, as elaborated upon later in this paper. Nevertheless, this, demonstrates the potential of affective computing in addressing the specific challenges faced by individuals with learning disabilities.

3.7 Age-Related Disabilities

Age-related disabilities pose unique challenges to individuals, impacting their ability to access and interact with various technologies and services. With the global population aging, there is a growing need to address the accessibility barriers faced by older individuals.

Affective computing offers the potential to develop adaptive user interfaces that dynamically adjust based on users' emotional states and abilities. For example, robotic companions like the German robot Pepper [15] or the Boston Dynamics chat robot [16], equipped with affective computing capabilities, can dynamically adapt their behaviour based on the user's emotional state and abilities. These robotic companions may adjust their pace, provide additional support for users with mobility challenges, or express empathy when detecting signs of frustration or confusion. Affective computing thus contributes to creating more inclusive and supportive technologies for an aging population.

4 Ethical Considerations in Affective Computing for Accessibility

Affective computing, the study and development of systems and devices that can recognize, interpret, and process human emotions, holds significant potential for enhancing the accessibility of technology for individuals with disabilities. By leveraging emotional data, these systems can offer more intuitive interactions, personalized experiences, and support for users with diverse needs. However, the use of affective computing also raises a number of ethical concerns, including privacy, consent, data security, bias, discrimination, transparency, accountability, and human oversight. The ethical integration of affective computing into accessibility technologies presents a complex but critical challenge. Addressing concerns around privacy, consent, data security, bias, and the need for transparency and human oversight is essential for harnessing the potential of these technologies to enhance the lives of individuals with disabilities. By prioritizing ethical considerations and involving diverse stakeholders in the development process, we can ensure that affective computing serves as a force for inclusion, empowerment, and equity [17]. Following, we present a brief description of each issue and how it can be addressed.

4.1 Privacy and Consent

One of the primary ethical concerns surrounding affective computing is the potential for privacy violations. Affective computing systems often rely on the collection of personal data, including facial expressions, vocal patterns, and physiological signals, in order to infer emotional states. This data can be highly sensitive and revealing, and its collection and use without proper consent can pose a significant risk to individuals' privacy.

To address this concern, it is essential that affective computing systems be designed with strong privacy protections in place. This includes obtaining informed consent from individuals before collecting their personal data, limiting the collection and use of data to what is necessary for the specific purpose, and implementing robust security measures to protect data from unauthorized access or disclosure.

4.2 Data Security

Data security is paramount, as emotional data can be highly sensitive and potentially exploitable. Safeguarding this data against unauthorized access, breaches, and misuse is essential. This involves implementing robust encryption, secure data storage practices, and regular security audits. Moreover, data minimization principles should be applied, collecting only what is necessary for the intended purpose and deleting it once it is no longer needed.

4.3 Bias in Affective Computing

Affective computing systems can inadvertently perpetuate bias and discrimination, particularly against individuals with disabilities or those from diverse cultural backgrounds [18]. Biases can manifest in the datasets used for training these systems, in the algorithms themselves, or in the interpretation of the data. For instance, facial expression analysis algorithms may misinterpret expressions of individuals with certain physical disabilities or cultural differences in emotional expression may lead to inaccurate readings. To mitigate this risk, it is important to ensure that affective computing systems are trained on diverse datasets that represent the full range of human emotions and experiences. Additionally, developers should be aware of the potential for bias and take steps to address it, such as by using algorithms that are designed to be fair and unbiased. Thus, mitigating bias requires a multifaceted approach, including diversifying training datasets, employing algorithms that are transparent and explainable, and regularly assessing and adjusting systems based on feedback from a broad range of users. Involving users with disabilities and from diverse cultural backgrounds in the design and testing processes can help identify and address potential biases early on.

4.4 Transparency and Accountability and Oversight

It is important to consider the ethical implications of transparency, accountability, and human oversight in the development and use of affective computing technologies. Affective computing systems are often complex and opaque, making it difficult for users to understand how they work or to hold developers accountable for any biases or errors [19].

Transparency in how affective computing systems are designed, what data they collect, and how they make decisions is crucial for building trust. Users should have access to information about the workings of these systems and their potential limitations. Accountability mechanisms must be in place to address any issues or harms that arise from the use of these technologies. This includes clear policies for data handling, user recourse in the event of errors or misuse, and external audits.

Furthermore, human oversight is essential to ensure that affective computing technologies are used ethically and effectively. This involves continuous monitoring of these systems in real-world settings, with humans in the loop to interpret ambiguous situations, make judgment calls, and intervene when necessary. Such oversight can help balance the benefits of automation with the need for human empathy and understanding, particularly in sensitive contexts [20].

5   Implications of the EU AI Act for Affective Computing in Accessibility

The European Union is currently developing an AI Act, which would establish a comprehensive regulatory framework for AI products and services within the bloc. This legislation would classify AI systems based on their risk level and impose specific requirements for each category. For example, high-risk AI systems would require mandatory conformity assessments and transparency reports. The EU AI Act aims to create a balance between fostering innovation in AI technologies like affective computing and ensuring these technologies are developed and used in ways that respect privacy, consent, and data security. The emphasis on transparency, accountability, and human oversight is particularly relevant for affective computing applications, as it addresses ethical concerns and potential biases, especially in contexts related to accessibility for individuals with disabilities or diverse cultural backgrounds.

However, the EU AI Act has significant implications for the development and deployment of affective computing technologies, particularly in the realm of accessibility. The Act introduces a risk-based regulatory framework that categorizes AI systems based on their potential risk to health, safety, and fundamental rights. Affective computing systems, which include emotion recognition technologies, are directly impacted by these regulations, especially if they utilize biometric data for identifying or inferring emotions.

One of the key aspects highlighted by the EU AI Act is the distinction made regarding emotion recognition systems. These systems are identified based on their use of biometric data, which includes physical, physiological, or behavioural characteristics that can uniquely identify a person. The Act emphasizes the need for transparency, mandating that any affective computing system must inform the user of its emotion recognition capabilities. This requirement aims to ensure users are aware when their emotional states are being processed, addressing concerns about privacy and consent [20].

The Act also affects academic researchers and developers of open-source software in the affective computing field. Even if software is distributed freely, it falls under the scope of the Act if it's intended for market placement or service provision, regardless of whether it's commercialized. This includes open-source software developed by researchers, which means that academic projects could also need to comply with the Act's provisions if they are shared or utilized outside of private research collaborations [20].

For high-risk AI systems, which could include many affective computing applications due to their impact on areas like health, education, and workplace monitoring, the Act imposes strict compliance requirements. These include conducting fundamental rights impact assessments, maintaining robust data governance practices, and ensuring transparency and human oversight. Systems classified as high-risk must undergo conformity assessments and be registered in an EU database, among other obligations.

The AI Act also introduces prohibitions on certain uses of AI that are deemed a high risk to fundamental rights, including specific applications of emotion recognition in workplaces and educational settings. Moreover, the Act promotes innovation through regulatory sandboxes, allowing for the development and testing of innovative AI technologies in a controlled environment, which could be beneficial for advancing affective computing technologies in a compliant manner.

The EU AI Act in the context of affective computing for accessibility, several areas emerge where the Act could be further strengthened to better address ethical challenges. These challenges primarily revolve around privacy, bias and discrimination, and transparency in how affective computing technologies are developed and implemented, as previously discussed.

5.1 Enhanced Privacy Protections

While the Act AI mandates transparency about the use of emotion recognition systems, there could be stronger provisions to protect individuals' privacy. This is especially pertinent for individuals with disabilities who might rely more heavily on affective computing technologies for daily tasks and social interactions. Enhanced privacy protections could include stricter regulations on data minimization and the anonymization of sensitive data, ensuring that the collection and processing of biometric and emotional data are limited to what is strictly necessary for the intended accessibility purposes.

5.2 More Rigorous Bias and Discrimination Mitigations

The Act AI's risk-based approach categorizes AI systems by their potential impact, imposing stricter rules on high-risk systems. However, there is a need for more explicit guidelines on identifying and mitigating biases in affective computing technologies, especially those used in accessibility contexts. For individuals with disabilities or those from diverse cultural backgrounds, biases in emotion recognition can lead to misinterpretation and discrimination. The Act could be strengthened by requiring more detailed impact assessments that specifically evaluate biases and the potential for discrimination, coupled with mandates for regular updates and refinements based on feedback from diverse user groups.

5.3 Clearer Standards for Transparency and Accountability

Transparency and accountability are crucial for building trust in affective computing technologies. The Act could introduce clearer standards for how transparency is achieved, especially in explaining the decision-making processes of AI systems to users. For accessibility technologies, understanding how and why a system interprets emotions in a certain way can be crucial for users to feel comfortable and in control. The Act could mandate the provision of easily understandable information to users about the AI's functioning, its limitations, and the logic behind its decisions.

5.4 Greater Emphasis on Human Oversight

While the Act AI mandates human oversight for high-risk AI systems, it could go further in specifying the roles and responsibilities of human supervisors, particularly in contexts involving vulnerable groups. Human oversight is essential to ensure that affective computing technologies are used ethically and responsibly. The Act could specify that oversight mechanisms must include experts in accessibility and disability rights, to ensure that these technologies are aligned with the needs and rights of all users.

5.5 Inclusive Design and Development Processes

The Act AI could promote more inclusive design and development processes by requiring the involvement of individuals with disabilities and those from diverse cultural backgrounds in the creation and testing phases of affective computing technologies. This involvement can help ensure that these systems are truly accessible and meet the needs of a broad spectrum of users. The Act could mandate stakeholder engagement as part of the conformity assessment for high-risk systems, ensuring that these technologies are developed with a user-centred approach from the outset.

5.6 Specific Provisions for Accessibility

The Act AI could include specific provisions that address the use of affective computing technologies for enhancing accessibility. This could involve guidelines for the ethical use of these technologies in educational, employment, and healthcare settings, ensuring they support rather than hinder the participation of individuals with disabilities in society. Such provisions would highlight the EU's commitment to accessibility and inclusivity, ensuring that the benefits of AI and affective computing are equitably distributed.

By addressing these areas, the EU AI Act could provide a more robust framework for the ethical development and use of affective computing technologies, particularly in enhancing accessibility for individuals with disabilities and those from diverse cultural backgrounds. Strengthening the Act in these ways would not only mitigate potential risks but also promote the development of more inclusive, equitable, and trustworthy AI systems.

6 Future Directions for Research and Development

As we venture further into the exploration of affective computing's potential to enhance accessibility, several future research directions emerge as pivotal. These avenues not only promise to unlock new capabilities within assistive technologies but also ensure that such developments proceed within a robust ethical framework, fostering collaboration across disciplines to achieve inclusive and equitable access to technology.

The following outlines future research directions, the development of ethical guidelines, and the importance of collaboration in the field of affective computing for accessibility.

6.1 Future Research Directions

Personalization and Adaptability: Investigate how affective computing can be tailored to individual needs and preferences, particularly for people with diverse types of disabilities. This includes developing adaptive systems that learn from user interactions to improve their support over time.

Cross-Cultural Emotional Recognition. Due to the diversity in emotional expression across cultures, research into developing culturally sensitive affective computing models is crucial. This involves collecting and analysing data from a wide range of cultural contexts to enhance the global applicability of these technologies.

Integration with Existing and Emerging Technologies. Explore how affective computing can be integrated with other technologies, such as augmented reality (AR), virtual reality (VR), and the Internet of Things (IoT), to create more immersive and accessible experiences for users with disabilities.

Real-World Applications and Impact Studies. Conduct longitudinal studies to assess the real-world impact of affective computing technologies on accessibility. This includes evaluating user satisfaction, independence, and overall quality of life improvements for individuals with disabilities.

Ethical AI and Algorithmic Transparency. Develop methodologies for ensuring that affective computing algorithms are transparent and explainable. This is key to building trust and understanding among users, particularly when these systems make decisions based on emotional data.

6.2 Importance of Collaboration

Interdisciplinary Research. Promote interdisciplinary research collaborations that bring together experts from computer science, psychology, ethics, disability studies, and other relevant fields. Such collaborations can drive innovation while ensuring that affective computing technologies are developed with a holistic understanding of user needs.

Engagement with Disability Communities. Foster partnerships with disability communities to ensure that the development of affective computing technologies is guided by the insights and experiences of those it aims to serve. This engagement is crucial for creating accessible and meaningful solutions.

Policy Development. Collaborate with policymakers to develop and implement regulations that ensure the ethical use of affective computing technologies. Such collaboration can help in creating a policy environment that supports innovation while protecting the rights and dignity of individuals with disabilities.

Global Standards. Work towards establishing global standards and best practices for the development and use of affective computing technologies in accessibility. International cooperation can facilitate the adoption of universally accepted ethical guidelines and promote equitable access to technology.

The future of affective computing in enhancing accessibility is bright, with vast potential to transform how individuals with disabilities interact with the world. By focusing on personalization, cultural sensitivity, integration with other technologies, and the real-world impact of these systems, researchers can contribute significantly to the field. Simultaneously, the development of ethical guidelines and the emphasis on collaborative efforts across disciplines will ensure that these technological advancements are achieved responsibly, promoting universal access and equity in the digital age.

7 Conclusion

The exploration of affective computing within the context of accessibility highlights both the transformative potential of these technologies and the ethical imperatives that must guide their development and deployment. This paper has underscored the delicate balance between harnessing affective computing to enhance accessibility for individuals with disabilities and the need to navigate the complex ethical terrain that accompanies the collection, analysis, and use of sensitive emotional data.

Affective computing holds remarkable promise for improving the quality of life for individuals with disabilities, offering nuanced technologies that can adapt to emotional states and provide more intuitive user experiences. However, the ethical dimensions of privacy, consent, bias, discrimination, and data security present significant challenges that must be navigated with care:

- Ethical challenges, including privacy concerns, the potential for bias and discrimination, and issues of consent and data security, are paramount. These challenges necessitate rigorous safeguards to ensure that the benefits of affective computing do not come at the expense of fundamental rights and freedoms.
- The EU AI Act represents a crucial step towards regulating AI technologies, including affective computing, by introducing a risk-based approach that categorizes and imposes obligations based on the level of risk to individuals' rights and safety. However, areas for enhancement were identified, including stronger privacy protections, more rigorous bias mitigation strategies, clearer transparency standards, and more inclusive design practices.

Balancing the potential benefits of affective computing for accessibility with ethical concerns is essential. While these technologies can offer unprecedented opportunities for individuals with disabilities, ensuring they do not exacerbate existing inequalities or introduce new forms of vulnerability is critical. This balance requires ongoing vigilance, research, and adaptation of regulatory frameworks to keep pace with technological advancements.

Ongoing research and development are vital to ensure that affective computing technologies evolve in ways that are both innovative and ethically responsible. This includes continuous efforts to improve the accuracy and inclusivity of emotion recognition algorithms, enhance privacy protections, and develop more robust mechanisms for human oversight. Moreover, engaging with diverse communities to understand their needs and concerns can inform the development of more accessible and equitable technologies.

Given the global nature of technology development and the cross-border impacts of AI, international cooperation is imperative. Collaborating to establish standardized ethical guidelines and frameworks can help harmonize regulatory approaches and ensure that affective computing technologies are developed and used in ways that respect universal human rights. This cooperation should include a wide range of stakeholders, including policymakers, technologists, ethicists, disability advocates, and the broader public, to ensure that diverse perspectives inform the creation of these guidelines.

The advancement of affective computing for accessibility presents a promising horizon for enhancing the lives of individuals with disabilities. However, realizing this potential requires a concerted effort to address the ethical challenges inherent in these technologies. Through ongoing research, development, and international collaboration, we can ensure that affective computing serves as a tool for empowerment and inclusion, fostering a more accessible and equitable digital world for everyone.

Disclosure of Interests. The authors have no competing interests to declare that are relevant to the content of this article.

References

1. Picard, R.: Affective Computing, 1st edn. The MIT Press, Cambridge (2000)
2. OECD AI Principles overview. https://oecd.ai/en/ai-principles. Accessed 30 Jan 2024
3. Artificial Intelligence Act: deal on comprehensive rules for trustworthy AI, News European Parliament. https://www.europarl.europa.eu/news/en/press-room/20231206IPR15699/artificial-intelligence-act-deal-on-comprehensive-rules-for-trustworthy-ai. Accessed 01 Feb 2024
4. Daily, S., et al.: Affective computing: Historical foundations, current applications, and future trends. Emot. Affect Hum. Factors Hum.-Comput. Interact., 213–231 (2017). https://doi.org/10.1016/b978-0-12-801851-4.00009-4
5. Ekman, P., Friesen, W.V.: Facial action coding system. PsycTESTS Dataset (1978). https://doi.org/10.1037/t27734-000
6. Heise, D.R.: Enculturating agents with expressive role behavior. In: Payr, S., Trappl, R. (eds.) Agent Culture: Human-Agent Interaction in a Multicultural World, pp. 127–142. Lawrence Erlbaum, Mahwah (2004)
7. Universal Declaration of Human Rights, United Nations (UN). https://www.un.org/en/about-us/universal-declaration-of-human-rights. Accessed 30 Jan 2024
8. Stephanidis, C.: The Universal Access Handbook, 1st edn. CRC Press, Boca Raton (2009)
9. Intel HOOBOX wheelchair, Intel. https://www.intel.com/content/www/us/en/artificial-intelligence/hoobox.html. Accessed 01 Feb 2024
10. Seeing AI, Microsoft Garage. https://www.microsoft.com/en-us/garage/wall-of-fame/seeing-ai/. Accessed 01 Feb 2024
11. Ava – Captions for all, Ava. https://www.ava.me/. Accessed 01 Feb 2024
12. El Kaliouby, R., Robinson, P.: Emotional hearing aid: an assistive tool for children with Asperger's syndrome. In: Designing a More Inclusive World, pp. 163–172 (2004). https://doi.org/10.1007/978-0-85729-372-5_17
13. Horvers, A., Tombeng, N., Bosse, T., Lazonder, A.W., Molenaar, I.: Detecting emotions through electrodermal activity in learning contexts: a systematic review. Sensors **21**(23), 7869 (2021). https://doi.org/10.3390/s21237869
14. Nagae, T., Lee, J.: Understanding emotions in children with developmental disabilities during robot therapy using EDA. Sensors **22**(14), 5116 (2022). https://doi.org/10.3390/s22145116
15. Pepper, Humanizing Technologies Group. https://humanizing.com/en/pepper-robot-humanoid-robot-by-softbank-robotics-for-retail-fairs-receptionist-showrooms-happiness-hero/. Accessed 01 Feb 2024
16. Robots that can chat, Boston Dynamics. https://bostondynamics.com/blog/robots-that-can-chat/. Accessed 01 Feb 2024
17. Iren, D., Yildirim, E., Shingjergji, K.: Ethical risks, concerns, and practices of affective computing: a thematic analysis. In: 2023 11th International Conference on Affective Computing and Intelligent Interaction Workshops and Demos (ACIIW), Cambridge, MA, USA, pp. 1–4 (2023). https://doi.org/10.1109/ACIIW59127.2023.10388171
18. Devillers, L., Cowie, R.: Ethical considerations on affective computing: an overview. Proc. IEEE **111**(10), 1445–1458 (2023). https://doi.org/10.1109/JPROC.2023.3315217

19. Ferraro, A.: Affective rights: a foundation for ethical standards. In: 2020 IEEE International Symposium on Technology and Society (ISTAS), Tempe, AZ, USA, pp. 1–11 (2020). https://doi.org/10.1109/ISTAS50296.2020.9462172
20. The New EU AI Act – the 10 key things you need to know now, Dentons. https://www.dentons.com/en/insights/articles/2023/december/14/the-new-eu-ai-act-the-10-key-things-you-need-to-know-now. Accessed 02 Feb 2024

Designing for Intersectional Inclusion in Computing

Anna Szlavi[1]([✉])[ID], Marit Fredrikke Hansen[1][ID], Sandra Helen Husnes[1][ID], Tayana Uchôa Conte[2][ID], and Letizia Jaccheri[1][ID]

[1] Norwegian University of Science and Technology, Trondheim, Norway
{anna.szlavi,maritfh,sandrahh,letizia.jaccheri}@ntnu.no
[2] Universidade Federal do Amazonas, Manaus, Brazil
tayana@icomp.ufam.edu.br

Abstract. Diversity, Equity, and Inclusion (DEI) is essential because it creates a more inclusive environment that benefits individuals, organisations and society as a whole. To gain a comprehensive understanding of DEI in computing, it is important to apply an intersectional lens to explore the complexities and nuances of the issues and possible solutions to these. This study aims to provide new knowledge about intersectionality in the computing field. According to the design and creation research strategy, we have developed a prototype for a website called "DiversIT", which aims to help increase inclusion by facilitating a supportive peer community and raising awareness. Then, 17 students and professionals in the field were involved in five rounds of usability tests and design iterations. DiversIT, designed to address intersectional perspectives in the computing community, led to a promising high-fidelity prototype in terms of increasing DEI in computing. According to our investigation, the impact of intersectionality needs to be acknowledged in the computing field.

Keywords: Intersectionality · Design · Diversity · Inclusion · Computing

1 Introduction

Technology is socially shaped and requires diverse perspectives and voices to ensure ethical and responsible development. Without a diverse development team, technology can perpetuate biases and reinforce systemic inequalities, leading to exclusionary outcomes [10]. For instance, the best speech-recognition software on the market in 2016 was from Google, but the product was excluding women as it had 70% more accuracy for male speech than female speech [17]. When Apple launched their health monitoring system in 2014, introduced as an advanced tracker, they had forgotten to think about the menstrual period, which excluded women from utilising the application fully [5]. Lack of diversity in training sets for machine learning and artificial intelligence (AI) algorithms has led

M. Antona and C. Stephanidis (Eds.): HCII 2024, LNCS 14696, pp. 122–142, 2024.
https://doi.org/10.1007/978-3-031-60875-9_9

to people not being recognised as humans, or autonomous cars not recognising people with dis/abilities as pedestrians [1]. Furthermore, no universally accepted methodology or standard exists for testing apps and assessing universal design principles, including techniques and common errors, internationally [18]. As the above examples show, diversity, equity, and inclusion (DEI) in computing is not only a social issue but a technological one as well. In order for teams to be more productive [4] and design more inclusive software, intersectional considerations are necessary [14].

Intersectionality, a concept originally coined by Crenshaw [3], emphasizes that a person's identity has numerous overlapping segments, such as gender, race, ethnicity, age, sexuality, socioeconomic status, ability, etc.), and discrimination can arise from the combination of (any of) these. Therefore, true DEI goes beyond addressing people as one-dimensional [8].

In the preliminary phase of this research, a Systematic Literature Review (SLR) was conducted to analyse literature related to intersectionality in computing [14]. Our findings show that there are severe obstacles for minoritized people in computing, but a peer network is one of the main success factors in overcoming barriers. Therefore, we developed a prototype specifically as a peer networking tool to increase a sense of belonging. DiversIT, designed based on the results of the SLR, was further developed by involving our user group. Using the principles of inclusive design [13,15,16], we created a website after five rounds of user testing.

2   Background

In the first phase of the project, a systematic literature review (SLR) was performed to identify current studies and the research gaps on intersectionality in CS [14]. The SLR's objective was to provide knowledge about intersectionality in CS at the university and professional level while contributing to research that considers the complexities of intersectional challenges beyond the one-dimensional narrative that is most prevalent presented within CS research in terms of DEI. Intersectionality in CS was investigated by examining what research existed on the topic and further analysing recurring patterns of intersectional challenges and success factors throughout the CS field identified in the papers. In total, 16 papers were selected as primary studies for the SLR.

The primary studies included in the SLR were published between 2018 and 2022. 75% of the papers were published in the last three years (2020–2022). 81% of the studies used data from the US and were based there. Most of the primary studies focused on the intersectional factors of gender and ethnicity. Four of the studies researched more than two intersectional factors but decided not to include them due to the low sample sizes. Two primary studies reflected on some intersectional factors that were not included in their research and deemed these as limitations to the study.

All of the 16 primary studies addressed challenges regarding intersectionality in CS. Stereotypes, discrimination and bias were common intersectional challenges found in the papers. Many of the primary studies also indicate that the lesser sense of belonging was a significant intersectional challenge.

The identified success factors can be grouped into three categories: mentorship, sense of belonging, or other. Multiple primary studies from the SLR call attention to the importance of the sense of belonging. Moreover, both mentorships and various forms of formal and informal networks can be used to improve belongingness and increase DEI, both of which were challenges identified in CS.

To sum up, most of the primary studies in the SLR used data from the US, and since intersectionality is a very complex topic, not having a more international scope and diverse research from different countries results in a higher probability of meaningful intersectional experiences in CS being ignored. In addition, as success factors to overcome challenges and increase DEI, the findings from our primary studies suggest mentorship and supportive networks in order to address the lack of sense of belonging amongst people of intersectional identities in CS. Since mentoring programs are less sustainable as they require more human resources, we decided to focus on peer networks. Professional and peer networks support diversity through building social, academic, and industry connections as well as contribute to career confidence and skill building. They proved to help promote retention and supportive communities in CS. As a consequence, we aimed to develop a website (DiversIT) for peer networking with an intersectional approach in mind, which is often lacking. We involved users of various genders, of different age groups, living in both the Global North (Norway) and the Global South (Brazil).

3   Methodology

Our chosen research strategy, *design and creation*, focuses on developing new technology. According to Oates [9], the design and creation strategy is grounded in the idea that knowledge is not only discovered but also created and that research can be a creative process where the results are new knowledge and an artefact. The strategy is the normally expected mode of research in CS, as a technological artefact is produced to show the researchers' effort rather than only abstract theories and other knowledge. The artefact then has a greater potential beyond the academic community. On the other hand, it is also important to show academic qualities and evaluate the product, not only technical skills [9]. Usability tests are applied to evaluate the product to ensure its quality. A challenge with the strategy regarding the evaluation is that the limitations should be acknowledged, as it can be difficult to generalise all user cases from a single test case [9]. For this reason, space triangulation was used to increase the validity of the evaluation.

The design and creation strategy is considered an iterative process for problem-solving [9]. The development and continuous evaluation of a digital artefact is an iterative and cyclical process, which consists of designing, testing, refining, and re-evaluating the prototype based on user feedback [9]; where prototyping and usability testing help provide a product that is more effective, efficient, and user-friendly [2, 6, 9, 11]. The development of the prototype followed five steps as detailed below.

Awareness: This step revolves around acknowledging and expressing the existence of a problem, which can be obtained through further research in studies, findings from another discipline, the expression of the need for something, field research, or new developments [9]. Based on the findings in the SLR, the CS field fails to acknowledge the impact of intersectionality, and there is a dearth of literature about intersectionality in CS.

Suggestion: This stage further builds upon the curiosity about the problem, from the awareness stage, to suggest a preliminary idea of how to address the problem [9]. The SLR was the base for the suggestion as it presented success factors to help overcome challenges related to intersectionality in CS. Feedback from the usability tests also added more to the suggestion phase through the different iterations.

Development: The implementation of the suggested design concept is conducted in this step [9]. A high-fidelity prototype was developed in *Figma*[1]. Given that Figma enables prototypes to operate in the same manner as coded prototypes, the authors posited that Figma should be classified as a constituent of the development phase rather than the suggestion phase.

Evaluation: The developed artefact was evaluated based on its value and variation from the expected outcome [9]. After each iteration, the prototype was tested through a usability test with relevant end-users, which provided new suggestions for improvements that looped the process back to the suggestion phase until all prototype iterations and usability tests were completed. Interviews were also conducted with the usability testing, and the evaluated results looped the process back to the awareness phase.

Consolidation: In this last step, the results from the entire process are consolidated and documented, and the new knowledge is identified and discussed together with suggestions for further research [9].

The methodology used in the design and creation process was a combination of methods from agile software development, prototyping, and human-centered design. A key element in the agile process is the *sprints*, several small iterations, where the prototyping focuses on gradually modifying a product until a satisfactory implementation is produced [9]. Figure 1 visualises the development phase with the iterations. The prototype was improved after each iteration of data gathering, which can be considered sprints, before being tested again and improved for the next sprint. The figure also illustrates that the usability tests

---

[1] https://www.figma.com/.

employed space triangulation, as we conducted interviews both in the Global North (Norway) and in the Global South (Brazil), for better intersectional considerations.

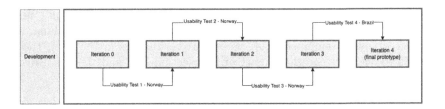

Fig. 1. Development iterations for the prototype.

4   Results

4.1   Participant Demographics

17 students and professionals participated in the usability testing for this research, with 11 participants in Norway and 6 participants in Brazil.

Most of the participants were professionals. One student in Norway, P10, had work experience through multiple internships, which made all participants capable of talking about their experience as a student and as a CS professional. In Brazil, there were four students and two professionals. All of the students worked beside their studies or had experience from internships. Therefore, all of the participants in Brazil could also relate to both user groups, student and professional, when it came to intersectionality in CS.

At the beginning of the test, each participant got the chance to describe their intersectional identity. A limitation with the existing literature that was found in the SLR is that none of the primary studies contained data or findings about people with dis/abilities, even though this is considered the world's largest minority. Two of the subjects in this research have a dis/ability. In addition to this, three of the subjects expressed that they are in contact with a psychologist or have a mental condition. It is important to acknowledge both physical and psychological challenges as part of intersectionality. Gender, as is common in the literature too, was mentioned by the participants. Regarding the other identity segments, one participant informed the researchers about the LGBTQIA situation in Brazil. The country is religious, and it can be challenging to be a part of this community. Two of the candidates interviewed in Brazil and two of the subjects in Norway identified as members of the LGBTQIA community. Age is a variable factor that everyone faces, and seven of the participants stated that they had experienced challenges related to their age. Two participants expressed a limitation with being the youngest in the team, and two participants expressed the challenge of being considered too old for new opportunities.

4.2   Observations

During each usability test, one of the authors was the test leader and another author was the observer. The test leader explained the process of usability testing and read the scenarios and tasks aloud to the participant. The observer took field notes when the participant solved the tasks from the usability test guide. Feedback from each usability test was then analysed, and the improvements to be done to the prototype were identified.

During the design and creation process, there were a total of five iterations. Iteration 0 was the first iteration based on findings from the SLR and brainstorming at the start of the development process, while Iteration 4 suggests the final prototype for this project.

Iteration 0. The first iteration was developed based on research findings in the SLR [7, 14], and not user feedback. However, this still aligns with the design and creation strategy, since Oates [9] argues that design and development should be based on research. The authors developed this Figma prototype version by brainstorming possible solutions to develop a product to support DEI in CS through an intersectional approach. Inspiration was found from similar websites related to the product and by following the design principles.

Figure 2 is the first page introduced to the user when entering the website DiversIT. While scrolling down the page, the user can read about what DiversIT is and what it offers as a product.

When pressing the "Log in"-button or "New to DiversIT? Sign up now"-button, a popup window appears on the screen to log in or create a new account as presented in Fig. 3. Figure 3a is the first popup window. Here the user can choose between logging in with an existing user, LinkedIn, Google or Facebook, or create a new account. If the "Create account"-button is clicked, the process continues to Fig. 3b where the user can start filling in an email address, username and password. Here it is still an option to instead log in with a third-party service, or log in with an existing account. By clicking the "Next"-button, the user can fill in the full name, birth date and preferred pronoun (see Fig. 3c). The pronouns are added to this page as DiversIT wants to focus on diversity and be inclusive to all intersectional identities in CS. Both Fig. 3d and Fig. 3e are versions of the third step in the process of creating a new account, depending on which radio button is chosen. The students can select their university in the dropdown menu, as seen in Fig. 3d, while the professionals can select their workplace in the dropdown menu, as seen in Fig. 3e. The last step of creating an account, presented in Fig. 3f, contains a text field where the user can describe their intersectional identity. When clicking the "Create account"-button, the user is then logged in with their new account.

When the user presses the "Community"- or "Articles"-tab, the popup to log in or register (see Fig. 3) appears as feedback to the button clicks, constraining the user from accessing *Community* and *Articles* without being logged in. This constriction is meant as a way to motivate new users to register to get access

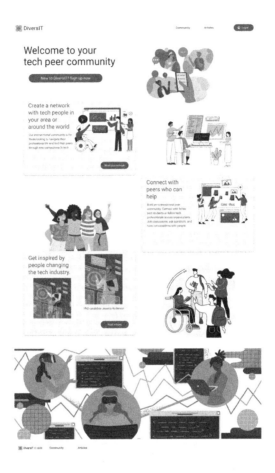

Fig. 2. Front page of DiversIT.

and build trust within the community, as it is only accessible to those who are registered.

When a user is logged in, the header changes. Now, if the user clicks the "Community"-tab, the *Community* is accessible. The *Articles* page is also available to the user when clicking the "Articles"-tab in the header. The *Articles* page contains articles about DEI in CS. On this page, role models with different intersectional backgrounds are presented to increase awareness of intersectionality. In general, it presents an intersectional platform where users can get inspired by reading others' stories, hearing about projects, and exploring initiatives focusing on DEI.

Figure 4 presents the *Community* page of DiversIT. The *Community* consists of different prompts posted by users. Arrows in the figure show different interactions that can be done in the forum. Users can add a new prompt by pressing

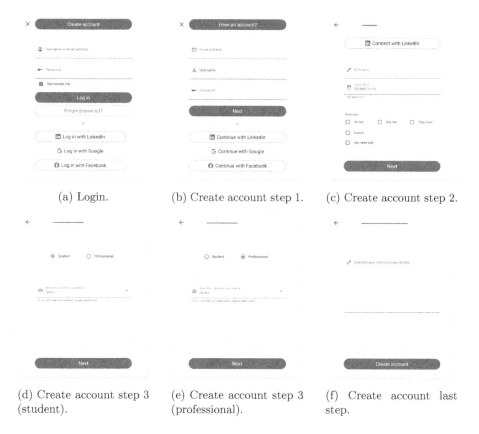

(a) Login.   (b) Create account step 1.   (c) Create account step 2.

(d) Create account step 3   (e) Create account step 3   (f) Create account last
(student).   (professional).   step.

Fig. 3. The process of logging in or creating a new account.

the "Add new prompt"-button, and others can interact with prompts by adding
a response.

Usability Test 1. Four participants, referred to as P1, P2, P3, and P4, usability
tested the initial prototype under the framework established in the usability
testing guide. This subsection presents the observations and feedback from the
tests.

The participants were initially introduced to the website's homepage. P4
favourably appraised the interface's aesthetic elements, noting the appeal of its
illustrations and colour scheme. From these illustrations, P3 stated *"I can see
that it is a website for people like me"*, which promoted a sense of belonging.
The participants commented that having DEI as a goal was something positive
since this made DiversIT more reliable compared to its counterparts. However,
P1 and P2 voiced uncertainties regarding the website's intent and what type of
community the website offered. This lack of clarity was also present for P4, who

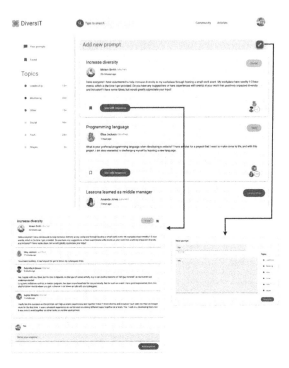

Fig. 4. The Community page shows how to add a new prompt and add a response to an existing prompt.

was explicitly looking for an *About* page informing about the purpose, but this did not exist.

Additionally, all the participants expressed reservations about immediate registration. P1 was looking for more information about the website and commented that the goal and purpose of the website were not clearly described. The limited content availability before registration was a source of frustration for P2, as P2 expected that there would be at least some articles and information to incentives the user to register. Resources should be on the website to get people interested and do something more exclusively. The participants, in general, were frustrated that there were too many constraints limiting interactions when a user first wanted to explore the website before registering. Also, P4 specifically wanted to get a clear understanding of the website before registering.

P2 was sceptical informing about which organisation the participant worked at to DiversIT during registration, highlighting the importance of addressing privacy concerns for both the workplace and intersectionality. P2 further asked about anonymity and how that would work if people have an identity connected to their users.

When asking the participants about the prototype's potential to increase DEI in CS, the participants expressed optimism, but some practical considerations needed to be encountered. P1 stated "*I could imagine myself using it to network to exchange ideas and get help*", and P3 thought it was an interesting concept, providing a low threshold to communicate with others in the field. In addition to the envisaged use of DiversIT for networking, P3 also lauded its potential to bridge the gap between students and professionals. However, they also acknowledged the inherent challenges community-based systems face and the importance of effective marketing strategies.

Iteration 1. Based on the feedback and observations from the first usability test, the Iteration 0 prototype was further developed in Iteration 1. A general theme from the test was that the participants were sceptical about registering, as the website's purpose needed to be clearly described. Therefore, an improvement made to the prototype was to create a separate *About* page with the vision and mission of the website, which one of the candidates was explicitly looking for during the test.

The header was updated to access the *About* page. A third button was added in the same format as *Community* and *Articles*, as all of these navigate to a new page. Based on feedback from the usability tests, these buttons now navigate to separate pages. To still offer the community exclusively to the registered users, this page is still not accessible without being logged in, but in this iteration, the user can navigate to an informative page about the community.

One participant was sceptical about giving away information about their workplace. The process of logging in or registering has been updated in this iteration. The number of popup frames is reduced from six to four. The last three frames in Fig. 3 were merged into one frame. So now, regardless of selecting student or professional, the only option further in the signup process is for the user to select their current or prior university. In addition to this change, the open text field describing the intersectional identity was moved to an earlier page to save space and shorten the process of registering to DiversIT.

Usability Test 2. Participants P5, P6, P7, and P8 were the candidates for the second usability test to examine the Iteration 1 of the prototype. It is important to note that P7, due to being blind, was unable to interact with the Figma prototype. Hence, an alternative usability test was conducted where the prototype was verbally described, and the participant reflected on the website based on the tasks from the usability test guide. The researchers considered this a valid alternative usability test as the goal of creating the prototype was to investigate if the prototype had the potential as a technical solution to increase DEI in CS. P7 also provided valuable insight into the developing process, particularly concerning the accessibility of visual content such as pictures and videos.

P7 would consider registering if DiversIT was an already existing platform, depending on how the participant first heard about the website. P7 also queried the necessity of this platform when alternatives exist. Later in the tests, P8 commented that the *Community* forum looks like other pre-existing forums, and it is not immediately clear why it differs from these. Although the second usability test participants had a better initial understanding of the website than those in the first test, they struggled to identify it as a distinct product.

Upon registration, P8 preferred following the signup process without using socials for registering. P8 appreciated the inclusion of pronouns in the registration form but would have preferred an example of what to write in the "Intersectional identity" open text field.

Opinions diverged concerning the website's perceived utility based on initial impressions. P7 expressed scepticism *"In general, I am not a big of things made for us who are 'easily discriminated', but if this covers a need where it feels safer and easier, then I could be positive"*, pointing out how this could be more excluding than including. P8, on the other hand, perceived potential value and could consider DiversIT helpful; *"I can find people based on similar interests and I can learn from them"*.

Overall, the participants demonstrated that the website was easy to navigate. P6 found the website purposeful, user-friendly, and easy to navigate, aligning with P5 underlined this by complementing the design aesthetics and intuitive UI. However, P6 and P8 stated that the front page came across as overwhelming, suggesting incorporating features such as hiding information behind buttons and making sure that information was not halfway visible at first glance due to long pages.

In Iteration 1, the *Community* was only accessible to those who were logged in, while *Articles* were open to all. P5 felt that this restriction was reasonable, showing that this implementation had a positive effect on the website's usability.

P5 saw the potential in DiversIT as a useful supplement to other initiatives for sharing experiences, an opinion supported by P6 if the website is marketed towards the target audience. However, P8 expressed scepticism about the website's novelty and questioned its capacity to affect change in the larger CS community.

Iteration 2. Due to time limitations between Iteration's 1 and 2, only a few improvements were made to the prototype. Feedback suggesting improvements not implemented during this iteration was added to the product backlog.

Now the user can here decide whether to publicly show the written intersectional identity to others in the *Community* or not. This improvement was added to motivate people to participate in the *Community* even if they were uncomfortable sharing all their information. Logout functionality was also added to the profile page, as it is critical to let the user be able to sign out.

The functionality to show others' profiles was also added to the prototype. When a user clicks the profile picture of someone in a prompt, then a popup appears showing the profile. The profiles of others look similar to the user logged in, but when viewing others' profiles, then the user cannot change the fields as in their own profile.

Usability Test 3. The third and last group of participants in Norway included participants P9, P10, and P11, testing the Iteration 2 of the prototype. The initial impressions of DiversIT were generally positive among two of the participants. P9 admired the website's aesthetics and UX, commenting on its professional look. P10 felt inspired to join the community due to its appealing appearance and representation of diverse individuals. However, P11 raised concerns about the broadness of the website's target audience, questioning the feasibility of building associations with such a diverse user base.

In previous usability tests, there was feedback that having pictures and information halfway visible on the front page made it look overwhelming. P10, on the other hand, understood the functionality of scrolling due to the pictures and information only being hallway visible at the bottom of the page. P11 appreciated the site's readability, finding the font size, colours, and background contributing to a good UX. However, P11 felt the design could have been clearer because too many pictures and elements were visible simultaneously, which points back to the feedback from previous usability tests of some elements being overwhelming.

Reflecting on the potential impact of DiversIT, P10 thought that the website could have helped the participant to earlier get motivated to battle for diversity in CS without the underlying fear concerning how boys would react. P9 reflected on the use of topics in the *Community*, suggesting that there should be subcategories of the topics to organise the posts more easily. P9 also stressed the need for increased visibility of intersectional issues, believing that current challenges are causing missed opportunities.

Iteration 3. Suggestions for improvements from the third usability test and issues from the product backlog were added to Iteration 3.

Previous feedback was conflicting on whether the front page was clear or not. In an attempt to make the page less overwhelming, the half-visible information on the page was moved further down, to give the front page a clean look at first glance. This change made more information visible only when scrolling. Since some commented that this half-visible information indicated to the user that there was a possibility to scroll on the page, an arrow pointing down at the bottom of the page was added to increase the affordance and visibility of the functionality.

Based on the changes made, the user will hopefully get the impression that it is a tech-peer community. The only visible text box is "Create a network with tech people in your area and around the world", which enhances the probability of the user focusing on this aspect to decide if DiversIT is a website to explore more or not.

From the first usability test, the question of anonymity was addressed. A checkbox was added as an option to allow the users to be anonymous when posting a new prompt or responding to an already existing prompt. The default mode was not checked, as DiversIT wants to promote intersectionality by being open in a supportive network. There is an understanding that some users can be uncomfortable posting vulnerable information. Still, hopefully, by adding the opportunity to be anonymous, more people can get comfortable sharing their experiences and challenges.

In addition, multiple issues were removed from the previous version based on the backlog and implemented in this iteration.

Usability Test 4. The fourth and final iteration of usability tests was conducted in Brazil, involving six participants, P12, P13, P14, P15, P16, and P17, examining Iteration 3 of the DiversIT prototype. The initial impressions were largely positive. P12 and P17 admired the design. P13 understood the website as a space for people from diverse backgrounds, as evidenced by the inclusive illustrations. P12 and P14 highlighted the website's potential for providing a variety of perspectives from different countries. P14 and P17 viewed DiversIT as a community-building tool, with P17 noting its role as an information source about the intersectional peer community.

P13 reflected that DiversIT is a place where the participant can learn. When navigating to the *About* page by clicking the "Learn more about us"-button on the front page, the participant was confused about who "us" were. While exploring the site, P13 appreciated the availability of articles even for unregistered users, and P15 found it interesting to see what others had contributed. According to P17, DiversIT is a place to get inspired. While still not being logged in, P13 and P17 provided positive remarks about the *Community* page.

Three of the participants tried to use the search functionality in the header when being on the front page. P13 and P15 commented that they did not know what it was for, and because of this, did not consider the search bar as an intuitive functionality.

P13 appreciated that the sign-up is a popup, not a separate page, and commented that the registration process was quick and easy. During registration, P12 appreciated the possibility of signing up with LinkedIn. Further in the registration process, P13 thought it was great with pronouns as an option, which P14 also commented on as a great feature. These comments indicate that the registration process showed elements of the UX goals effectiveness and utility. However, the participants also pointed out issues, which showcased poor consistency, affordance, and visibility. The top button in the popup, when creating an account or logging in, confused P15 as it both looked like a button and a heading.

P13 could personally see himself asking questions and answering in the *Community*. At the same time, P16 was more sceptical of the possibility of being anonymous; "*I don't know if it's good to have the option to be anonymous. It seems contradictory to the site's purpose.*". P14 was critical to the number of prompts the *Community* possibly could contain; hence it could be hard to find specific prompts when there are many users. P14 further reflected that the existing functionality for saving prompts is suitable for structuring the information overload when having many users.

When asked if they wanted to join DiversIT, P12 expressed interest, while P13 and P17 were interested with the condition of getting recommendations or the site's popularity. Regarding DiversIT's potential to increase DEI, P12, P13, and P16 voiced positive opinions. P16 agreed that the concept presented through the prototype has potential as "*[m]any people with intersectional factors (e.g., gay) look for peers online. When you can talk with people who understand, it's easier, compared to having to explain to people*". The participant thought that DiversIT looked like a social network for people in tech to find others in CS and aims to be more inclusive. P16 further commented on *Articles* as a positive feature, which can show different experiences, such as mental health or diversity in CS education. However, P15 was uncertain about DiversIT's value on its own, and saw it more as a blend of LinkedIn and Twitter, suggesting the concept needed differentiation from existing social media platforms.

Iteration 4. In Iteration 4 the final prototype was completed and can be viewed *here.*[2] Improvements implemented to the prototype based on feedback are presented in the first part of this section, while the entire prototype is presented in the rest of this section.

Some participants found it confusing whether the labels on the front page under "Content Topics to Explore" were clickable buttons. This was improved in the previous iteration, but were not updated with the new design on the front page. In this last iteration, these were updated in order to make the design of the labels similar to those in *Community* and achieve consistency. Other improvements done to the landing page of DiversIT were removing the search bar on this page and reformulating the text on one button from "Learn more about us" to "Learn more about DiversIT". In addition, as creating a new user is a process with multiple steps, the progress bar was added to the first popup page in addition to the existing pages of the process.

The Final Prototype
DiversIT aims to increase DEI in CS by creating a supportive intersectional community online where peers worldwide can communicate, ask questions, discuss topics relevant to the field and be supportive of each other. With a focus on intersectionality, the researchers want to express a website that is welcoming and appealing to individuals of intersectional backgrounds by showing diversity in the illustrations and example prompts presented in the prototype. The high-fidelity Figma prototype aims to test DiversIT as a concept to be further coded and developed.

Figure 5 presents an overview of DiversIT. The first page a user sees is Fig. 5a, giving a first impression of the website and its functionalities. The user can scroll down the page to read more information in the text boxes. Figure 5b shows the *Articles* page. Here the user can read articles from the field where role models of diverse backgrounds will be presented. Based on the findings from the SLR [7,14] and the conducted interviews, role models who people can identify with, especially intersectional role models, are essential. The *Articles* page tries to assist in this, in addition to motivating, engaging, and raising awareness of intersectionality. A separate *About* page was added to DiversIT not to overwhelm the user with information on the front page. Figure 5c informs the user about the vision and mission of DiversIT. As a prominent part of DiversIT is a *Community*

---

[2] https://tinyurl.com/245n6em5

where the users can interact with each other, Fig. 5d was added to the prototype, informing the users about the code of conduct for the website. All pages presented in Fig. 5 are accessible through links on the front page, the header, or the footer.

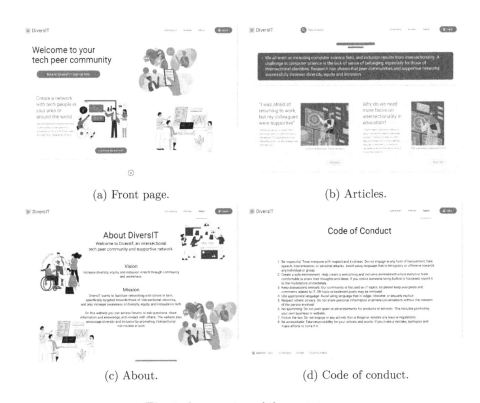

(a) Front page.

(b) Articles.

(c) About.

(d) Code of conduct.

Fig. 5. An overview of the prototype.

As mentioned, the *Community* part is an essential factor of DiversIT as a prototype. Figure 6 presents the *Community* where the logged-in users can interact with each other. As the *Community* is only visible to those who have registered an account, Fig. 6a provides a user who is not logged in with information about what the user can expect when logging in without sharing any prompts of existing users. Figure 6b presents the *Community* when the user has logged in and has full access to it. All the prompts are grouped into different topics, which work as a filtering system to easier find relevant prompts. A user can also save a prompt for easier access at a later time. By clicking on the "See/add response"-button, the user navigates to Fig. 6c, where the user can read responses made by other users and contribute to the discussion by adding a response. A user can also add a new separate prompt by clicking the "Add new prompt"-button in Fig. 6b, navigating to Fig. 6d.

This process of logging into DiversIT got simplified and clarified. A progress bar has been added and instead of the four steps, now it only takes three. Users

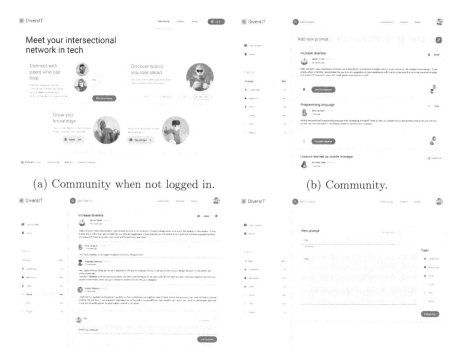

(a) Community when not logged in.   (b) Community.

(c) See and add responses to a prompt.   (d) Add a new prompt to the Community.

Fig. 6. Overview of the Community.

can log in or sign up through the popup shown using their username and password or using third-party accounts. They can select Student/Professional, provide their institution and their intersectional identity.

5   Discussion

This chapter discusses and evaluates the findings from the design and creation process. DiversIT, the prototyped website, is evaluated and discussed in Subsect. 5.1 based on findings from the usability tests. Lastly, a review of the limitations of this research is presented in Subsect. 5.2.

5.1   Evaluation of DiversIT as Digital Support to Increase DEI

In the prototyping stage of design and creation, DiversIT was developed in five iterations, with usability tests conducted after each design sprint. Each iteration and the results of each usability test are presented in Subsect. 4.2.

Findings from the SLR, underline how a supportive intersectional peer network [12] strongly correlates to a strong sense of belonging, indicating that there is a potential market demand for DiversIT as a digital product. During the interviews, the participants were generally optimistic about the idea of a networking platform, and the majority remained positive about the concept after interacting with the prototype during the usability test. These findings indicate the potential of DiversIT to help strengthen DEI within CS.

Despite the generally favourable impressions of the prototype, some participants were more critical of the website. Notably, those who reported fewer intersectionality related challenges in the interviews tended to be more critical of DiversIT. On the other hand, participants who experience challenges related to their intersectional identity seemed enthusiastic about DiversIT, envisioning themselves as regular users. As one participant stated, it can be hard to develop a product tailored for everyone, as the target group is wide because intersectionality varies greatly. Therefore, as the majority liked DiversIT, it could be considered a valuable product for further development.

In the first usability tests, participants focused more on the website's functionality, noting that the site's purpose was not immediately clear. The prototype was subsequently improved through multiple iterations and feedback from the usability tests, resulting in a better high-fidelity prototype than the one presented in Iteration 0. As a testament to this improvement, later usability tests garnered less negative feedback regarding the website's purpose, indicating enhanced usability.

The prototype underwent testing in Norway and Brazil, facilitating space triangulation that provided feedback from users with different cultural backgrounds and perspectives, which helped identify potential usability issues and areas for improvement. Having such geographical diversity in the testing also helped in evaluating the adaptability of the product in different environments, which is essential as DiversIT want to create a networking platform connecting peers in CS who identify with intersectionality from all over the world. Although space triangulation was time-consuming, its significant benefits made the researchers want to prioritise it, since it can lead to a better-designed prototype that meets the needs and expectations of a diverse range of users.

Evaluation Based on User Experience Goals. In alignment with the UX goals, the prototype demonstrates effective interaction design. Following, is an enumeration of the desirable aspects achieved based on the observations and feedback from the usability tests:

- **Engaging**: DiversIT came across as engaging for the participants, where multiple participants explicitly expressed that the provided information made them want to interact with the website.
- **Helpful**: Based on the impressions from the participants, the website came across as helpful. DiversIT can be divided into two main parts; the *Community* and *Articles*. The *Community* works as a supportive network to help those who feel a connection to intersectionality increase their sense of belonging. The *Articles* provides articles to inspire and help increase the awareness of intersectionality in the field.

- **Motivating**: The users can find motivation from other users in the *Community* or by reading articles.
- **Enhancing sociability**: The website provides an increased sense of belonging through the *Community* and the articles promoting diverse, intersectional role models.
- **Cognitively stimulating**: DiversIT can come across as cognitively stimulating as the users may discuss challenges related to CS and intersectionality in addition to reading articles.
- **Provocative**: Articles are thought to be provocative and inspiring.
- **Emotionally fulfilling**: The participants expressed engagement over the website due to its focus on DEI. The users can contribute positively to an online community.

In contrast, the potential undesirable aspects and associated risks to DiversIT include:

- **Frustrating**: Some participants expressed that the website was difficult to understand, but this was improved through multiple iterations.
- **Making one feel guilty**: It was commented that sensitive information may be difficult to discuss online, and intersectionality revolves around sensitive information.
- **Unpleasant**: As the website handles sensitive information, the website could feel unpleasant or unsafe to use, and therefore a code of conduct was added to the prototype.
- **Patronising**: This could occur if a user does not feel supported in the *Community*.

By evaluating the desired and undesired aspects, the developed prototype comes across as a website with good interaction design. However, in further development of DiversIT into a fully functional website, it is crucial to remember that the website handles sensitive data and acknowledge the risks this brings.

5.2   Limitations

The greatest limitation regarding the interviews was that they needed to be held in English. In Norway, some of the participants asked to conduct the interview in Norwegian, and since both researchers also speak Norwegian, this was not an issue as it made the interviewee more comfortable. In Brazil, there was a language barrier, since none of the researchers spoke Portuguese, and therefore, could not help if a participant struggled with expressing themselves in English. To minimise the barrier as much as possible, the researchers got assistance from a person in Brazil who spoke Portuguese and English and could help during the interviews. Since the interviews potentially discussed sensitive topics, each interviewee was asked prior to their interview whether they wanted additional assistance from the person who spoke Portuguese.

Other possible limitations identified during the usability test sessions were stress caused by time constraints and interruptions, affecting the researchers and the participants. In Brazil, the researchers did not have full control of the room used to execute the interviews and usability tests. This was noticeable during one interview in particular, where multiple people entered the room and interrupted the session. Every time someone interrupted, the interview was paused, but these interruptions happened outside the researchers' control. This resulted in significantly less time to complete the interview and usability test as planned, and the participant was noticeably stressed in the situation.

A limitation related to using Figma as a tool for designing the prototype for DiversIT is that users cannot write in input fields within the prototype. Through the usability tests, this confused the participants when they e.g. tried to create an account. To reduce this limitation as much as possible, dummy text was added to the input fields when the user clicked on the fields. The limitation made it challenging to test the overall usability of the input elements. Another limitation is the fact that if the user pressed somewhere in the prototype, then it became visible where the user could click. This could potentially spoil the honest UX as it made the prototype feel less like a real application, resulting in the user being less critical of the UI. In one usability test, this was a distracting factor and took the focus away from the actual design and interactions being tested.

Lastly, this study does not look into perspectives from e.g., transgender and non-binary people, because no participants with these intersectional identities expressed interest. Although the findings provide some perspectives from the LGBTQIA community, these do not fully encompass these experiences, nor do they reflect experiences outside the gender binary.

6   Conclusions

The study presented in this paper focused on the potential of a peer networking website on intersectional challenges in computing. The design process included multiple user test interviews looking into intersectionality in both Norway and Brazil.

The website prototype, DiversIT, got promising feedback after the usability tests, which also opens up for further development of the concept. Although some issues suggested for improvements during the usability tests were not implemented in the prototype, the final version of the product backlog has these listed. As DiversIT focuses on intersectionality and the fact that personal data related to this is sensitive, it is important to have accessibility and security as quality attributes, in addition to usability, when further developing the prototype into a fully functioning website. Following a universal design approach, using guidelines from Web Content Accessibility Guidelines (WCAG) and the Authority for Universal Design of ICT[3] is highly recommended to ensure the usability and accessibility of the website. Furthermore, scalability, for supporting increased user activity; and interoperability, for easily integrating this solution with other existing products; could be other quality attributes to consider.

---

[3] https://www.uutilsynet.no/english/websites/906.

References

1. Allen, R., Masters, D.: Artificial intelligence: the right to protection from discrimination caused by algorithms, machine learning and automated decision-making. ERA Forum **20**, 585–598 (2020). Springer
2. Bass, L., Clements, P., Kazman, R.: Software Architecture in Practice, 3rd edn. Pearson Education, New Jersey (2013)
3. Crenshaw, K.: Demarginalizing the intersection of race and sex: a Black feminist critique of antidiscrimination doctrine, feminist theory and antiracist policies. Univ. Chic. Leg. Forum **1989**(1), 139–167 (1989)
4. Diversity in Tech: The benefits of diversity in tech (2022). https://diversityintech.co.uk/the-benefits-of-diversity-in-tech
5. Duhaime-Ross, A.: Apple promised an expansive health app, so why can't I track menstruation? (2014). https://theverge.com/2014/9/25/6844021/apple-promised-an-expansive-health-app-so-why-cant-i-track
6. Gomoll, K., Nicol, A.: User observation: guidelines for Apple developers. Apple Human Interface Notes **1** (1990)
7. Hansen, M.F., Husnes, S.H.: Intersectionality in computer science: a systematic literature review (2022)
8. McCall, L.J.: The complexity of intersectionality. Signs: J. Women Cult. Soc. **30**, 1771–1800 (2005)
9. Oates, B.J., Griffiths, M., McLean, R.: Researching Information Systems and Computing, 2nd edn. SAGE, Thousand Oaks (2022)
10. Perez, C.C.: Invisible Women: Data Bias in a World Designed for Men. Abrams Press, New York (2019)
11. Sharp, H., Rogers, Y., Preece, J.: Interaction Design: Beyond Human-Computer Interaction, 5th edn. Wiley, New Jersey (2019)
12. Spencer, B., Rorrer, A., Davis, S., Moghadam, S.H., Grainger, C.: The role of 'intersectional capital' in undergraduate women's engagement in research-focused computing workshops. In: Research on Equity and Sustained Participation in Engineering, Computing, and Technology, RESPECT - Conference Proceedings (2021). https://doi.org/10.1109/RESPECT51740.2021.9620576
13. Stumpf, S., et al.: Gender-inclusive HCI research and design: a conceptual review. Found. Trends Hum.-Comput. Interact. **13**(1), 1–69 (2020). https://doi.org/10.1561/1100000056
14. Szlavi, A., Hansen, M.F., Husnes, S.H., Conte, T.U.: Intersectionality in computer science: a systematic literature review. In: IEEE/ACM 4th Workshop on Gender Equity, Diversity, and Inclusion in Software Engineering (GE@ICSE), pp. 9–16. Association for Computing Machinery (2023). https://doi.org/10.1109/GEICSE59319.2023.00006
15. Szlávi, A., Landoni, M.: Human computer interaction-gender in user experience. In: Stephanidis, C., Antona, M., Ntoa, S. (eds.) International Conference on Human-Computer Interaction, HCII 2022. CCIS, vol. 1580, pp. 132–137. Springer, Cham (2022). https://doi.org/10.1007/978-3-031-06417-3_18
16. Szlavi, A., Guedes, L.S.: Gender inclusive design in technology: case studies and guidelines. In: Marcus, A., Rosenzweig, E., Soares, M.M. (eds.) Design, User Experience, and Usability, vol. 14030, pp. 343–354. Springer, Cham (2023). https://doi.org/10.1007/978-3-031-35699-5_25

17. Tatman, R.: Google's speech recognition has a gender bias (2016). https://makingnoiseandhearingthings.com/2016/07/12/googles-speech-recognition-has-a-gender-bias/
18. Tilsynet for universell utforming av IKT: Apps (na). https://www.uutilsynet.no/english/apps/909

Mapping Gamification Elements to Heuristics and Behavior Change in Early Phase Inclusive Design: A Case Study

Alicia Julia Wilson Takaoka$^{(\boxtimes)}$ and Letizia Jaccheri

Norwegian University of Science and Technology (NTNU), Trondheim, Norway
{alicia.j.w.takaoka,letizia.jaccheri}@ntnu.no

Abstract. This paper identifies the connection between heuristics, gamification, and system visualization in the early design phase of a mobile application in order to create what we call *environmental behavior change*. Participant motivations, abilities, and triggers are identified as a part of the design process using Fogg's behavior model. Through purposive focus groups and the design of wireframes, features that can enable environmental behavior change are identified and turned into design goals. Example User stories, or personas, were generated for each goal. These goals are also mapped to heuristics for interface design, white hat drives for motivation using the Octalysis framework, and aspects of behavior change. The gamification of these aspects are discussed. Network features and competition were elements identified by participants as motivating factors that may enable environmental behaviour change. Key heuristics identified by participants include: 1. a match between the system and the real world, 2. user control and freedom, and 3. recognition rather than recall. These factors align with Fogg's Hope, social acceptance, and social rejection.

Keywords: environmental behaviour change · design and creation · heuristics · inclusive HCI · participatory design

1 Introduction

In the Green Deal, the European Commission states that tackling climate and environmentally related challenges is the defining duty of this generation[1]. The Green Deal outlines a just and inclusive transformation of communities, where zero greenhouse gas emissions are achieved in 2050. In addition, users' health and well-being are protected from environmental-related threats [19]. The UN Sustainable Goals (SDGs)[2] reinforce the idea that people and systems are responsible for reaching climate neutrality in an ethically inclusive and just way. The

---

[1] https://commission.europa.eu/strategy-and-policy/priorities-2019-2024/european-green-deal.

[2] https://sdgs.un.org/goals.

© The Author(s), under exclusive license to Springer Nature Switzerland AG 2024
M. Antona and C. Stephanidis (Eds.): HCII 2024, LNCS 14696, pp. 143–161, 2024.
https://doi.org/10.1007/978-3-031-60875-9_10

objective of this research is to address these intersecting issues by influencing behaviors and examining how people interact with the environment, called *environmental behaviour change*, through the early stage design and creation process, often used for new IT artifacts [44]. Through purposive focus groups to co-design wireframes and prototypes, gamification elements, heuristics, and motivation factors that can facilitate environmental behaviour change are presented.

1.1   Smart Cities

The concept of smart cities includes technologies and digital infrastructure as inclusive solutions to challenges created by urbanisation and the rapid growth of city populations [59,60]. In smart cities, technology will be designed to address needs from carbon reduction and energy consumption to inclusion in governmental processes. Digital technology is set to play a crucial role in the outcomes of smart cities and climate neutrality [58] under the Green Deal.

However, women are often omitted from the creation process of software development [27] and the use of their likeness [57] in software applications. Women are also excluded from discussions around the creation and adaptation to achieve the goals of climate transition [17]. This is in spite of women exhibiting an increased adoption of information communication technologies (ICT), which include mobile phones and internet access [12]. To date, there is minimal research about the barriers women experience as a result of the transition to smart cities [63]. The non-participation and exclusion of women [4,9] significantly impacts the governance of smart cities, which requires collaboration between relevant stakeholders like governments, citizens, and the systems being integrated [2]. Furthermore, refugee and immigrant women are often not citizens of their place of residence for years and can experience negative impacts during their period of residence [64].

1.2   Inclusion in Smart City Research

Inclusion, particularly of women and other marginalized voices from an intersectional perspective [14,37], is an integral part to our research. In this project, inclusion is in the purposive selection of focus group participants; however, transition to climate neutrality excludes many inhabitants, residents, and citizens from participation by the nature and cost of creating change (e.g. [29] and [40]), even in the design of mobile applications.

Mobile Applications. Mobile internet use has significantly increased in recent years, and the development of mobile applications are increasing as well. A mobile application (app) is created specifically for mobile devices like smartphones and tablets[3]. Some notable features of apps include sending push notifications, using offline, and using location-based or navigation elements [25]. Social

---

[3] https://www.techopedia.com/definition/2953/mobile-application-mobile-app.

media, games, and messaging apps are common examples of this rapidly growing area [65], indicating that apps may continue to hold influence with the increase of smartphone users [5]. This study focuses on designing a mobile application to promote environmental behavior change using purposive, inclusive focus groups to examine the intersections of motivation, heuristics, and behavior change.

Inclusive Design. Inclusive design is a process that empowers people from various backgrounds and abilities are referred to as inclusive design to participate in the design process. From an intersectional perspective, inclusive traits include accessibility, age, financial position, location, language, race, and more. Joyce explains inclusive design should be done in all phases of design and creation research, and both the product and the process should be inclusive [30]. While the app designed in this study aims to be inclusive, the focus of this paper the process of inclusion in early design phases to identify elements that will help create environmental behavior change.

1.3   Fogg Behaviour Change Model

Connecting the design of a mobile application to environmental behavior change requires embedding a behavior model into the design process [23,48]. Cognitive behavior models imply that the behaviour is driven by conscious mechanisms, usually conveying convincing messages about the importance or outcomes of performing a behaviour. Behavior change interventions have been used in health [24], but they can also be used to encourage environmental behavior change [56]. The Fogg Behavioral Model was selected for early design and creation activities because it presents dichotomous motivation factors to illicit response and provoke change [23].

Fogg [20] addresses three factors that influence behavior: motivation, ability, and triggers. To change a behaviour, the individual must be intrinsically motivated, possess the required skills, and be triggered to perform the behaviour. The FBM is useful to design and analyze apps because each factor can be identified through their sub-components. The motivation elements in the FBM are [20]:

1. *Pleasure/Pain* - functions adaptively and may be related to self-preservation
2. *Hope/Fear* - anticipation of what will happen
3. *Social acceptance/rejection* - desire for connectedness and inclusion (p. 4)

The six elements of ability are: time, money, physical effort, brain cycles, social deviance, and non-routine [21]. These traits may impact environmental behavior change because they may be barriers to entry. Finally, Fogg introduces three types of triggers. Spark can be applied when a person lacks the motivation to perform a behaviour. Facilitator can be applied when a person lacks the ability to perform a behaviour, and signal can be applied when a person has both motivation and ability to perform a behaviour. These triggers can be manipulated through gamification elements in early phase app design.

1.4   Fogg in Software Engineering

FBM is used in software engineering. Rist examines FBM related to energy savings because it is a validated model with over 20 years of testing [52]. Sugarman and Lank state that studies in human-computer interaction (HCI) use FBM to consider how technology can increase ability and also trigger users [56] for different actions. In this study, FBM is used in planning, conducting, and evaluating the early stage design.

1.5   Octalysis Gamification Framework

Gamification is the use of game design elements in non-game contexts [15, p. 9]. Gamification may promote inclusion and environmental behavior change though gameplay or a gamified experience, and can potentially increase engagement with environmental behavior change [49]. Some implemented game design elements include Points, Badges and Leaderboards (PBL). These three elements are often paired together because of their breadth, adaptability, and user familiarity [3]. Other examples of game elements include levels, storytelling, chance, goals, feedback, rewards, progress, challenge, avatar, and status are also used to harness motivation and provide a captivating UX [47]. These elements align with core drives for designing gamified systems.

The Octalysis framework [13] is used to design and evaluate applications in reference to motivational drivers. Figure 1 shows an octagon with eight areas of motivation, called core drives. Each core drive lists activities and characteristics. As Ådlandsvik and Doveland [1] explain, the octagon can be divided both horizontally and vertically to further group core drives with similar attributes. Vertically, the right-side drives represent intrinsic motivators and creativity while the left-side drives are extrinsic and logical. Horizontally, the top half are white-hat gamification drives that use positive techniques to drive users to interact with the application. The bottom drives are black-hat which use negative traits for engagement. The Octalysis framework bridges psychology and gamification [41,61], making it appropriate for app development [32] in the design and creation process [61].

The implemented core drives in the design phase in this project are *1: Epic Meaning & Calling, 2: Development & Accomplishment* and *5: Social influence and relatedness*. These drives are all white-hat. Users will maintain a sense of control and minimize the risk of users developing unhealthy habits or technology addiction. Additionally, by not employing any black-hat techniques, the risk of user drop out is reduced [13].

1.6   Heuristics

There are ten principles of usability, called heuristics [42,43]. These principles are used to identify and solve problems. This is often done in the user testing phase, but recently has been employed in developing apps [34] and addressing real world problems [31] in a bespoke manner [16]. These heuristics are:

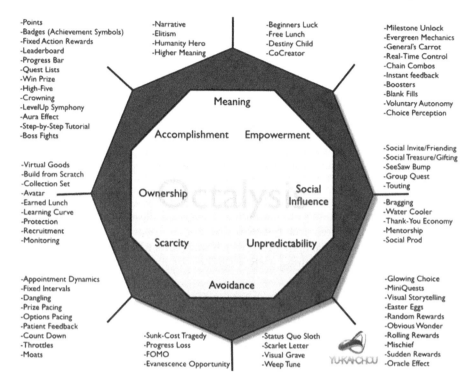

Fig. 1. Core Drives in the Octalysis framework [13]

1. Visibility of system status
2. Match between system and the real world
3. User control and freedom
4. Consistency and standards
5. Error prevention
6. Recognition rather than recall
7. Flexibility and efficiency of use
8. Aesthetic and minimalist design
9. Help users recognize, diagnose, and recover from errors
10. Help and documentation

These heuristics provide a framework for our thematic analysis during early phases of design and creation for mobile applications. Incorporating FBM, the Octalysis gamification model, and heuristics, as previously stated, led to the development of the following research question: *To what extent can design goals, white hat core drives, and heuristics of design be identified using purposive inclusive sampling?*

Finally, this framework also guided the early stage design methods, presented in the next section.

2 Methods

Design and Creation was selected as the process for data collection. According to Oates, the design and creation research strategy focuses on the development of new IT artefacts [44] across disciplines like HIV prevention [8], eco-adventure [28], virtual museum tours [7], and process simulations [26,46]. The five stages are: Awareness, Suggestion, Development, Evaluation, and Conclusion. While this study includes usability testing, observations, and validated usability instruments, they are not the focus of this paper. This paper explores the alignment of heuristics within the suggestion and early development phases of design and creation.

Data management was handled through a national interactive platform, and a notification form outlining our handling of personal data was submitted and assessed by the national research review board. For this paper, we focus on Step 2 and 3, Suggestion and Development, in which we conduct focus group interviews to design wireframes and address early stage heuristic concerns and elements of environmental behavior change.

2.1 Focus Group Interview

Focus group interviews were selected because they allow interaction and informal discussion between participants [33,62]. Questions for the focus group were in the areas of citizen participation, gamification, and usability and tested for construct validity. These questions also allowed for discussion about the gamification of application elements to promote environmental behavior change and inclusion. This included barriers to use, features to promote inclusion, and Nielsen's heuristics. The focus group was one hour, and participants sat in a circle so they could interact with each other. Tangible items like paper and pens were available to help foster and explain ideas.

2.2 Participants

Purposive sampling was employed to select six participants. These participants were selected based on their age, education, ethnicity, country of origin, experience with technology as a user, and coding knowledge as a developer [39]. All participants identified as women. The participants were recruited through a convenience sampling technique because a familiarity within the group could create an ease of conversation that may not have been achieved with a group of strangers.

2.3 Data Collection

The focus group interview followed a semi-structured protocol in which participants were asked to imagine a scenario where they were participating in volunteer clean up activities around their city. Time was allotted for exploring emergent questions and discussions [50]. Data was collected via note taking and automatic translation using Microsoft Teams[4]. This led into collaborative ideation through thematic analysis.

2.4 Data Analysis

Thematic analysis is frequently used in UX research [10,53], and collaborative analysis thematic analysis sessions employing open and axial were conducted to analyze the transcripts. Organization was managed on Miro[5].

Themed data was later categorized using pattern and protocol coding to align themes with heuristics, FBM, and the Octalysis core drives using Saldana [54]. An example of data segments and theme can be seen in Table 1. A visualisation of thematic analysis grouping is shown in Fig. 2.

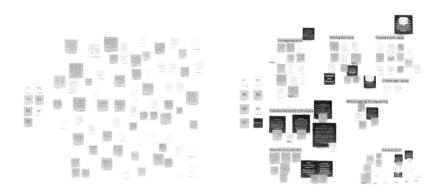

Fig. 2. Theming in Miro, Rounds 1 and 2

2.5 Wireframes

After thematic analysis, the wireframe design phase began by developing paper prototypes in alignment with the focus group data. These were created both on paper and digitally [55]. Paper prototypes were selected as a preliminary artifact to evaluate the FBM and Heuristics before constructing digital wireframes.

3   Results

Participants imagined a scenario in which they volunteer in city-wide cleanups. They had to imagine an application that would feel inclusive and help them participate in both the app and more clean up activities. Participants also explored

---

[4] https://www.microsoft.com/en-us/microsoft-teams/group-chat-software.
[5] https://miro.com/.

barriers to participation. This began the discussions around motivating factors. Participants should not feel high pressure to participate, as stated by Participants 5 and 6. There was group consensus about flexibility being a motivating factor for participation and contribution. A sample of responses contributing to this theme can be seen in Table 1.

Table 1. Motivation factors

Part.	Data segment	Fogg
1	..during the pandemic we were able to travel less. So we felt like we were also maybe doing more (for the climate) and then by 2021 people started travelling again and which isn't that great for the climate obviously	Hope, Social Acceptance, Social Rejection
2	So for me in general it's related to the values and the things that I believe in. But it's also about people joining at the events as well, for example, if I am passionate about a topic and I see an event that I like and I know there are some people that I know there, I join.	Hope, Social Acceptance
2	I like to share activities with [friends].	Social Acceptance
4	I think like the social aspect of the ones sharing is important. Just like as you said. To meet more people and kind of being together	Social Acceptance
3	For me, its motivating to wanting to make a change, so when I noticed that there's something wrong, then instead of, you know, waiting for it to be solved, somehow trying to be part of the solution	Hope
5	And also that it is low pressure. So you can participate in it when you have time, and don't need to use a specific amount of time every week for example	Pleasure
6	The volunteer work should be more flexible. If I feel like I'm bound to do this, then maybe it will not interest people to come for the work, so it should be a bit flexible.	Pleasure, Pain

3.1   Features for Motivation

Based on the Fogg behavior model, participants identified mobile features that may contribute to environmental behavior change. These elements were analyzed using pattern coding and protocol coding [45] and aligned with development goals for environmental behavior change, Octalysis core drives, and Nielsen's heuristics for usability, which can be seen in Table 2.

To promote environmental behavior change, these motivation factors should be integrated into app design. Participant 4 summarised: *'Again, it's just connecting with people and see if you can do something that is small but has a value'*. The importance of highlighting the problem in a tangible way, in a way the user can relate to, was very important according to Participant 3. Participant 1 highlighted gamification elements as important motivational factors. These include badges and leaderboards.

Table 2. Alignment of Development Goals for Environmental Behavior Change, Octalysis Core Drives, elements from the Fogg Behavior Model, and Nielsen's Heuristic Elements

Environmental Behavior Change Dev. Goals	Core Drives	Fogg Behavior Model	Nielsen's Heuristics
Register on and continued use of the app	CD1, CD5	Motivation: Social Acceptance/Rejection, Trigger: Spark	Visibility of system status
Network on the app	CD2, CD5	Motivation: Social Acceptance/Rejection, Ability: All	User Control and Freedom
App Purpose: Contribute to a sustainable city	CD1, CD2	Motivation: Any, Ability: All, Trigger: All	Match Between the System and the Real World
See scores and ranks among friends	CD2	Motivation: Social Acceptance/Rejection	User Control and Freedom
Accessibility and inclusion of diverse users	CD1, CD5	The app must prove that this is a place for these users.	Match Between the System and the Real World

3.2   Design Features

Both the negative and positive sides of notifications and pop-ups were discussed. These notifications can be helpful reminders as well as annoying. Notifications are not just limited to sounds or buzzing. Reminder e-mails are negative notifications. Participant 5 highlighted dark design and manipulation, or the feeling that an application collects a lot of sensitive data, as a factor that could prevent this participant from using an app while Participant 2 warned against conflating notifications with engagement. Table 3 shows statements expressed by participants and their alignment with themes.

3.3   White-Hat Core Drives and Participation

Participants mentioned many different gamification elements which can help motivate them. Participant 3 highlighted rank, leaderboards, and rewards, Participant 4 outlined a preference for short games that can be played whenever reasonable, Participant 6 outlined levels as a motivational element, Participant

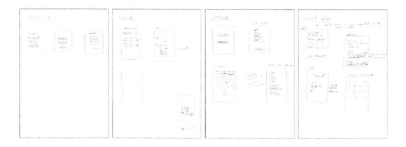

Fig. 3. Paper Prototype

Table 3. Design features for motivation

Data segment	Themes
Participant 1: *"I guess one thing is like this those apps that have like ads popping up all the time or just like super annoying pop up elements in general."*	Design features to motivate users
Participant 2: *"In general if I don't feel like using an app anymore, it's mostly because I'm bored, not because they do something that like annoys me, so it's a matter of how engaging the application is and what can I do with the application."*	Design features to motivate users Motivational factors for behavioural change
Participant 2: *"So if you decide that an app should be used two times a day, then it should be designed to being used two times a day"*	Design features to motivate users
Participant 3: *"I really hated that when I stopped using Duolingo for Norwegian, it still continued sending me emails. 'Ohh you're letting us down'. It was annoying."*	Design features to motivate users
Participant 2: *"So if you dont use it, then it can be annoying. But if for example I get a notification because of an update of something that I like, I will open it and check out the update. I like this use of notifications"*	Motivational factors for behavioural change Design features to motivate users
Participant 6: *"For me, these notifications from Duolingo sometimes helps. If i forget to use the app for some days, and I get a notification saying "Are you forgetting us? Why dont you use Duolingo?", then i remember that I should use the app, and use it. So for me it works sometimes"*	Motivational factors for behavioural change Design features to motivate users
Participant 3: *"I agree that it is good with notifications when you want to keep the streak, but when I have decided that I want to stop using the application, it is annoying"*	Design features to motivate users
Participant 5: *"I think if an app has some kind of dark design and is trying to manipulate you, or if you feel that the app is collecting a lot of sensitive data about you, then I don't want to use that"*	Motivational factors for behavioural change Design features to motivate users
Participant 2: *"For storytelling I like graphics and animations, because they keep you engaged, just like Duolingo"*	Design features to motivate users
Participant 1: *"If the app is a socially geared app or one with gamification elements, I would like it to be more complex and have animations."*	Gamification elements
Participant 2: *"I can have notifications, but if they are too many, I get angry and just delete the app"*	Design features to motivate users
Participant 1: *"I think the user should have some kind of options to set the notifications settings. If I want notifications, I can switch it on if I don't want it then I keep it odd. It should also be possible to choose what kind of notifications you get."*	Design features to motivate users

5 highlighted some features that show how much of a given task has been completed as motivating, Participant 2 highlighted the importance of how the game is connected to the actual goal that is pursued, and Participant 1 outlined point systems. In summary, the participants had many different opinions on which gamification elements were motivating, but seemed to agree that gamification is motivating if used in a reasonable way. Table 4 shows how these expressions align with heuristics, and some of the prototypes can be seen in Fig. 3.

Table 4. Gamification Elements and Heuristic Alignment

Data segment	Heuristics
Participant 3: *"For example in Duolingo, I find it good to have gamification elements like the ranks, leaderboards and rewards"*	Visibility of status
Participant 3: *"I don't know how specific this is to language learning, but I felt that sometimes gamification overrode the initial function of the specific app. Because sometimes I just did the practice in order to gain points, instead of focusing on what will benefit my language learning. So sometimes I mean it helped me keep my streak and if you say that for language learning it is important to have consistency, then it is good. But I have mixed feelings about gamification"*	Match between system and real world
Participant 4: *"I think I prefer games that are short, so I can play them whenever I want to."*	Flexibility and efficiency of use User control and freedom
Participant 6: *"If the game has multiple levels, then maybe I'll feel the push to have to go to the next level. So there is some motivation to play the game and [fix mistakes] the game so I can move forward"*	Help users recognize, diagnose, and recover from errors
Participant 5: *"I prefer some features that show how much you have completed. For example, if it's a game about steps, if you want to go 10000 steps each day, then you can see how many steps you have left in a sort of progression bar. To see the percentage you have left to complete a task, I think that is really motivating"*	Visibility of system status Match between system and the real world

3.4   Application Requirements

The developed application requirements were constructed with inclusion in mind. These requirements will guide the design of the application and also provide a framework for further development in order to foster engagement of diverse participants, especially of women. Each of the five goals is accompanied by several user stories, which can be seen in Table 5.

Goal 1. Registering on and continued use of the app is the first goal of the design, as seen in the literature and the focus group. A potentially powerful approach to affecting behaviour change is to surround oneself with others that normalise desired behaviours, and online spaces have shown the potential to foster the growth of social communities with a common interest in climate change. Lee et al. state that having a publicly viewable profile as one of the features that create a community [35].

Goal 2. Goal 2 is about social engagement and networking. The desire to network accompanied by a change in social network dynamics may impact environmental behaviour change by changing motivation factors like social acceptance [20]. For networking, Lee et al. highlight viewing other users' activity in a feed, reacting to others, and giving and receiving positive feedback as features to promote discussion, the sharing of knowledge, and user-generated contribution [35].

Table 5. Application Requirement Goals and Example User Stories

Goal	User Stories Example
Goal 1 A new user should be able to register and add relevant personal information that will be shown on a publicly viewable profile	(1.2) As a User, I want to be able to log in and out, so that I can choose when I want to be active on the application
Goal 2 A user should be able to create a network to interact with other users	(2.6) As a User, I want to be notified when a friend completes a challenge or participates in an event, so that I can be motivated by my friends' activity
Goal 3 A user should be able to make contributions for a more sustainable city	(3.1) As a User, I want to be able to create inclusive events, so that I can facilitate social meetings for climate-neutrality
Goal 4 A user should be able to see their score and rank and compete with their friends	(4.4) As a User, I want to show my badges on my profile, and also see others badges on their profiles, so that I can show my achievements and also be motivated by others
Goal 5 The design of the application should be inclusive, providing equal opportunities for all users	As a User, I want to be able to choose among different languages in the application, so that I can use my preferred language

Goal 3. Goal three addresses the purpose of the app. A user's contributions towards a more sustainable city is the third goal of this application. Magalhães et al. [38] state that the contributions of users can produce better social and environmental results. Lee et al. also note that offering practical and readily applicable information could be an effective strategy to motivate individuals to lasting environmental behavior change choices [35].

Goal 4. Competition is the fourth goal of the application. Users should be able to see their score and rank among their friends or opt out. Implementing gamification as a method to motivate users was supported by both a paper from the SLR [51] and the focus group. Participant 2 said, "As a user, I want to be able to see my own points in a leaderboard, so that I can compare myself to friends." Participant 5 echoed this as a motivational aspect for tracking their own progress.

Goal 5. The last goal concerns accessibility to ensure the inclusion of potential users. As mentioned, an important part of reaching the climate goals is that no one is left behind and can use the mobile application to create environmental behaviour change. This study focused on the inclusion of women with emphasis of some intersectional traits in the design process, but other groups need to be prioritized as well. Ballantyne et al. highlight the importance of mobile applications being usable by users with disabilities, especially because of the increased amount of mobile device users [5], and present universal guidelines to ensure the accessibility of mobile apps. Participant 4 stated, "As a User, I want to use an application following the WCAG, so that I can use the application even though

I have a disability" while Participant 5 explained, "As a User, I want to use an application portraying human diversity, so that I recognize others like myself within the application." In further application development, such a framework is followed strictly to ensure inclusion for all users.

4   Discussion

Based on the discussions held during the focus group, there are clear indications that a developed mobile application platform will help motivate users to contribute to a sustainable and inclusive city. This study examines the effects purposive sampling has in early phase design as demonstrated by RQ1: *To what extent can design goals, white hat core drives, and heuristics of design be identified using purposive inclusive sampling?*. Identifying women using an intersectional perspective to participate in a focus group helped to identify key features of gamification for white hat motivation factors in app design. These choices may help promote environmental change. Through the process of focus groups and prototyping, valuable insights about the connections between motivation, heuristics and Fogg's behavior model were gathered. The findings indicated motivational factors intrinsic to the app like networking, events, and flexibility as well as those intrinsic to the user like the desire to make a difference. The results also demonstrate how gamification elements can influence environmental behaviour change. Rank, leaderboards, rewards, and task completion tracking were identified as effective elements. By incorporating these findings into the development goals, apps may effectively engage and motivate users toward active participation in creating sustainable and inclusive cities.

The purposive sampling of women using an intersectional lens revealed important information about app design and motivation. While motivation should be included in all aspects of design goals, the app itself should not press motivation in its content. Fogg explains, "persuasive design succeeds faster when we focus on making the behaviour simpler instead of trying to pile on motivation" [20, p. 6]. By demonstrating and normalizing the desired behavior through ease of use in an app, the behavior should become easier to perform. Perceived ease of use was mentioned throughout the design process.

While 75% of participants expressed that social features provide motivation, 25% indicated that solely relying on social aspects is not adequate motivation for use. The app needs to offer more than social aspects. Additional incentives and features to enhance motivation should be incorporated. These may include in-app currency and progress-related badges and rewards. Participants of the focus group discussed gamification elements that work for them individually. This relates to Neilsen's heuristic User Control and Freedom, which in its strict interpretation is related to having planned exit points. This heuristic in practice also allows an app user to participate at their own pace and not feeling forced to participate in events. This can be through planned exits of events and challenges as well as the deletion of tasks without shame.

Aligning with the findings of Ferron et al. [18], individual challenges were the most well-received design feature. Challenges can promote environmental behaviour change, but they can dissuade use, especially if accompanied by unwanted notifications. Individual challenges are designed to contribute to a sustainable city that aligns with the Octalysis framework. Overcoming challenges is an integral aspect of Core Drive 2, which provides motivation for engaging in specific activities.

The focus group mentioned that information about the specific purpose of the app is a motivational factor. In this case, information about climate change and volunteering activities may impact intrinsic motivation of users. Rajanen and Rajanen explain that traditional mass media communication has shown low effect on environmental behavior change for individuals because the issue is perceived as both not personally relevant and a distant problem [49]. Therefore, information about the problem should be stated in local and immediate scope using white hate drives [36].

Some features may deter use of the app. First, ads and pop-ups should be used sparingly if at all. Other funding streams should be secured in order to not have these features deter use. Next, the repetition of tasks may lead to lack of engagement. Tasks and challenges should be fun and engaging. Finally, dark design and manipulation techniques were raised in the focus group. Gray et al. defines *dark patterns* as "instances where designers use their knowledge of human behavior (e.g., psychology) and the desires of end users to implement deceptive functionality that is not in the user's best interest" [22, p. 1]. An application should be designed ethically without embedded dark patterns to promote inclusion, safety, use.

4.1   Limitations

This research project has several limitations. One limitation is the limited number of focus groups in the design phase. While the group was intentionally designed to be gender inclusive and inclusive of age, country of origin, and education, the replication of focus groups would only strengthen results through triangulation. Another limitation is the use of purposive sampling for participant recruitment. Due to the limited time period of this research project, and the aim of answering the research question as precisely and thoroughly as possible, design was prioritized over development. Finally, developing a coded MVP of the app may have produced different results in the focus group.

4.2   Future Studies

The future design of this mobile application is an area of future research. Replication of this study is also necessary to triangulate the results of purposive sampling in the early design phase. These studies should be about apps that promote environmental change as well as apps in different domains. In relation to this project, a high fidelity prototype was developed and tested using usability tests and the system usability score (SUS) [6,11]. An MVP should also be designed and tested.

5 Conclusion

The results of this study indicate that a mobile application is a suitable digital platform to motivate users to contribute more toward reaching the goals of the European Green Deal, namely reaching zero greenhouse gas emissions by 2050 in a just and inclusive way. The developed application requirements and mobile application prototype presented in this study contribute to knowledge on how to design such a mobile application and on which specific design elements should be included.

While it is demonstrated that displaying information alone may not be sufficient to convey the problem's significance to individuals, it is emphasised that doing so plays a crucial role in inspiring users to contribute. Participants have expressed the importance of receiving clear and relatable information that illuminates the reasons they should be concerned and outlines ways in which they can contribute to the cause. The application should incorporate functionalities that promote consciousness, enhance awareness, and offer insights into sustainable behaviours and initiatives, and the implementation of a feed where other users' contributions appear, information about initiatives through a blog in the application and facilitation of events are found to be suitable ways to incorporate these functionalities in the application.

Acknowledgments. We would like to acknowledge the work of Ferdinand Ward Ådlandsvik and Eivind Dovland who chose the models and conducted the sessions with participants.

References

1. Ådlandsvik, F.W., Dovland, E.S.: Motivating positive environmental behaviour change for sustainable and inclusive cities: a study on mobile application design and gamification. Master's thesis, NTNU (2023)
2. Al Sharif, R., Pokharel, S.: Smart city dimensions and associated risks: review of literature. Sustain. Urban Areas **77**, 103542 (2022)
3. Alcântara, A.S., Rodrigues, E., Oliveira, S., Junior, R., Cardoso, W.: The use of PBL (points, badges and leaderboards) components and game mechanics for teaching and learning of knowledge management. In: XXIV Conferência Internacional de Informática Educativa (TISE 2019), vol. 16 (2019)
4. Asteria, D., Jap, J.J., Utari, D.: A gender-responsive approach: social innovation for the sustainable smart city in Indonesia and beyond. J. Int. Women's Stud. **21**(6), 193–207 (2020)
5. Ballantyne, M., Jha, A., Jacobsen, A., Scott Hawker, J., El-Glaly, Y.N.: Study of accessibility guidelines of mobile applications. In: Proceedings of the 17th International Conference on Mobile and Ubiquitous Multimedia, pp. 305–315. ACM International Conference Proceeding Series, 1601 Broadway, Times Square, New York City (2018). https://doi.org/10.1145/3282894.3282921
6. Bangor, A., Kortum, P.T., Miller, J.T.: An empirical evaluation of the system usability scale. Int. J. Hum.-Comput. Interact. **24**(6), 574–594 (2008). https://doi.org/10.1080/10447310802205776

7. Besoain, F., Jego, L., Gallardo, I.: Developing a virtual museum: experience from the design and creation process. Information **12**(6), 244 (2021)
8. Besoain, F., et al.: Prevention of HIV and other sexually transmitted infections by geofencing and contextualized messages with a gamified app, UBESAFE: design and creation study. JMIR Mhealth Uhealth **8**(3), e14568 (2020)
9. Bleja, J., Langer, H., Grossmann, U., Mörz, E.: Smart cities for everyone–age and gender as potential exclusion factors. In: 2020 IEEE European Technology and Engineering Management Summit (E-TEMS), pp. 1–5. IEEE (2020)
10. Braun, V., Clarke, V.: Using thematic analysis in psychology. Qual. Res. Psychol. **3**(2), 77–101 (2006). https://doi.org/10.1191/1478088706qp063oa
11. Brooke, J.: SUS: a quick and dirty usability scale. Usability Eval. Ind. **189**, 4–7 (1995)
12. Bululukova, D., Wahl, H., Ballner, M.: European academic smart cities network–renewable urban energy systems, sustainable mobility and ICT technology nexus for smart cities studies. J. Real Corp. 207–215 (2014)
13. Chou, Y.K.: Actionable gamification: Beyond points, badges, and leaderboards. Packt Publishing Ltd, 30 N Gould Street STE 4000 - 82801 SHERIDAN (WY) - USA (2019)
14. Crenshaw, K.W.: On intersectionality: essential writings. The New Press, 120 Wall Street, 31st Floor New York, NY 10005 (2017)
15. Deterding, S., Dixon, D., Khaled, R., Nacke, L.: From game design elements to gamefulness: defining "gamification". In: Proceedings of the 15th International Academic MindTrek Conference: Envisioning Future Media Environments, pp. 9–15. ACM (2011). https://doi.org/10.1145/2181037.2181040
16. Drake, J.H., Kheiri, A., Özcan, E., Burke, E.K.: Recent advances in selection hyperheuristics. Eur. J. Oper. Res. **285**(2), 405–428 (2020)
17. Ertl, T., et al.: Ethical future environments: smart thinking about smart cities means engaging with its most vulnerable. In: Proceedings of the 10th International Conference on Communities & Technologies-Wicked Problems in the Age of Tech, pp. 340–345 (2021)
18. Ferron, M., Loria, E., Marconi, A., Massa, P.: Play & go, an urban game promoting behaviour change for sustainable mobility. Interact. Des. Archit. J. IxD&A **1**(40), 24–45 (2019). https://doi.org/10.55612/s-5002-040-002
19. Fetting, C.: The European green deal. ESDN report 53 (2020)
20. Fogg, B.: A behavior model for persuasive design. In: ACM International Conference Proceeding Series, vol. 350. ACM (2009). https://doi.org/10.1145/1541948.1541999
21. Fogg, B.J.: A behavior model for persuasive design. In: Proceedings of the 4th international Conference on Persuasive Technology, pp. 1–7 (2009)
22. Gray, C.M., Kou, Y., Battles, B., Hoggatt, J., Toombs, A.L.: The dark (patterns) side of UX design. In: Conference on Human Factors in Computing Systems - Proceedings, vol. 2018-April (2018). https://doi.org/10.1145/3173574.3174108
23. Heimlich, J., Ardoin, N.: Understanding behavior to understand behavior change: a literature review. Environ. Educ. Res. **14**, 215–237 (2008). https://doi.org/10.1080/13504620802148881
24. Hollands, G.J., Marteau, T.M., Fletcher, P.C.: Non-conscious processes in changing health-related behaviour: a conceptual analysis and framework. Health Psychol. Rev. **10**(4), 381–394 (2016). https://doi.org/10.1080/17437199.2015.1138093
25. Huy, N.P., et al.: Selecting the right mobile app paradigms. In: 2012 Fifth IEEE International Conference on Service-Oriented Computing and Applications (SOCA), pp. 1–6. IEEE (2012)

26. Iriondo Pascual, A., et al.: Multi-objective optimization of ergonomics and productivity by using an optimization framework. In: Black, N.L., Neumann, W.P., Noy, I. (eds.) IEA 2021, pp. 374–378. Springer, Cham (2021). https://doi.org/10.1007/978-3-030-74614-8_46

27. Jaccheri, L., Pereira, C., Fast, S.: Gender issues in computer science: lessons learnt and reflections for the future. In: 2020 22nd International Symposium on Symbolic and Numeric Algorithms for Scientific Computing (SYNASC), pp. 9–16. IEEE (2020)

28. Jego, L., Gallardo, I., Besoain, F.: Developing a virtual reality experience with game elements for tourism: Kayak simulator. In: 2019 IEEE CHILEAN Conference on Electrical, Electronics Engineering, Information and Communication Technologies (CHILECON), pp. 1–6. IEEE (2019)

29. Jian, I., Luo, J., Chan, E.: Spatial justice in public open space planning: accessibility and inclusivity. Habitat Int. 102122 (2020). https://doi.org/10.1016/j.habitatint.2020.102122

30. Joyce, A.: Inclusive Design (2012). https://www.nngroup.com/articles/inclusive-design/. Accessed 15 May 2023

31. Juan, A.A., et al.: A review of the role of heuristics in stochastic optimisation: from metaheuristics to learnheuristics. Ann. Oper. Res. **320**(2), 831–861 (2023)

32. Karać, J., Stabauer, M.: Gamification in E-commerce. In: International Conference on HCI in Business, Government, and Organizations, pp. 41–54 (2017). https://doi.org/10.1007/978-3-319-58484-3_4

33. Kitzinger, J.: Qualitative research: introducing focus groups. BMJ **311**(7000), 299 (1995). https://doi.org/10.1136/bmj.311.7000.299

34. Kumar, B.A., Goundar, M.S.: Usability heuristics for mobile learning applications. Educ. Inf. Technol. **24**, 1819–1833 (2019)

35. Lee, J., Ceyhan, P., Jordan-Cooley, W., Sung, W.: GREENIFY a real-world action game for climate change education. Simul. Gaming **44**, 349–365 (2013). https://doi.org/10.1177/1046878112470539

36. Luger-Bazinger, C., Hornung-Prähauser, V.: Innovation for sustainable cities: the effects of nudging and gamification methods on urban mobility and sustainability behaviour. GI Forum **9**(2), 251–258 (2021). https://doi.org/10.1553/giscience2021_02_s251

37. Lunn, S., Zahedi, L., Ross, M., Ohland, M.: Exploration of intersectionality and computer science demographics: understanding the historical context of shifts in participation. ACM Trans. Comput. Educ. (TOCE) **21**(2), 1–30 (2021)

38. Magalhães, M., Duarte, R.P., Oliveira, C., Pinto, F.C.: The role of the smart citizen in smart cities. In: International Conference on Computational Science and Its Applications, ICCSA 2021, vol. 12952, pp. 295–310 (2021). https://doi.org/10.1007/978-3-030-86973-1_21

39. Masadeh, M.A.: Focus group: reviews and practices. Int. J. Appl. Sci. Technol. **2**(10), 63–68 (2012)

40. Mohajermoghari, N.: Socially-mixed Affordable Housing in Nyhavna. Master thesis, NTNU (2021). https://ntnuopen.ntnu.no/ntnu-xmlui/handle/11250/2825087

41. Morschheuser, B., Hassan, L., Werder, K., Hamari, J.: How to design gamification? A method for engineering gamified software. Inf. Softw. Technol. **95**, 219–237 (2018). https://doi.org/10.1016/j.infsof.2017.10.015

42. Nielsen, J.: How to conduct a heuristic evaluation. Nielsen Norman Group **1**(1), 8 (1995)

43. Nielsen, J.: Ten usability heuristics. Nielsen Norman Group (2005)

44. Oates, B.J., Griffiths, M., McLean, R.: Researching Information Systems and Computing. Sage (2022)
45. Onwuegbuzie, A.J., Frels, R.K., Hwang, E.: Mapping saldana's coding methods onto the literature review process. J. Educ. Issues **2**(1), 130–150 (2016)
46. Pascual, A.I., Högberg, D., Syberfeldt, A., Brolin, E., Hanson, L.: Optimizing ergonomics and productivity by connecting digital human modeling and production flow simulation software. Adv. Transdisc. Eng. **13**, 193–204 (2020)
47. Lombriser, P., Dalpiaz, F., Lucassen, G., Brinkkemper, S.: Gamified requirements engineering: model and experimentation. In: International Working Conference on Requirements Engineering: Foundation for Software Quality (2016). https://doi.org/10.1007/978-3-319-30282-9_12
48. Pinder, C., Fleck, R., Díaz, R., Beale, R., Hendley, R.: Accept the banana: exploring incidental cognitive bias modification techniques on smartphones. In: Proceedings of the 2016 CHI Conference Extended Abstracts on Human Factors in Computing Systems, pp. 2923–2931 (2016). https://doi.org/10.1145/2851581.2892453
49. Rajanen, D., Rajanen, M.: Climate change gamification: a literature review. In: CEUR Workshop Proceedings, vol. 2359, pp. 253–264 (2019). https://ceur-ws.org/Vol-2359/paper22.pdf
50. Recker, J.: Scientific Research in Information Systems: A Beginner's Guide. Springer, Cham (2013). https://doi.org/10.1007/978-3-642-30048-6
51. Remelhe, E., Cerqueira, M., M., F.P., Paiva, S.: Sustainable smart parking solution in a campus environment. EAI Endorsed Trans. Energy Web **9**(39) (2022). https://doi.org/10.4108/ew.v9i39.1191
52. Rist, T., Masoodian, M.: Promoting sustainable energy consumption behavior through interactive data visualizations. Multimodal Technol. Interact. **3**, 56 (2019). https://doi.org/10.3390/mti3030056
53. Rosala, M.: How to Analyze Qualitative Data from UX Research (2022). https://www.nngroup.com/articles/thematic-analysis/. Accessed 12 May 2023
54. Saldaña, J.: The Coding Manual for Qualitative Researchers. Sage (2021)
55. Snyder, C.: Paper Prototyping: The Fast and Easy Way to Design and Refine User Interfaces. Morgan Kaufmann (2004). https://doi.org/10.1016/B978-1-55860-870-2.X5023-2
56. Sugarman, V., Lank, E.: Designing persuasive technology to manage peak electricity demand in ontario homes. In: Proceedings of the 33rd Annual ACM Conference on Human Factors in Computing, pp. 1975–1984 (2015). https://doi.org/10.1145/2702123.2702364
57. Takaoka, A.J.W.: Reality pregnancy and the online recolonization of the female body. In: Coman, A., Vasilache, S. (eds.) HCII 2023. LNCS, vol. 14026, pp. 276–291. Springer, Cham (2023). https://doi.org/10.1007/978-3-031-35927-9_20
58. Takaoka, A.J., Ahlers, D., Ådlandsvik, F.W., Dovland, E.S., Jaccheri, L.: Towards understanding digital support contributing to climate neutral, inclusive, and beautiful cities: a systematic literature review. In: 2023 IEEE/ACM 7th International Workshop on Green and Sustainable Software (GREENS), pp. 30–37. IEEE (2023)
59. Toçilla, A.: The use of IoT for future smart sustainable cities: its perspectives and challenges. In: International Conference on Recent Trends and Applications in Computer Science and Information Technology, vol. 2872, pp. 211–214 (2021). https://ceur-ws.org/Vol-2872/short10.pdf
60. Umamaheswari, S., Priya, K.H., Kumar, S.A.: Technologies used in smart city applications - an overview. In: 2021 International Conference on Advancements in Electrical, Electronics, Communication, Computing and Automation (ICAECA), pp. 1–6. IEEE (2021). https://doi.org/10.1109/ICAECA52838.2021.9675707

61. Weber, P., Grönewald, L., Ludwig, T.: Reflection on the Octalysis framework as a design and evaluation tool. In: GamiFIN Conference (2022)
62. Wilkinson, S.: Focus group methodology: a review. Int. J. Soc. Res. Methodol. **1**(3), 181–203 (1998). https://doi.org/10.1080/13645579.1998.10846874
63. Wong, S.: Gendering information and communication technologies in climate change. In: Research Anthology on Environmental and Societal Impacts of Climate Change, pp. 764–779. IGI Global (2022)
64. Ylipulli, J., Hämäläinen, J.: Towards practice-oriented framework for digital inequality in smart cities. In: Proceedings of the 11th International Conference on Communities and Technologies, pp. 180–190 (2023)
65. Zhang, D., Adipat, B.: Challenges, methodologies, and issues in the usability testing of mobile applications. Int. J. Hum. Comput. Interaction **18**, 293–308 (2005). https://doi.org/10.1207/s15327590ijhc1803_3

When Users Dislike Tech: Assessing Inclusivity and Common Themes with the PTPI Scale

Carmen A. Van Ommen[(⊠)], Brandon D. Dreslin, Joseph R. Keebler, and Barbara S. Chaparro

Department of Human Factors and Behavioral Neurobiology, Embry-Riddle Aeronautical University, 1 Aerospace Blvd., Daytona Beach, FL 32114, USA
rescoc@my.erau.edu, barbara.chaparro@erau.edu

Abstract. This research seeks explore the factor structure of the PTPI and provide insight into what product design features contribute to perceptions of dislike. The PTPI was administered to 965 participants who were asked to either evaluate a technology they liked, or one they disliked. A confirmatory factor analysis (CFA) was conducted to assess model fit, and participant comments were analyzed to determine how feelings of dislike mapped to PTPI subscales, as well as what design features were mentioned when a product was disliked. The CFA results indicated that the PTPI has acceptable model fit. The thematic analysis of participant comments reveals key design themes that are consistently referenced when consumers dislike technology products, offering valuable insights for product designers to enhance both satisfaction and inclusivity. Participant comments also give insight into why consumers may persist in using disliked products.

Keywords: Product Inclusivity · Consumer Satisfaction · Product Design · Technology Products · Consumer Insights

1 Introduction

Consumer satisfaction with products is a highly researched area of both marketing and user experience [1–3]. Satisfied consumers are more likely to repurchase a product, recommend it, and buy from the same company [4]. Models of consumer satisfaction with products show that satisfaction can be influenced by several factors, including product usage, product performance, brand expectations, and brand attitudes [5–7].

Consumer satisfaction has been shown to be influenced by product alignment with self-identity and values and fostering a sense of belonging to a specific user group, which may contribute to a perception of inclusivity [8, 9]. Additionally, if a product is not inclusive, consumers may not be able to use a product well, or at all, which may cause feelings of dissatisfaction [10]. For example, a website that does not give descriptions of images may still be navigable to someone using a screen reader, but they may not have the same quality of experience as someone who is able to visually perceive and understand the images. This is especially true if the images are integral to the experience of a website, like images of clothing that a consumer may wish to purchase.

M. Antona and C. Stephanidis (Eds.): HCII 2024, LNCS 14696, pp. 162–178, 2024.
https://doi.org/10.1007/978-3-031-60875-9_11

When applied to product design, the term "inclusive design" has been defined by designer Susan Goltsman as "designing a diversity of ways for users to participate so that everyone has a sense of belonging" [11]. Perceived inclusivity may be influenced by a variety of aspects, including the ability of a product to fulfill aspects of our psychological needs, if the product promotes a sense of belonging, if a consumer trusts the product, as well as how pleasurable the product experience is [12].

While research highlights consumer satisfaction's importance, it is equally important to understand why dissatisfaction may occur. Research in consumer satisfaction often focuses on the positive [1, 3]. If dissatisfaction is discussed, it is either unclear what the dimensions are, or it is seen as the direct opposite of satisfaction [1–3, 13]. Therefore, assessing consumer perceptions of inclusivity and satisfaction with both liked and disliked products and understanding what contributes to those factors is crucial.

The Perceptions of Technology Product Inclusivity (PTPI) scale is a psychometrically validated instrument to assess user perceptions of inclusivity [12]. The 25-item scale includes five factors reflecting inclusivity. These include Personal Connection, Product Challenges, Confidence in Usage, Meets Expectations, and Company Empathy (Table 1).

Table 1. Description of Each Subscale

Subscale	Description
Confidence in Usage	Perceptions of confidence and self-efficacy when using the product
Personal Connection	Having a sense of belonging or personal connection to the product
Meets Expectations	Perceptions of how well the product works to meet users' needs
Product Challenges	Challenges or demands experienced when using a product
Company Empathy	Perceptions of the company in terms of trust and their intentions to design for diverse audiences

The PTPI was validated with a sample of over 2000 participants who chose technology products in over 25 categories. While there was a wide range of technology products included in the original validation study, the vast majority of products that participants chose were technology products they liked.

1.1 Purpose

The purpose of this study is to explore the factor structure of the PTPI with a more balanced distribution of liked and disliked technology products and provide insight into what product design features contribute to perceptions of dislike. By conducting this study, we seek to provide evidence that the scale items are suitable for measuring perceptions of technology product inclusion with products that are disliked, as the reasons for dissatisfaction or lack of inclusivity may vary in those cases. Additionally, we explore reasonings for why people dislike a technology product, as well as how those feelings relate to perceptions of inclusivity.

2 Method

2.1 Participants

Participants were from the United States and were recruited from Prolific, an online platform utilized for survey distribution. After filling out the survey, participants were split into two groups. The Like group (n = 562) contained responses from participants who answered that they felt satisfied with their technology product. The Dislike group (n = 403) contained responses from participants who answered that they felt dissatisfied with their technology product. Older adults comprised 15.7%, people with disabilities 12.7%, 53% were people of color, and participants ranged in age from 18–83. A detailed breakdown of participant demographics is included in Table 2.

2.2 Materials and Procedure

Qualtrics Online Survey Software was used to create the survey which included the following sections:

1. Consent form
2. Make and model of the technology product under evaluation (participants entered the name in a text field)
3. Questions about product ownership
4. Questions about familiarity and frequency of use of the product
5. Open ended questions about what the participants disliked about the product and how it could be improved (Only displayed to Dislike group)
6. Product evaluation statements. These statements were randomized and five statements per screen were displayed to minimize scrolling. Each statement was evaluated on a 7-point rating scale (1 = strongly disagree, 7 = strongly agree; N/A option at the end of the scale)
7. Overall satisfaction rating (1 = extremely dissatisfied, 7 = extremely satisfied)
8. Overall inclusion rating ("Overall, I feel included as a user of this product."; 1 = strongly disagree, 7 = strongly agree)
9. Net Promoter Score (NPS)
10. System Usability Score (SUS; [14])
11. Basic demographic questions (e.g., age, gender, disability)

Before entering in the make and model of the technology product, participants were presented with a screen that asked them to think about a technology product they had personally interacted with. Participants in the Dislike group were specifically asked to think about a product that they disliked, and were given prompts to help them recall a time where they may have interacted with a product that they disliked, such as if they had returned or stopped using a product, or used a product only out of necessity.

Before distribution of the survey, the study was approved by the University's Institutional Review Board (IRB). Information about the study and the survey link were shared on the survey distribution platform Prolific. Participants who completed the survey were compensated for their time.

Table 2. Demographics of Participants (N = 965)

Variable	Value
Age in Years (M $\mp$ SD)	37.38 $\mp$ 15.40
Age Range in Years	18–83
Gender (%)	
Male	51.4%
Female	46.2%
Transgender	0.3%
Nonbinary	1.9%
Prefer to self-describe	0.0%
I prefer not to answer	0.2%
Ethnicity (%)	
American Indian/Alaskan Native	0.9%
Asian/Pacific Islander	18.6%
Black/African American	16.7%
Hispanic/Latino	10.2%
White (not of Hispanic origin)	46.0%
Biracial/multiracial/mixed	6.5%
I prefer not to answer	1.0%
Education Level (%)	
High school	14.9%
Some college	20.4%
Associate's Degree	7.5%
Vocational/Technical College	2.1%
Bachelor's Degree	41.0%
Master's Degree	11.4%
Doctorate or Professional Degree	2.2%
I prefer not to answer	0.5%
Self-identify as having a disability	
Yes	12.7%
Physical	6.2%
Visual	1.8%
Auditory	1.7%
Cognitive/Mental	6.6%

(*continued*)

Table 2. (*continued*)

Variable	Value
Emotional	3.4%
Other	0.3%
No	84.2%
Prefer not to answer	3.0%

Note: Participants could select more than one disability type, so percentages of disability type may sum to more than total percentage of disability

2.3 Technology Products Chosen

The majority of the technology products participants chose to evaluate in the Like group were used daily and had been purchased at least one year prior to taking the survey. The mean ratings for overall satisfaction were 6.20, with a standard deviation of 0.66 (1 = extremely dissatisfied, 7 = extremely satisfied).

The majority of the technology products participants chose to evaluate in the Dislike group had also been used daily and had been purchased at least one year prior to taking the survey. The mean ratings for overall satisfaction were 2.20, with a standard deviation of 0.88 (1 = extremely dissatisfied, 7 = extremely satisfied).

Table 3 provides a summary of the technology products chosen overall, and by each group. Overall, the technology products evaluated covered 30 categories containing a variety of products within those categories.

Data Analysis. Both quantitative and qualitative data were analyzed. For the quantitative data, a confirmatory factor analysis (CFA), correlation, and ANOVAs were performed. for the qualitative data, a two-stage thematic analysis of 2,733 comments received from participants was conducted to understand (a) which subscale(S) aligned with each comment and (B) the specific factors that influenced subscale mappings. Responses were separated into individual sentences or phrases to ensure accurate analysis of each distinct thought. During the first stage of analysis, comments were mapped (I.E., associated) to relevant PTPI subscales. Sentences and phrases were cross-checked against the criteria for each subscale. Responses were considered mapped to a subscale when a sentence or phrase met at least one criterion. There was no limit to how many subscales a sentence, phrase, or overall response could be mapped to. some responses were not mapped to a subscale because they either failed to meet the subscale's criteria or contained insufficient information. During the second stage of analysis, all comments were re-analyzed to generate product design themes. These themes were extracted from sentences and phrases that directly discuss how a product's design affected participants' usage and feelings of the product. All product design themes were defined according to the relationship between participants and the product (E.G., some definitions began with "how poorly a user can..." and "the degree to which..."). The list of product design themes was gradually refined as more comments were re-analyzed.

To establish a shared understanding of the coding guidelines, the authors collaboratively examined the first 50 provided comments and developed coding principles.

Table 3. Percentage of Technology Products Chosen by Group

Technology Product Category	Like	Dislike
Smartphone	25.51%	9.26%
Computer	16.16%	8.63%
Gaming Device	10.37%	4.84%
Smart Speaker	8.16%	10.74%
Smart Watch	7.31%	6.32%
Smart TV	5.61%	4.63%
Headphones	4.42%	9.47%
Tablet	4.08%	3.79%
Other	3.06%	6.11%
Fitness Tracker	2.38%	6.32%
Software	2.04%	5.26%
Smart Doorbell	1.87%	1.47%
Home Products	1.70%	3.16%
Security System	1.70%	2.74%
Computer Accessories	1.19%	3.79%
Speaker/Sound System	1.02%	2.95%
Audio Equipment	1.02%	0.42%
Vehicle	0.68%	0.84%
Smart Thermostat	0.51%	0.63%
eReader	0.34%	1.68%
Smart Display	0.34%	1.26%
Smart TV Remote	0.17%	1.05%
Drone	0.17%	0.63%
TV Accessories	0.17%	0.63%
GPS	0.00%	1.05%
Digital Camera	0.00%	0.63%
Music Player	0.00%	0.63%
Office Equipment	0.00%	0.42%
Video Game	0.00%	0.42%
Tool	0.00%	0.21%

Responses were categorized based on one or more of the PTPI subscales and product design themes or marked as not applicable or not enough information. The subsequent responses were evenly divided and assigned to two authors to code. Each author independently scrutinized every response to determine which PTPI subscale and product design theme it aligned with. After coding, the authors discussed their outcomes and collectively addressed any questions or inconsistencies to arrive at a consensus.

3 Results

3.1 Confirmatory Factor Analysis

To validate the PTPI with a more balanced distribution of technology products people like and dislike, a CFA was performed using data from both participant groups to evaluate the suitability of the 5-factor model proposed in a prior study [12].

Missing Data. N/A responses were treated as missing data. In total, 1.88% of the data was missing. Little's MCAR test results ($\chi^2 = 3082.485$, $df = 2137$, $p < .000$) indicated that the data was not missing completely at random. All variables or scale items (n = 25) and 20.7% of cases, or participants (n = 200) contained at least one missing value. The percentage of missing values for each variable ranged from 0.19% to 5.08%.

To address the missing data, the expectation maximization method was used. As the overall missing data and data for each variable was less than 10%, the expectation maximization method used to replace the data to be consistent with how missing data was dealt with during the original validation study [12].

Model Fit Assessment. To evaluate model fit, the model and the three fit indexes used in the original validation process for the PTPI were evaluated. After inputting the data, the modification indices were examined, and correlations were added to the model between items with highly correlated errors. This helps to ensure the best model fit and account for questions with related errors. The model with the same factor structure as in the original validation study, with revised error correlations is displayed in the Appendix. The three fit indexes used were the Comparative Fit Index (CFI; [15]), root mean square error of approximation (RMSEA; [16]), and the Tucker Lewis Index (TLI; [17]). The results of the model fit assessment are displayed in Table 4, along with the recommended cutoff values for acceptable fit for each index.

Table 4. Model Fit Statistics (N = 965)

Fit Index	Value	Recommended Cutoff Values	References
χ^2	$\chi^2 = 1357.82$, $df = 257$, $p < .001$	N/A	N/A
CFI	.95	0.90–0.95 indicates acceptable fit, > 0.95 indicates good fit	[15, 18]
RMSEA	0.063 [0.06, 0.067]	0.06–0.08 indicates acceptable fit, < .06 indicates excellent fit	[19, 20]
TLI	.942	0.90–0.95 indicates acceptable fit, > 0.95 indicates good fit	[18]

3.2 Scale Reliability and Validity Assessment

Following the evaluation of model fit, the scale's reliability, convergent validity, and discriminant validity were assessed [21]. The reliability values for all factors or subscales are presented in Table 5, and were above the suggested threshold of 0.7, indicating consistent measurement across all individual scale factors.

To examine construct validity, average variance extracted (AVE) values and maximum shared variance (MSV) were analyzed. AVE helps determine convergent validity, and it was observed that one factor (Product Challenges) fell slightly below the suggested threshold of 0.5 [22].

For MSV, which assesses discriminant validity, the values should be less than AVE values. The results revealed that the factors of Company Empathy and Personal Connection had MSV values greater than their corresponding AVE values. The detailed results of the validity analysis are displayed in Table 5.

Table 5. Reliability, Convergent, and Discriminant Validity Results

	CR	AVE	MSV
Factor 1: Personal Connection	0.897	0.687	0.691
Factor 2: Product Challenges	0.870	0.492	0.469
Factor 3: Confidence in Usage	0.913	0.677	0.469
Factor 4: Meets Expectations	0.954	0.778	0.738
Factor 5: Company Empathy	0.834	0.627	0.738

Note: CR = Composite Reliability, AVE = Average Variance Extracted, MSV = Maximum Shared Variance

3.3 Relationship Between Inclusivity and Satisfaction

The relationship between perceptions of inclusivity and satisfaction with the technology product was investigated using Pearson's product-moment correlation coefficient. There was a strong, positive correlation between the two variables, $r = .773$, $n = 965$, $p < .001$, with high levels of satisfaction with a technology product associated with a high perception of inclusivity.

3.4 PTPI Subscale Scores

Subscale scores from the PTPI were analyzed to determine if there are differences between the Like and Dislike group. The top technology product categories from the Like group were Smartphone, Computer, Gaming Device, Smart Speaker, and Smart Watch. The top technology product categories from the Dislike group were Smart Speakers, Headphones, Smartphones, Computers, and Smart Watches.

A mixed-design ANOVA was conducted to analyze the mean differences of the subscale scores between liked and disliked products. The ANOVA revealed that there were significant main effects ($p < .05$) of user satisfaction and subscale category, and a significant interaction between the two, where the subscales of Personal Connection, Meets Expectations, and Company Empathy are reduced the most when a participant does not like the product.

Overall, across all the product categories analyzed, Meets Expectations had the greatest difference between groups and was the lowest in the Dislike group. Figure 2 illustrates these subscale differences, where all scores are reduced, but Personal Connection, Company Empathy, and Meets Expectations are reduced more than Product Challenges and Confidence in Usage, and Meets Expectations has the greatest reduction in scores when a product is disliked.

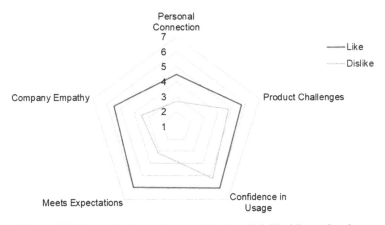

Fig. 1. PTPI Subscale Scores Between Liked and Disliked Smart Speakers

3.5 Qualitative Analysis

Mapping Participant Comments to PTPI Subscales. Respondents evaluating a product they disliked were presented with five open-ended questions that asked them to reflect on a product that they disliked:

1. "Why do you no longer own this product?"
2. "Why do you no longer use this product?"
3. "Why do you still use this product?"
4. "Why do you dislike this technology product?"
5. "What could improve the product to make your experience better?"

Overall, Meets Expectations was the subscale most comments were mapped to (67.5%), followed by Company Empathy (13.2%), Product Challenges (10.8%), Confidence in Usage (4.6%), and Personal Connection (3.8%). Table 6 provides mapping frequencies across each survey question for a more comprehensive perspective of subscale mapping results.

Looking at the participant comments may show the effect of a subscale being impacted (Table 7). When asked why they no longer own their product, Meets Expectations had the highest frequency of comments mapped to it, and many participants shared that their experiences with the product failed to align with their expectations. For example, desired features either did not function as expected or were not present.

Product Challenges was often referenced when participants no longer used their product. Specifically, aversion towards proprietary technological ecosystems (e.g., Apple, Android) and frustration due to the lack of seamless connectivity between two or more ecosystems appear to be the two greatest product challenges. However, many participants continue to use their product because they have a personal connection with it. Responses emphasized psychosocial factors (e.g., they must use it at work, they received it as a gift, etc.) and perceived value (e.g., it is expensive, it is the only option they have, etc.) as reasons for continued usage.

Company Empathy had a large number of comments mapped to it when a participant was asked why they disliked their product. Participant comments showed that they dislike their product because of concerns about the company's trustworthiness and their commitment to consider the needs of all customers. For example, companies' ethical values (specifically surrounding user privacy and collection of personal information) was questioned. Additionally, some participants preferred products from other brands.

When looking at how Confidence in Usage was referenced when participants were asked how their product could be improved, many identified that their products can be improved by making more intuitive interfaces that allows them to feel more confident during usage. For example, companies can holistically approach product improvement by better integrating hardware with software and making products less complicated and easier to set up/use.

Table 6. Mapping of User Comments to PTPI Subscales

PTPI Subscale	Ownership	Usage (No)	Usage (Yes)	Dislike	Improvement
Meets Expectations	171	453	178	798	378
Company Empathy	40	100	3	107	136
Confidence in Usage	7	31	5	44	50
Personal Connection	12	24	10	33	31
Product Challenges	18	106	10	130	53
Total Mappings	248	714	206	1,112	648

Product Design Themes. When analyzing participant comments, a total of 24 product design themes were identified. Table 8 lists each design theme along with its corresponding definition.

Design Themes Identified by Technology Type. Design themes identified in participant comments were matched to the top technology product categories from both groups

Table 7. Example Quotes from Mapping of User Comments to PTPI Subscales

PTPI Subscale	Example Quote
Personal Connection	"It felt very hostile to own and be part of that economy." - *Participant reviewing an Apple product, mapped to Personal Connection and Company Empathy*
Product Challenges	"The system on the Android drove me crazy. I couldn't text friends with iPhones, I had issues with email, just using it was continual frustration." - *Participant reviewing an Android phone, mapped to Product Challenges and Meets Expectations*
Confidence in Usage	"It was too complicated compared to another GPS unit I have. So I sold it." - *Participant reviewing a TomTom GPS, mapped to Confidence in Usage*
Meets Expectations	"It didn't have as many features as I wanted." - *Participant reviewing a Fitbit, mapped to Meets Expectations*
Company Empathy	"Can't create custom widgets." - *Participant reviewing an iPhone, mapped to Meets Expectations and Company Empathy*

Table 8. Product Design Themes and Definitions

Product Design Theme	Definition
Accuracy	A product does not provide correct output or response
Aesthetics	Comments about how a product looks
Does Not Align with Values	Degree to which a product does not matches a user's personal values
Lack of Brand Loyalty	Users' inconsistent preference for one brand over others
Discomfort	Physical and ergonomic dissatisfaction of a product
Incompatibility	The lack of ability of a product to integrate with other devices or platforms
Inconvenience	The degree to which users find it burdensome or troublesome to use the product
Customer Service	Quality of support and assistance for a product
Lack of Customization	Users' inability to personalize a product to their preferences
Difficulty of Use	How difficult a product is to operate
Easy to Lose	The likelihood of a product being misplaced
Unfamiliarity	A product's misalignment with users' habits and expectations
Lack of Features	A product's insufficient or limited set of functionalities and capabilities

(continued)

Table 8. (*continued*)

Product Design Theme	Definition
Exclusivity	Not made for a variety of user groups
Intrusive	A product's impact on user privacy and personal space
Does Not Meet Needs	How poorly a product fulfills a user's requirements
Obsolete	Product is outdated or no longer being updated
Performance	How a product works (slow, fast, well, poorly, etc.)
Lack of Physical Fit	More than uncomfortable, was not made for the person (e.g., "doesn't fit in my ears," "too small for my hand")
Privacy Concerns	Apprehensions about how a product handles personal data
Quality	Quality of a product's materials and design
Reliability	Product is or is not consistent in how it works
Unwanted Promotions	Presentation of unsolicited promotional content
Lack of Value	Lack of perceived worth and benefit from using a product

(Smartphones, Computers, Smart Speakers, Gaming Devices, Smart Watches and Headphones) to determine whether design themes identified differed between technology product groups. Differences were found when looking at the top design themes referenced per technology product category. For example, the top theme that participants disliked for computers was performance, and the top theme participants disliked for headphones were discomfort. Table 9 shows the design themes most frequently referenced by technology category type.

Table 9. Design Theme Most Frequently Referenced by Technology Category Type

Technology Product Category	Design Theme Most Referenced	Percentage Referenced
Computer	Performance	**31.55%**
Gaming Device	Does Not Meet Needs	**24.58%**
Headphones	Discomfort	**20.57%**
Smart Speaker	Privacy Concerns	**23.89%**
Smart Watch	Does Not Meet Needs	**28.33%**
Smartphone	Difficulty of Use	**19.21%**

Continued Product Usage. Participants were asked why they continued to use a product they disliked, and the qualitative comments from that question were analyzed. 10 comment themes were identified that matched 5 or more comments (Table 10). Out of 187 total comments, 129 were matched to a theme, 8 comments were categorized as "Other" as the themes they belonged to did not have 5 or more comments matching that theme, 9 were considered to not have enough information, and 41 were not applicable. Overall, the top five responses for why a participant continued to use the product were because they were forced to, due to financial constraints, the product was necessary for a specific task, it was more convenient to use the product instead of replacing it, and there were no better alternatives for purchase.

Table 10. Themes Identified in why Participants Continued to Use a Technology Product

Theme and Explanation	Comment Example
Forced Usage: The participant was required to use this device such as for a job or for a task	"It's the only option for interpreter services in my hospital." - *Participant reviewing a Stratus Video Interpreter*
Financial Constraints: Could not replace the device due to financial reasons	"I can't afford to buy a new TV right now" - *Participant reviewing a TCL Roku TV*
No Better Alternatives for Purchase: The participant did not know of a better product that could be purchased	"I can't find a product that will do any better." - *Participant reviewing a bluetooth waterproof speaker*
Convenience: Participants found it more convenient to use the product than to search for and purchase a replacement	"It is occasionally convenient [to use] but I use it with a much lower frequency" - *Participant reviewing Facebook*
Necessity for Specific Tasks: The device was useful to accomplish a specific task	"I can't use another controller for the game console." - *Participant reviewing a Nintendo Switch joy-con controller*
Don't Own Other Alternatives: The participant used the product because they didn't own an alternative	"[I use it] because it's all I have right now." - Participant reviewing a computer
Partial Utilization: The participant reduced the usage of the product to certain features	"I mainly just use [the Amazon Alexa] now as a timer next to the oven." - *Participant reviewing an Amazon Alexa*
Functioned for the Task: The participant continued to use the product because it still worked	"[I continue to use it because] it functions as described." - *Participant reviewing a Wyze Camera*
Already Purchased: The participant continued to use the product because they had already purchased it	"I am still trying to give it a chance since I own it." - *Participant reviewing an Amazon Echo*
Gift: The participant had been gifted the product	"I received it as a gift and feel bad about returning it." - *Participant reviewing a Google smartwatch*

4 Discussion

While consumer satisfaction is highly studied and provides valuable insight into purchasing behavior of consumers, it's equally important to study consumer dissatisfaction with products. In the same vein, while it is important to understand what makes a consumer feel a sense of inclusion when using a technology product, factors that contribute to a sense of exclusion are also important to understand.

Previous studies have shown that the PTPI is appropriate for use with products that consumers generally like. Results from the CFA indicate that the PTPI is also appropriate for use when measuring consumer perceptions of inclusivity in a more balanced sample of technology products that users like and dislike.

When mapping participant comments about their reasonings for disliking a technology product and what can be improved to the subscales they reference, the Meets Expectations subscale of the PTPI is referenced most often. This is generally because the Meets Expectations subscale contains the statement items "This product meets my expectations.", "This product works well for me.", and "There is a good fit between what this product offers me and what I am looking for in this product.", which are generally not met when a participant dislikes a technology product. An analysis of the scores on the PTPI subscales also show that the Meets Expectations subscale scores the lowest when a technology product is disliked. However, subscale scores also show that Personal Connection and Company Empathy are notably lower in products that participants dislike, and this is not reflected in participant comments. For example, when asked why a participant dislikes a product, they may say "It's very buggy and rarely works as expected. It lags terribly and was a pain to set up." All of these thoughts may map to the Meets Expectations subscale, but the participant may also indicate that they do not feel a personal connection to the product, and feel that the company did not consider their needs when designing the product, when prompted by the items on the PTPI. Thus, quantitative scores from the PTPI may show additional areas of impact to perceptions of inclusivity with technology products that are disliked that participants may not reference.

When examining participant comments, insights into what design themes are most frequently referenced when a consumer dislikes a product provides product designers more direction into what can be improved about technology products in general to affect both consumer satisfaction and feelings of inclusivity. The overall design theme most referenced when a product was disliked was "does not meet needs", referencing how a product fails to fulfill a user's requirements. Since participants chose a wide range of technology products, this finding indicates what design theme is most frequently referenced when a participant dislikes a technology product in general. When looking at specific technology product categories, however, the design theme most referenced differs between technology product categories. For example, the design theme most referenced for computers was poor performance, while the theme most referenced for headphones was discomfort. This provides insight into what design themes are most referenced when a participant dislikes a technology product in a specific category, which may help product designers prioritize different design features, depending on what technology product they are designing.

A thematic analysis of comments about why consumers continue to use products they dislike show that the most common themes are because they were forced to, due to financial constraints, the product was necessary for a specific task, it was more convenient to use the product instead of replacing it, and there were no better alternatives for purchase. There is little research on the impact to a company of a consumer continuing to use a product they dislike, so it is not known what the effects may be. However, it is possible that continuing to use a product that a consumer dislikes will increase the negative feelings that a consumer may have about that brand. If the consumer is able to quickly return a product or does not have to continue using it, it is possible that the negative feelings may be changed due to being satisfied with the customer service or return process, or the negative feelings about the brand will be lessened, due to the experience with the product they dislike being short. Identifying themes of why consumers continue to use products they dislike may allow consumers to reduce barriers in some areas, so the consumer can have a better experience or perception of the brand.

In conclusion, this discussion highlights the importance of studying not only consumer satisfaction but also consumer dissatisfaction with products, and the significance of understanding factors contributing to both inclusion and exclusion in the context of technology products. This study demonstrates that the PTPI is a valuable tool for measuring consumer perceptions of inclusivity, even when users dislike a technology product. It is important to note that the Meets Expectations subscale of the PTPI plays an important role in assessing inclusivity, as it is frequently referenced when consumers dislike a product. However, other subscales, such as Personal Connection and Company Empathy, also impact perceptions of inclusivity, even if not explicitly mentioned by participants. The thematic analysis of participant comments reveals key design themes that are consistently referenced when consumers dislike technology products, offering valuable insights for product designers to enhance both satisfaction and inclusivity. Additionally, an understudied area is why consumers persist in using disliked products.

5 Future Research

The results of this study show that, when a consumer dislikes a product, comments about why they dislike that product generally map to the Meets Expectations subscale of the PTPI. Future research should gather qualitative data from consumers as to why they like a product, to see if there are any insights to inclusivity, other than that the product meets their expectations. Future research should also explore what aspects contribute to an opinion that a product is better than just acceptable, as it is possible that acceptable products are ones that meet consumer expectations, and products that consumers consider to be high quality or great products, may have other factors.

When looking at the difference between scores in liked and disliked products, results show that Confidence in Usage and Product Challenges had less of a difference in scores than the other three subscales. Since participant comments did not give insight into this reason, future research should explore why these subscales are less negatively impacted than other subscales when participants dislike a product.

This research and previous research conducted did not specify that consumers choose a product they use for any particular reason, and it is possible that most products were not products that were essential for a consumer to use. For example, gaming devices may be used for recreation, and not necessarily for work or health reasons, which may be considered more of a necessity. Future research could specify a use case for products, to see if perceptions of technology product inclusivity change when a product is used for enjoyment versus out of necessity.

Appendix

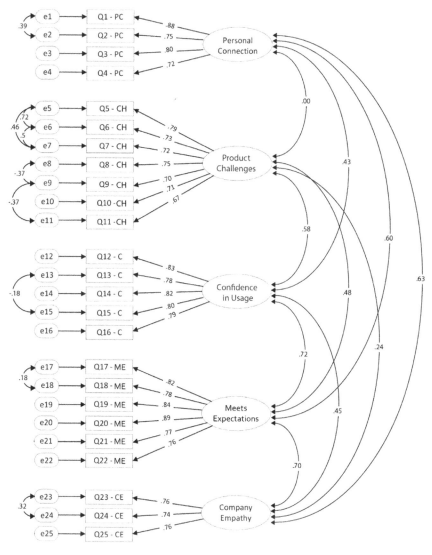

Fig. 2. PTPI Scale Model

References

1. Czeplel, J.A., Rosenberg, L.J.: Consumer satisfaction: concept and measurement. J. Acad. Mark. Sci. **5**(3), 403–411 (1977)
2. Giese, J.L., Cote, J.A.: Defining consumer satisfaction. Acad. Mark. Sci. Rev. **1**(1), 1–22 (2000)
3. Borsci, S., Federici, S., Bacci, S., Gnaldi, M., Bartolucci, F.: Assessing user satisfaction in the era of user experience: comparison of the SUS, UMUX, and UMUX-LITE as a function of product experience. Int. J. Hum.-Comput. Interac. **31**(8), 484–495 (2015)
4. Anderson, E.W., Fornell, C., Lehmann, D.R.: Customer satisfaction, market share, and profitability: findings from Sweden. J. Mark. **58**(3), 53– (1994)
5. Ram, S., Jung, H.-S.: How Product Usage Influences Consumer Satisfaction. Mark. Lett. **2**(4), 403–411 (1991)
6. Tse, D.K., Wilton, P.C.: Models of consumer satisfaction formation: an extension. J. Mark. Res. **25**(2), 204–212 (1988)
7. Woodruff, R.B., Cadotte, E.R., Jenkins, R.L.: Modeling consumer satisfaction processes using experience-based norms. J. Mark. Res. **20**(3), 296–304 (1983)
8. Shin, S.-A., Jang, J.-O., Kim, J.-K., Cho, E.-H.: Relations of Conspicuous Consumption Tendency, Self-Expression Satisfaction, and SNS Use Satisfaction of Gen Z through SNS Activities. International Journal of Environmental Research and Public Health **18**(22), 11979 (2021)
9. Lee, Y.: A study on the effects of the SNS use focused on the social relationships on the self-expression in SNS, off-line activity, and the life satisfaction. J. Convergence Culture Technol. **6**(1), 301–312 (2020)
10. Patrick, V.M., Hollenbeck, C.R.: Designing for all: Consumer response to inclusive design. J. Consum. Psychol. **31**(2), 360–381 (2021)
11. Holmes, K.: Mismatch: How inclusion shapes design. The MIT Press (2018)
12. Van Ommen, C., Chaparro, B. S., Keebler, J. R., Batra, S., Lu, M.: Development and validation of a scale to assess consumer perceptions of technology product inclusivity (PTPI). Available at SSRN: https://ssrn.com/abstract=4416085. Manuscript under review (2022)
13. Erevelles, S., Leavitt, C.: A comparison of current models of consumer satisfaction/dissatisfaction. Journal of consumer satisfaction, dissatisfaction and complaining behavior **5**, 104–114 (1992)
14. Brooke, J.: SUS-A quick and dirty usability scale. Usability Eval. Ind. **189**(194), 4–7 (1996)
15. Bentler, P.M.: Comparative fit indexes in structural models. Psychol. Bull. **107**(2), 238 (1990)
16. Steiger, J.H.: Statistically based tests for the number of common factors. In: Paper presented at the annual meeting of the Psychometric Society, Iowa City, IA (1980)
17. Tucker, L., Lewis, C.: A reliability coefficient for maximum likelihood factor analysis. Psychometrika **38**, 1–10 (1973)
18. Hu, L., Bentler, P.M.: Cutoff criteria for fit indexes in covariance structure analysis: conventional criteria versus new alternatives. SEM **6**(1), 1–55 (1999)
19. Browne, M.W., Cudeck, R.: Alternative ways of assessing model fit. Sage Focus Editions **154**, 136 (1993)
20. Fabrigar, L.R., Wegener, D.T., MacCallum, R.C., Strahan, E.J.: Evaluating the use of exploratory factor analysis in psychological research. Psychol. Methods **4**, 272–299 (1999)
21. Gaskin, J.: "ValidityMaster", Stats Tools Package. http://statwiki.gaskination.com (2016). Accessed 10 Jan 2024
22. Hair, J., Black, W., Babin, B., Anderson, R.: Multivariate data analysis, 7th edn. (2010)

Usability Study and Design Implications for Novice AR-Based 3D Model Design Tools

Tzu-Yang Wang$^{(\boxtimes)}$, Zhaoxin Zuo, and Takaya Yuizono

Graduate School of Advanced Science and Technology, Japan Advanced Institute of
Science and Technology, Nomi, Japan
research@wang-tzuyang.info, yuizono@jaist.ac.jp

Abstract. This study explores how novices of 3D model designing can
use an AR-based 3D model design tool. In the experiment, users used
Microsoft HoloLens2 and Microsoft Mesh App to complete two 3D model
design tasks. In Task 1, participants were given an image of a 3D model
and asked to create the same 3D model; in Task 2, participants were
asked to freely design three 3D furniture models. The participants' experience was evaluated using the System Usability Scale and the NASA
Task Load Index. Simultaneously, the task process was videotaped for
later analysis. After task completion, video analysis was performed, and
user actions, gestures, and interface interactions were manually annotated to identify human errors that occurred. Based on the results of the
two questionnaires and video analysis, in this paper, we provide some
insights into challenges and opportunities associated with AR-based 3D
model design applications, particularly for novices. Furthermore, we proposed some design ideas and solutions to help AR-based 3D model application designers in the future.

Keywords: 3D model design · Augmented Reality · Video analysis ·
Usability · Implications for design

1 Introduction

"Augmented reality" or "AR" is a modern technique in which virtual objects
are displayed on top of the real world. With AR, users may manipulate virtual
objects within the real world and receive immediate feedback. Among multiple usages, researchers have focused on AR-based 3D model design [4,15] since
the nature of AR provides a more intuitive and immersive design experience.
Especially for novice users, compared to conventional 3D design tools, which
only allow them to observe through 2D displays, they can manipulate and refine
their models directly in the context of the environment, gaining a deeper understanding of scale, proportion, and spatial relationships.

However, novices still often encounter challenges in effectively utilizing modern AR-based 3D model design tools (AR design tools). In addition to system

M. Antona and C. Stephanidis (Eds.): HCII 2024, LNCS 14696, pp. 179–193, 2024.
https://doi.org/10.1007/978-3-031-60875-9_12

defects and the limitation of specification of current AR devices, there are many user interface issues that worsen the learning curve, and users may struggle with the interactions during designing.

Since the ultimate goal is to design a useful AR design tool, in this paper, we posed the following research questions: 1) do current AR design tools have good usability? 2) what errors are most often occurred while using such AR design tools? 3) can such AR design tools be used in varied 3d model design tasks?

To answer the above questions, we conducted an observational experiment to observe users' behavior while using an off-the-shelf AR design tool. Questionnaires and detailed video analysis were used to identify common human errors that affect the usability of current AR design tools. Later, we also provided guidelines for overcoming these problems while developing a new AR design tool.

2   Related Work

For 3D model design, although skilled designers can create complex models using off-the-shelf software such as 3DS Max, it requires a long time for novices to learn how to use these complicated tools. Therefore, many researchers have paid attention to creating 3D model design applications using immersive technologies, such as VR and AR. Related studies can be categorized into two types: 3D sketching and 3D modeling.

3D sketching is the drawing of lines and shapes in the air; one of the challenges of 3D sketching tools is their accuracy. Arora et al. indicated that the inaccuracies are caused by the lack of physical drawing surfaces [2]. One idea to solve this problem is to allow users to sketch in a 2D platform and project the sketch into 3D spaces. For example, Arora et al. developed SymbiosisSketch, which allows 3D sketching and 2D sketching together, to integrate the accuracy advantages of 2D sketching into 3D sketching [1]. Many other researchers have also focused on improving the 2D to 3D projection experience [7,9].

3D modeling is to create polygonal surface models. Research about 3D modeling focused on developing new interaction allowing user to efficiently generate and manipulate 3D objects. For example, Mendes et al.'s system allowed users to perform union, intersection, and difference manipulation of multiple 3D models through gestures [13]. Compared to VR-based 3D modeling, AR-based 3D modeling is more challenging since the 3D models should seamlessly integrate with real world. Reipschläger et al. combined AR with 2d displays; users can first design prototypes of 3D models through the 2d display and generate 3D models with Microsoft Hololens [15].

Although many previous studies on the design of VR/AR 3D models have developed new interactive functions for users to achieve a variety of manipulations, many of them have limited usability. In addition, for the usability of AR design tools, it is necessary not only to consider the interactive functions, but also to evaluate all other aspects, such as UI design and human error caused by hardware defects. Therefore, in this paper, we conducted a user study to comprehensively investigate all types of issues that occur in an AR design tool.

3 Experiment

An observational study was conducted to explore the problem in AR design tools. The participants had to complete two 3D design tasks using an AR design tool. Their behavior was recorded, and perceived usability and workload were assessed through questionnaires.

3.1 Apparatus and Materials

In this experiment, Microsoft HoloLens2 was used as the AR device. The Microsoft HoloLens 2 is a standalone holographic computer, and as an optical see-through AR device, it has fewer 3D sickness problems. In this study, among the applications available on hololens2, Microsoft Mesh App (Preview) was selected as the AR design tool.

This experiment included two tasks. Task 1 is a visualization task, and Task 2 is a creation task. Visualization and creation are two valuable functions that augmented reality may contribute in 3D model prototyping [8]. Visualization using AR supports designers to investigate complex elements of a design effectively. Thus, we included it in our tasks to examine whether users can create a 3D model from a 2D image. Creation is a process in which people creatively design models, and as we explained in Sect. 1, the three dimensions of AR allow people to design in a more trivial way. Thus, we also included it in our tasks.

3.2 Experimental Procedure

Seven male and three female students from the Japan Advanced Institute of Science and Technology were recruited to participate in this experiment. Their average age were 30.5 years old (SD = 7.06). All participants completed an informed consent form and agreed that their data, including video and audio, could be used for academic publication.

For each participant, a one-hour-long individual experiment was carried out. Initially, the participants first received a brief (15-min) explanation of the experiment from a experimenter along with slides, which covered using HoloLens 2 and an overview of the capabilities of the Microsoft Mesh App (only those functions required for this experiment (Fig. 1). In the next step, each participant was free to practice and get familiar with the operation and functions for a maximum of 30 min at the discretion of the participant. After the practice, the experiment with two tasks started.

In Task 1, a castle picture was presented to the participant (Fig. 2). The participant had to create a 3D castle model by using the functions in the software, and the model's shape, color, and the decorative brush all had to match the sample. Task 1 had a 15-min time limit for participants to finish (the experiment was terminated when time was up). Following a 5-min break, participants completed two questionnaires (detail is shown in Sect. 3.3) based on their opinions about Task 1.

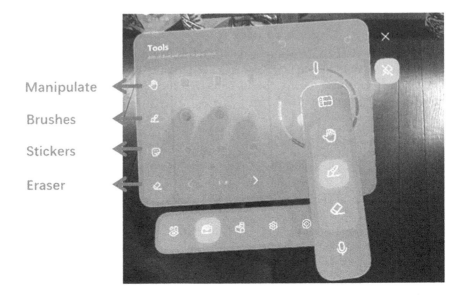

Manipulate

Brushes

Stickers

Eraser

Fig. 1. The main functions in the Microsoft Mesh App used in this experiment

Task 1:Design according to the prescribed style

models   brush   castle

Fig. 2. Content of task1

In Task 2, participants were asked to build three pieces of furniture (a chair, a table, and a bookshelf) in 20 min, using three or more 3D objects and one brush for each piece (Fig. 3). The color and shape of the models were left up to the participants. After Task 2, participants completed the same two questionnaires about their perceptions.

After the two tasks, a participant interview was be held and documented in accordance with the findings of the two tests as a whole.

Task 2: Furniture Design

Fig. 3. Content of task2 and the example of completed models

3.3 Analysis Methods

The System Usability Scale (SUS) was used to analyze the usability of the AR design tools. SUS was first released in 1996 [3], and it contains a total of 10 items, of which 5 are positive items and 5 of which are negative items. Lewis and Sauro have examined that it has a high-reliability rating (0.92), and it contains two factors: eight of the items were labeled as "Usable" while the other two were classified as "Learnable" [10].

SUS can be used to compare the usability of different systems, and it can also be used to rate a system with a single score on a scale of 0–100. Lewis and Sauro created a scale of 11 from F (51.7) to A+ (¿84.1) by combining the SUS correlation tests [10].

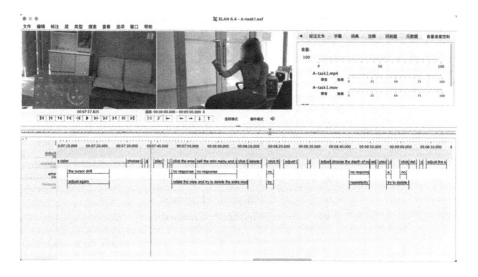

Fig. 4. Using ELAN to annotate the video files

The NASA Task Load Index (NASA-TLX) was used to measure participants' perceived workload. As a well-known questionnaire [6], the NASA-TLX measures six dimensions: mental, physical, temporal, performance, effort, and frustration. The participants first rated the six dimensions on a scale of 0–100, and they made a paired comparison of which of the dimensions played a greater role in workload. The weight of the dimension and the dimension score were multiplied to obtain the final workload score.

We used the HoloLens2 to record the screen continuously throughout the experiment, and we used the phone to capture the participants' movements in real-time. After the experiments, the video files from this experiment were integrated into a video analysis tool, ELAN (Fig. 4). Each operation was segmented (e.g., select the star model, adjust the color, draw the brush, etc.), and for each human error that occurred, the error and resolution methods were annotated.

4   Result

4.1   Completion of Task

Regarding the overall completion of this experiment, it can be roughly divided into three categories: completed, not completed, and basically completed but with some flaws (Table 1). The results indicated that half of the novice participants were not able to finish Task 2.

Table 1. Completion of Task 1 & 2; * indicates that the task was basically completed but with some flaws (e.g., wrong choice of brush type or deviation in the choice of color in task1).

Participant	Task 1	Task 2
1	Finished*	Timeout
2	Finished*	Finished*
3	Finished	Timeout
4	Finished*	Finished
5	Timeout	Timeout
6	Finished	Finished
7	Finished	Timeout
8	Timeout	Timeout
9	Finished	Finished*
10	Finished*	Finished

4.2 Usability and Workload

The results of the two questionnaires were first counted and examined. The participants rated the usability of the system in Task 1 and Task 2 with a combined score of 58.5 and 52.25 (Table 2). Based on Lewis and Sauro's rating scale, both ratings were D's, exceeding 15–34% of the products. It indicated that the system has a low usability for both training and creating usage.

One sample t-tests were applied to examine whether the item score was lower than the average score. Since 68 is the center of the curved grading scale [11], we compared whether the item score was lower than 3.4 for positive items and higher than 2.6 for negative items. The result showed for Item 4, 6, and 8, the scores were significantly lower than average. Among those, the low score of item 4 indicated that perceived consistency was low [11].

Table 2. Result of SUS. Even items are negative items. For each column, the first number represents the number of participants in Task 1; the second number represents the number of participants in Task2.

	1	2	3	4	5	Avg.	Test
1: I think that I would like to use this system frequently.	0/0	2/0	3/4	3/4	2/2	3.5/3.8	$t(19) = 1.79$; $p = .12$
2: I found the system unnecessarily complex.	1/0	4/4	5/3	0/2	0/1	2.4/3.0	$t(19) = 0.48$; $p = .32$
3: I thought the system was easy to use.	0/0	2/2	5/4	1/4	2/0	3.3/3.2	$t(19) = 0.74$; $p = .24$
4: I think that I would need the support of a technical person to be able to use this system.	1/0	3/3	1/2	3/3	2/2	3.2/3.4	$t(19) = 2.48$; $p = .01$
5: I found the various functions in this system were well integrated.	0/1	1/0	2/3	4/5	3/1	3.9/3.5	$t(19) = 1.3$; $p = .10$
6: I thought there was too much inconsistency in this system.	1/0	2/0	1/5	6/3	0/2	3.2/3.7	$t(19) = 3.81$; p¡.001
7: I would imagine that most people would learn to use this system very quickly.	0/1	2/2	3/1	1/3	4/3	3.7/3.5	$t(19) = 0.68$; $p = .25$
8: I found the system very cumbersome to use.	0/0	2/2	5/3	3/4	0/1	3.1/3.4	$t(19) = 3.42$; $p = .001$
9: I felt very confident using the system.	0/1	3/0	2/4	2/4	3/1	3.5/3.4	$t(19) = 0.20$; $p = .47$
10: I needed to learn many things before I could get going with this system.	1/0	4/4	3/2	2/4	3/0	2.6/3.3	$t(19) = 0.94$; $p = .18$

For the result of the NASA-TLX, the average total workload score for Task 1 is 56.97, and the average total workload score for Task 2 is 59.9. There was no significant difference between the two tasks. Based on the meta-analysis of the NASA-TLX [5], the workload of the two tasks was higher than 75% of the cognitive tasks (54.66%). It indicated that the participants were subjected to a high workload when using this system.

4.3 Video Analysis

We categorized the operations and analyzed the problems encountered by the participants based on the video data recorded during the experiment. In this experiment, the regular operations include clicking buttons or selecting models, selecting buttons or models for dragging, adjusting the position or size of models, opening and hiding menus, deleting models, etc. The errors were categorized into 15 types and shown in Table 3, and the errors were categorized into two types: System (errors caused by system defects) and UI (errors caused by unfamiliarity or misuse of the system).

Table 3. Classification of errors and their occurrences

Type of Error	Total Number	Task 1	Task 2	Cause
Operation failure	472	224	248	System/UI
Miscreated objects/brush marks	187	72	115	UI
Misselection	173	92	81	System/UI
Accidentally deleted objects	15	7	8	UI
Unrelated menu changed/appeared	15	3	12	System/UI
Failed to click any button	9	0	9	System
Color changed Accidentally	3	3	0	System
Failed to move/delete unwanted objects	3	0	3	System/UI
Brush disconnected	3	3	0	System
Mini menu disappears	2	0	2	System
Objects disappeared	2	0	2	System
App crashes	1	1	0	System
Automatic refresh of the interface	1	1	0	System
Unwanted objects appeared	1	0	1	System
Low battery status	1	0	1	System

Among the errors counted in Table 3, most of the errors happened due to the UI. The three common mistakes are operation failure, miscreated objects/brush marks, and misselection. These three mistakes were frequent and occurred on every participant's task. Combined with the operations, the three most frequent errors mainly occurred in the following operations.

- Interaction with buttons in the mini menu
- Altering the model's dimensions and orientation
- Interaction with the color palette's adjustment buttons
- Creating and putting together the 3D models
- Drawing on the 3D model with brushes

The three major types of error were further analyzed together to discover the causes, and it is summarized as follows.

Operation Failure. Operation failure is an umbrella situation in which participants correctly performed the gestures (e.g., air-tap to click a button on the menu or drag an object) but did not receive correct feedback or the operation did not proceed. It is the most frequent error, which occurred 23.6 times for each task. This happened due to three reasons: slow or failed calibration, gesture interference, and unclear operation status.

Slow or Failed Calibration. The extensive computation of spatial information required by AR devices has given rise to a notable issue of real-time calibration. When participants moved their fingers across the interaction interface to perform actions, there was a significant likelihood that the cursor may exhibit a slow reversion. For instance, during task 1, participant 2 encountered difficulties adjusting the color by moving the button on the palette. Although their fingers were aligned with the button, the selection did not work until their fingers had been recognized by the AR device. Another important finding is that the computation time depended on the environment. When the participants moved against a background, such as a wall or floor, it resulted in an improvement in the operation recognition rate. On the other hand, the error increased when the participants faced excessive background clutter.

Gesture Interference. Gesture interference occurred due to the design of HoloLens2 interaction methods. HoloLens2 allowed users to use gestures to perform multiple operations. However, the gestures are too general, and the same gesture corresponds to a wide range of functions. For example, when the participants raised their palm to move the 3D objects with the palm up or open the mini-menu, the start menu was unintentionally opened instead (Fig. 5), which even led to a certain chance that the participant accidentally closed the software. This suggests that the current interaction design is not in line with the user's usage habits and requires a process of adaptation.

Unclear Operation Status. Because the design involved many operations and required multiple gestures, and the objects and menu were spatially distributed, the participant was often confused about the current state, such as not knowing whether a prior operation had been performed or not. This is due to the lack of visual feedback or textual support. Especially when multiple objects were stacked, the lack of feedback made the participant confused about which one was selected. Even with audio feedback turned on, there is still a chance that the user was unsure whether they had selected a model, clicked a button, etc.

Miscreated Objects/Brush Marks. During the tasks, participants often created many objects and brush marks unintentionally, and they spent much time removing those objects.

Narrow Field of View. Another reason that the participants created extra objects is because the field of view of the HoloLens2 is narrow. During designing, the participants had difficulty observing all objects at the same time. The

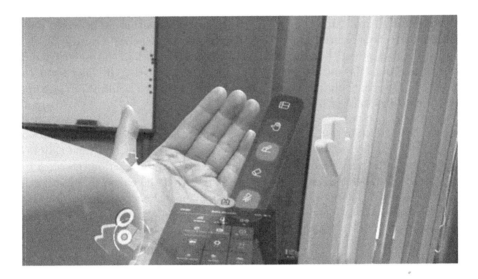

Fig. 5. The start menu appeared when opening the mini menu (participant 8)

narrow field of view required participants to turn their heads to see the entire scene. In addition, it was hard for the participants to remember whether any object was created or not. Therefore, the participants often repeatedly created the same objects (Fig. 6). This problem not only increased the time of that operation itself but also sometimes affected other operations. That is, the reductant objects often occluded other objects and made the participants recreate those objects, too. Consequently, adjustments to the spatial arrangement are necessary to accommodate the limitations of the visual area and enhance the overall user experience.

Fatigue-Induced Incorrect Gestures. Fatigue is another cause that increases the miscreated objects/brush marks. Based on the video analysis, after performing air-tap gestures to click buttons several times, it is observed that the participants' gestures slowed down, and the angle of the finger lift gradually became smaller or bent. Since the air-tap gesture was only recognized when the participants tapped and retracted their index fingers in a short period, the slow or incomplete gestures made it impossible for the system to recognize the gestures. For example, participant 8 did not lift his index finger after performing the air-tap, and the system recognized his gesture as a long press instead of a click. This fatigue-induced incorrect gesture would further increase the fatigue when repeating the operations.

Misselection. Misselection is another important error in that the participants failed to select the objects or functions they wanted. Misselection happened mainly due to the following causes: slow rendering and poor user interface layout.

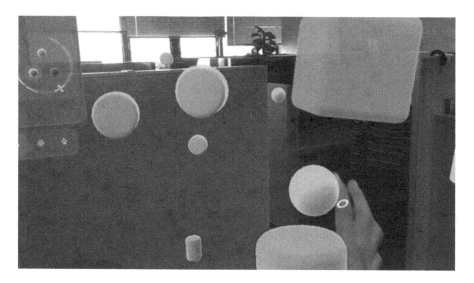

Fig. 6. Due to the narrow field of view, Participant 10 did not realize that objects have been already created and created reductant objects

Slow Rendering. During the design process, participants moved back and forth, and the heavy computation caused the Hololens to not render all objects at the same time. Therefore, participants tended to select an object that they saw, but when they actually selected it, the selection switched to another object that was rendered slower but physically in front of the former object.

Poor User Interface Layout. Another cause is due to the combination of cursor drifting and user interface layout design. The HoloLens2 cursor was controlled by head movement, and when there was a small movement of the head, the cursor would jump significantly. In addition, the buttons in the menu panel were too close to each other; for instance, the color palette buttons and the color block for adjusting color brightness in the Microsoft Mesh App were too close to each other, and the cursor easily moved out of the original option range and jump to the adjacent option (Fig. 7).

Furthermore, other occasional but significant errors occurred during the experiments. For example, participant 1 encountered an application flashback that caused the menu to disappear. Participant 7 experienced a scenario where the menu became non-interactive and required a restart. In addition, participant 9 experienced a computational slowdown due to a drop in the device's battery level during the experiment. These sporadic issues had a noticeable impact on the participants' interactions and highlighted the need for system optimization and stability.

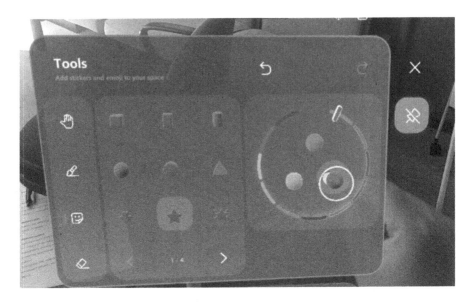

Fig. 7. When the color palette button is selected to adjust the color, the color shade is mistakenly clicked (participant 1)

5   Discussion

5.1   Summary of the Experiment

AR design tools bring users a new mode of human-computer interaction, but in the current experiment, the low usability and high perceived workload suggested that it may still contain many problems. The results also indicated that the participants made various errors in performing both the visualization task and the creation task. The high error rate seriously affected the user experience. In the interview, the participants also pointed out that although it is enjoyful to use AR design tool to design, the low usability made them feel tired.

In Sect. 4.3, we have listed up to seven types of causes inducing three main errors. Three of them are mainly related to the system defects: slow or failed calibration, slow rendering, and narrow field of view; four of them are mainly related to the user interface: gesture interference, unclear operation status, poor user interface layout, and fatigue-induced incorrect gestures. The main errors contributed to 93% of the defects, so it is important to find solutions to reduce their causes.

5.2   Design Implications

Based on the experiment's results, we offered some design concepts and directions that might address these difficulties.

Continuous Feedback. AR devices often have the drawback of heavy computation, so to compensate for the long computation time, it is critical to provide useful feedback in any interactive interface as one of the seven fundamental design principles proposed by Don Norman [14]. AR design tools should continuously provide immediate feedback on how the user is interacting with the system so that the user can understand his or her ability to control the system. If users don't receive immediate feedback, they will assume that the system didn't understand their input and repeat it, which will hinder the progress of the experiment and the completion of the task. Continuous feedback can improve errors caused by "slow calibration", "slow rendering", and "unclear operation status". In future system design, it is recommended to use rich effects to provide timely and effective real-time feedback to users.

Input Visualization and Tolerance. Natural inputs, such as gestures or head movements, have the disadvantage of limited precision, so it is important for the user to be able to determine whether the input was successful or not. Otherwise, it is easy for the user to lose patience with the operation if there is no visible change after the input. For example, the AR design tool should inform the user of the recognized gesture and its operation with visual or audio feedback. Visualizing the input may improve the "gesture interference" that occurred in this experiment.

In addition, the user interface design should consider fault tolerance of natural inputs. In this experiment, the participant's head movement often caused the cursor to drift, which resulted in the wrong selection of objects. To resolve such a problem, both user studies and ergonomics theory, such as Fitts's law, should be taken into consideration [12].

Multimodal Feedback. In this experiment, the gestures were recognized by visual (highlighting when the cursor reaches the target) or auditory (sound effect when the click or grasp is successful) effects. However, there were cases in which the participants failed to receive the feedback because the visual feedback was blocked by other objects. Thus, it is necessary to include multimodal feedback, such as vibration + visual or visual + auditory, in future design.

One-to-One Correspondence of Input and Operation. For HoloLens2 and the Microsoft Mesh App, the same input may trigger two different operations. For instance, when the participants called up the mini menu, their palms were opened, which was also recognized as a process from gathering to scattering and vice versa. Such one-to-many correspondence may harm the learning curve and should be avoided. This design concept may improve the "gesture interference".

Reduce Fatigue. Muscle fatigue easily accumulates when a user has to maintain a raised arm posture throughout the process. Fatigue not only affects the accuracy of gesture recognition, but in the interviews, participants reported that the single and repetitive gestures put much strain on their dominant hand, which led to an increase in irritation. Therefore, to reduce the need for repetitive actions, it is necessary to consider the amount of gesture input and try to add different gesture operations to reduce fatigue.

Simplify Process. When utilizing HoloLens2, engaging with the target involves two operations: initial interaction through eye tracking, followed by issuing commands through gesture interaction. This two-step process, compared to the conventional touch control mode of a two-dimensional interface, can occasionally result in a higher number of operations, potentially impacting user experiences and also increasing the error rate.

Thus, it is essential to reduce the operational steps required. In this experiment, for instance, when attempting to access the operation menu of a single 3D object, the user had to first select the object and then double-click on it. This operation proved to have a high error rate and low success likelihood. A more user-friendly approach would be to consolidate the functionality of fixed items into a common menu interface, allowing users to click and select them directly. Such a modification would simplify the process, decrease the frequency of user actions, and consequently reduce the error rate.

Gentle Variation. The rapid presence or removal of an object from the user's visual field annoys them. Because most users are sensitive to acceleration objects in space (including angular acceleration and displacement acceleration), it is preferable to move in or out of the plane direction as much as possible while developing the animation of object changes rather than performing the action on the Z-axis.

6   Conclusion

Computer scientists and information scientists have paid much attention to AR-based 3D model design tools. Nowadays, researchers in design fields have also started to explore the possibility of integrating such tools into the design process. Hence, the development of a practical AR-based 3D model design tool is essential.

For this, this paper focused on novice users and carried out an observational study to explore potential user interface issues that appear in the Microsoft Mesh App, an off-the-shelf AR design tool. A combination of objective video analysis and subjective surveys and interviews indicated the current AR design tool still requires much improvement. We also provided several design concepts for future developers to design a better AR design tool.

In this study, we only focused on HoloLens2 and Microsoft Mesh App; however, we believe that most of these issues can be seen in many AR design tools, and it is necessary to take into consideration even AR devices with better specification are carried out.

Acknowledgments. We thank for all the participants to participate in this study.

Disclosure of Interests. The authors have no competing interests to declare that are relevant to the content of this article.

References

1. Arora, R., Habib Kazi, R., Grossman, T., Fitzmaurice, G., Singh, K.: Symbiosissketch: combining 2d & 3d sketching for designing detailed 3d objects in situ. In: Proceedings of the 2018 CHI Conference on Human Factors in Computing Systems, pp. 1–15 (2018)
2. Arora, R., Kazi, R.H., Anderson, F., Grossman, T., Singh, K., Fitzmaurice, G.W.: Experimental evaluation of sketching on surfaces in VR. In: CHI, vol. 17, pp. 5643–5654 (2017)
3. Brooke, J.: Sus: a "quick and dirty"usability. Usabil. Eval. Ind. **189**(3), 189–194 (1996)
4. Dudley, J.J., Schuff, H., Kristensson, P.O.: Bare-handed 3D drawing in augmented reality. In: Proceedings of the 2018 Designing Interactive Systems Conference, pp. 241–252 (2018)
5. Grier, R.A.: How high is high? a meta-analysis of nasa-tlx global workload scores. In: Proceedings of the Human Factors and Ergonomics Society Annual Meeting, vol. 59, pp. 1727–1731. SAGE Publications, Los Angeles (2015)
6. Hart, S.G.: Nasa-task load index (nasa-tlx); 20 years later. In: Proceedings of the Human Factors and Ergonomics Society Annual Meeting, vol. 50, pp. 904–908. Sage publications, Los Angeles (2006)
7. Jackson, B., Keefe, D.F.: Lift-off: using reference imagery and freehand sketching to create 3D models in VR. IEEE Trans. Visual Comput. Graph. **22**(4), 1442–1451 (2016)
8. Kent, L., Snider, C., Gopsill, J., Hicks, B.: Mixed reality in design prototyping: a systematic review. Des. Stud. **77**, 101046 (2021)
9. Kovacs, B.I., Erb, I., Kaufmann, H., Ferschin, P.: Mr. sketch. immediate 3D sketching via mixed reality drawing canvases. In: 2023 IEEE International Symposium on Mixed and Augmented Reality (ISMAR), pp. 10–19. IEEE (2023)
10. Lewis, J.R., Sauro, J.: The factor structure of the system usability scale. In: Kurosu, M. (ed.) HCD 2009. LNCS, vol. 5619, pp. 94–103. Springer, Heidelberg (2009). https://doi.org/10.1007/978-3-642-02806-9_12
11. Lewis, J.R., Sauro, J.: Item benchmarks for the system usability scale. J. Usabil. Stud. **13**(3), 1–10 (2018)
12. MacKenzie, I.S.: Fitts' law as a research and design tool in human-computer interaction. Hum.-Comput. Interact. **7**(1), 91–139 (1992)
13. Mendes, D., et al.: Mid-air modeling with Boolean operations in VR. In: 2017 IEEE Symposium on 3D User Interfaces (3DUI), pp. 154–157. IEEE (2017)
14. Norman, D.: The Design of Everyday Things: Revised and Expanded Edition. Basic Books, New York (2013)
15. Reipschläger, P., Dachselt, R.: Designar: immersive 3D-modeling combining augmented reality with interactive displays. In: Proceedings of the 2019 ACM International Conference on Interactive Surfaces and Spaces, pp. 29–41 (2019)

AI for Universal Access

Style-Based Reinforcement Learning: Task Decoupling Personalization for Human-Robot Collaboration

Mahdi Bonyani⬚, Maryam Soleymani⬚, and Chao Wang⁽✉⁾⬚

Bert S. Turner Department of Construction Management, Louisiana State University,
Baton Rouge, USA
chaowang@lsu.edu

Abstract. Intelligent robots that are intended to engage with people in real life must be able to adjust to the varying tastes of their users. Robots can be taught personalized behaviors through human-robot collaboration without the need for a laborious, hand-crafted reward function. Instead, robots can learn rewards based on human styles between two robot movements that are called style-based reinforcement learning (SRL). However, existing SRL algorithms suffer from low exploration in the reward and state spaces, low feedback efficiency, and poor performance in complicated interactive tasks. We incorporate past information of the activity into SRL in order to enhance its result. In particular, we separate the activity in human-robot collaboration from the style. We employ an imprecise task reward based on task priori to guide robots in performing more efficient task exploration. Next, the robot's policy is optimized using a learned reward from SRL to better match human styles. Additionally, reward shaping allows for the organic fusion of these two components. The outcomes of the experiment demonstrate that our approach is a workable and efficient means of achieving customized human-robot collaboration.

Keywords: Human-Robot Collaboration · Task Decoupling Personalization · Reinforcement Learning

1 Introduction

The possibility of achieving human-robot symbiosis lies at the frontiers of artificial intelligence and robotics. Robots are designed to help people live safer, easier lives, and become more independent in a variety of ways in human social situations [15]. In order to accomplish this aim, robots are being designed with the ability to comprehend and communicate with people in extended, real-world contexts. This presents a number of difficulties for learning from and respecting human uniqueness. Every person has a different nonlinear movement for learning, growth, and care. For robots to adjust to various users, they need to have individualized talents.

M. Antona and C. Stephanidis (Eds.): HCII 2024, LNCS 14696, pp. 197–212, 2024.
https://doi.org/10.1007/978-3-031-60875-9_13

A solution to tailored human-robot collaboration is provided by interactive machine learning [5]. Among the representative interactive machine learning techniques is reinforcement learning (RL). Deep reinforcement learning (DRL), which makes use of deep learning's high-capacity function approximation capability, has been used in a variety of difficult domains, including robots and games like Go and Atari [9,16]. Still, the effectiveness of these strategies relies on carefully designed incentive structures. Sadly, a lot of activities have unclear, complex goals. An inaccurate reward function might result in reward hacking, when an agent maximizes the given reward without completing the original activity. Even worse, in human-robot collaboration, user styles are unpredictable.

SRL eliminates the need for hand-crafted rewards and relies on learning directly from the behavior of the system, making it a powerful data-driven approach to sequential decision-making and learning a reward function from external feedback, allowing it to adapt to changes in the environment [4,26–28]. Rather than optimizing long-term custom rewards, the agent learns the desired approach that aligns with human styles based on qualitative input, typically represented as human styles between two robot paths. One of the basic methods of SRL [4] helps robots learn tasks from human input. It learns a reward function that rewards the robot for taking steps that will lead to a successful outcome, and then optimizes it by adjusting the robot's behavior accordingly. This technique has been expanded to off-policy RL to increase for sampling effectiveness [13]. However because these SRL methods try to use human feedback for optimizing a reward function, they are incredibly inefficient. Obtaining good state space coverage by haphazard search directed by human styles is challenging. Therefore, utilizing SRL alone to optimize a robot to do intricate activities as well as adhere to human styles is impractical.

While human styles cannot be predicted in human-robot collaboration, it is useful to have some previous information about interactive activity. For instance, it's unclear how much power a robot should apply while shaking hands with a person, but we do know how to push the robot to do it. Motivated by this discovery, we develop individualized human-robot collaboration by integrating the activity-prior information into the SRL. In particular, we separate the activity in human-robot collaboration from the style. We use a rough reward function that we inferred from the activity information in order to guide the robot through more efficient activity exploration. The robot strategy is then optimized to match human styles using a trained reward function from SRL. Our tests show that on a challenging human-robot collaboration activity, the suggested strategy greatly outperforms SRL techniques [13]. Furthermore, the suggested approach is more resistant to illogical human input. This paper's primary contributions are twofold:

1. The performance of SRL is enhanced by utilizing the activity from style and integrating the activity's past information.
2. Sufficient experimental findings demonstrate the effectiveness of the suggested approach as a tailored human-robot collaboration solution.

This is how the remainder of the paper is structured. In Sect. 3, we methodically provide the suggested approach after a discussion of the relevant work in Sect. 2. The tests involving human-robot collaboration are carried out in Sect. 4, and the outcomes show that the suggested approach is successful. Section 5 provides conclusions.

2   Related Work

2.1   Personalized Human-Robot Collaboration

The way that various people respond to the same robot activity shows how humans are individualized. Robots should be able to process each person's unique information in order to meet their individualized demands. A current dynamic model of the environment may include unique information that allows us to create an ideal robot policy. For instance, using optimization, customized cooperative plans were put into place for robot-assisted dressing [11]. Taking into account individualized machine learning approaches, we may apply multitask learning strategies [24] or cluster users based on their attributes, training a different machine learning model for each cluster [21]. These techniques do, however, need an in-depth understanding of the relevant topic. Recently, reinforcement learning (RL) has demonstrated its promise for individualized human-robot collaboration. It has been applied to learn personalized proxemics by optimizing the parameters of the collaboration model [20], as well as to assist robots in choosing the right action to make tea [17]. In individual styles, each person's distinct information is reflected in the reward function for robots. The secret to this method's effectiveness is a carefully thought-out reward function design. To maximize individualized exoskeleton gait, human paired styles were utilized as a source of learning instead of a hand-crafted incentive [25, 26].

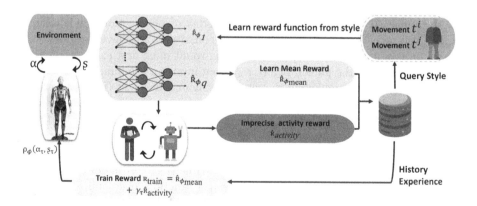

Fig. 1. This figure shows an example of our approach. The robot adjusts its collaboration strategy to suit human tastes by adding the optimized mean reward, $\hat{R}_{\phi\,mean}$, and the imprecise activity reward, $\hat{R}_{activity}$.

2.2   Human Feedback

Human pairwise style feedback has been effectively used in a number of works to train agents [7,27]. One of the possible approaches is to learn a reward function from input from humans and then optimize it [1]. Using contemporary deep learning techniques, SRL was extended from this fundamental strategy to more complicated domains, such as robotics activities in MuJoCo and Atari games [4]. The primary issues with SRL are low sample efficiency and feedback efficiency as real-world human feedback is highly costly. Through unsupervised pre-training and relabeling past experience, an off-policy SRL method was recently presented to increase sample efficiency and feedback efficiency [13]. Furthermore, it has been demonstrated that integrating paired styles with expert demonstrations may effectively boost SRL's effectiveness [10,18]. By taking into account the reward function's ambiguity, an effective exploration strategy was put forth [14]. A style predictor was trained to produce pseudo style labels in a number of studies that reduced the requirement for human feedback without compromising performance [3,19,29].

3   Methodology

An agent that interacts with its surroundings can learn under the paradigm of reinforcement learning [23]. The policy $\rho\left(\alpha_\tau \mid \mathbf{s}_\tau\right)$ is then used to determine the action α_τ that the agent will take, which is then updated state s_τ in accordance with the agent's observations. Within the traditional reinforcement learning paradigm, the agent aims to maximize the discounted return $\mathcal{D}_\tau = \sum_{m=0}^{T} \lambda^m \mathrm{R}\left(\mathbf{s}_{\tau+m}, \alpha_{\tau+m}\right)$, where the environment provides a numerical reward $\mathrm{R}\left(\alpha_\tau, \mathrm{S}_\tau\right)$.

But with human-robot contact, human styles are unpredictable, thus there won't be any manually created effective rewards. Therefore, we look at SRL, which substitutes the styles between two robot behavior activities for the numerical reward [28]. Formally, a series of observations and actions $\{(\mathbf{s}_m, \alpha_m), (\mathbf{s}_{m+1}, \alpha_{m+1}), \ldots, (\mathbf{s}_{m+n}, \alpha_{m+n})\}$ constitutes a behavior segment Ω. When a human and a robot communicate, the robot must first execute a activity in order to assist the person before receiving input on the human's styles. In this study, we suggest employing the whole behavior movement (Eq. 1) to probe human styles instead of using a brief behavior segment Ω. The human demonstrates which movement is selected (i.e., $y = \left(t^0 > t^1\right)$ or $\left(t^1 > t^0\right)$), that the two movements are equally selected $y = \left(t^0 = t^1\right)$ or that the two movements are unmatched. The robot exhibits two behavior movements $\left(t^0, t^1\right)$ to interact with Human. Every style feedback is kept as a triple $\left(t^0, t^1, y\right)$ in dataset F. SRL uses human style feedback to develop a reward function, overcoming the lack of a numerical payoff. Subsequently, the robot is guided to maximize the policy using the learnt reward function [4,10,13,14,19,28].

$$\tau = \{(\mathbf{s}_1, \alpha_1), (\mathbf{s}_2, \alpha_2), \ldots, (\mathbf{s}_T, \alpha_T)\} \tag{1}$$

Deep neural networks parametrize both the policy ρ_θ and the reward function $\hat{R}_\phi$. Three procedures are used to update these networks:

- **Phase 1**: Using supervised learning, the reward function $\hat{R}_\phi$ is tuned to match the style feedback that is provided by people.
- **Phase 2**: The policy ρ_θ engages with the surroundings to gather a collection of movements $\{t^0, t^1, \ldots, t^i\}$. It is then modified using traditional reinforcement learning techniques to maximize the total learned reward $\hat{R}_\phi$.
- **Phase 3**: From the gathered movement dataset, the robot chooses pairs of movements (t^i, t^j) and executes them to inquire about human styles.

Style-Based Reward Learning: It seems to sense that the movements exhibiting more appealing behaviors would receive greater total rewards. This requirement must be met by the learned incentive function. A pair of movements' style predictor is modeled as Eq. 2, in accordance with the Bradley-Terry model [2], using the learned reward function $\hat{R}_\phi$ as the basis. α_τ, S_τ

$$\pi_\phi \left[t^i > t^j\right] = \frac{\exp \sum_{\tau=0}^{T} \hat{R}_\phi \left(s_\tau^i, \alpha_\tau^i\right)}{\sum_{m \in \{i,j\}} \exp \sum_{\tau=0}^{T} \hat{R}_\phi \left(s_\tau^m, \alpha_\tau^m\right)} \tag{2}$$

where the occurrence that the movement t^i is better than the movement t^j is indicated by the notation $t^i > t^j$. By converting the problem to a binary classification, SRL methods simplify the optimization of the reward function in order to match style predictor with style feedback from humans. In particular, the following cross-entropy loss is minimized by updating the reward function $\hat{R}_\phi$, which is parametrized by ϕ:

$$\ell_R = - \mathop{\varepsilon}_{(t^i,t^j,y) \sim F} \left[\mathbb{I}\left\{y = \left(t^i > t^j\right)\right\} \log \pi_\phi \left[t^i > t^j\right] \right.$$
$$\left. + \mathbb{I}\left\{y = \left(t^j > t^i\right)\right\} \log \pi_\phi \left[t^j > t^i\right]\right] \tag{3}$$

where F denotes the dataset of style feedback.

Policy: After optimizing the reward function $\hat{R}_\phi$ based on human styles, a traditional reinforcement learning issue remains. Most RL algorithms that are currently in use can be used to teach robots. On-policy methods [22] as well as off-policy methods [8] are the two groups into which RL methods fall, based on whether the behavior policy and the target policy match. All that is required for on-policy methods is to substitute the learned reward function $\hat{R}_\phi$ that utilized the hand-crafted reward function [4]. On the other hand, off-policy algorithms will not benefit from this approach. We adjust the reward function $\hat{R}_\phi$ throughout training, so there's a chance that it's not stationary. The previously learned reward function is applied to past events stored in the replay buffer in off-policy algorithms. Consequently, off off-policy methods' learning process will be unstable. While the reward function $\hat{R}_\phi$ is changed, we may relabel the entirety of the robot's experience to address this problem [13]. Through the reuse of prior experiences, off-policy algorithms achieve greater sample efficiency than on-policy algorithms. In this study, we build our tests on two on-policy as well as off-policy methods to more thoroughly verify our strategy.

Queries: SRL aims to use the least amount of style input while training an agent to exhibit actions that a human would find desirable. All historical movements are saved in annotation buffer β throughout training, and at every feedback session, the robot should provide N_{query} pairs of movements to inquire about human styles. How should the robot approach queries to lighten the load on humans? The simplest approach is uniform sampling, which involves selecting uniformly and randomly from N_{query} pairs of movements as well as buffer β. However, in complicated domains, uniform sampling is insufficiently efficient. An efficient query technique to elicit styles in order to optimize the amount of information collected is ensemble-based sampling [4,12,13]. Also, we choose queries using the ensemble-based sampling approach. The reward functions are train as ensemble (q reward function $\left\{ \hat{R}_{\phi_1}, \hat{R}_{\phi_2}, \ldots, \hat{R}_{\phi_q} \right\}$), using replacement sampling of $|F|$ triples from style feedback dataset F. As the ensemble outcome, we use their average to facilitate policy optimization. In order to choose queries, the initial batch of N_{init} pairs of movements $\mathcal{G}_{\text{init}}$ is created by the robot uniformly randomly based on the buffer β. Next, it predicts styles $\left\{ \pi_{\phi_1} \left[t^i > t^j \right], \ldots, \pi_{\phi_q} \left[t^i > t^j \right] \right\}$ from each pair $\left(t^i, t^j \right)$ using every reward predictor in our ensemble. Ultimately, N_{query} ($N_{\text{query}} \leqslant N_{\text{init}}$) of movements are chosen to query human styles, meaning that the predictions for these pairs have the maximum variance according to ensemble items (Var $\left\{ \pi_{\phi_1} \left[t^i > t^j \right], \ldots, \pi_{\phi_q} \left[t^i > t^j \right] \right\}$).

3.1   Decoupling Activity from Style

In general, numerical incentives provide more information than binary-style feedback. As a result, traditional RL algorithms with numerical rewards are more efficient than SRL algorithms. Long-term human-robot contact presents a difficult challenge: assigning credit to the reward function. Moreover, SRL finds it challenging to achieve adequate space of the state as well as action coverage by probe randomly, particularly in high-dimensional human-robot collaboration challenges. We integrate activity-prior information into SRL to enhance its performance in human-robot collaboration. Our approach's main concept is to separate the activity from the user's desire while interacting with a robot. In order to convey the desired activity behavior, we create a rudimentary reward function, which is then utilized to provide the robot instructions on how to explore activities more successfully. The learned reward function helps the robot understand how its actions result in rewards and consequences. By optimizing the robot strategy, it is able to reduce the search space and find the most optimal strategy that matches the human style. In particular, this paper uses reward shaping to integrate the specified imprecise activity reward into style-based. Figure 1 depicts our method's structure.

Activity and Style Hypotheses for Collaboration: In tailored human-robot collaboration, the robot must not only successfully engage in dynamic interaction with humans but also devise a tailored approach to match human styles. For instance, when completing a handshake assignment, a robot must choose how much force to use in addition to physically shaking hands with a person. These two objectives are referred to as the task goal and the style goal in this study. Moreover, in the actual world, the activity objective and the style goal are frequently combined. The robot should use SRL to acquire individualized abilities through human collaboration in order to fulfill the preferred objective. Because human styles are unpredictable, traditional reinforcement learning techniques are not relevant. SRL finds it challenging to teach a robot to accomplish both objectives at the same time, nevertheless. Human styles are unpredictable, but we can learn some background information about the work beforehand. For instance, in a handshake challenge, the robot's hand should approach a human hand closely. Motivated by this, in human-robot collaboration, we separate the activity from style. To convey the desired activity behavior, we create a rough reward function, $\hat{R}_{activity}$, based on the prior information about the activity. To sum up, our approach is predicated on these two conjectures:

1. Style hypothesis: since human styles are unpredictable, robots should interact with people to acquire individualized abilities.
2. Activity hypothesis: Given some previous information about the activity, we may build a rough reward function, $\hat{R}_{activity}$, based on that information.

Activity Priori-Decoupled SRL: After optimizing the reward functions $\left\{\hat{R}_{\phi_l}\right\}_{l=1}^{q}$ based on human styles, SRL often uses standard RL algorithms to train the robot, with guidance from the mean reward function that it has learned.

$$\hat{R}_{\phi_{mean}} = \frac{1}{q}\sum_{l=1}^{q}\hat{R}_{\phi_l} \tag{4}$$

SRL integrates past activity knowledge by learning the mean reward $\hat{R}_{\phi_{mean}}$ and the specified imprecise activity reward $\hat{R}_{activity}$, then trains a policy of the robot to maximize the below equation:

$$R_{train}\left(S_\tau, \alpha_\tau\right) = \hat{R}_{\phi_{mean}}\left(S_\tau, \alpha_\tau\right) + \gamma_\tau \hat{R}_{activity}\left(S_\tau, \alpha_\tau\right), \tag{5}$$

where the balance between the activity as well as the style goal at the timestep τ during training may be found using the activity reward rate, $\gamma_\tau \geqslant 0$. The $\hat{R}_{activity}$ is imperfect and should only be considered an estimate of the activity reward that is determined by ground truth. Therefore, if γ_τ stays high for the whole training session, the activity incentive that was provided might skew the preferred approach. We utilize a reward rate that drops throughout the training period to prevent this scenario:

$$\gamma_\tau = \frac{T-t}{T}\gamma_0 \tag{6}$$

where γ_0, the starting activity reward rate, is likewise a hyperparameter in this study, and T is the training step.

4   Experiments

We plan our experiments on a simulation environment [6] in order to assess the effectiveness of the suggested strategy on individualized human-robot collaboration, specifically addressing the following queries:

Q1: By separating activity from style, is it possible for the suggested approach to outperform current SRL techniques in customized human-robot collaboration?
Q2: Is there a high level of resilience in the suggested strategy to use flawed human feedback?
Q3: What is the impact of reward rate γ_τ on performance?

4.1   Setups

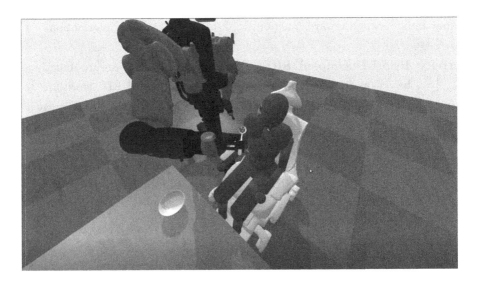

Fig. 2. This figure shows the assistive gym's feeding activity.

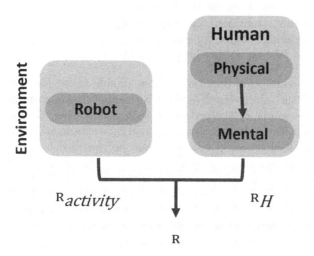

Fig. 3. This figure shows a model of the world with human styles. With AssistiveGym, the environment may deliver a human-style reward R_H by evaluating how people's physical and mental states interact. The robot's activity reward, R_R, and the human style reward, R_H, combine to form the output reward, R.

We test our approach on a feeding activity from Assistive-Gym for assistive robotics [6], as seen in Fig. 2. Within the simulated setting, a Baxter robot is utilized for feeding food to a human without letting it spill. The food is represented by little spheres on the spoon. In addition, the robot's actions have to be in line with human tastes. For instance, the robot must move slowly and interpretively, and it must not exert excessive force on the human body. As seen in Fig. 3, a unique RL environmental model [6] was provided to mimic human styles. The R_H value then determines the degree to which the robot is successfully imitating human behavior at each time step. The robot's activity reward, $R_{activity}$, is then combined with the human style reward, R_H, to provide an R. In particular, the R_H is calculated as

$$R_H = \omega \odot [C_d(\text{ s}), C_e(\text{ s}), C_v(\text{ s}), C_f(\text{ s}), \\ C_{hf}(\text{ s}), C_{fd}(\text{ s}), C_{fdv}(\text{ s})], \tag{7}$$

where $Cx(\text{ s})$ is utilized to calculate the cost of departing from human style in the s and the vector ω is a weight for each style. $\omega = [0.5, 0.5, 0.25, 0.3, 0.1, 2.5, 10.0]$ is used in this study, and C.( ) are defined as

- The distance the robot has to travel to reach the target assistance location affects the cost for the robot's movement is shown by $C_d(\text{ s})$.
- Feeding food to a human without letting it spill is $C_e(s)$.
- Cost for high robot end effector velocities is expressed as $C_v(\text{ s})$.

- Applying force away from the intended aid site is $C_f(\text{s})$.
- $C_{hf}(\text{s})$: exerting strong force close to the object.
- $C_{fd}(\text{s})$: splattering food on a person.
- $C_{fdv}(\text{s})$: food feeding quickly into the mouth.

We use the assumption that the robot is unable to see the real reward (R) in order to test the effectiveness of SRL in learning from non-numerical input. Rather, With the guidance of a programmed human teacher, the robot is able to develop a human-like understanding of human interaction, as in previous efforts [4,10,13,14]. Styles between robot paths can be provided by the programmed human instructor based on the real R. Since the ground truth reward of the environment is perfectly reflected in the styles of the programmed human instructor, we can measure the true average return to assess the effectiveness of our system. Additionally, in order to assess if our approach is in line with human styles, we may obtain the underlying human style reward, or R_H.

$$R_{\text{activity}} = -\|d\|_2, \tag{8}$$

In our approach, SRL is integrated with the activity's past information. The robot's objective in the feeding challenge is to use a spoon to deliver food to a human mouth. The imprecise activity reward is defined as

where d is the distance between the mouth and the spoon. We note that our approach may be integrated with any SRL algorithm by substituting its backbone method's policy optimization process with ours. In this study, we select as our backbone method cutting-edge on-policy [13] as well as off-policy [13] method in order to thoroughly evaluate our approach.

5   Result and Discussion

Our method's result is assessed by comparing it with a number of different approaches, including state-of-the-art SRL approaches and traditional RL methods (RL with real reward and imprecise activity reward) . The following is a list of all the techniques' settings:

1. **RL with real reward**: We use traditional RL methods like SAC and PPO to maximize the predicted ground truth output. The robot achieves ground truth reward R from the environment.
2. **RL with an activity incentive**: The robot achieves the imprecise R_{activity} from its environment. To optimize the imprecise activity return, we train the robot using PPO and SAC.
3. **RL based on styles**: The robot utilizes the reward function it has learned to maximize its policy after learning it based on the programmed human teacher's style input. In this study, we specifically implement PrefPPO and PEBBLE.

4. **decoupled SRL(Our approach)**: We combine the learned reward function from SRL with an imprecise activity reward, denoted as $R_{activity}$. We present two decoupled SRL algorithms, named Decoupled PrefPPO and PEBBLE, respectively, using PrefPPO and PEBBLE as our foundational algorithms.

Our goal in comparing our technique to the RL with real reward (as baseline) is to perform as close to or better than RL with real reward, rather than to outperform it. Equation 2 is used to build an ensemble of reward functions for all style-based algorithms. During the training phase, 50000 questions are produced. We set q = 3. Specifically, we take into account $\gamma_0 = 1.0$ and $\gamma_0 = 15.0$ for Decoupled PEBBLE and Decoupled PrefPPO. Figure 4 presents the experimental data, including the mean and standard deviation over the course of three experiments.

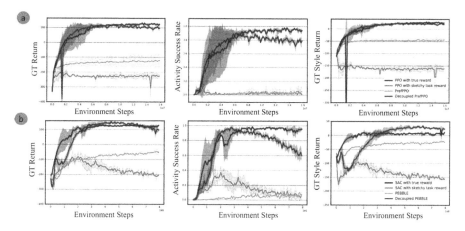

Fig. 4. The subfigure (a) shows the feeding activity's on-policy case learning curves. Subfigure (b) shows the feeding activity's off-policy case learning curves. The activity success rate, GT (Ground Truth) style return, and GT return are used to measure the experimental outcomes. The standard deviation and mean across three trains are shown by the shaded areas and the solid line, respectively.

Figure 4 demonstrates lacking access to numerical reward information, our approaches are able to perform almost like RL in the feeding problem when using the real reward. We use a learning reward function and a vague activity reward to direct the robot to probe effectively for the activity as well as human styles, respectively, and decoupled activity from style in personalized human-robot collaboration compared to SRL algorithms. The outcomes demonstrate that our techniques can enhance SRL's performance on challenging interactive activities and demonstrate that they are a fruitful attempt at individualized human-robot collaboration. Furthermore, while the hazy activity reward appears insignificant in traditional reinforcement learning, it is a valuable tool in our techniques.

5.1   Robustness of Our Method

$$\pi\left[t^i > t^j; \beta, \lambda_{iy}\right] = \exp\left(\beta \sum_{\tau=1}^{T} \lambda_{iy}^{T-\tau} R\left(s_\tau^i, \alpha_\tau^i\right)\right) / $$
$$\left(\exp\left(\beta \sum_{\tau=1}^{T} \lambda_{iy}^{T-\tau} R\left(s_\tau^i, \alpha_\tau^i\right)\right) + \exp\left(\beta \sum_{\tau=1}^{T} \lambda_{iy}^{T-\tau} R\left(s_\tau^j, \alpha_\tau^j\right)\right)\right) \qquad (9)$$

In reality, a human's choices and feedback are influenced by a multitude of potential irrationalities. Therefore, comparing our approach to the idealized scripted human teacher is impractical. We look to more accurate scripted human teacher models created by [12]:

- Random style model is designed to accommodate human noisy styles.
- where the likelihood of choosing movement i over movement j is indicated by $\pi\left[t^i > t^j\right]$, β is a constant, as well as $\lambda_{iy} \in (0, 1]$ is a scale parameter to mimic shortsighted actions.
- Humans can occasionally be myopic, so a teacher may recall and concentrate on the conduct at the conclusion of the movement he observed. Equation 8 is modified to incorporate a weighted total of rewards with a scale parameter λ_{iy}, so modeling the shortsighted actions.
- Question skipping: A human would like to designate both movements as incomparable and remove this inquiry if they represent undesirable behaviors. Skipping a query is modeled as follows: $\max_{m \in \{i,j\}} \left(\sum_\tau R\left(S_\tau^m, \alpha_\tau^m\right) - 0_{\min}\right) < \left(0_{\text{avg}}\left(\rho_\tau\right) - 0_{\min}\right) \delta_{\text{skip}}$, where $0_{\text{avg}}\left(\rho_\tau\right)$ is the average output of the $0_{\min}$ and ρ_τ as the minimum return and current policy, respectively.
- Equally desirable: A human wants to label two movements as similarly successful if they are both equally good. An uniform distribution

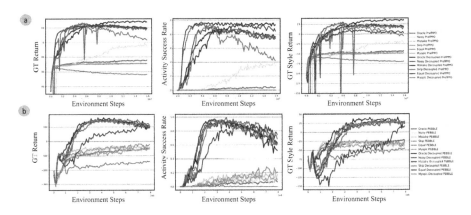

Fig. 5. The subfigure (a) shows the PrefPPO and Decoupled PrefPPO learning curves with different scripted human trainers. Subfigure (b) shows the PEBBLE and Decoupled PEBBLE learning curves with different scripted human teachers. The activity success rate, GT style return, and GT return are used to measure the experimental outcomes.

(0.5, 0.5) should be given if two movements have same rewards like $\left| \sum_\tau R\left(s_\tau^i, \alpha_\tau^i\right) - \sum_\tau R\left(s_\tau^j, \alpha_\tau^j\right) \right| < \left(0_{avg}\left(\rho_\tau\right) - 0_{min}\right)\delta_{equal}$.

- Erroring: Errors can happen to humans occasionally. The styles are reversed with the likelihood of ϵ to reflect this.

We apply our approach to several realistic scripted human instructors (whose attributes are specified in Table I) in order to assess the robustness. We make one change to the human teacher's oracle at a time. The performance of the experiment is displayed in Fig. 5. Despite the limitations of the scripted human teachers, our approaches can nevertheless achieve good performance in both on-policy and off-policy scenarios. This demonstrates the resilience of our techniques against illogical human feedback and their enormous potential for scaling to real-world human collaboration (Table 1).

Table 1. The type of human teachers utilized are realistically scripted.

Type	δ_{equal}	ϵ	λ_{my}	δ_{skip}	β
Equal	0.1	0	1	0	∞
Oracle	0	0	1	0	∞
Skip	0	0	1	0.1	∞
Mistake	0	0.1	1	0	∞
shortsighted	0	0	0.99	0	∞
Noisy	0	0	1	0	1

5.2 Effect of γ_τ on Reward

An essential parameter called γ_τ is utilized to calculate the balance between the optimized and imprecise activity reward. We create two decay methods for γ_τ in our experiments - a linear approach and a nonlinear strategy-in order to examine the effects of γ_τ.

Linear strategy: as training time increases, γ_τ falls linearly. Equation 5 illustrates that the only hyperparameter that has to be found is γ_0.

Non-linear strategy: γ_τ decays exponentially according to $\gamma_\tau == (1 - \mu)^\tau \gamma_0$, where μ is a decay rate. This is similar to [14].

We examine employing $\gamma_0 \in \{1.0, 5.0, 10.0\}$ and $\gamma_0 \in \{10.0, 15.0, 20.0\}$ in Decoupled PrefPPO and PEBBLE as a linear technique, respectively. This paper examines employing $\mu = 0.00001, \gamma_0 \in \{5.0, 10.0, 30.0\}$ and $\mu = 0.000001, \gamma_0 \in \{5.0, 10.0, 30.0\}$ in Decoupled PEBBLE and PrefPPO as nonlinear strategies. Figure 6 shows the experimental outcomes that we reported. We should make sure that the imprecise activity reward $R_{activity}$ applies on an extended length of time, e.g., utilizing non-linear or linear method based on the $\mu = 0.000001$, in order to aid robot in exploring activities more successfully and acquiring activity skills more rapidly. Nevertheless, we still need to carefully modify γ_0.

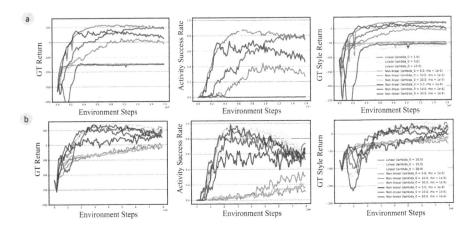

Fig. 6. The subfigure (a) shows the Decoupled PrefPPO learning curves for various decay techniques. Subfigure (b) shows the Decoupled PEBBLE learning curves with various decay tactics. The activity success rate, GT style return, and GT return are used to measure the experimental outcomes.

6   Conclusion

Our objective is to create a robot with customized abilities that can interact with humans in a variety of ways. We introduce decoupled SRL in this research, a unique SRL approach that takes activity information into account. In tailored human-robot collaboration, we disentangle the activity from style. We leverage a learned reward from SRL to update the policy of the robot to match human styles, and the proposed method leverages an imprecise activity reward generated from the previous information of the activity to manage the robot probe the activity efficiently. We merge them naturally via reward shaping. The outcomes of the experiment demonstrate that the suggested approach is a practical means of enabling customized human-robot collaboration and can perform admirably in a challenging interactive activity.

Acknowledgement. This material is based upon work supported by the National Science Foundation under Grant No. 2222881. Any opinions, findings, conclusions, or recommendations expressed in this material are those of the author(s) and do not necessarily reflect the views of the National Science Foundation.

References

1. Akrour, R., Schoenauer, M., Sebag, M.: APRIL: active preference learning-based reinforcement learning. In: Flach, P.A., De Bie, T., Cristianini, N. (eds.) Machine Learning and Knowledge Discovery in Databases: European Conference, ECML PKDD 2012, Bristol, UK, 24–28 September 2012, Proceedings, Part II 23, pp. 116–131. Springer, Cham (2012). https://doi.org/10.1007/978-3-642-33486-3_8
2. Bradley, R.A., Terry, M.E.: Rank analysis of incomplete block designs: I. the method of paired comparisons. Biometrika **39**(3/4), 324–345 (1952)
3. Cao, Z., Wong, K., Lin, C.T.: Weak human preference supervision for deep reinforcement learning. IEEE Trans. Neural Netw. Learn. Syst. **32**(12), 5369–5378 (2021)
4. Christiano, P.F., Leike, J., Brown, T., Martic, M., Legg, S., Amodei, D.: Deep reinforcement learning from human preferences. In: Advances in Neural Information Processing Systems, vol. 30 (2017)
5. Clabaugh, C., Matarić, M.: Robots for the people, by the people: personalizing human-machine interaction. Sci. Robot. **3**(21), eaat7451 (2018)
6. Erickson, Z., Gangaram, V., Kapusta, A., Liu, C.K., Kemp, C.C.: Assistive gym: a physics simulation framework for assistive robotics. In: 2020 IEEE International Conference on Robotics and Automation (ICRA), pp. 10169–10176. IEEE (2020)
7. Fürnkranz, J., Hüllermeier, E., Cheng, W., Park, S.H.: Preference-based reinforcement learning: a formal framework and a policy iteration algorithm. Mach. Learn. **89**, 123–156 (2012)
8. Haarnoja, T., Zhou, A., Abbeel, P., Levine, S.: Soft actor-critic: off-policy maximum entropy deep reinforcement learning with a stochastic actor. In: International Conference on Machine Learning, pp. 1861–1870. PMLR (2018)
9. Hwangbo, J., et al.: Learning agile and dynamic motor skills for legged robots. Sci. Robot. **4**(26), eaau5872 (2019)
10. Ibarz, B., Leike, J., Pohlen, T., Irving, G., Legg, S., Amodei, D.: Reward learning from human preferences and demonstrations in Atari. In: Advances in Neural Information Processing Systems, vol. 31 (2018)
11. Kapusta, A., et al.: Personalized collaborative plans for robot-assisted dressing via optimization and simulation. Auton. Robot. **43**, 2183–2207 (2019)
12. Lee, K., Smith, L., Dragan, A., Abbeel, P.: B-Pref: benchmarking preference-based reinforcement learning. In: Neural Information Processing Systems (NeurIPS) (2021)
13. Lee, K., Smith, L.M., Abbeel, P.: PEBBLE: feedback-efficient interactive reinforcement learning via relabeling experience and unsupervised pre-training. In: International Conference on Machine Learning, pp. 6152–6163. PMLR (2021)
14. Liang, X., Shu, K., Lee, K., Abbeel, P.: Reward uncertainty for exploration in preference-based reinforcement learning. In: Deep RL Workshop NeurIPS (2021)
15. Liu, M., Xiao, C., Chen, C.: Perspective-corrected spatial referring expression generation for human-robot interaction. IEEE Trans. Syst. Man Cybern. Syst. **52**(12), 7654–7666 (2022)
16. Mnih, V., et al.: Human-level control through deep reinforcement learning. Nature **518**(7540), 529–533 (2015)
17. Moro, C., Nejat, G., Mihailidis, A.: Learning and personalizing socially assistive robot behaviors to aid with activities of daily living. ACM Trans. Hum.-Robot Interact. (THRI) **7**(2), 1–25 (2018)

18. Palan, M., Shevchuk, G., Charles Landolfi, N., Sadigh, D.: Learning reward functions by integrating human demonstrations and preferences. In: Robotics: Science and Systems (2019)
19. Park, J., Seo, Y., Shin, J., Lee, H., Abbeel, P., Lee, K.: SURF: semi-supervised reward learning with data augmentation for feedback-efficient preference-based reinforcement learning. In: Deep RL Workshop NeurIPS (2021)
20. Patompak, P., Jeong, S., Nilkhamhang, I., Chong, N.Y.: Learning proxemics for personalized human-robot social interaction. Int. J. Soc. Robot. **12**, 267–280 (2020)
21. Rudovic, O., Lee, J., Dai, M., Schuller, B., Picard, R.W.: Personalized machine learning for robot perception of affect and engagement in autism therapy. Sci. Robot. **3**(19), eaao6760 (2018)
22. Schulman, J., Wolski, F., Dhariwal, P., Radford, A., Klimov, O.: Proximal policy optimization algorithms. arXiv preprint arXiv:1707.06347 (2017)
23. Sutton, R.S., Barto, A.G.: Reinforcement Learning: An Introduction (2018)
24. Taylor, S., Jaques, N., Nosakhare, E., Sano, A., Picard, R.: Personalized multitask learning for predicting tomorrow's mood, stress, and health. IEEE Trans. Affect. Comput. **11**(2), 200–213 (2017)
25. Tucker, M., et al.: Human preference-based learning for high-dimensional optimization of exoskeleton walking gaits. In: 2020 IEEE/RSJ International Conference on Intelligent Robots and Systems (IROS), pp. 3423–3430. IEEE (2020)
26. Tucker, M., et al.: Preference-based learning for exoskeleton gait optimization. In: 2020 IEEE International Conference on Robotics and Automation (ICRA), pp. 2351–2357. IEEE (2020)
27. Wilson, A., Fern, A., Tadepalli, P.: A Bayesian approach for policy learning from trajectory preference queries. In: Advances in Neural Information Processing Systems, vol. 25 (2012)
28. Wirth, C., Akrour, R., Neumann, G., Fürnkranz, J.: A survey of preference-based reinforcement learning methods. J. Mach. Learn. Res. **18**(136), 1–46 (2017)
29. Zhan, H., Tao, F., Cao, Y.: Human-guided robot behavior learning: a GAN-assisted preference-based reinforcement learning approach. IEEE Robot. Autom. Lett. **6**(2), 3545–3552 (2021)

User Profile: Changed in the Era of Artificial Intelligence

Laura Burzagli[✉] and Pier Luigi Emiliani

CNR IFAC, Via Madonna del Piano 10, Sesto F. no., Firenze, Italy
l.burzagli@ifac.cnr.it

Abstract. It is commonly accepted that communication and information technology can be used to support people. The paper reviews the different forms that this support has taken on over time. It is clarified that support applications have become increasingly complex and require more and more detailed user knowledge, available in real time. This requires the use of artificial intelligence not only at the application management but also at the profile generation level.

Keywords: User profile · Ambient intelligence · Artificial Intelligence

1 Introduction

Information and communication technology has always had an important impact on people, both offering new important services (as the telephone or the television) and being flexible enough to be adaptable when their use was not possible. As examples, the development of speech recognition for access of deaf people to the telephone and of speech synthesis to add descriptions to images for blind people, can be cited. At the beginning, the main problem was to give access to information and communication. Now the situation is changing. From the technological perspective, the development of the concepts of Ambient Intelligence has made possible the implementation of complex applications, addressing individual activities in everyday life. From a political/social point of view, the WHO and the UNO recommend the use of technology to support all people, contributing to their well-being. This means that for an appropriate and efficient use of technology, the application needs to know the person who will use it and therefore her user profile. The work describes the development of the concept of user profile, from when it was enough to know that the user was blind to the current situation in which the applications must know every detail of the user's abilities and needs, even their variations in real time. Fortunately, this is made possible using artificial intelligence techniques.

2 Assistive Technology Approaches

When ICT began to develop, it immediately became clear that it offered the possibility of supporting connection and exchange of information between people, facilitating such activities for certain groups of people with activity limitations. Examples include the

© The Author(s), under exclusive license to Springer Nature Switzerland AG 2024
M. Antona and C. Stephanidis (Eds.): HCII 2024, LNCS 14696, pp. 213–223, 2024.
https://doi.org/10.1007/978-3-031-60875-9_14

telephone for blind people and image transmission for deaf people. At the same time, it was clear that such services, once commonplace, could create additional problems for some people, such as the telephone for deaf people and television for blind people.

At that time, accessibility to information in the ICT environment was mainly considered a problem of the human interface. Solution for specific abilities limitations (e.g., blind, or deaf people) were developed, based on a correct structuring of the information and its transduction with the use of specific technologies (as text to voice for blind people and voice to text for deaf people) [1]. This means that redundancy of the information must be used to allow different presentations) and that this information must be correctly structured to be interpreted by all the access technologies. Specific solutions were also developed for certain user groups, such as screen readers for access to computers by blind people.

The situation supported the development of assistive technology, i.e. a technology able to solve, normally, single problems of users. Examples are voice synthesizers, the voice recognizers, the text-telephone, the screen readers for access of blind people to computers. Now, all these technologies have become commonly available, on mobile phones as well. Screen readers are available as free software.

For the access to the Web, due the complexity of available sites, guidelines for correct production of material accessible to all users, including people with limitations of activities, various versions of Web Accessibility Guidelines (WCAG) [2] have been produced. This required a first rigorous effort in conceiving technological solutions that would allow to accommodate in the web sites information in all its forms (images, text, sounds). This means that the information to be provided must be available in a redundant form and that this information must be correctly structured to be interpreted by all the access technologies available. This implies that the production of the pages is supposed to be supported by authoring tools, which are able to combine all the modalities of presentation, and that the obtained results are checked with suitable evaluation tools. The user is supposed to interact with a browser and media players with the support of assistive technologies as shown in Fig. 1.

The version 1.0 of the web Accessibility Guidelines were published by the W3C/WAI (Web Accessibility Initiative) group in 1999 [2] Each guideline has several checkpoints with a priority level assigned on the base of the checkpoint's impact on accessibility. If Priority 1 checkpoints are not satisfied, one or more groups will find it impossible to access information in the document. Priority 2 implies that if not satisfied one or more groups will find it difficult to access information in the document. Finally, with the satisfaction of Priority 3 one or more groups will find it somewhat difficult to access information in the document. WCAG 2.0 were published in 2008. Their emphasis is shifted from technique-centered checkpoints to guidelines and success criteria rooted in four core principles that provide the foundation for Web accessibility: information must be perceivable, operable, understandable, robust, each of which obtainable with the use of specific guidelines (12 in total) and testable with success criteria. WCAG 2.1, the current sub-version of WCAG 2, was adopted in 2018. It did not replace WCAG 2.0 in the same way WCAG 2.0 replaced 1.0. Instead, it adds new success criteria, especially for mobile devices. All success criteria from 2.0 remain unchanged, as do the four core principles. Therefore WCAG 2.1 b is backwards compatible with WCAG

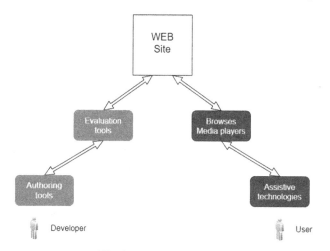

Fig. 1. Web interface steps

2.0, meaning that web pages that conform to WCAG 2.1 also conform to WCAG 2.0. The development was initiated with the goal to improve accessibility guidance for three major groups: users with cognitive or learning ability limitations, users with low vision, and users with ability limitations on mobile devices.

Through the application of these guidelines, which became an international standard, it was made possible, in principle, for everyone to use information in electronic format, using techniques of redundancy of information, such as, for example, the textual description of the graphic elements present, which allowed access the information even to those who were unable to use their sight. Using this approach, users are supposed to overcome numerous barriers to inclusion. In fact, interaction with devices is transformed from an access problem to a resource for social interaction. Unfortunately, the situation is that the technology used for transductions is widely available, but the guidelines are not universally used.

Obviously, in the activity aimed to make possible the use of ICT technologies with the production of information in a suitable form and the implementation of AT equipment for people support, the user profile has always been considered a key element. It was supposed to be integrated in the authoring tools and assistive technology blocks presented in Fig. 1. It considered the physical, sensory, and cognitive state of the person and based on these elements it provided a solution for accessing electronic devices and information in electronic format. However, the user was defined by a static profile, which was essentially a list of existing limitations of abilities [2], an on this base an optimal solution was constructed. The user was defined as a blind, or low vision, deaf etc. person, with guidelines on how the information should be adapted and what AT equipment should be used.

3 Adaptivity and Adaptability

With the development of technology, a second approach to accessibility of information and communication was based on research about the possibility of implementing the design for all approach [3], i.e. an approach not based on the needs of the average user, but, in principle, those of all potential users. A considered possibility was based on constructing adaptivity and adaptability in the systems, aimed to guarantee accessibility to the produced interfaces and contents. One example was developed in the PALIO (Personalized Access to Local Information and Services for Tourists) [4], funded by the EC's IST Programme from 2000 to 2003. The main challenge of the PALIO project was the creation of an open system for accessing and retrieving information without constraints and limitations (imposed by space, time, access technology, etc.). Mobile communication systems played an essential role in this scenario because they enabled access to services from anywhere and at any time. Moreover, the PALIO system envisaged the adaptation of both the information content and the way in which it is presented to the user, as a function of user characteristics.

The PALIO information system consists of the following main elements (Fig. 2):

- A communications platform that includes all network interfaces, to inter-operate with both wired and wireless networks.
- The AVC center, which is composed of the main adaptation components, a service control center, and the communication layers to and from the user terminals and the information services.
- Distributed Information Centers in the territory, which provide a set of primary information services.

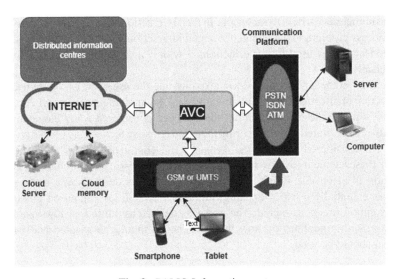

Fig. 2. PALIO Information system

The AVC centre is the architectural unit which manages diversity and implements the mechanisms for universal access. The AVC is perceived by users as a system which groups together all information and services that are available in the city. It serves as an augmented, virtual facilitation point from which different types of information and services can be accessed. The context- and location- awareness, as well as the adaptation capabilities of the AVC, enable users to experience their interaction with services as a form of 'contextually-grounded' dialogue: e.g. the system always knows the user's location and can correctly infer what is 'near' the user, without the user having to explicitly provide information to the system.

The fundamental changes in the user profile necessary to support the Palio system are evident. The system must know all the characteristics of the user (e.g. abilities, needs, requirements, interests), the user location (with the use of different modalities and granularities of the information contents), the context of use, the current status of interaction (and previous history), and, lastly, the used technology (e.g., communications technology, terminal characteristics, special peripherals) used. Therefore, the user profile becomes a component that is not only complex but able to change, to guarantee adaptation with the individual user when the system is accessed and adaptability to the different situations during use.

4 The Emerging Situation

In the new millennium, important changes have emerged, both from the political/social and the technological perspectives. From the user perspective the World Health Organization (WHO) published the International Classification of Functioning, Disability and Health, known more commonly as ICF, a classification of health and health-related domains. Since functioning and/or disability of an individual occurs in a physical context, ICF also includes a list of relevant environmental factors. ICF was officially endorsed by all 191 WHO Member States in the Fifty-fourth World Health Assembly on 22 May 2001 (resolution WHA 54.21) as the international standard to describe and measure health and disability.

Moreover, the support systems in the society, according to UN and WHO [5, 6], must not only be considered as a means for making living possible, but an approach to improve the quality of life of people, aiming to increase their well-being, whose meaning may be different for each person.

From the technology perspective, several trends in the supply of new products and services could be identified, to meet the above changing demands in the Information society, as: increased scope of information content and supporting services; emergence of novel interaction paradigms (e.g. virtual and augmented realities, ubiquitous computing); shift towards group-centered, communication-, collaboration- and cooperation-intensive computing. Now there are no longer only terminals to communicate or access information, but most of the objects that surround us have intelligence on board (at least one computer) and can be connected to each other. These devices include computers, standard telephones, cellular telephones with built-in displays, television sets, information kiosks, special information appliances, and various other "network-attachable" devices. This allows the creation of complex applications to support people, all people, in the tasks they need to perform to live independently.

In order to clearly describe the changing impact of technology on people, let us consider a typical activity necessary for living, namely the ability to access the external environment, where accessibility is not only defined as being able to go from one site to another, but also of being informed about where services of interest (e.g., a pharmacy or a postal office) are located [7]. Individual users' experience in going around to find what is necessary for them, their abilities in interacting with the environment and with the support system are particularly important. Moreover, if, for example, elderly people are considered, it is evident that their situation is really a continuum from an (almost) complete availability of all necessary abilities to an almost complete lack of them. For many of them the problems can be caused by a not sufficient knowledge of the surrounding environment and the organization of functionalities of the application that support mobility and interaction. From this perspective, it must be emphasized that the situation may be different for each person.

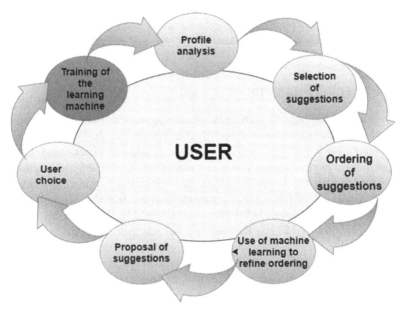

Fig. 3. Loop of processing

Twenty years ago, the information society mainly included people from research, industry, and business, that is professionals with at least knowledge of the basis of information technology and able and willing to learn. In this group of people there could be someone with physical or/and sensory limitations and it was only necessary to find adaptations to allow them to be integrated in their well-defined environments. Today, information and communication technology are widely distributed and useful, sometimes fundamental, for all people. The active members of the information society are all citizens. It should not create obstacle to any one and, instead, it should help all to reach their well-being.

The rapid aging of population is a particularly influential factor in this respect, resulting in a considerable proportion of the future technological environments. Old people may perceive technology differently, due to functional limitations and age-related changes in cognitive processes [8, 9]. However, AAL environments have the potential to support independence and quality of life of older adults. Assisted living systems can also contribute in addressing emergency situations, which are expected to have a dramatic increase with age. At the same time, following a similar strategy, ambient assisted working can foster adaptations of the workplace, thus ensuring that the population aging and/or with limitations are active and participate for the longest possible in the workforce [10]. Finally, it is necessary that public environments, for example transportation systems are revisited and redesigned in order to be age-friendly and age-ready [11].

From user profile perspective, precisely because the use of support services is extended to all people (as far as possible avoiding the adoption of specific Assistive Technologies), their varying abilities, correspondingly needs, and preferences expressed by single users are very important and their variations needs to be made available to the support system in real time (see Fig. 3).

5 Industry

Unfortunately, the design for all approaches was not very successful, since industry did not consider the number of potentially interested new users sufficient to justify their investment.

Now the situation is potentially more favorable, and it is interesting to report the reactions, at the industrial level, to the development of the previously reported attitudes at the regulatory and political levels about people who may need support, mainly connected to the access to technology and to the environment, with the use of the ambient intelligence paradigm.

From an analysis, albeit partial, different visions emerge: Apple focuses heavily on the dissemination of the resources it has developed for the accessibility of its devices to different categories of people, Google immediately highlights different approaches for different roles such as developers, users and research, IBM and Microsoft highlight an activity that goes beyond simple adherence to the accessibility rules, but seeks to develop a broader approach, which, in the case of Microsoft, is aimed at making accessibility a business and for IBM on the idea of a cultural approach to the problem, for which it also proposes a toolkit.

Industry is starting to take into account that ICT technology for user support is used not only for accessibility of devices and systems, but also for the creation of smart environments. In the literature reference is made to this field of activity which different denominations: Ambient Intelligence, Intelligent environments, Pervasive Computing, Internet of Things, Smart Objects. The terms are not equivalent, but they are connected by the shared vision of a processing of information no longer concentrated in specific points of the environment, such as a PC or a tablet, but in objects distributed in the environment and interconnected.

Since the integration of different components into a common platform is therefore one of the most technologically critical elements, there are efforts aimed at developing open standards, such as "Connected Home over IP", with the cooperation by Amazon, Apple, Google, Zigbee (https://en.wikipedia.org/wiki/Connected_Home_over_IP). Interesting examples can then be found in many specific application fields. As examples, the home and health environments are considered.

For the home, LG proposes ThinQ (https://thinq.developer.lge.com/en/), defined as a brand of LG that brings together AI products and services as well as those with connectivity capabilities, in order to elevate the quality of life with Smart/AI-powered appliances and electronics. LG ThinQ is supposed to evolve over time by learning about the users. SAMSUNG offers the SmartThings ecosystem, that in their site is described as a platform (https://smartthings.developer.samsung.com/docs/platform-bas ics.html, https://www.smartthings.com/) that enables people to build integrated and IoT devices, services, and Automations on SmartThings Cloud, to be integrated on the Smart-Things catalog. SIEMENS presents its own home interconnection system, which is also capable of managing household appliances and functionalities, even with voice interaction (https://www.home-connect.com/gb/en/). The description shows how several functionalities can help people in their daily life activities. For example, with children, the possibility of giving vocal commands allows them to manage home appliances without leaving babies alone.

As a general comment, most of the activity in this field has been first at the level of setting up smart objects and architectures to connect them in different environments and then to the implementation of applications aimed at specific aims. However, the concept of the intelligent environment as a general support to people in their life is starting to be considered at the industrial level.

6   AI - The Support System

New perspectives are arising, which emphasize the role of intelligent environments towards providing useful means to all support people in their daily life activities, including older people and for people with limitations of activities [12]. In this context, accessibility and usability, although necessary, are not sufficient. In order to achieve the above objective, it is necessary that: (i) the design of Intelligent Environments is centered around the well-being of people, roughly intended as the possibility of executing the (everyday) human activities necessary for living (independently), thus emphasizing usefulness in addition to usability; (ii) the technological environment is orchestrated around such activities and contains knowledge about the abilities necessary to perform them and how people need to be supported to perform them, when some abilities are limited; (iii) the environment makes use of monitoring and reasoning capabilities in order to adapt, fine-tune and evolve over time the type and level of support provided, and this process takes place considering ethical values; (iv) the applications also support the possibility of contact with other people, who in many cases may be the only effective help.

This shift has two main consequences. First, a richer architectural approach must be considered, where a control component is introduced. Devices and smart objects need to be integrated to obtain a system able to support people in their activities. This control is not seen from the perspective of the communication and interoperability of the technologies but has the specific objective of embedding the knowledge about technology and users and being able to match the implementable functionalities with the different and often continuously varying needs of users. The envisaged environment usability does not only imply ease of use, ease of learning and effectiveness in use of a system, but also the necessary adaptations of the service itself, because different people may need or prefer to carry out the same activity in different ways, or need to receive different types of information, as, for example, in the case of older people with mild cognitive limitations.

This can be obtained by introducing Artificial Intelligence in the system, with the evolution of the control component to include two main blocks: a knowledge base and a reasoning system [13]. The knowledge base needs to contain information about the activities to be carried out in the environment, the necessary functionalities, the available technologies, the interoperability issues (i.e. interfaces and communication protocols), the user profiles (abilities of individual users and their requirements and preferences), the interaction issues: available interaction devices and modalities.

The implementation, maintenance and run-time use of the system must be carried out under the control of a reasoning system (intelligence in the environment) capable of:

- Enriching the knowledge base, acquiring, and integrating information already received in a formal representation (rule-based AI) and/or extracting it (machine learning) from informal information (for example from natural language text).
- Using the information in the knowledge base to adapt, in an unobtrusive and anticipatory way, the functionalities made available in their interfaces.
- Learning from usage to refine the knowledge base, introducing the necessary updates.
- Evolving the functionalities according to the evolution of technology.
- Suggesting to the user alternative suitable means of interaction.

For the interaction with this environment and the services made available by it, there is an emphasis on "natural" user interfaces, meaning interactions based on modalities and media typical of human-human interaction (e.g. using speech, the body language, gestures, facial expressions and so on), possibly with simplifications or additions necessary to meet the abilities of people. Finally, social networks can be fruitfully embedded in the very fabric of the intelligent environment. The information coming from social networks and any other application such as a forum, if conveniently processed, may contribute to the available knowledge, and contribute to limit possible social segregation. Therefore, support systems in the environment must be useful to all citizens and be adapted to their individual user profile. Therefore, the profile does not only need to contain a static list of deficient skills. The system must be able to follow the persons over time, adjourning, also in real time, their profile with information about their sensory characteristics (physical, motor, cognitive), their interests, and their behavior. This is necessary to plan a strategy for the support and to reason about the changes in skills/abilities and the changes in the context. For elderly people, for example, it must be able to recognize the level of autonomy during their life and in real time.

To clarify the necessary functions of the support system, which emphasize the need of an intelligent management of the user profile, let start with an example, the generation of information to find a service in the environment and to go from a site to another. I am in a hotel. I need a pharmacy and to be informed if the pharmacy is reachable for a pedestrian. Therefore, the system should know the environment at two levels. First it needs to know the services that are around the hotel. Is a pharmacy available at a pedestrian distance? Then it must be able to find a path to it that is suitable for my abilities to walk. The problem seems trivial because many navigation systems are available. However, not all the available services are reported in the systems and, normally, the information about accessibility is limited to the lack of architectural obstacles. For example, there is no information about the slope or the bad conditions of the sidewalks.

Therefore, in principle, the support system should be able to explore the network trying to find the necessary additional information of what is available in the environment and the state of the path between the hotel and the pharmacy to inform me about the real situation. Then, it should consider my habits and preferences. It should consider if I normally prefer to be informed about the shortest walk to the service or I like to use the longest route if it passes through a garden or near a shop of interest, as a bookshop. My reaction to possible unexpected difficulties, due to the environment not corresponding to the available information, or my physical or psychological changed situation should be used to give me additional help. Any change from the normal habit should be considered as a possible integration in my profile and controlled in time. Finally, from the perspective of interaction any suggestion should be organized to be presented on different devices, such as smart phones, tablets, computers, according to my present abilities.

7   Possible Application of Recommendation Systems

It is interesting to discuss if and how available tools, as recommender systems, which are a widely used tool in the commercial field, may be of interest in relation to the personalization of the support service. Born in the commercial field, they are based on different technological approaches and aim to recommend the most suitable products or services to the person who explores the Web site of a shopping organization.

The ability to advise the user about a product or an action is undoubtedly part of the criteria of personalization, although with necessary distinctions and attentions when used in services as the ones that are discussed in the paper.

The important problem is accuracy. Concerning the case of the user seen as a buyer, the suggestion provided may also contain elements of inaccuracy. An incorrect offer to purchase a non-interesting item is rejected by the user. In the case of personal support services, the use of this type of product, even if powerful from a technological point of view, may present problems. When the service offers a recommendation and the available user profile contains elements of limitations of abilities, even mild ones, the response must in any case be certainly consistent with the support to overcoming of the barriers due to reductions of abilities. However, since the profile will have a part related to the user's preferences, at this level one could also suggest that the proposed suggestion is not only based on the user's previous choices, but also on the choices of users with a similar profile. In any case, the suggestion must be absolutely consistent with the psychophysical profile, otherwise it cannot be of real help.

The situation is different if the information of the support service is not only provided to final user, but its recommendations are considered as a support for a caregiver as well. In this case, the suitability of the response is evaluated by human support, before going to the end user. In this case the recommender system is a support to the caregiver. A use of this kind already occurs in professional environments, such as in the legal field, or in the artistic field, when the amount of data to be managed can lead to disorientation of the person. Help from the systems facilitates the final decision.

8 Conclusions

It is clear that technology can presently be used to support people not only in accessing information and communication but in most activities in ambient intelligent environments. However, to be really useful it must know the user, their needs, preferences, and possible limitations of activities, being also able to note the some of the information that it has at its disposal must be changed momentarily or forever. The problem of building and maintaining the user profile is very complex. However, with the help of artificial intelligence techniques the problem can be addressed, as demonstrated in the applications implemented in IFAC for access to mobility and support for loneliness.

References

1. Billi, M., et al.: A unified methodology for the evaluation of accessibility and usability of mobile applications. Universal Access Inf. Soc. **9**, 337–356 (2010)
2. WAI. https://www.w3.org/WAI/. Accessed 06 Feb 2024
3. Burzagli, L., Emiliani, P.L., Gabbanini, F.: Design for All in action: an example of analysis and implementation. Expert Syst. Appl. **36**(2), 985–994 (2009)
4. Palio project. https://cordis.europa.eu/project/id/IST-1999-20656. Accessed 06 Feb 2024
5. WHO (2015) Global strategy and action plan on ageing and health (2016 - 2020). WHO (2015)
6. UN (2020) UN Decade of Healthy Ageing: Plan of Action 2021-2030. UN
7. Burzagli, L., Emiliani, P.L.: From accessible interfaces to useful and adapted interactions. In: Antona, M., Stephanidis, C. (eds.) Universal Access in Human-Computer Interaction. Design Approaches and Supporting Technologies, HCII 2020. LNCS, vol. 12188, pp. 19–32. Springer, Cham (2020)
8. Charness, N., Boot, W.R.: Aging and information technology use: potential and barriers. Curr. Dir. Psychol. Sci. **18**(5), 253–258 (2009)
9. Czaja, S.J., Lee, C.: The impact of aging on access to technology. Univ. Access Inf. Soc. **5**, 341–349 (2007)
10. Bühler, C.: Management of Design for All. In: The Universal Access Handbook 2009, pp. 1–12. CRC Press, Boca Raton
11. Coughlin, J.F., Brady, S.: Planning, Designing, and Engineering Tomorrow's User-Centered, Age-Ready Transportation System. The Bridge, 49 (2019)
12. Burzagli, L., Emiliani, P.L., Antona, M., Stephanidis, C.: Intelligent environments for all: a path towards technology-enhanced human well-being. Univ. Access Inf. Soc. **21**(2), 437–456 (2022)
13. Burzagli, L., Emiliani, P.L.: Implementation of applications in an ambient intelligence environment: a structured approach. In: Miesenberger, K., Fels, D., Archambault, D., Peňáz, P., Zagler, W. (eds.) Computers Helping People with Special Needs. ICCHP 2014. LNCS, vol. 8548, pp. 11–18. Springer, Cham (2014)

Artificial Intelligence Support to the Accessibility to the Environment

Laura Burzagli[1]($\boxtimes$), Pier Luigi Emiliani[1], and Simone Naldini[2]

[1] CNR IFAC, Via Madonna del Piano 10, Sesto F.no, Firenze, Italy
l.burzagli@ifac.cnr.it
[2] MATHEMA, Via Torcicoda 29, Firenze, Italy

Abstract. ICT technology and Artificial Intelligence can be used to facilitate people's daily activities, including elderly people and/or people with activity limitations. One of the activities classified by WHO ICF for people's well-being is mobility, including pedestrian mobility. The paper analyzes the problem of supporting mobility and describes an application developed at IFAC to propose to people the paths suitable for their abilities, to reach points of interest in the area where the user is headed, with main reference to old people.

Keywords: Mobility · Accessibility · Artificial Intelligence

1 Introduction

According to the current definition an accessible environment [1] is a space where all the necessary services are available [2], and it is possible to move where they are placed, independently from limitations of activities of people. Therefore, accessibility is not only a problem of architectural barriers, but also of the possibility of knowing what is around and to be guided to the site of interest through a suitable path. This is currently made possible by the development of the smart environment technologies, which include artificial intelligent components to collect data, to reason about needs and to learn from the person's behavior. This approach is in accord with the attitude of all international organizations as the UN and WHO [3], which assert that technology must be used to support all people during their entire life, and not only people who have activity limitations. In the paper a particular reference will be made to old people due to the present interest at the international level due to the increasing number of this component in the present societies.

2 Mobility and Accessible Environments

In planning living spaces (urban planning) accessibility is defined as "the potential for interaction", i.e. the potential of the environment to provide services to people, while mobility is defined as "the potential for movement", i.e. the potential of people to move to points of interest (PoIs), i.e. the places where the services are available [4]. From the perspective of mobility, this means that it is necessary to guarantee physical accessibility, i.e., absence of physical obstacles (e.g., stairs). Consequently, the availability and efficiency of personalized information services, capable of advising people about the availability of services and guiding them in the external environment, affects the person's autonomy level. For example, paths on uneven ground are particularly dangerous for a lame person, while paths not known in advance or not signaled with tactile or sound aids are dangerous for a person with vision problems.

Mobility is important for all people. In the description of human activities, as pointed out previously, the ICF classification (International classification of functioning disabilities and health) [5] dedicates a specific chapter of the ontology of human activities to "Activities and Participation". The specific section related to mobility exhibits an accurate and extensive description ranging from the ability to change the position of the body (d410-d429), to that of walking to move from one place to another, up to the use of means of transport (d470) or the ability to move objects from one place to another. In a narrow sense, mobility can be interpreted as one of the person's abilities, i.e., the ability to move the various parts of the body, or to move it from one place to another. From a broad perspective, mobility also represents the support for conducting daily activities, such as reaching healthcare places, purchasing goods, cultivating social relationships, or even dedicating to leisure activities, without the necessity of mediation by the means of communication. The possibility of conducting these activities substantially affects the person's level of autonomy, which depends on several factors: the person's physical and mental condition, the characteristics of the physical environment where she lives and last, but not least, the knowledge of the environment.

Pedestrian mobility plays an even more key role because it addresses the wider pool of people, including those, who see the possibility of using means of transport diminishing over time, Appropriate management of this activity assumes even greater importance if the reference group is elderly people. In fact, over the years there is a reduction in the length of the person's journeys. The difficulty of using means of transport, both public, such as buses, trains, or planes, and private, such as cars or taxis, is increasing. This implies that older people reduce the area of their movements, preferably in the area around their homes. The presence of services in this area, therefore, becomes fundamental for the autonomy of the person who can reach them without the aid of means of transport, but simply by walking. It increases the importance of the presence of clinics, pharmacies, gardens, shops, and in any case of all the services required by daily life in this reduced space.

Studies about mobility of old people are available [6], and the main characteristics as their key travel patterns, their travel mode preferences, the possibility of transport access, infrastructure solutions, mode choice model have been clarified. It appears that most people prefer to age in their houses, even though it may have some disadvantages such as loneliness and social isolation. Most of their trip destinations are at short distance and in the time interval between 9.30 a.m. to 3 p.m. The main purposes are shopping, health care, voluntary activities, pick-up and drop-off of children, banks, post office, and chemist. Positive attitudes for social purposes are present for religious places, restaurants, and hairdressers.

The investigations have shown that when old people need to move on longest distance, for short trips they prefer driving, when possible, even if there are concerns about congestion of traffic, road safety, and navigational problems. The main problems with public transport are the identification of the services, walking to the stop, boarding, finding a seat, deciding where to descend, coping with interchanges. As a summary, the links are manageable if they are accessible, coherent, compatible, and continuous. Possible improvements are: ticketing and fare concessions, special public services, improvement of vehicles, improvement of shops, elderly housing planning, and alternative transport. The main barriers are the lack of railings at ramps, steps, gaps, and lack of wheelchair slopes.

3   AI Contribution to Mobility Support Applications

It is evident that, due to the use of ICT and information technology, the entire society is undergoing a transformation into an environment where people are surrounded by interconnected intelligent objects. In the field of support for people, especially elderly or disabled people, Artificial Intelligence could be in the future the controlling element of support ecosystems, which, even without the need for specific Assistive Technology, can favor the emergence of complex applications for the well-being of people. For example, in mobility applications AI can be used to construct and manage the profile of the user; to monitor her mood (e.g., voice analysis); to collect and organize information about the route (e.g., from the perspective of a pedestrian); to suggest itineraries and to discuss with the user about different possible itineraries.

Therefore, new possibilities of proposing reasonable solutions for support to mobility can be obtained introducing Artificial Intelligence in the system in a control component including two main blocks: a knowledge base and a reasoning system [7]. The knowledge base needs to contain information about:

- The activities to be conducted in the environment (e.g., shopping or walking in a park).
- The abilities necessary to conduct the possible activities.
- The available technologies, which can be used to support the walking person.
- Their interoperability issues, i.e., interfaces and communication protocols.
- The user profiles: abilities of individual users and their requirements and preferences.
- The interaction issues: available interaction devices and modalities.

The implementation, maintenance and run-time use of the system must be conducted under the control of a reasoning system (intelligence in the environment) capable of:

- Enriching the knowledge base, by acquiring and integrating information received in a formal representation (rule-based AI) and/or extracting it (machine learning) from informal information (for example, from a natural language text).
- Using the information in the knowledge base to adapt, in an unobtrusive and anticipatory way, the functionalities made available in the interfaces.
- Learning from usage to refine the knowledge base, introducing the necessary updates about PoIs and the abilities of people. This must be possible also in real time, due to the possible variations of abilities, e.g., due to fatigue.

- Evolving the functionalities of the application according to the evolution of technology.
- Suggesting to the user alternative suitable means of interaction.

It is necessary to consider the fact that the process of the creation of paths does not consist in obtaining the shortest path between two points or nodes, but of generating many paths that can be used by the neural network to choose the most suitable to the user. When these paths are available it is necessary to examine them considering the user profile. Following the "human in the loop" approach, the end user is placed at the center of the entire system. All decisions and proposals coming from the system must be calibrated according to the individual user who is requesting them. The strength of the whole application lies in the possibility of implementing a dynamic system capable of customizing the proposals not only based on data from the outside world but based on the user's profile. Profile attributes are not equally important at all levels. These have been divided into two separate areas. The first is the level of physical attributes, including all data relating to the user's psychophysical health, considering also mild cognitive problems: They are:

- Motor deficits – major difficulties in walking or even problems in climbing uphill or covering stretches of bumpy roads.
- Visual impairment - Problems identifying objects or road signs, or oncoming cars on the road.
- Health deficit: health problems that can affect walking (heart problems, blood pressure…).
- Cognitive impairment: difficulties interacting with the surrounding world.

However, data about psychophysical health are not the only attributes that must be considered. There are also the personal preferences of individual users, which do not directly impact a person's health, but rather their mood or quality of life (well-being). In this category of characteristics, the following have been selected:

- Love of nature: preference to pass through parks or near public green areas.
- Sociability: preference to spend time with other people, in meeting places or places of aggregation, or to walk on uncrowded roads.
- Shopping: in a broad sense, preference to walk in places with shops or markets.
- Services: personal services such as banks, post offices, pharmacies ….

4   Support System

The components necessary for the development of a system to support accessibility are (Fig. 1):

- An interaction block incorporating the user profile and the user interfaces to introduce requests and comments about the proposals.
- A communication component collecting and storing information about the environment.
- A block for a possible interaction with a community of users and/or supporting people.
- A control element, based on AI, able to reason about the situation and learn from the interaction and the additional information made available.

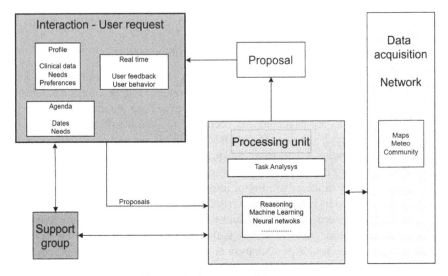

Fig. 1. Block diagram of the system

4.1 Interaction Block

From the perspective of the user the interaction unit is the core of the system. It is the interface, where the user, using a keyboard and a screen, or interacting with voice, can communicate its needs. For example, she can tell the system that she needs to buy vegetables or visit a pharmacy.

The user profile in the interaction block is the starting point for being able to adapt any suggestion about a service and/or place to access to any user. The interaction block must be able to consider:

- The static profile of the user (including her limitation of activities if present).
- Her preferences (e.g., she could prefer a longer walk, if along the path toward the PoI satisfying her needs, she can walk through a park or an environment where a set of shops of interest are located).
- Her real time emotions as made available by sensors.

The block must be able to present suggestions to the user and to adapt them according to the reaction of the user herself and to the real time evolution of the situation.

Suggestions may be presented to the user in different forms. If she is able to take advantage of it, a graphic representation can be used, as presented in Fig. 2, and used as a choice in the implemented prototype. Using it the user can easily have an intuitive idea of the possible paths, with the perception of the distances, the areas to be crossed and the existing difficulties (represented by the distinct colors of the paths on the map).

Of course, such a presentation is only offered if the user is described in her profile as able, in principle, to use it. However, the system must monitor the user's behavior, and if after a reasonable interval, it does not receive any reaction, it is allowed to try other forms of interaction. So, it must be able to observe not only her reactions, but also her behavior.

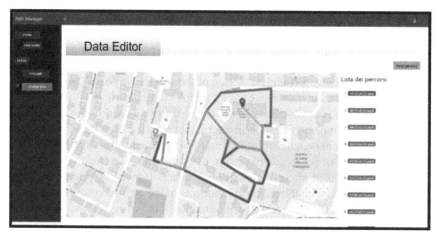

Fig. 2. A representation of the paths.

The interaction block consists of several workspaces. The first is dedicated to the user's profile, where all the data is collected that will then be passed to the system to compose the vector of the user's characteristics. Through the interface, it is possible to select dis/abilities and upgrade them when necessary. When a person uses this possibility, the system reaction helps the user to effectively assess the neural network's reaction preferences of the subject who is using the platform.

Once the profile of the user has been set, it is possible to proceed with the calculation of the routes: through the interface it is possible to set two points, one at the start (green marker) and one at the end (red marker), and the system takes care autonomously of the following actions:

- Transfer of information to the neural network.
- Construction of the routes.
- Transfer to the interface of the data relating to the route suggested by the neural network.
- Represent routes on the interface map.

4.2 Data Acquisition Component

The communication and storage components are supposed to collect information about the structure of the environment (points of interests, barriers, public services) and its possible real time situation (e.g., a traffic jam could slow down the public services).

Sources of information are the Open Data of Municipalities or Metropolitan Cities, which provide users with the possibility of accessing data directly from their site. The provided data is often in Excel/CSV format or in GIS formats, which therefore must be converted before being used by the described application. This data is subject to variable updates, based on the availability of the source: in some cases, the data is updated on an annual basis, in others, they do not have a clear updating plan.

It is evident that other sources are all online services that provide maps and manage cartographic data, such as OpenStreetMap [8], Bing Maps, Google Maps, MapQuest, Here WeGo, Apple Maps, Yandex Maps. From this perspective it is important to consider that important applications as Google Map do not make available all information necessary for constructing a complete picture of the services available and the state of the itineraries to reach them if someone has a particular limitation in mobility. Moreover, when the information is available (as in the OpenStreetMap used in the implemented prototype), it is not simple to extract it in a form that makes it easy the integration into the system. The dynamic nature of online platforms guarantees an almost continuous updating of the data, but not its completeness: often the data is limited to the geographical position of a point of interest without other details (timetable, price, goods sold, etc.).Therefore, reasoning and learning components of the control system must be also able not only to look for the necessary information, but, when relevant, extract and restructure it according to format used in the system.

Two additional information components must be considered for the implementation of a useful application. The first is the ability to access weather information that is of fundamental importance to some users. The second is the ability to interact with other people in the environment. For example, it can be important to contact people who live in the place the user wants to reach to find out the situation at that precise moment. It can also be convenient to contact a store to find out if a product is available or if the queue is not too long. People can be able to contribute to the fill the data acquisition system with information about changes of the situation of PoIs in the environment and the state of the paths to reach them.

When convenient, the user can introduce additional information on the map with the interface shown in Fig. 3.

Fig. 3. User interface for introduction of information on the map

4.3 Community of Users – Support Group

Another key component of individual mobility is that in real situations it is presently possible that communities of volunteers and/or relatives and friends are available to support people when they plan to move around. Therefore, the system needs an additional set of interfaces through which they can have access to the suggestions of the system and intervene if they consider it necessary. The suggestions of the control AI system will consider the requests of the user, her comments and the information and comments produced by the support people.

The system for generating itinerary proposals (all the possible ones) can consider two possibilities: that the user is able to move on her own or that she needs support from the community. In both cases, the system must consider all viable options, evaluating their characteristics and selecting those possible according to the user's characteristics and preferences. If community intervention is required, the system must access information about people available to give support and select the possible solutions according to the profile of the user and the availability and characteristics of the people presently available for support.

4.4 Control

The AI-based control block is obviously the heart of the entire system, where the memorized information is used, and proposals are produced. During its use it must be able to produce suggestion by reasoning about the requests of the user considering: the knowledge of their physical and intellectual abilities, their habits and preferences about different in principle suitable services and routes, the comments of supporting people, and the continuously varying situation of the environment. Moreover, it is supposed to learn by observing the behavior of the user, to produce variations of information about habits and preferences. When not in use it must check the situation in the environment through the analysis of maps and, for example, of news from municipalities referring to works in the streets, possible public events and so on. It is evident the increase of complexity of AI services that must put together information about a person and/or the environmental situation, advise about the way of solving a specific problem, offer possibilities of visiting places that appear of possible interest according to previous exits, and guide actions considering the average behavior of people in similar situations.

The control block is directly connected to the interface that is continuously transferring data about users and their requests, receiving requests of itineraries, and suggesting useful solutions. The user can react to the proposals by accepting them or offering comments about the reason why she is not satisfied.

The ordering and proposal of a particular path is delegated to the recommendation system, which relies on a neural network implemented in Python, using the Tensorflow framework [9]. The system takes all the data available as input, and then outputs the list of paths sorted by the results of the neural network.

5   Experimental Implementation

A first prototype has been implemented in IFAC for the suggestion of pedestrian paths. The task is complex due to the variety of situations from a starting point to an arrival point: e.g., sidewalks on both sides of a road, state of the sidewalk, existing pedestrian crossings, routes within public parks (when reported), available services along the path and so on. The system offers the user three different levels of interface to be used in different situations: the first for the input of geographical data (where the user is presently located), the second for introduction of user data (she has a pain in the back), the third, based on an AI reinforcement learning approach, for input on the map of the required arrival point. The output is an ordered list of the possible paths, based on the user's characteristics. When selected from the list, the route is activated on the map.

The application was implemented on two machines of IFAC-CNR: one in the IFAC laboratory, which was entrusted with the development, and the online server AMI (also within IFAC), on which the last version open to the public was made available. In addition to the algorithmic and decision-making components, the interfaces dedicated to the application were also created, which served both as a basis for conducting the tests and better evaluating the results, and as a demonstrator of the state of the work.

Both machines have been aligned from the point of view of software requirements: in particular, particular attention has been devoted to the management of the versions of Python [10] installed on the machines. This is because many packages used in the execution of the algorithms (path calculation and Neural Network) require specific versions and development environments, otherwise stability, correct functionality or, in some cases, the installation of the packages is precluded. Now both machines have working environments set to Python version 3.6, which guarantees the best compatibility on all the packages used.

The data used during the execution of the application are based on a relational database MySQL [11], which can be directly queried by the developed algorithms.

6   Conclusions

Artificial intelligence applications seem in principle the most promising suggestion for the implementation of applications in supporting people, all people not only people with limitations of activities, in conducting activities in emerging technological society. This is since many applications address complex tasks and need the use and cooperation of complex components. With reference to environmental accessibility, according to the present definition, the problem is not the identification of a path without obstacles for a person who moves in a wheelchair, but to construct a representation of the environment in which the person must move and identify a route that is satisfactory for her needs and preferences.

Finally, it must be considered that for the approval of a real adoption of a system like the one proposed, problems of ethics and of compatibility with existing legislation must be considered.

References

1. Hansen, W.G.: How accessibility shapes land use. J. Am. Inst. Plann. **25**(2), 73–76 (1959)
2. Burzagli, L.: Smart cities: a new relationship between people and technologies. In: Monteriù, A., Freddi, A., Longhi, S. (eds.) Ambient Assisted Living. ForItAAL 2019. LNCS, vol. 725, pp 161–166. Springer, Cham (2021). https://doi.org/10.1007/978-3-030-63107-9_12
3. UN Decade of Healthy Ageing: Plan of Action 2021–2030. UN (2020)
4. Handy, S.: Is accessibility an idea whose time has finally come? Transp. Res. Part D: Transp. Environ. **83**, 1–6 (2020)
5. WHO: ICF International Classification of Functioning, Disability and Health. World Health Organization, Geneva (2001)
6. Kaniz, F.: Elderly sustainable mobility: scientific paper review. Sustainability **12**, 1–17 (2020)
7. Burzagli, L., Emiliani, P.L.: Structured knowledge: a basic aspect for efficient user applications. In: Stephanidis, C., Antona, M. (eds.) Universal Access in Human-Computer Interaction. Design and Development Methods for Universal Access. UAHCI 2014. LNCS, vol. 8513, pp. 11–18. Springer, Cham (2014). https://doi.org/10.1007/978-3-319-07437-5_2
8. OPEN STREET MAP Home Page. https://www.openstreetmap.org/. Accessed 31 Jan 2024
9. Abadi, M., et al.: TensorFlow: large-scale machine learning on heterogeneous systems, 2015. http://tensorflow.org. Accessed 31 Jan 2024
10. Python Homepage. https://www.python.org/. Accessed 31 Jan 2024
11. MySQL Homepage. https://www.mysql.com. Accessed 31 Jan 2024

Model Based Control System for Outdoor Swimming Pools

Cristiano Cabrita[1,2(✉)], Jailson Carvalho[1], Jânio Monteiro[1,2], Armando Inverno[1], and Miguel Oliveira[1]

[1] ISE, Universidade do Algarve, Algarve, Portugal
ccabrita@ualg.pt
[2] CISCA, Universidade do Algarve, Algarve, Portugal

Abstract. Swimming pools are closely associated to leisure activities, especially in touristic areas, and both indoor and outdoor swimming pools can be found worldwide in large quantities. With their fast growth, an increasing stress has been also placed on both energy and water resources they require to operate. In this scope renewable energy sources, especially those that use sun's radiation are of paramount importance. Exploring alternative, green and sustainable energy sources to replace traditional sources has become one of the main points in the European Union's actions over the last decade. In this context, this paper proposes a control approach where smart decision is made based on predictions made by models representing sustainable thermal systems (local renewable energy source) and on information gathered from an array of sensors. The aim is to regulate the water temperature of an outdoor swimming pool. The information obtained from both environmental variables and from the modelling of sub-systems internal transfer function, is then combined with an optimization framework which goal is to ultimately, reduce the human intervention in the swimming pool maintenance and provide resource savings in terms of financial costs to the final user but also in terms of natural resources, contributing to environmental sustainability. The research work is developed within the scope of the Ecopool+++ project: Innovative heated pools with reduced thermal losses with the integration of SMART energy and water management systems.

Keywords: Energy Efficiency · Outdoor Swimming Pools · Renewable Energy Sources · Thermal Systems · Model Predictive Control

1 Introduction

According to US Census Bureau [1] swimming is the fourth most popular sports activity in the United States and a good way to get regular aerobic physical activity. Besides sports and health benefits, swimming pools are also closely related to leisure activities, especially in tourist areas [2]. For these main reasons, both indoor and outdoor swimming pools can be found worldwide, and as stated in [3], statistics indicate that about 140 million people swim in Europe (roughly 20% of the population) for a universe of 13 million swimming pools on a global level. Approximately 29% of these in Europe and

59% in North America, with the rest of the world registering about 12% of the whole world.

The European Union and its national governments have set clear objectives to guide European environmental policy up to 2020 and a longer-term vision (for the next 30 years). Specific research programs, legislation and funding intend to protect, conserve and enhance the European Union's (EU) natural capital, to transform it into a green, competitive, low-carbon and resource-efficient economy. These guidelines aim at protecting European citizens from pressures and risks to health and promoting well-being related to the environment.

In this context, a significant portion of research is dedicated to exploring the usage of wind power, biomass and solar power for replacing conventional energy sources, as they pose many advantages such as reduced environmental impacts and are envisaged as a means to comply to European and global environmental norms [4].

Indeed, there is an increasing interest on decarbonisation of the electricity generation with special focus on the penetration of Renewable Energy Resources (RES).

Taking into consideration the power consumption data, supplied by Portuguese statistics portal Pordata [5], in Portugal and during the 2022 year, the energy consumption corresponded to a total of 21,315 thousand of toe (Tons of Oil Equivalent), among which 6,557 thousand of toe were generated from renewable energy sources. These latter figures identify Portugal as one of the European countries where the effective penetration of renewable energy is significant (as it is responsible for 30.0% of the overall energy consumption) with a higher impact when compared with the average value of 11.7% in the EU. Therefore, demand for new sources of flexibility and growing recognition of the multi-energy nature of regions are increasing interest in the interaction between energy sectors, like electricity, heating/cooling and gas and in the significant amount of flexibility supported by heating systems [6, 7].

The efficiency of solar energy depends on the availability and intensity of solar radiation. In an urban environment, especially, in large cities the use of solar energy has been confronted with many obstacles as a result of neighboring tall buildings. Thus, air-source heat pumps are widely used in this situation to supply heat to outdoor swimming pools. Further, most of the existing swimming pools are largely inefficient due to water and heat losses, having a considerable impact on the associated environmental footprint. At this level, in [8] the average environmental impact of a residential swimming pool in the state of Arizona (USA) and other warmer regions is calculated highlighting an energy footprint ranging from 2400 to 2800 kWh/year, a water footprint of as high as 185 m^3/year and 1400 kg $\pm$ 50 kg of CO_2e/year.

Factors such as 1) evaporation, 2) radiation to the sky; 3) convection close to the surface of the water and 4) and convection through the walls and floor to the ground are closely related to the high energy consumption demand for heating outdoor swimming pools. The water of the pools is an excellent medium for the accumulation of heat, so when the solar radiation is high, particularly in the summer months, the conditions for its use improve. However, outside these periods, environmental conditions tend to cause lower gains of free heat and simultaneously greater thermal losses.

The most common way of using solar power is to convert sunlight into heat energy to produce hot water, using solar thermal collectors. In such case, the basic mechanism uses the incident solar radiation for generating heat as it converts the irradiated energy into thermal energy. There are many different applications where solar heat energy can be used, such as domestic water-heating systems, pool-heaters, and space-heating systems [7].

The work presented by Lam [9] proposes a new heating system for outdoor swimming pools that integrates an air-source heat pump (for heat supply), and a phase change material (PCM) storage tank (for heat storage). Also, in [10] a PCM integrated heating system for outdoor swimming is studied. The results show that compared with traditional heating system operational cost can be reduced in nearly 85%.

In this scope, this paper proposes a new scheme to increase and control a swimming pool's water temperature using sustainable thermal systems (local renewable sources generation devices). The aim of the control system is to coordinate the functioning of a set of thermal energy sources and thermal storage, to adjust the water temperature of outdoor swimming pools according with the user requirements. It relies on information gathered from an array of sensors. The information (environmental variables and sub-systems internal transfer function modelling) is then combined with an optimization framework which goal is to ultimately, reduce the requirements for human intervention in the swimming pool maintenance and provide resource savings for the final user in terms of financial and natural resources, contributing to environmental sustainability.

The system implemented goes way beyond traditional systems [9–12] where typically only efficiency is addressed and the number of systems is small (solar and gas based thermal systems).

In the present work we address the development of methods for system identification and future time-based forecasting, using machine learning methods, and employ optimization based in simulated data, to control the water temperature in the swimming pool's tank. The control of the water temperature is set according to a setpoints as specified by the user.

The remainder of this work has the following structure. A description on the problem is made in Sect. 2. Section 3 presents a background theory on model based predictive control and systems identification. Section 4 introduces the functionalities and layout of the SMART platform and, Sect. 5 presents the results with real data scenarios. Finally, Sect. 6 draws results and presents perspectives on future work.

2 Problem Formulation

In its simplest description, the system here considered (see Fig. 1) is composed of the main water tank (Swimming Pool), the water filtering system and several renewable energy thermal sub-systems, which include: (1) Phase Change Material (PCM) accumulator, (2) solar collectors (SC), (3) Floor/soil Heat collectors (FHC), and (4) Geothermal accumulator or Soil Heat exchanger. The PCM circuit has no direct circulation of pool water and so an additional circuit was added which includes its reservoir and a heat exchanger. To perform the control a set of water pumps are activated and deactivated, which then promote the water flow at a constant rate and preestablished direction regarding the retention valves setup.

The various thermal sub-systems are connected by one or several ducts, three water pumps, flowmeters and pressure retention valves. While pump 1 is responsible for pumping water through the PCM exchanger secondary circuit and pump 2 forces water to run through the solar collectors, pump 3 is dedicated to the PCM primary circuit.

Given the fact that the main goal is to implement a water temperature control strategy, it is obvious that the system is highly complex because of: (1) the multitude of systems (i.e., high number of inputs to the plant – the swimming pool) and (2) the external factors such as climate that determine the system response in many different ways. As such, for the control strategy the authors considered that the inclusion of weather variables is recommended as long as they can in some way be foreseen or predicted.

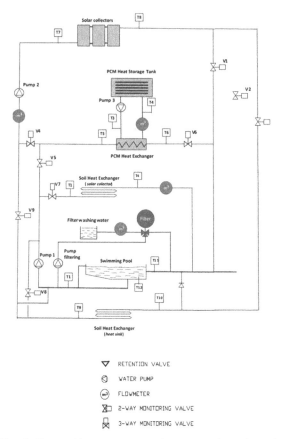

Fig. 1. Renewable energy system interconnection schematic

Due to the multitude of sub-systems, several scenarios of operation (or *setups*) can be considered during the system operation. For example, to make the water circulate through the solar collectors and the Pool, the opening of valves V_1 and V_9 is obligatory, as it makes pump 2 to operate. A second scenario, which involves holding both V_1 and V_7 valves open, is when the water circulation is required simultaneously at the solar collector and at the Soil Heat exchanger. Flow into the duct system of the Soil Heat Exchanger sub-system, requires having both the primary and secondary circuits from the PCM heat exchanger "active", i.e., not only pump3 must be on but valves V_5 and V_6 have to remain open.

Since the goal is to regulate the water temperature at the Pool, readings of the sensors T_i ($i = 1...10$) allow monitoring the temperature in each of the sub-systems and provide additional information to allow the control mechanism to decide which setup is the most effective at a given moment.

3   Model Based Predictive Control

In scenarios where the right conditions are met, the application of predictive control makes it possible to anticipate the control action in advance, taking into account the correct identification of the system and, consequently, the model's ability to predict the system's operation for future instants. In its typical approach, the methodology embraces the concept of optimization by defining the effective control input value (u) to be applied to the system (see Fig. 2).

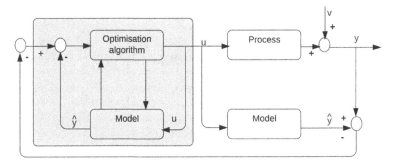

Fig. 2. Flow diagram for Model Predictive Control

As shown in Fig. 3, and using the past N_e sampled data an estimation of the best model is carried out. The model is then used to provide a sequence of control signals to the system for the prediction horizon, or Np future steps.

Using the optimizer (based on evolution and natural selection for example) a solution can be determined among a set of alternatives that best satisfy the restrictions imposed and, in the end, selecting the best one.

It should be noted that renewable sources may not provide immediate availability of the required control signals so an alternative approach must be adopted instead.

From the standpoint of optimal control the present system features some drawbacks. (1) each and every sub-system features slow *input-output* responses, and (2) limited range of inlet water temperature into the Pool (i.e., though water flow regulation is possible, water temperature regulation is not). In this regard, the generalized predictive control from Fig. 3 is the basis for a second stage of the proposed control scheme which resembles to a task scheduling problem. That said, each sub-thermal system will be

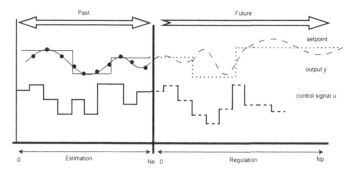

Fig. 3. System response based on generalized model predictive control

identified with a particular response (or a control setup) and the aim is to find the best time slot where to place each of the setups.

A genetic algorithm (GA) is used as an optimizer to help determine the best control scenarios time sequence for a pre-defined prediction horizon. The best sequence is found if the system output returns the closest response to the desired Pool water temperature defined as setpoint.

Figure 5 shows the flow diagram illustrative of this methodology (Fig. 4).

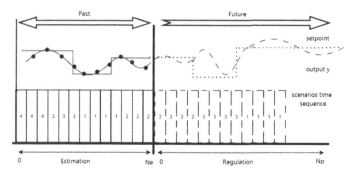

Fig. 4. Time diagram representation of the proposed approach

Under the aforementioned conditions the control strategy to adopt must consider modelling each of the sub-systems. The next sub-section will give insight into systems identification.

3.1 Systems Identification

Systems identification concerns to finding the appropriate model for a "real" system. This includes finding the appropriate inputs and estimating the appropriate parameters values that define the model. If seen as a black-box, the model application becomes simple and provides alternative control techniques in order to identify the best control signal to apply at the input of the system.

The dynamic system features the *inputs,j* which are commonly associated with the external signals and can be manipulated by the observer and, the *Disturbances* which correspond to signals which may not be measured. Then, there are the *outputs* of particular interest to the observer. Figure 5 illustrates the relations between the inputs, disturbances and outputs of a typical dynamical system.

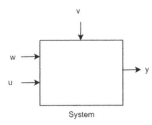

Fig. 5. System with output *y*, input(s) *u*, measured disturbance *w* and unmeasured disturbance *v* (adapted from [13]).

A mathematical formulation for a dynamical system, where the next sample for the future output value is related to the past inputs and external disturbances is:

$$y(t) = f(y(t-1), y(t-2), \ldots y(t-n), u(t-1), u(t-2), \ldots$$

$$\ldots u(t-m), w, v) \tag{1}$$

In the specific case of this work, systems identification can be performed through the analysis of time-series records for each of the scenarios/setups previously mentioned. Appropriate estimation algorithms help define a ARMA (Auto-Regressive-Moving-Average), ARIMA (Auto-Regressive-Integrated - Moving-Average), or SARIMA (Seasonal ARIMA with exogenous inputs) models.

The choice of an autoregressive model depends on the compromise between the simplicity of the model and the properties of a time series. Under a stationary time series (i.e., if its properties are not affected by a change in the time source) the models chosen are normally the Autoregressive with Exogenous Input (ARX) and/or the Autoregressive Moving Average with Exogenous Input (ARMAX) [14]. ARMAX is more complex than ARX due to the fact that it has the ability to deal with stationary time series whose error regression is a linear combination. If a time series is non-stationary, the Autoregressive Integrated Moving Average with exogenous input (ARIMAX) and/or the Seasonal Autoregressive Integrated Moving Average with exogenous input (SARIMAX) model can be used. Both models, ARIMAX and SARIMAX, are capable of handling both stationary and non-stationary series. However, if the time series has seasonal elements, the best option may be SARIMAX.

In [15], an analysis was made to forecast load demand in the context of smart grids, using ARX, Artificial Neural Networks (ANN) and Artificial Neural Networks optimized by Genetic Algorithm (ANN-GA). In this same analysis, the ARX presented lower execution time and a higher mean absolute percentage error when compared to the ANN and ANN-GA solutions.

In [16], a hybrid model was developed to predict electricity demand as a function of outdoor air temperature. It then was compared with the ARMAX model. Despite the good performance of both, ARMAX presented higher forecast errors than the hybrid model.

In the current work, it was found that the modelling the system using ARMAX produced acceptable results.

Autoregressive Moving Average with Exogenous Input (ARMAX) includes the moving average component. ARMAX modelling is, again, applied when a time series has regression characteristics, and the error is a linear combination [17]. The ARMAX model is ruled by the following equations:

$$\phi(L)y(t) = \sum_{i=1}^{n} \beta_i(L)u_i(t) + \psi(L)e(t) \tag{2}$$

with

$$\phi(L) = 1 + \phi_1 L^{-1} + \cdots + \phi_p L^{-p} \tag{3}$$

$$\beta_i(L) = \beta_{i1} + \beta_{i2}L^{-1} + \cdots + \beta_{ip}L^{-p+1} \tag{4}$$

$$\psi(L) = 1 + \psi_1 L^{-1} + \cdots + \psi_q L^{-q} \tag{5}$$

where

- $\psi(L)$ is the *moving average* component;
- q is the order for the *moving average* component;

  and,

$$\phi_t = \left[\phi_1, \phi_2, \ldots, \phi_p\right]^T \tag{6}$$

$$y_t = \left[y(t-1), y(t-2), \ldots, y(t-p)\right], \tag{7}$$

The coefficients of the ϕ, β and ψ polynomials are defined by Eqs. 9–11, and estimated using the CSS-MLE method.

3.2 System Modelling

One aspect that makes useful using a *smart* system is the fact that such a system incorporates the ability to make a prediction into a specified time step into the future depending on the actuation of the thermal system in action. In this sense we assume that the variables influencing the model parameters are known (predictable and available) for the prediction horizon of the controlling scheme.

When possible simulation data can be advantageous for making preliminary testing with the models, and so the TRNSYS 18.0 [18] simulation tool was applied for employing the mathematical models for some of the thermal sub-systems that comprise the global system.

In a second stage every sub-system is employed at a local testbed, the modelling approach requires using sampled data (at a specified sampling period.) to perform model identification.

The system identification procedure carried on this work is summarized by algorithm 1. The goal is to find an ARMAX model for each one of the sub-thermal systems.

Algorithm 1: System modelling

Input: a matrix of the past sampled data for the n_inp input (includes three weather variables, wind velocity, ambient temperature, relative humidity) and the one output sampled data, size of the training data (Train_size), size of the testing data (Test_size)   **Output:** the best representation of the system according to its forecasting performance on forecasting the testing data (Best_model)

Generate a set of N ARMAX models with randomly chosen polynomials order
 For each ARMAX model
   Estimate the polynomial parameters using the Maximum-LikeLihood-Estimator (MLE)
   Calculate the Sum-of-Squared-Error (SSE) and R^2 on the training data.
   Calculate the prediction values over the testing data
   Calculate MSE value for the predicted values (MSE_predict)
 Best_model = the model with the lowest MSE_predict
 return Best_model

4   SMART Platform

A remote access is provided to the user allowing the interaction with the proposed system. It gives the user the ability to indirectly control some of the actuating devices, by only setting the desired temperature. In this platform the user has also the ability to observe the water temperature within a time span, the water flow rate, estimate power consumption and the operational status of the electrical devices of the system.

As can be seen in Fig. 6 the SMART platform is composed of several components. On one end, there is the *Cloud Server*, which includes the online services supplied by OpenWeather® and, an open source web-application dedicated to data logging, processing, and visualization, EmonCMS [19]. Running as a standalone application, the smart control system (or optimizer) makes up the decisions relative to the control steps undertaken. Note that its success depends on retrieving forecast weather variables in steps of one hour into the prediction horizon. These forecasts are collected through API requests over to the server (located at https://openweathermap.org/api). The data retrieved includes the humidity, wind speed and ambient temperature. These variables are used as inputs to the swimming pool's tank model and were chosen after preliminary analysis on the simulated data.

Additionally, a local controller acts as a core unit which is also configured as a Modbus Master and is responsible for: (1) providing fresh data for updating the *Cloud Server*, (2) resolving requests made by the HMI interface, namely access control, system parameters customization, and (3) accessing the sensors and actuators for periodic reading of values referring to, for example, water flow, water temperature, water pressure, and water level in different parts of the system.

The local controller is running in *Python*, and uses the HTTP protocol as a uniform interface for handling Web resources among different platforms.

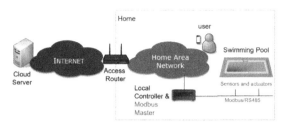

Fig. 6. The SMART Platform

4.1 SMartAPP

As a part of the SMART platform (see section ahead), the SMartAPP is the interface responsible for the interaction of the user with the system. The HMI interface is illustrated in **Error! Reference source not found.** Where the user can carry most operations. Upon authentication, the user is given the choice for consulting instantaneous or historical data, define whether the control system switches to manual or remains in automatic mode, or even define the control parameters such as water temperature setpoint.

In summary, the HMI presents the user with the following operations (see Fig. 7):

– Register or login
– Consulting real-time data from the pool system
– Consulting real-time as recorded in the IoT platform/server
– View real time data within a range of time instants. This includes temperature, rates, time of operation, etc.
– Alarm history with logs related to unexpected abnormal operation in the system, for example, hydraulic overheating or low water pressure.
– System Logout

The SmartAPP is based on the REST (REpresentation State Transfer) software architectural style which is commonly used for applications in the World Wide Web. This architectural style is simplified by Fig. 8

The main point for having chosen this architecture is related to its simplicity, scalability and stateless [20] (Fig. 9).

Every communication is processed on a server-client architecture based on the HTTP protocol to uphold requests served by *Flask* Web services coded in Python computing language and executed in a machine that lodges the Server & API component. The API implemented for this *webservice* are:

- /read_plc. This API activates a ModBus/IP connection to the local programmable controller and return back to the client (or *browser*) the current data saved temporarily in memory. Therefore, it allows the user to access and view pool information in real time.
- /read_emcms. This API uses the HTTP protocol to connect through WebApi to the IoT remoteServer based on the CloudServer (Fig. 5) and requests the latest real-time data available at the IoT platform. It thus, allows the user to view information instantly on the IoT platform

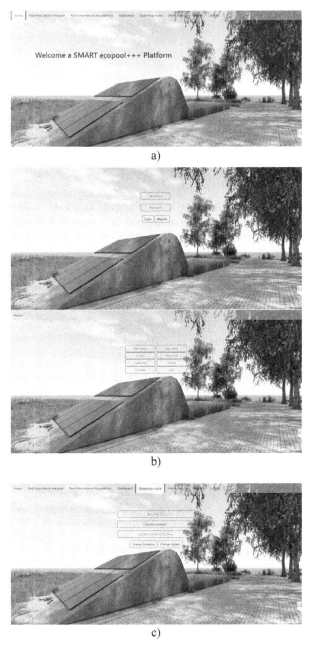

Fig. 7. Example of the HMI interface. a) the *sign in* and *register* pane, b) the main menu pane. c) specification of control parameters

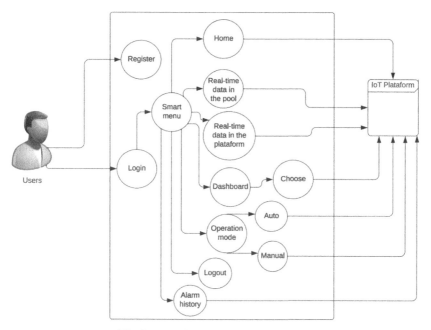

Fig. 8. HMI flow chart with user (client)

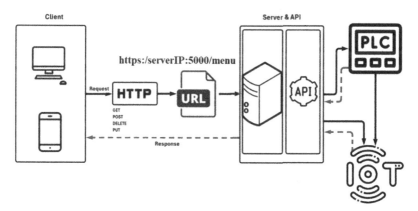

Fig. 9. REST architecture based SmartAPP flow chart

- /register: captures personal and login security information, through a web page form which allows new users to sign in on the platform.
- /dashboard. After validating the current user's access this API allows the user to view graphs with information within a time range, such as the day, week, month and year, upon request.
- /operation_mode. This API delegates on the HMI core the possibility to run either the control Allows the user to choose the operating mode, which can be manual or automatic

- /login: Allows the user to access the platform

Simulation Tests and Results

In the previous section, the remote access and operation guidelines were presented. Though interaction between the user and HMI, the user has the ability to intervene directly with some of the actuating devices by only adjusting the desired temperature.

Two different exterior pool water temperature control approaches are implemented and used to show and assess the system inter-operability. These are:

1. no form of control is performed. Basically, it simulates a typical outdoor swimming pool installation where water temperature regulation is solely depending on the external ambient conditions and no external heating source is applied. Figure 10 shows the profile for the water temperature as registered across the first days of December 2023.

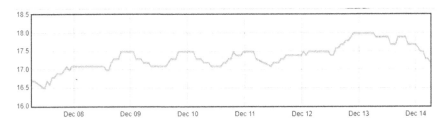

Fig. 10. Pool's water temperature with no control. Water temperature regulation depends exclusively on weather conditions. No heating system is applied

2. control based on best effort. Regulation of the water temperature in the pool depends on the combined effort of the thermal systems, where the decision upon which is used depends on the actual and expected conditions and season of the year. In this approach, regulation of the water temperature in the pool tank depends also on the solar collector and the combination of solar and floor solar collectors which heating ability is highly dependent on the weather conditions. The expectation is that over the day, the thermal systems contribute to a gradually increasing temperature of the pool's water. This scenario is depicted in Fig. 11. Along this period, the sequence of thermal sub-systems was applied regarding the availability of 4 setups: (1) the pool at rest, (2) the solar collectors active and feeding the pool, (3) the PCM circuit active and feeding the pool, (4) the solar collectors and floor solar collectors combined to feed the pool.

Starting at 8:00 am, the control sequence applied by the SMART platform is given from the combination of the setups in the following order (in steps of 30 min):

Setup: [2, 4, 2, 4, 2, 4, 2, 4, 2, 4, 2, 4, 2, 4, 2, 4, 2, 4, 2, 4, 2, 4, 2, 4, 3, 3, 1, 1].

Time of the day: [8:00 … …. 13:00 … … 20:00 …].

By the end of the day, i.e., by 9:00 pm the pool is left at rest for the night hours. The cycle repeats itself each day, from the 22nd until the 28th December.

This control strategy results in the response of the system in Fig. 11 and shows that users specifications will still not be attended in the absence of the SMART component. The strategy applies ON/OFF control based on a preset timer and a timetable for each of the sub-systems, using as reference or desired value, $T_{setpoint}$.

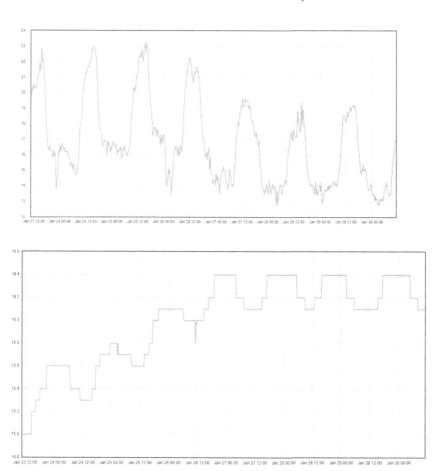

Fig. 11. Scenario scheduling approach along several days in December 2023. Top: the air temperature profile; bottom: the temperature of the water at the pool

5 Conclusions

This paper proposed a new scheme for setting up the swimming pool's water temperature through the usage of sustainable thermal systems (local renewable sources generation devices). The performance of this system was compared to a setup where the traditional heating systems such as boiler are applied.

The results have shown that not always is the system able to satisfy the specifications set by the user but the inclusion of the renewable based system (solar collector) can make the system more eco-sustainable while ensuring desired water temperature under very specific ambient conditions.

This approach of control based on scenarios and having the system a degree of autonomy, lower human intervention in the swimming pool maintenance is gradually attained.

Future work will address the application of improved SMART control approach where the selection of the setup scenario will be accounted for within a pre-defined prediction horizon. In that case the model forecast ability here addressed will be prominent for defining which of the setups will be prioritized ahead as to guarantee that the best combination of setups will be applied.

It is the authors conviction that incorporating this methodology will provide resources savings for the final user in terms of financial and natural resources, contributing to a sustainable environment.

References

1. US Census Bureau. Statistical Abstract of the United States: 2012. Arts, Recreation, and Travel: Participation in Selected Sports Activities 2009. https://www.cdc.gov/healthywater/swimming/swimmers/health_benefits_water_exercise.html. Accessed 18 Dec 2023
2. Gössling, S., et al.: Tourism and water use: supply, demand, and security. Int. Rev. Tourism Manage. **33**(1), 1–15 (2012). ISSN 0261-5177, https://doi.org/10.1016/j.tourman.2011.03.015
3. Final report summary—POOLSAFE (A novel swimming pool water treatment for the detection and elimination of excess cyanuric acid). https://cordis.europa.eu/project/id/604884/reporting. Accessed 18 Dec 2023
4. Official site of the European Union. https://european-union.europa.eu/priorities-and_actions/actions-topic/environment_en. Accessed 17 Dec 2023
5. Pordata, Consumo de energia primária: total e por tipo de fonte de energia. https://www.pordata.pt/Portugal/Consumo+de+energia+prim%C3%A1ria+total+e+por+tipo+de+fonte+de+energia-1130. Accessed 17 Dec 2023
6. Solar Heating and & cooling programme, international energy agency. https://www.iea-shc.org/solar-heat-worldwide-2020. Accessed 13 Dec 2023
7. Abdunnabi, M., Tawil, I.H., Benabeid, M., Elhaj, M.A., Mohamed, F.: Design of solar powered space heating and domestic hot water system for Libyan common house. In: 2021 12th International Renewable Energy Congress (IREC), pp. 1–6 (2021). https://doi.org/10.1109/IREC52758.2021.9624800
8. Tyler, G., Harrison, T., Hulverson, R., Hristovski, K.: Estimating water, energy, and carbon footprints of residential swimming polls. Water Reclamation and Sustainability, pp. 343–359 (2014). https://doi.org/10.1016/b978-0-12-411645-0.00014-6
9. Lam, J.C., Chan, W.W.: Life cycle energy cost analysis of heat pump application for hotel swimming pools. Energy Convers. Manage. **42**, 1299–1306 (2001)
10. Li, A., Huang, G., Wu, H., Xu, T.: Feasibility study of a PCM storage tank integrated heating system for outdoor swimming pools during the winter season. Appl. Thermal Eng. **134**, 490–500 (2018). ISSN 1359-4311, https://doi.org/10.1016/j.applthermaleng.2018.02.030
11. Popa, C.-D., Ungureanu,C.: Analysis of a hybrid water heating system for a swimming pool. In: 2021 International Conference on Electromechanical and Energy Systems (SIELMEN), pp. 521–526 (2021). https://doi.org/10.1109/SIELMEN53755.2021.9600361

12. Fahmy, F.H., Nafeh, A.A., Ahamed, N.M., Farghally,H.M.: A simulation model for predicting the performance of PV powered space heating system in Egypt. In: 2010 International Conference on Chemistry and Chemical Engineering, pp. 173–177 (2010). https://doi.org/10.1109/ICCCENG.2010.5560389

13. Ljung, L.: System Identification, theory for the user, University of LinKöping Sweden, (1987). ISBN 0-13-881640-9

14. Awaludin, R.I., Rama Rao, K.S.: Conventional ARX and Artificial Neural networks ARX models for prediction of oil consumption in Malaysia. In: 2009 IEEE Symposium on Industrial Electronics & Applications, Kuala Lumpur, 2009, pp. 23–28 (2009). https://doi.org/10.1109/ISIEA.2009.5356496. http://ieeexplore.ieee.org/stamp/stamp.jsp?tp=&arnumber=5356496&isnumber=5356402

15. Campos, B.P., da Silva, M.R.: Demand forecasting in residential distribution feeders in the context of smart grids. In: 2016 12th IEEE International Conference on Industry Applications (INDUSCON), Curitiba, 2016, pp. 1–6 (2016). https://doi.org/10.1109/INDUSCON.2016.7874464

16. Ruslan, F.A., Haron, K., Samad, A.M., Adnan, R.: Multiple Input Single Output (MISO) ARX and ARMAX model of flood prediction system: case study Pahang. In: 2017 IEEE 13th International Colloquium on Signal Processing & its Applications (CSPA), Batu Ferringhi, 2017, pp. 179–184 (2017). https://doi.org/10.1109/CSPA.2017.8064947. http://ieeexplore.ieee.org/stamp/stamp.jsp?tp=&arnumber=8064947&isnumber=8064908

17. "Statsmodels.tsa.arima_model.ARMA.fit", Statsmodels. https://www.statsmodels.org/stable/generated/statsmodels.tsa.arima_model.ARMA.fit.html#statsmodels.tsa.arima_model.ARMA.fit. Accessed 20 Jan 2019

18. Trnsys 18.0–Transient Simulation Tool; Doc04-MathematicalReference; Doc07-Programmers Guide; Solar Energy Laboratory, Univ. of Wisconsin-Madison

19. https://emoncms.org/. open-source web-app for processing, logging and visualising energy, temperature and other environmental data

20. REST Api tutorial. https://restfulapi.net/. Accessed 22Jan 2024

A Multimodal Approach to Understand Driver's Distraction for DMS

Andrea Generosi[1(✉)] 📵, Josè Yuri Villafan[1] 📵, Roberto Montanari[2],
and Maura Mengoni[1] 📵

[1] Department of Industrial Engineering and Mathematical Sciences, Università Politecnica delle
Marche, Ancona, Italy
a.generosi@univpm.it
[2] Re-Lab Srl, Reggio Emilia, Italy

Abstract. This study introduces a multimodal approach for enhancing the accuracy of Driver Monitoring Systems (DMS) in detecting driver distraction. By integrating data from vehicle control units with vision-based information, the research aims to address the limitations of current DMS. The experimental setup involves a driving simulator and advanced computer vision, deep learning technologies for facial expression recognition, and head rotation analysis. The findings suggest that combining various data types—behavioral, physiological, and emotional—can significantly improve DMS's predictive capability. This research contributes to the development of more sophisticated, adaptive, and real-time systems for improving driver safety and advancing autonomous driving technologies.

Keywords: Driver Monitoring Systems · Deep Learning · Attention Recognition

1 Introduction

Advanced Driver-Assistance Systems (ADAS) have been thriving and widely deployed in recent years. They are human-machine systems that assist drivers in driving and parking functions, providing partial automation applications like adaptive cruise control, lane departure warning, pedestrian detection, and avoidance, etc. to improve a safe and effortless driving experience [1]. They receive sensor data, compute driving decisions and output control signals to the vehicles. Some open issues in ADAS regard their reliability to reduce malfunctions and critical consequences, precise and real-time measurements, multi-sensor data fusion to avoid that incorrect fusion logic can lead the vehicle to critical accidents.

One of the most challenging applications of ADAS is the Driver Distraction and Drowsiness Recognition (DDR), which warns the driver of drowsiness or other distractions. It is crucial that these systems begin to be incorporated into mass production vehicles, as demonstrated by studies such as [2] and [3].

Real-time Driver Monitoring Systems (DMS) represent a solution to address key behavioural risks as they occur, particularly distraction and fatigue. Their integration in proactive ADAS opens new frontiers in vehicular safety and autonomous driving

M. Antona and C. Stephanidis (Eds.): HCII 2024, LNCS 14696, pp. 250–270, 2024.
https://doi.org/10.1007/978-3-031-60875-9_17

technologies. DMS and ADAS communication allow multi-sensor data to be fused and processed to assess the level of driver's attention, mental workload and fatigue and then to ensure possible hand-over/hand-back actions to achieve full autonomous and safe driving [4]. These systems commonly aim to offer adaptive Human Machine Interfaces (HMI) to alert the driver to potential risks and take immediate action to prevent a collision based on the level of risk associated with the driver's state [5].

The huge amount of data to be processed by ADAS and DMS includes parameters like the steering wheel movement, the brake pressure, the acceleration patterns, and high-dimensional data extracted by computer vision from images and videos captured by embedded cameras in the cabin, i.e. eye movement, facial expressions, driver's posture etc. The first data allows the DMS to assess the driver's physical interaction with the vehicle, while the second to understand his/her cognitive and emotional state.

This paper examines the correlations between various types of data that can be extracted from an automated DMS and vehicle dynamic data. The aim is to propose a multimodal approach to enhance the reliability of driver recognition of distraction states while driving for ADAS systems.

This research starts with a review of the state-of-art multimodal approaches for multi-sensor data fusion to enhance the assessment of the driver's state, particularly concerning distraction. Most studies explored using signals originating from the vehicle's electronic control unit and various types of sensors, including biometric ones, to analyse the existing correlation between the physical and cognitive aspects of the driver's state. However, previous studies have not assessed the correlations between driving signals extracted from the control unit and behavioural signals processed by RGB-based computer vision software, including facial expression analysis. Despite a similar approach being proposed in [6], where an adaptive Human-Machine Interface capable of responding to user-expressed emotions to enhance driving safety has been introduced, this gap in the literature still needs to be addressed.

This preliminary study results in an overview of current approaches and investigates how to merge physical, cognitive and emotional aspects to have a complete understanding of the driver's status. Testing involves a driving simulator with advanced computer vision and Deep Learning technologies, capturing detailed control unit data and employing state-of-the-art algorithms for facial expression recognition, head rotation analysis. By statistically correlating data from the control unit and computer vision, a better understanding of the driver's state can be achieved. This can lead to advancements in automotive safety systems and autonomous vehicle technology. The main contributions of the paper are as follows:

- A comprehensive analysis of the current state-of-the-art, focusing on the critical parameters and processing techniques essential for the development of effective DMS.
- The introduction of a multimodal approach for data processing. This approach integrates data from the vehicle's control unit and vision-based information, thereby enhancing the accuracy and reliability of the DMS.
- The research also involves the compilation of a substantial dataset, gathered using a driving simulator. This dataset is used to test the potential of Deep Neural Networks (DNN) algorithms with control unit data in the context of distraction recognition.

2 Literature Review

2.1 Driving Monitoring Systems

The evolution of ADAS marks a significant leap in automotive technology, underpinned by the integration of advanced sensors and artificial intelligence. The current trend emphasises the essential role of in-vehicle DMS as a core component of efficient ADAS platforms. However, the journey towards creating an effective and reliable DMS involves numerous challenges and limitations, which are critical to address for the advancement of this field.

The current scientific literature on DMS underscores the critical importance of a multimodal approach to effectively assess driver states. As driving is fundamentally a visual task, the peril posed by visual distractions to safe driving performance is particularly highlighted. Instances of frequent lane deviations, abrupt steering movements, and slow reaction times to braking events underscore the significant risks associated with visual distractions. The European Commission in 2015 emphasised that "activities that cause visual distraction seem to be the most dangerous" [7], underscoring the necessity for systems capable of assessing the driver's visual attention state determining when the driver is visually distracted.

Despite advancements, the state of the art indicates a gap in comprehensive solutions, even among systems utilising advanced artificial intelligence, to accurately evaluate these parameters. Challenges such as occlusions that prevent eye-tracking and the limitations of using only facial behaviour metrics (head movement and/or face orientation) for approximate gaze direction assessment are notable [8].

However, the feasibility of countering distraction through innovative driver analysis systems is supported by research. Direct and non-intrusive psychophysiological monitoring of drivers, such as eye closure, could significantly improve the detection of distraction and drowsiness [9].

At the same time, it is necessary to go beyond the simple use of these systems based on cameras and artificial intelligence software (mostly based on computer vision and deep learning), as is currently the case for a large part of the products integrated by car manufacturers in their cars [10], and to develop multimodal approaches based on different types of data and sensors.

The pioneering work of Daza et al. [11] set a benchmark by introducing non-intrusive methods to monitor driver drowsiness through a mix of physical and driving performance indicators, albeit within the confines of simulated conditions. Sandberg et al. [12] expanded the range of indicators to 35, utilising stochastic optimization algorithms to enhance detection, yet facing the challenge of processing large datasets in real-time.

Zhang et al. [13] provided insights into the correlation between vehicle dynamics and driver fatigue, emphasising the challenge of individual variability, which calls for personalised or adaptable DMS.

In the continued effort to refine DMS [9], introduced a multimodal analysis system that adeptly integrated physiological, behavioural, and vehicle signals. This system's high accuracy rates underscored the efficacy of a holistic approach, considering the full spectrum of a driver's condition, and set a benchmark for future systems.

[14] took a practical approach, analysing one vehicle with different drivers and routes, with the system implemented on a mobile application. This study highlighted the critical role of context variability in DMS and embraced the trend of harnessing mobile technology to broaden the accessibility and integration of DMS applications.

However, a challenge identified in [15] was the lack of a freely available, comprehensive database containing complex driver and vehicle data, including stress or fatigue annotations. This limitation in data availability is a hurdle that continues to impede the development of universally applicable and effective DMS.

2.2 Drowsiness and Distraction Parameters

One aim of this study is to investigate the correlation between different signals and their effectiveness in the future development of DMS. After conducting extensive research on the current state of the art, a wide range of parameters has been evaluated to improve the accuracy of detecting drivers' attention states. A key finding from this research highlights the importance of integrating multiple parameters, as singular metrics are insufficient in accurately capturing the complex nature of driver distraction. Consequently, studies are increasingly examining a wider range of parameters, both within the same category (such as physiological, video, vehicle dynamics, or ocular dynamics) and across different categories. These parameters are primarily used to identify states of distraction and/or fatigue, which often overlap. The table categorises each parameter reflecting the nuanced approach required to accurately monitor driver attention and safety (Table 1).

Table 1. State-of-the-art analysed parameters for distraction detection.

CATEGORY	VARIABLE	DESCRIPTION	REFERENCE
Physiological	Electroencephalogram measures (EEG)	There is good evidence that rising alpha (8–11Hz) and theta (4–7 Hz) EEG activities indicate increasing sleepiness and thus the potential for lapses in attention and behaviour	[16, 17]
Physiological	Heart rate variability (HRV)	Elevated HRV can indicate increased mental workload or stress, while a lower HRV is often associated with fatigue or drowsiness	[18, 17]
Physiological	Electrodermal activity (EDA)	Refers to the variation of the skin's electrical conductance in response to sweat secretion. Skin conductance can be a measure of emotional response	[19]

(continued)

Table 1. (*continued*)

CATEGORY	VARIABLE	DESCRIPTION	REFERENCE
Physiological	Skin Temperature	Can signify a driver's stress or relaxed state, impacting their attention and alertness	[19]
Ocular dynamics	Visual fixation	Used to indicate a loss of focus on the road. Alert drivers frequently shift their gaze, actively engaging with their surroundings	[20, 21]
Ocular dynamics	Pupil diameter	Changes in pupil size can indicate changes in alertness, helping to detect moments of distraction or drowsiness	[20]
Ocular dynamics	Eye glance position	Prolonged or frequent glances away from the road, as indicated by eye glance position, suggest the driver is not paying attention to the driving task	[21]
Vehicle behaviour	Steering wheel variability	Variability is greater as drivers become more distract	[22, 17]
Vehicle behaviour	Steering wheel reversal rate (SWRR)	Variability in SWRR indicates a change in steering behaviour that is symptomatic of both distraction and fatigue	[23]
Vehicle behaviour	Standard deviation of lane position (SDLP)	Lane-tracking variability was observed to be related to the amount of distraction and drowsiness in drivers	[24, 17]
Vehicle behaviour	Steering wheel rapid movement (SWRM)	High variability in SWRM can indicate a lack of smooth steering control, often due to a driver's divided attention or the onset of fatigue, leading to more frequent and erratic steering corrections	[22, 17]

(*continued*)

Table 1. (*continued*)

CATEGORY	VARIABLE	DESCRIPTION	REFERENCE
Vehicle behaviour	Mean square of the lane deviation	It is considered to be an accurate and reliable measure for the detection of distraction	[22, 17]
Vehicle behaviour	Time to line crossing (TLC)	Used to predict driver impairment due to drowsiness and distraction, representing how much time before the vehicle drifts out of the lane	[25, 17]
Vehicle behaviour	Lane keeping offset	When the driver performs a secondary task, her/his lane keeping ability degrades. A road segment is described by speed limit and road curvature	[26, 23]
Vehicle behaviour	Standard deviation of speed (SDS)	When the driver performs secondary task, her/his speed maintenance ability degrade	[26]
Vehicle behaviour	Brake pedal angular position	The physical response of braking can be correlated with attention levels while performing various driving manoeuvres	[19]
Vehicle behaviour	Gas pedal angular position	Changes in gas pedal position, such as sudden acceleration, can reflect the driver's response to external stimuli or a lapse in attention	[19]
Video based	Observation of body motions	Driver alertness decreases over time; initially, drivers are more active in checking mirrors and the road. Over an hour, these behaviours reduce	[27, 17]
Video based	Face position	Determining face pose involves analysing the orientation and position of the face, and head movements. Normal face orientation while driving should be forward-facing, deviations suggest distraction	[20]

(*continued*)

Table 1. (*continued*)

CATEGORY	VARIABLE	DESCRIPTION	REFERENCE
Video based	Drivers' Interaction with Car Interior	Quantifying the number, the type, and the conditions of events and interactions between car and driver	[19]
Video based	Emotions detection	Facial expression analysis in drivers assesses their emotional state, which can significantly impact driving behaviour and potentially lead to accidents	[28, 29, 30]

Physiological Parameter. Detecting distraction in drivers relies on a set of physiological parameters that provide insights into their cognitive and physical states.

These indicators include variations in heart rate, which can escalate during periods of distraction [17, 18]. Skin conductance gauges changes in the electrical conductance of the skin, reflecting alterations in the autonomic nervous system that occur during distraction [19].

In addition, the monitoring of electroencephalography (EEG) signals can provide valuable information about brain activity. Sudden shifts in beta waves, for example, can suggest drowsiness and distraction [16]. Moreover, alterations in skin temperature can indicate changes in the autonomic nervous system, revealing physiological responses to distraction or drowsiness. The temperature fluctuates based on blood flow and sympathetic nervous system activity. Increased distraction can result in heightened sympathetic nervous system activity and vasoconstriction, causing a drop in skin temperature [19].

Ocular Dynamics Parameters. Parameters related to ocular dynamics can provide a more comprehensive understanding of the driver's alertness and focus. Measuring blink rate and amplitude provides valuable insights into cognitive workload and attention levels [20]. Tracking gaze direction is another essential parameter, as shifts in focus away from the road suggest distraction [20, 21]. The analysis of saccades, which are rapid eye movements between fixations, can help assess the ability to shift attention efficiently. Pupil diameter is also a sensitive indicator, with dilation often associated with increased cognitive load. Variations in pupil size can reveal fluctuations in alertness, helping to identify moments of distraction or drowsiness [20]. In addition, evaluating eye movement patterns, including smooth pursuit, can determine the driver's capacity to track moving objects. Jerky or irregular movements may indicate impaired concentration [20, 21]. PERCLOS, which stands for Percentage of Eye Closure, measures the percentage of time a person's eyes are closed over a specific duration, usually expressed as a percentage.

Vehicle Dynamics Parameters Vehicle dynamics parameters include factors that contribute to understanding the state of the vehicle and the driver's attentiveness. These factors include steering wheel movement, acceleration, deceleration, and lateral movements, which provide valuable insights into the driver's engagement with the driving task [23].

To examine steering behaviour, it is necessary to analyse the frequency, amplitude, and smoothness of steering inputs. Abrupt or erratic steering changes may indicate distraction or drowsiness [23]. Additionally, acceleration and deceleration patterns are critical, as sudden or inconsistent changes in speed may suggest a lack of focus [23, 26]. Lateral movements, such as lane deviations or drifting, can also provide further clues about the driver's state [23, 26].

Furthermore, the analysis of vehicle dynamics encompasses parameters such as yaw rate, which measures the vehicle's rotation around its vertical axis. Abnormal yaw behaviour, such as excessive swaying or instability, can be associated with impaired driving attention [23, 26].

Moreover, examining brake usage, gas pedal, and other control inputs contributes to a comprehensive evaluation of driver vigilance [19].

Video-Based Parameters Video-based parameters involve the analysis of various visual cues within the captured video feed. The driver's posture is assessed for any unusual slouching or body movements that deviate from the norm [27]. Additionally, head movements can be scrutinised, with a focus on the head orientation that may indicate a lack of attentiveness [20, 23, 27]. Another kind of analysis examines the driver's overall spatial awareness and responsiveness to the surrounding environment [19]. Another interesting aspect that has only recently begun to interest the DMS sector is driver emotion recognition. The correlation between drivers' emotional states and attention levels has been extensively studied, with research indicating that emotions significantly influence driving behaviour and cognition. Emotions like happiness and anger not only impact attentional demands but can also lead to aggressive driving behaviours [28]. Recognizing the importance of real-time detection of drivers' emotional states, the DMS field has developed systems to mitigate potential driving risks associated with negative emotions. For instance, Wu et al. [29] designed a DMS that uses a deep convolutional neural network for facial emotion recognition and audio resources to alleviate negative emotions, thereby reducing driving risks. The system has shown promising results in accuracy and reliability. Building on this, [6] proposed an emotion-aware vehicle architecture that adjusts the car's dynamics in response to the driver's emotions, linking negative emotional states to driving performance.

In summary, while modern DMS proposals in the literature highlight the significance of a multimodal approach, they struggle to introduce a system that truly evaluates all the aspects discernible from driver analysis through modern sensors. The aspiration for such a comprehensive system is to not only align with regulatory mandates but to significantly enhance road safety by mitigating risks associated with driver distraction and fatigue.

The literature also reveals a reliance on control unit data in DMS development. While these data provide valuable insights into vehicle dynamics, it does not provide a complete picture as it does not capture the physiological and behavioural nuances of the driver's state. Taken together, these studies highlight the importance of a multimodal, comprehensive approach that takes into account the myriad aspects of the driving experience, from the physical to the behavioural and from the individual to the universal, but also highlight various limitations, such as the difficulty in accurately detecting and differentiating between types of distraction and levels of fatigue. Most existing systems rely heavily on physical indicators, often neglecting cognitive aspects. There is also the ongoing challenge of ensuring accuracy and reliability in diverse and dynamic driving environments. Another limitation is the lack of integration between different types of indicators. Current systems often operate in silos, analysing specific data sets (such as visual cues or driving performance metrics) independently. In addition, many of these systems struggle to process data in real-time, which is essential for timely intervention and accident prevention.

In summary, while current research in DMS has laid a solid foundation, our work aims to overcome the existing limitations by creating a more integrated, adaptive, and real-time system. This advancement not only contributes significantly to the field of driver safety but also paves the way for the development of more sophisticated ADAS and autonomous driving technologies.

3   Material and Methods

Our research aims to address the limitations and gaps identified in these studies by defining a comprehensive multimodal approach to interpreting and understanding data on dynamic vehicle behaviour during driving, and data collected through the use of cameras and analysis software based on computer vision and artificial intelligence. In this way, the potential of DMS and ADAS systems, in general, will be explored, where it is possible to use data fusion approaches to integrate different types of data with the common goal of detecting distraction while driving.

The study entails a systematic approach encompassing several key stages:

1. **Parameters analysis**: First, in-depth research is conducted to identify relevant parameters from existing literature and studies related to distraction video analysis and signal correlation during distracted driving.
2. **Selection of parameters**: Parameters essential for the assessment of distracted driving have been selected based on the literature review and the specific objectives of the study.
3. **Data collection**: Experimental studies have been carried out using a driving simulator to record participants' actions in various driving scenarios. The data collected included video footage processed using computer vision and deep learning software developed to analyse facial expressions, and degree of head rotation.
4. **Manual video analysis**: This stage involves observing and annotating driver behaviour during periods of distraction in the video footage. Key visual cues such as head direction have been examined for qualitative insights.
5. **Data pre-processing**: Raw data from the experimental phase are pre-processed, including cleaning, filtering, and organising, to prepare them for subsequent analysis.
6. **Algorithmic parameters calculation**: Algorithms are used to calculate specific parameters previously identified. This automated approach aimed to extract new information from the data for a more objective and consistent analysis.

7. **Correlation analysis**: The final phase focuses on exploring correlations between different types of signals during instances of driver distraction. Statistical methods were used to identify relationships between facial expressions, and vehicle dynamics parameters.

In this study we have chosen to experiment with a select few parameters identified from the state of the art: Time to Line Crossing (TLC), Steering wheel reversal rate (SWRR), Steering wheel rapid movement (SWRM), Engagement from emotional analysis, and head orientation measures such as yaw. This selection was made by referring to the most representative parameters in the state of the art to assess the driver's level of distraction:

1. Time to Line Crossing (TLC).
2. Steering wheel reversal rate (SWRR).
3. Steering wheel rapid movement (SWRM)
4. Engagement from the Emotional Analysis component assesses the "excitement" associated with the driver's affective state, which can influence driving behaviour.
5. Head orientation Significant deviations in yaw and pitch values from the normative range can indicate distractions, as the driver may be looking away from the road.

By selecting these parameters, we aim to create a multi-dimensional profile of the driver's state that is accurate and comprehensive, ensuring that our experimental setup is focused, manageable, and aligned with the key variables that will be empirically validated to affect driving performance. The inclusion of emotional engagement and attentional cues in the integration of these parameters offers a novel approach to DMS development that is sensitive to both the cognitive and affective dimensions of the driving task (Fig. 1).

Fig. 1. Considered categories of data for the proposed multimodal approach

3.1 Computer Vision and Deep Learning Software

This work incorporates computer vision and deep learning algorithms capable of processing large datasets in real-time. This enables the system to adapt to individual driver characteristics, potentially providing personalised assessments and warnings: 33.

- Emotion Recognition Module: This module, based on a Convolutional Neural Network (CNN) tested and described in [30], was trained using a merged dataset with both lab-based and real-world data. The CNN was trained with public datasets like CK + [31] and FER + [32], and the "in the wild" dataset provided by Affectnet [33]. The final dataset composed of 250k photos was split using an 80–20 proportion for training and validation phases. In the final layer of the CNN architecture, a softmax function computes the scores for Ekman's emotions from each video frame captured by the camera, with the results normalised to a sum of 100 percent. Building on Russel's Circumplex model [34], which categorises Ekman's emotions based on valence and arousal, we calculate engagement from the emotion percentages. Engagement scores span from 0 for completely neutral expressions to 100 for highly engaging ones.

$$Engagement = Happiness(\%) + Surprise(\%) + Anger(\%) + Fear(\%) - Sadness (\%) \qquad (1)$$

- Head Direction Module: This module, tested in [35], detects driver attentiveness from the estimation of head orientation with respect to the camera, using an approach similar to the one described in [36] to estimate yaw, pitch, and roll parameters. Eye Aspect Ratio (EAR) is also utilised, calculated based on the eye blinking detection method outlined in [37]. Originally designed for eye closure detection, the EAR has also proven to be useful in identifying frontal head tilting by users. This module returns yaw, pitch and roll values related to the degree of head rotation relative to the camera view.

4 Experimental Procedure

While this research endeavours to explore the correlations between signals typically associated with driver distraction, it is important to note that the experimental phase did not simulate drowsiness states. This omission was a deliberate methodological choice, primarily due to the challenges inherent in inducing a state of drowsiness in a controlled environment. Simulating drowsiness can be complex and requires careful monitoring to ensure the safety and well-being of participants, which may not always be feasible within the constraints of an experimental setting.

The explored case study was conducted using a driving simulator operating on the SCANeR Studio 1.7 platform, which is adept at simulating sensors and automated driving functionalities, essential for a realistic and controlled testing environment. The static driving simulator is equipped with an engine simulation and authentic car controls, such as a driver's seat, pedals, and gearbox. Additionally, it features a SensoDrive steering wheel with haptic force feedback to emulate real driving conditions. The simulation environment is enhanced with visual aids, including a video projector and a 15.6″ display behind the steering wheel, presenting a full digital Human-Machine Interface. Synchronisation is accomplished by using the simulator machine timestamp, which enables a distributed system architecture that is necessary for testing and validating the AI algorithms involved. The vehicle's various parameters could be monitored and controlled by drivers through a tablet located on the dashboard. This interface served as both a

Fig. 2. The driving simulator

control mechanism and a means of introducing distraction events, simulating the impact of external factors on the driver's attention (Fig. 2).

The driver was captured from multiple angles using strategically positioned HD cameras. One of the cameras was connected to an Intel NUC11PAHi7, which ran the software for emotion analysis and head analysis. Other cameras provided additional cabin perspectives. This enabled a comprehensive analysis of the driver's reactions and engagement.

The key hardware integrated into the simulator included:

- Hikvision Digital Technology DS-2CE16H0T-ITF HD cameras for high-definition recording
- A Samsung Galaxy Tab A8 used for vehicle interaction and distraction induction.
- Onboard dedicated processing modules, integrated with the simulator, to monitor vehicle dynamics in real time, supporting a lifelike driving simulation and enabling crucial data collection.

The AVSimulation SCANeR software has been used to create two environmental scenarios for the driving simulation: highway and urban. The highway scenario incorporated random behaviours and overtaking capabilities to simulate real traffic conditions. The urban setting was characterised by a dense network of traffic signals, roads, and pedestrian crossings, with diverse road users including cars, motorcycles, bicycles, and pedestrians. These environments were designed to simulate varying traffic and weather conditions, challenging drivers to adapt their behaviour to the complexities of the road.

Within these simulations, three specific contexts were crafted to elicit different emotional and cognitive states in drivers. The first context mimicked the urgency of a parent late to collect their child from school. The second scenario envisioned the driver setting off on a much-anticipated vacation, aiming to induce a sense of relaxation and joy. The third scenario involved the driver being called into work on their day off for an urgent meeting, intended to provoke feelings of frustration and stress (Fig. 3).

To further engage the drivers and introduce elements of distraction, five secondary tasks were integrated into each driving session. These tasks required drivers to interact

Fig. 3. An example of a simulated scenario

with various objects within the vehicle and execute specific actions such as interacting with a simulated Human-Machine Interface (HMI) of the car's dashboard, in this case a tablet. These interactions involved completing various tasks to simulate potential distraction activities in real-world scenarios, including:

- Answering the phone
- Sending messages on the phone
- Talking on the phone while holding it to the ear
- Drinking

These were employed to mimic realistic distractions and observe the drivers' responses. Through a systematic combination of these distraction events and the sequence in which they were performed, paired with different driving conditions, five distinct scenarios emerged that were colour-coded for clarity. These scenarios, labelled with the colours blue, yellow, orange, green, and purple, provided a comprehensive list of distraction levels and driving conditions for analysis.

Nineteen participants, 9 males and 10 females aged between 21 to 53, were enlisted for the study. Each participated in three separate 10-min sessions, each presenting one of the three contexts. Throughout these sessions, participants engaged in the prescribed tasks to simulate distraction, allowing for a comprehensive assessment of their reactions within the simulated driving environments.

5   Experimental Results

5.1   Qualitative Analysis

The findings of our study are here analysed using visual data, highlighting the behaviour of certain indices across the five colour-coded test scenarios designed to study driver distraction under varying traffic conditions. The data encompassed telemetry metrics, facial expressions analysed through Ekman's framework, and head orientation movements measured in yaw, pitch, and roll.

We'll analyze how these data, retrieved during the distracting scenarios, compare with the data outside these events.

The aim of this qualitative analysis is, in fact, to spot particoular trends in these parameters, especially during moments of distraction.

First step regards the observations from the facial expression analysis software, which identified notable changes in engagement and valence among subjects during distractions, identifying patterns that suggest a relationship between certain expressions and decreased driving performance.

For example, subject 16 showed a significant shift in engagement during specific distraction tasks, such as responding to messages and using a tablet. This variability in emotional responses underscores the complexity of driver reactions to distractions and highlights the potential for emotional states to influence driving behaviour (Fig. 4).

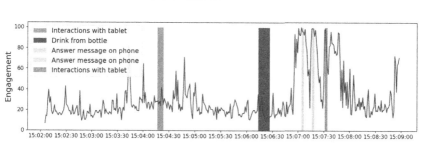

Fig. 4. Engagement and Valence data of subject coded "16" showing their trends across distractions events highlighted by the coloured vertical bars

Similarly, the analysis of data collected by the software to gauge driver attention based on head orientation reveals that significant yaw deviations correspond to decreased attention levels, as anticipated, since yaw rotation signifies turning around the vertical axis. Consequently, elevated values of this measurement suggest that the driver's head is turned away from the front. During the tests, most distraction activities required the user to turn right since the standard driving position in Europe is on the left of the car, resulting in the highest deviations observed either during these activities or at the beginning and end phases of the test when drivers typically glance around (Fig. 5).

Some subjects exhibited peaks in emotional engagement before the distraction event occurred, suggesting that anticipation or reaction to the instruction itself could be a distraction. However, for many subjects, no clear trends were identified, possibly due to inaccuracies in data collection, particularly with camera-based measurements. Factors such as inadequate lighting and improper camera angles could have compromised the data quality, affecting the reliability of emotion detection based on facial expressions.

Vehicle dynamics data further elucidated the impact of distractions on driving performance. The analysis of telemetry data shows a recurring trend highlighted in the literature. When drivers become distracted or anticipate distraction, they typically exhibit a decrease in vehicle speed. Such speed reduction is commonly associated with a protective instinct wherein drivers preemptively slow down upon recognizing the impending

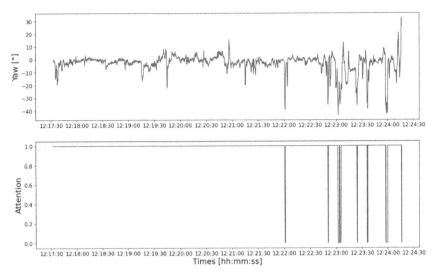

Fig. 5. Yaw and Attention data of subject coded "2" showing their trends across the driving simulation

engagement in a secondary task that will divert their attention from driving. This behavior was consistent across subjects, with notable deviations in speed trends observed during distraction scenarios. Subject 2 exhibits this trend in the most clear and evident manner during the "Drink from bottle" distraction event, where cognitive engagement is required to locate and open the bottle (Fig. 6).

5.2 Quantitative Analysis

A quantitative analysis has been then conducted to explore correlations between the available data and indicators, specifically focusing on steering wheel reversal rate (SWRR), steering wheel rapid movement (SWRM), and time to lane crossing (TLC). The aim was to determine whether data from non-distraction periods could predict outcomes during distraction events, offering insights into the predictive potential of these metrics across varying levels of driver distraction. Our analysis also involved a meticulous categorization of driving behaviour data, separating it into two groups: 'data with events,' captured during distraction periods, and 'data without events,' representing normal driving conditions. This segmentation facilitated a targeted examination of how distraction events influence driving behaviour. From these groups, we conducted additional subdivision based on thresholds exceeded by the specific indicators TLC, SWRR, and SWRM. The primary objective was to discern differences between the datasets with and without events across all combinations of indicators: this granular classification resulted in fourteen distinct subsets, seven corresponding to 'data with events' and seven to 'data without events'. This comparative analysis aimed to identify behavioral changes during distraction events, providing insights into how such events alter driving patterns.

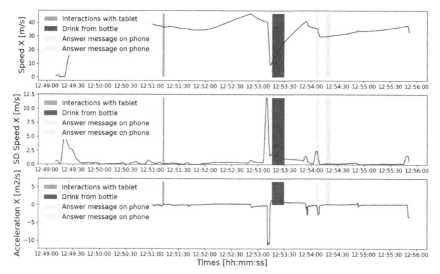

Fig. 6. Telemetry data of subject coded "2" showing their trends across distractions events highlighted by the coloured vertical bars

Through this approach, we sought to understand the specific impact of distraction events on driving behavior, independent of individual indicators, allowing for a comprehensive examination of the driving dynamics under varying conditions of attention. The boxplots in Fig. 7 serve to illustrate the dataset subdivision utilized as the foundation for subsequent analysis. At the top, we present the complete dataset without events on the left, alongside a subset extracted from it where all indicators exceeded their respective thresholds as indicated in the boxplot (e.g., TLC < 6.4 s, SWRM > 13°/s, and SWRR > 6°) on the right. The bottom row mirrors this setup, but now exclusively features data collected during distraction events. In particular, we show Speed Y data in the boxplots with the described subdivision (Fig. 7).

This investigation sought to determine which combinations of indicators most closely mirrored the 'data without events', suggesting their potential utility in predicting key variables like Speed X or steering wheel angle during distraction events. This approach was grounded in statistical analyses, including Mann-Whitney, Kolmogorov-Smirnov, and t-Tests, to accommodate the non-normal distribution of our data, despite its large volume.

Variable	N. KPI combinations
acceleration_y	33
steeringWheelAngle	26
speed_y	23
speed_x	14
acceleration_x	11
tlc	10
roadInfo_laneGap	8
steeringWheelSpeed	1

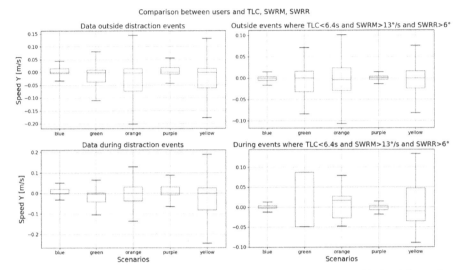

Fig. 7. Boxplots of 'data without events' (top) and 'with events' (bottom). To the right a subset from each dataset shown on the left is taken under the condition that the three indicators go over the thresholds indicated

These results illustrate the frequency of different variables appearing in combinations that could potentially predict distraction events based on various indicators. Acceleration in the y-direction appears most frequently, with 33 combinations across the several driving scenarios performed by the users, followed by steering wheel angle with 26 combinations and speed in the y-direction with 23 combinations. Other variables such as speed in the x-direction, acceleration in the x-direction, time to lane crossing (TLC), and road lane gap information also show notable occurrences. These findings suggest that certain variables may play a more prominent role in predicting distraction events, providing valuable insights for further analysis and mitigation strategies in enhancing driver safety. For instance, specific KPI combinations that yield y-axis acceleration values similar to those observed during distraction events indicate the occurrence of such events. This finding is instrumental in delineating the most effective combinations of indicators for predicting distraction, ranging from individual thresholds like TLC < 6.4 s, SWRM > 13°/s, SWRR > 6°, to composite thresholds involving multiple indicators.

In conclusion, the quantitative analysis underscores the significance of y-axis acceleration and steering wheel angle as key variables for detecting driver distraction. Through meticulous statistical testing and data segmentation, we've identified specific indicator combinations that offer a predictive lens for monitoring and potentially mitigating distraction-induced impairments in driving performance.

6 Discussion and Conclusion

This study aims to improve the understanding and development of DMS through a meticulous analysis of state-of-the-art parameters and processing techniques. Our primary objective was to investigate the essential components that underpin the effectiveness of DMS. To achieve this, we introduced a multimodal approach to data processing that seamlessly integrates information from the vehicle's control unit with vision-based data. This innovative fusion has significantly improved the accuracy and reliability of DMS. The findings from the experimental investigation provide a compelling narrative on the nature of driver distraction. The correlations observed among the diverse signals—ranging from steering patterns to emotional cues—demonstrate a significant alignment with the actual states of distraction as reported by participants, validating the ground truth data. These results underscore the potential of multi-signal analysis as a reliable indicator of distracted driving behaviors. Crucially, the study has shown that by integrating various data streams, such as the Standard Steering Wheel Reversal Rate (SWRR), Time to Line Crossing (TLC), Steering wheel rapid movement (SWRM), along with emotional engagement, and face orientation, we can achieve a robust detection system. The consistency of these signals with self-reported distraction instances strengthens the argument for a multimodal DMS capable of discerning subtle shifts in driver focus and engagement. This research contributes to the growing body of evidence that supports the use of complex data fusion in DMS. By leveraging a combination of behavioural, physiological, and emotional signals, we can enhance the predictive power of these systems, potentially leading to more responsive and adaptive safety mechanisms in vehicles. Moving forward, these conclusions not only pave the way for more advanced DMS development but also highlight the importance of continuous data validation against real-world scenarios. Future research can build on these foundations, exploring broader signal sets and refining detection algorithms to cater to the nuanced spectrum of driver behaviours. Although no states of drowsiness were simulated in the experiment, the findings related to distraction are still highly relevant, as the behaviours exhibited during distracted driving can share similarities with those observed in drowsy driving, such as delayed reaction times and decreased vehicle control. We acknowledge this limitation in our research design and propose that future studies could incorporate physiological measures, such as EEG or more accurate eye-tracking metrics that do not require the actual induction of drowsiness but can infer the state based on known biomarkers. Moreover, the development of advanced simulation technologies and safer experimental protocols could eventually allow for the inclusion of drowsiness simulations in a manner that is both ethical and effective. However, while the current study does not include drowsiness simulations, the insights gained from the analysis of distraction signals contribute valuable knowledge to the field of DMS and lay the groundwork for future research to build upon.

References

1. Antony, M.M., Whenish, R.: Advanced Driver Assistance Systems (ADAS) in AKathiresh, M., Neelaveni, R. (eds) Automotive Embedded Systems. EAI/Springer Innovations in Communication and Computing. Springer, Cham, pp. 165–181 (2021). https://doi.org/10.1007/978-3-030-59897-6_9

2. Owens, J., Dingus, T., Guo, F., et al.: Prevalence of Drowsy-Driving Crashes: Estimates from a Large-Scale Naturalistic Driving Study. AAA Foundation for Traffic Safety, Washington, DC (2018)

3. Fitzharrris, M., Liu, S., Stephens, A.N., Lenné, M.G.: The relative importance of real-time in-cab and external feedback in managing fatigue in real-world commercial transport operations. Traffic Inj. Prev. 18(1), 71–78 (2017)

4. Ortega, J.D., Canas, P.N., Nieto, M., Otaegui, O., Salgado, L.: Challenges of large-scale multi-camera datasets for driver monitoring systems. Sensors 22(7), 2554 (2022)

5. Hasenjäger, M., Heckmann, M., Wersing, H.: A survey of personalization for advanced driver assistance systems. IEEE Trans. Intell. Veh. 5(2), 335–344 (2019)

6. Ceccacci, S., Mengoni, M., Andrea, G., Giraldi, L., Carbonara, G., Castellano, A., Montanari, R.: A preliminary investigation towards the application of facial expression analysis to enable an emotion-aware car interface. In: Universal Access in Human-Computer Interaction. Applications and Practice: 14th International Conference, UAHCI 2020, Held as Part of the 22nd HCI International Conference, HCII 2020, Copenhagen, Denmark, July 19–24, 2020, Proceedings, Part II 22 (pp. 504–517). Springer International Publishing (2020). https://doi.org/10.1007/978-3-030-49108-6_36

7. European Commission: Road safety thematic report – Serious injuries. European Road Safety Observatory. Brussels, European Commission, Directorate General for Transport (2021)

8. Gardony, A.L., Lindeman, R.W., Brunyé, T.T.: Eye-tracking for human-centered mixed reality: promises and challenges. In: Optical Architectures for Displays and Sensing in Augmented, Virtual, and Mixed Reality (AR, VR, MR), (Vol. 11310, pp. 230–247). SPIE (Feb 2020)

9. Dehzangi, O., Sahu, V., Taherisadr, M., Galster, S.: Multi-modal system to detect on-the-road driver distraction. In: 2018 21st International Conference on Intelligent Transportation Systems (ITSC), (pp. 2191–2196). IEEE (Nov 2018)

10. Muhammad, K., Ullah, A., Lloret, J., Del Ser, J., de Albuquerque, V.H.C.: Deep learning for safe autonomous driving: Current challenges and future directions. IEEE Trans. Intell. Transp. Syst. 22(7), 4316–4336 (2020)

11. Daza, I.G., Bergasa, L.M., Bronte, S., Yebes, J.J., Almazán, J., Arroyo, R.: Fusion of optimized indicators from advanced driver assistance systems (adas) for driver drowsiness detection. Sensors 14, 1106–1131 (2014)

12. Sandberg, D., Akerstedt, T., Anund, A., Kecklund, G., Wahde, M.: Detecting driver sleepiness using optimized nonlinear combinations of sleepiness indicators. IEEE Trans. Intell. Transp. Syst. 12(1), 97–108 (2010)

13. Zhang, H., Wu, C., Huang, Z., Yan, X., Qiu, T.Z.: Sensitivity of lane position and steering angle measurements to driver fatigue. Transp. Res. Rec. 2585(1), 67–76 (2016)

14. Khandakar, A., et al.: Portable system for monitoring and controlling driver behavior and the use of a mobile phone while driving. Sensors 19(7), 1563 (2019)

15. Nemcova, A., et al.: Multimodal features for detection of driver stress and fatigue. IEEE Trans. Intell. Transp. Syst. 22(6) (2021)

16. Dinges, D.F.: An overview of sleepiness and accidents. J. Sleep Res. 4(2), 4–14 (1995)

17. Kircher, A., Uddman, M., Sandin, J.: Vehicle control and drowsiness. Statens väg-och transportforskningsinstitut (2002)

18. Bunji, A: Evaluation of Mental Condition on Drivers by Analysis of Heart Rate Variability. Journal of the Society of Automotive Engineers of Japan No. 9437601, 1994
19. Milardo, S., Rathore, P., Amorim, M., Fugiglando, U., Santi, P., Ratti, C.: Understanding drivers' stress and interactions with vehicle systems through naturalistic data analysis. IEEE Trans. Intell. Transp. Syst. **23**(9), 14570–14581 (2021)
20. Bergasa, L.M., Nuevo, J., Sotelo, M.A., Barea, R., Lopez, M.E.: Real-time system for monitoring driver vigilance. IEEE Trans. Intell. Transport. Syst. **7**(1), 63–77 (2006)
21. Çetinkaya, M., Acarman, T.: Driver impairment detection using decision tree based feature selection and classification. Results Eng. **18**, 101025 (2023)
22. Wylie, C.D., Shultz, T., Miller, J.C., Mitler, M.M., Mackie, R.R.: Commercial motor vehicle driver fatigue and alertness study: Technical summary (1996)
23. Doudou, M., Bouabdallah, A., Berge-Cherfaoui, V.: Driver drowsiness measurement technologies: current research, market solutions, and challenges. Int. J. ITS Res. **18**, 297–319 (2020)
24. Sagberg, F.: Road accidents caused by drivers falling asleep. Accid. Anal. Prev. **31**, 639–649 (1999)
25. Verwey, W.B., Zaidel, D.: Predicting Drowsiness Accidents from Personal Attributes, Eye Blinks, and Ongoing Driving Behaviour. Report TM-97-B009. Soesterberg. TNO Human Factors Research Institute, The Netherlands (1997)
26. Aksjonov, A., Nedoma, P., Vodovozov, V., Petlenkov, E., Herrmann, M.: Detection and evaluation of driver distraction using machine learning and fuzzy logic. IEEE Trans. Intell. Transp. Syst. **20**(6), 2048–2059 (2018)
27. Bittner, R., Hána, K., Poušek, L., Smrka, P., Schreib, P., Vysoký, P.: Detecting of Fatigue States of a Car Driver. In: Brause, R.W., Hanisch, E. (eds.) ISMDA 2000. LNCS, vol. 1933, pp. 260–273. Springer, Heidelberg (2000). https://doi.org/10.1007/3-540-39949-6_32
28. Sârbescu, P.: Aggressive driving in Romania: psychometric properties of the driving anger expression inventory. Transport. Res. F: Traffic Psychol. Behav. **15**(5), 556–564 (2012)
29. Wu, Y.L., Tsai, H.Y., Huang, Y.C., Chen, B.H.: Accurate emotion recognition for driving risk prevention in driver monitoring system. In: 2018 IEEE 7TH Global Conference on Consumer Electronics (GCCE) (pp. 796–797). IEEE (Oct 2018)
30. Talipu, A., Generosi, A., Mengoni, M., Giraldi, L.: Evaluation of deep convolutional neural network architectures for emotion recognition in the wild. In: 2019 IEEE 23rd International Symposium on Consumer Technologies, pp. 25–27, 2019. IEEEhttps://doi.org/10.1109/ISCE.2019.8900994
31. Lucey, P., Cohn, J.F., Kanade, T., Saragih, J., Ambadar, Z., Matthews, I.: The extended cohn-kanade dataset (ck+): A complete dataset for action unit and emotion-specified expression. In: 2010 IEEE Computer Society Conference on Computer Vision and Pattern Recognition-Workshops (2010). https://doi.org/10.1109/CVPRW.2010.5543262
32. Barsoum, E., Zhang, C., Ferrer, C.-C., Zhang, Z.:"Training Deep Networks for Facial Expression Recognition with Crowd-Sourced Label Distribution" (2016). https://doi.org/10.1145/2993148.2993165
33. Mollahosseini, A., Hasani, B., Mahoor, M.H.: Affectnet: a database for facial expression, valence, and arousal computing in the wild. IEEE Trans. Affect. Comput. **10**(1), 18–31 (2017)
34. Feldman Barrett, L., Russell, J.A.: Independence and bipolarity in the structure of current affect. J. Pers. Soc. Psychol. **74**(4), 967 (1998)
35. Ceccacci, S., Generosi, A., Cimini, G., Faggiano, S., Giraldi, L., Mengoni, M.: Facial coding as a mean to enable continuous monitoring of student's behavior in e-Learning. In: teleXbe (Jan 2021)

36. Mallick, S.: Head Pose Estimation using OpenCV and Dlib | LearnOpenCV #. LearnOpenCV – Learn OpenCV, PyTorch, Keras, Tensorflow With Examples and Tutorials (May 2021). https://learnopencv.com/head-pose-estimation-using-opencv-and-dlib/
37. Soukupova, T., Cech, J.: "Eye Blink Detection Using Facial Landmarks." 21st Computer Vision Winter Workshop, Rimske Toplice, Slovenia (2016)

The Social Consequences of Language Technologies and Their Underlying Language Ideologies

Maria Goldshtein[1]([✉]) [iD], Jaclyn Ocumpaugh[2] [iD], Andrew Potter[1] [iD], and Rod D. Roscoe[1] [iD]

[1] Arizona State University, Mesa, AZ 85212, USA
maria.goldshtein@asu.edu
[2] University of Pennsylvania, Philadelphia, PA 19104, USA

Abstract. As language technologies have become more sophisticated and prevalent, there have been increasing concerns about bias in natural language processing (NLP). Such work often focuses on the effects of bias instead of sources. In contrast, this paper discusses how normative language assumptions and ideologies influence a range of automated language tools. These underlying assumptions can inform (a) grammar and tone suggestions provided by commercial products, (b) language varieties (e.g., dialects and other norms) taught by language learning technologies, (c) language patterns used by chatbots and similar applications to interact with users. These tools demonstrate considerable technological advancement but are rarely interrogated with regard to the language ideologies they intentionally or implicitly reinforce. We consider prior research on language ideologies and how they may impact (at scale) the large language models (LLMs) that underlie many automated language technologies. Specifically, this paper draws on established theoretical frameworks for understanding how humans typically perceive or judge language varieties and patterns that may differ from their own or their perceived standard. We then discuss how language ideologies can perpetuate social hierarchies and stereotypes, even within seemingly impartial automation. In doing so, we contribute to the emerging literature on how the risks of language ideologies and assumptions can be better understood and mitigated in the design, testing, and implementation of automated language technologies.

Keywords: Language Technologies · Standard Language Ideologies · Bias · Artificial Intelligence (AI)

1 Introduction

Language technologies have become more prevalent and sophisticated. For instance, numerous tools for revising and improving grammar, writing style, tone, and vocabulary (e.g., Grammarly, WhiteSmoke, and WordTune) are publicly available via mobile phone applications and browser plugins. In educational settings, many contemporary technologies purport to teach reading and writing while enabling automated writing evaluation, computerized adaptive testing, and formative assessment (Ben-Simon & Bennett, 2007; Burner, 2016; Deane, 2013; Gardner et al., 2021; Graham et al., 2015; Krishnan et al., 2021; Heritage, 2021; Peng & Spector, 2019; Teng, 2022; Thompson & Weiss, 2019; Van der Linden & Glas, 2000; Wingate, 2014).

Commonly used language technologies—whether for personal or educational use—shape our language learning experiences and contexts for language use (e.g., in the workplace, higher education, and personal life, Ajisoko, 2020; Alharbi, 2023), and their prevalence has begun to motivate researchers to examine these effects. However, the ways in which these systems may reinforce normative or biased assumptions about language and people are often unexplored (Blodgett et al., 2020). Human-computer interaction (HCI) researchers and developers need to be aware of how language attitudes and biases may manifest within or as the result of using language technologies. For example, understanding deeply entrenched myths about "standard" English may inform how HCI experts effectively serve (and avoid excluding or harming) a broader range of technology users. In this paper, we first briefly explain the nature of language ideologies (Sect. 1) and the impact of standard language ideologies within language technologies (Sect. 2). We conclude by discussing ways to potentially mitigate those issues and illustrate how those ways may be used to counteract some negative effects of standard language ideologies (Sect. 3).

2   Understanding Language Ideologies

2.1   Language Ideologies

Language ideologies are deeply held but often unarticulated and unexamined beliefs about the nature of different varieties of language (Lippi-Green, 2012; Milroy, 2001; Chen, 2018; Lawton & Kleine, 2020). Such ideologies arise both from the attitudes people have about the *nature of language* as well as the stereotypes people hold about *language users*. For example, English language ideologies have typically crystalized around beliefs about "purity" and "correctness" of standardized language (Milroy, 2007), with variations from idealized norms perceived as "tainted", "incorrect", or "broken." Examples of these ideologies are demonstrated by various myths and misconceptions about dialect (Wolfram & Schilling-Estes, 1998). Such beliefs may assume that (a) so-called "standard" English represents a singular, uniform, and unchanging dialect; (b) which must be protected from deviations introduced by careless or uneducated speakers; and that (c) stigmatized English dialects deserve lower status because they are linguistically more variable and nonstandard (e.g., in spelling, pronunciation, usage, syntax, or semantics).

Attitudes toward language varieties also often reflect attitudes toward the users (i.e., speakers and writers) of those varieties. For instance, in English, research demonstrates that standardized varieties may be associated with Whiteness and wealth, whereas nonstandard varieties are associated with lower socioeconomic status, minoritized, and marginalized populations (e.g., racial and ethnicity minority groups, less educated people, and immigrants with "foreign" accents) (Kutlu et al., 2022; Milroy, 2002). In parallel, research suggests that stereotyped beliefs about nonstandard English speakers can lead to discriminatory practices. Spence et al. (2022) found that the presence of social stereotypes (e.g., about gender) compounded biases against job candidates who also spoke with a nonstandard accent. Similarly, investigations of U.S. court cases have found that defendants who spoke African American Vernacular English (AAVE) were judged to be less credible and received more guilty verdicts (Kurinec & Weaver, 2019).

In sum, language ideologies describe beliefs about language and language users. Standard language ideologies further describe beliefs that certain language varieties (or a single variety) are correct or ideal, whereas "nonstandard" varieties are incorrect and undesirable. These ideologies are intertwined with social stereotypes.

2.2 Standard Language Ideologies in Academic Settings

In academic settings, standard language ideologies acquired from informal sources (e.g., social media, news media, parents, friends, and everyday conversation, e.g., Kidd, 2016; Silber Mohamed & Farris, 2020) are mingled with language ideologies embedded in instructional materials. In schools, language serves both as the vehicle for instruction and, in certain classes, the topic of instruction. Thus, language ideologies that appear in educational settings may be more strongly reinforced by the formalized nature of education (e.g., curricula, learning objectives, assessment, and testing). Schooling emphasizes the acquisition of ideas normatively perceived as "accurate" and "factual" (e.g., correct word spellings) whereas deviations are penalized as "mistakes" (e.g., dialectical spelling variations). Indeed, for much of the 20th century, language ideologies in United States education systems were influenced by themes of social and linguistic purity (Ayres-Bennett, 2016; Curzan, 2014; Drake, 1977).

Currently, alternative approaches to teaching with and about nonstandard language varieties are gaining popularity (e.g., Dalton et al., 2011; McSwan, 2020; Snell, 2013). Such work recognizes that learners think and thrive in a variety of languages and dialects, and incorporating authentic language variance in instruction supports effective learning. However, such work is still rather scarce. The social and instructional processes that give rise to preferential and biases language ideologies are still very much present, and technology designers must remain vigilant about potential biases reinforced by their work. For example, when implementing generative artificial intelligence (gen AI) and large language models (LLMs), developers will have to make choices about which language(s) and corpora to use when training models or reporting output. One temptation will be to emphasize supposed "clarity" or "consistency" by focusing on only one imagined "standard" dialect. Focusing on "standard" language may also seem simpler or more affordable and may appear to benefit students by reinforcing more socially acceptable ways of speaking and writing. These rationalizations, however, run the risk of perpetuating or reinforcing the myriad stereotypes and social stigma (i.e., language ideologies) that underlie the "standard" language variety in the first place.

In the following section, we explore the impact of language ideologies on technology development and use more directly.

3 The Impact of Language Ideology on Technology

Despite considerable evidence that there is not one standard English (Lippi-Green, 2012; Trudgill & Hannah, 2013), standard language ideologies continue to influence both humans and the technologies we produce (e.g., grammar recommendations in popular writing tools and the style of generative AI outputs). As language technologies expand, it is imperative that we understand both how biases and other functional shortcomings might undermine their reach and efficacy. These challenges are particularly crucial for technologies designed for education, which can formally entrench certain ideologies and/or gatekeep opportunities for learning and career goals. For example, automated writing evaluation software that penalizes "nonstandard" English when grading standardized exams could negatively impact students' ability to graduate.

As briefly described in Sect. 1, many biases and language ideologies are learned implicitly via exposure to language and language patterns. Such patterns can be "built into" language technologies based on how underlying models are trained. Indeed, research on language technologies has revealed biases against nonstandard English that mirror common human biases. Table 1 summarizes several instances of bias found among humans and language technologies spanning phonology (e.g., sounds and pronunciation), syntax (e.g., grammar and structure), pragmatics (e.g., practices and context), and lexical and semantic (e.g., word choices and meanings).

Table 1. Parallel language-based biases observed among humans and technologies

Linguistic Level	Human Biases	Language Technology Biases
Phonetics and Phonology	Baratta, 2017; Munro, 2023; Silaj et al., 2023	Mason & Carson-Berndsenm 2023; Chan et al., 2022; DiChristofano et al., 2022; Martin & Wright, 2023; Markl, 2022; O'Neill 2017; Spence et al., 2022; Schleef, 2017; Wassink et al., 2022
Lexical and Semantic	Haig & Oliver, 2003;	Caliskan et al., 2017; Gururangan et al., 2022; Reyero Lobo et al., 2023
Pragmatic	Strickland & Young, 1999; Economidou-Kogetsidis, 2016;	Kotek et al., 2023; Koenecke et al., 2020
Syntactic	Gupta, 2010; Strickland & Young, 1999	Liang et al., 2023; Martin & Tang, 2020; Tan et al., 2020; Santiago et al., 2022; Koenecke et al., 2020

Researchers have begun to develop machine learning techniques for detecting and mitigating bias (see Sects. 3.1 and 3.2), such as disparate outcomes for diverse technology users (e.g., scoring that is less accurate for certain demographic groups). However, to our knowledge, very little work is being conducted that directly confronts biases related to language ideologies and marginalized language varieties. Without careful consideration, language technologies may continue to perpetuate or even amplify assumptions about normative language standards and people (Blodgett et al., 2020), thus undermining any effort to "de-bias" automated technologies.

3.1 Language Technologies and Education

As alluded to previously, the education sector represents a substantial audience for language technologies. Such tools are being used to support teaching, learning, formative assessment, evaluation, and other decision making. A wide range of technologies are available, including ubiquitous word processing tools (e.g., Microsoft Word and Google-Docs), systems for proofreading and editing (e.g., Grammarly, Hemingway, Ludwig, WordTune, and WhiteSmoke), language learning apps (e.g., DuoLingo and Babbel), and intelligent tutoring or automated writing evaluation systems designed to teach writing (e.g., Writing Pal, Roscoe & McNamara, 2013; McNamara et al., 2014, and MI Write, Wilson et al., 2021). Currently, with the advent of gen AI and LLM, we are witnessing an even greater proliferation of literacy-related technologies to support the above examples. For example, Kahn Academy has recently launched Kahnmigo—a chatbot that embeds ChatGPT into a wrap-around system to provide hints to students using their online services. Whether these systems are helping students to develop their language specifically or not, they appear to be targeting and using very similar language patterns.

Biases about nonstandard language varieties are widespread and typically associated with stereotypes about language users (Preston, 2017; Curzan, 2014). In education, for instance, language ideologies might manifest with regard to prescriptive grammar rules and beliefs about "correctness," which in turn might conflict with nonstandard English varieties or foreign language heritage (e.g., verb tenses and word orders). Knowing and using "proper" grammar is frequently interpreted as a signal of "intelligence" or "being educated." Due to formal educational activities of instruction and assessment, we argue that the language uses and rules embodies in educational language technologies are likely to be interpreted as "correct English" and perpetuate impressions of nonstandard dialects as substandard (Haig & Oliver, 2003). Research suggests that both teachers and students are susceptible to these sorts of biases (Cushing, 2021; Rose & Galloway, 2017); students may be more vulnerable because they are the targeted audience of instruction and beholden to assessment criteria (i.e., following "the rules" or else receiving a failing grade).

Innovative language technologies have the potential to dramatically improve individualized instruction and assistance on a scale that was previously impossible, but they must be used cautiously. For example, the "garbage in/garbage out" problem (GIGO; Gieger et al., 2021) of machine learning applies to how language technologies are created and trained (e.g., biased input corpora), and we must also consider issues of sampling and transparency. These examples are not exhaustive of the myriad issues encountered by language technologies (e.g., we do not address *pedagogical* principles or needs), but nonetheless help to appreciate the scope of the challenge.

3.2 Biased Training Data (Garbage in, Garbage Out)

A well-known problem in machine learning—garbage in/garbage out (or GIGO)—describes the impact of training data quality and features on resulting models, algorithms, and outputs. In short, if the training data used to generate the system are flawed, those flaws will be (at best) replicated in the technology. In our work, we explicitly consider biases and biased language ideologies as the "garbage." One example of this problem was demonstrated by the Microsoft *Tay* chatbot deployed on social media in 2016. Within 24 h of release, the chatbot began to acquire and use racist, misogynistic, and nonfactual claims and had to be shut down (Wolf et al., 2017). It was discovered that social media users were able to intentionally train Tay to use such language by feeding it inflammatory language and ideas, thus tuning the algorithm to rely on that input as legitimate language content. More recent LLM-based systems have attempted to implement filters and "guardrails" to prevent such outcomes, such as preventing systems from learning from new input data (i.e., only original training data are used to generate responses).

The *Tay* example is somewhat misleading, however, because it represents *intentional* attempts to insert bias into a language-based technology. Developers and users may be acting with the best of intentions yet still generate bias. In educational contexts, GIGO problems may manifest due to the limited range of language varieties used to train instructional and assessment systems. For example, to create a system that assesses student writing and gives feedback for improvement, developers may create a training corpus of tens of thousands of pre-scored and annotated essays. Despite such a large sample, one must consider the varieties of writing and writers that are included or excluded in the corpus. Moreover, we must consider how the essays were annotated and what assumptions are present in the rubrics (i.e., what forms of language are explicitly labeled as "high scoring" versus "low scoring").

Similarly, metaphors and other forms of figurative language also differ from one culture to the next (Gupta et al., 2024; Parks, 2010). Without attention to such varieties, language technologies may be even less equipped to capture the culturally diverse ways that humans express themselves (Liu et al., 2023).

3.3 Sampling

Another challenge related to training and development pertains to *whose* data is collected for such purposes. Research indicates that LLMs are still primarily trained on American, Canadian, and UK English, and subsequently are not performing well on "nonstandard" English (Choudhury, 2023) or even Englishes that represent different national backgrounds (e.g., Australian English; Horvath, 2008; Moore, 2008). Importantly, simply training on *all* available language data is typically not feasible for LLMs—a subset of texts or materials must be curated. Historically, many corpora for NLP have consisted of newspaper articles, published literature, and similarly formal texts, despite recognition that these materials differed significantly from spoken language (Lindquist & Levin, 2000). Fortunately, this practice has changed substantially over the two decades, yet there are still sampling biases related to genre, style, age, language background, socioeconomic status, and other demographic factors (Gururangan et al., 2022; Hovy & Yang, 2021).

Intentions to "be inclusive" when developing a language technology are not sufficient. First, data are not always readily available for different groups present in the population (i.e., representational bias, Baker & Hawn, 2021), they represent a smaller proportion of the population and/or often ignored in decision making and design (Barocas & Selbst, 2016; Lerman, 2013). In addition, relevant information about language users may be missing, thus negating our ability to inspect for inclusion or bias (i.e., measurement bias, Baker & Hawn, 2021). For example, existing training data often lacks information regarding North-African and Middle Eastern speakers of Arabic because demographic questionnaires typically do not include options for identifying as such (Magbouleh et al., 2022). Many current race and ethnicity questions force Arabic speakers of Middle Eastern and North African backgrounds to choose race and heritage options such as "White," "Asian," "African," "other," or "prefer not to say." Overall, concrete steps may be needed to reach and involve underrepresented populations and relevant data that is not being collected as a source of training data, and to be able to correctly identify those persons who do participate. Valid conclusions about populations affected by an algorithm cannot be drawn without representation of populations and relevant information about them (Krishnamurthy, 2019).

3.4 Transparency

Many automated tools lack transparency—their underlying code, computations, variables, rubrics, and decision-making algorithms are neither visible nor accessible to most users (Blattner, 2021; Prinsloo, 2020). This challenge can muddle or create distrust in the educational value of technologies (e.g., to teach, assess, or improve writing), and can make it difficult or impossible to detect or diagnose biases. Moreover, a lack of access to internal judgments and rubrics makes it difficult for students to understand how to succeed. Students may spend time trying to satisfy the mysterious demands of the technology that engaging in their own meaningful work (Knesek, 2022).

With respect to language and language technologies, a lack of transparency can also contribute to relatively narrow perspectives of language, genre, registers, and varieties. In such cases, it is unclear whether and what diverse kinds of language are being assessed. For instance, although tools like *Grammarly* offer several options for setting the "tone" of writing, the systems do not necessarily disclose the norms or assumptions that define those styles. Walsh (2022) has argued that *Grammarly* perpetuates White-centered raciolinguistic norms despite offering several national English dialects for users to choose from (e.g., American, British, Canadian, and New Zealand). However, other nonhegemonic varieties of natively spoken English are missing (e.g., Singapore English)—*Grammarly* is thus likely to "correct" their standard usage. Within American English, the tool also does not include different dialects that are natively spoken in the U.S. (e.g., AAVE, Chicano English, and Southern varieties). Consequently, users of these tools are subtly and invisibly nudged to adopt certain societal and contextual language norms (e.g., academic English) and ideologies.

4 Improving Language Technologies in Education

Language technologies already participate in numerous aspects of education, teaching, and learning, and ongoing innovations (e.g., LLMs and gen AI) have the potential to further transform educational practices. Consequently, there was *already* a need to interrogate and address biases in language technologies, and those needs will only *grow* in the coming years. Existing language technologies embed social stereotypes, biases, and standard language ideologies in their models. We thus contend that improving the language technologies embedded in educational systems will benefit all learners, and particularly students whose language(s), culture(s), and identities may be excluded or marginalized in the classroom.

Developers who seek to improve educational technologies will need to conscientiously employ a range of methods to prevent or address these threats. This section offers several considerations for language technology developers, researchers, and evaluators who seek more inclusive and equitable tools. These considerations can be advanced with inclusive design techniques such as participatory design (Bang & Vissoughi, 2016; Bødker et al., 2021; Borges et al., 2016; Mukhija et al., 2021; Spinuzzi, 2005), particularly when those methods are implemented mindfully. Care should be taken to support and not overburden co-designers, and to welcome contributions rather than merely "extract" data and information (Delgado et al., 2023; Pierre et al., 2021; Sloane et al., 2022). Finally, we recognize that a robust effort to prevent language technologies from perpetuating biases will require increasing the technological awareness and knowledge of teachers, students, and the general public. We thus also include considerations that extend to participants and stakeholders beyond only the developers.

The field of HCI providers an inventory of methods and existing research compatible with acknowledging the permeation of standard language ideologies to language technologies. Participatory design and annotation, along with the evaluation of tools by a diverse user population can help catch biased behaviors and improve tool interfaces (e.g., Chien & Yao, 2020; Menter & Hasirci, 2018; Nekoto et al., 2020; Hannon et al., 2022). Beyond design and user-experience concerns, the literature on participatory design offers critical theory that allows researchers to critically examine the ways in which societal power relations get perpetuated within education and technology and outlining applied approaches for creating transformative social change (Fine et al., 2003; Paris & Winn, 2013; Tuck & Yang, 2021; Zavala, 2013). The next section outlines a few solutions for the issues discussed in Sect. 2 and provides participatory design examples illustrating how these solutions could manifest. The list of solutions and examples is not exhaustive but is meant to illustrate how one may begin to address standard language ideology issues in language technology through participatory design.

4.1 Addressing Training Data and "GIGO" Threats

Language ideologies are present in many aspects of language and perceptions of language users, which interweave beliefs about language (e.g., the belief that there are standard or "correct" varieties of a language) and potentially racist, misogynistic, classist, and similar social stereotypes. Because these problems exist throughout our everyday conversation, news and entertainment media, literature, and more, they are necessarily part of the GIGO problem for language technology development (Bender & Koller, 2020; Shaffer et al., 2023). Without care, existing language ideologies *will* be fully adopted and integrated into any language technology, without any mitigation.

Developers have produced algorithmic techniques for mitigating well-documented socially discriminatory biases (Milios & BehnamGhader, 2022). However, less research is examining the kinds of cultural biases that might emerge from training data selection (see review in Talat et al., 2022) or how they impact the treatment of nonstandard languages. In the last ten years, research on the training and development of LLMs has grown so fast that communities working on this space are still converging on both the techniques and the terms necessary to describe them. Early failures appear to have provided important lessons for the development (and redevelopment) processes. Broadly, these practices now include (a) selecting training data, (b) pretraining models, and (c) task adaptation techniques that allow the models to be statistically modified to address GIGO problems.

First, in educational language technologies, data selection that includes texts from speakers of nonstandard dialects will be critical to ensuring the students' cultural and linguistic knowledge are recognized as valid by automated technologies. We need to develop and curate data sets that more thoroughly document the language varieties of marginalized groups. Some efforts are currently being explored to develop new corpora that encompass a wider variety of dialects. For example, Eisenstein et al. (2023) have collected a spoken language dataset with several dialects of English (from India, Nigeria, and the United States). The aim of that dataset, which is available to the public, is to train automated systems to incorporate linguistic variance. Kendall & Farrington (2018) report a similar effort with a publicly available dataset representing a variety of spoken African American English dialects from the US. These data include language features that can be filtered out in standard datasets (e.g., phonology, syntax, morphology) and a range of contextual context from the speakers.

Importantly, LLM creation involves multiple stages where algorithms may incorporate human biases. Simply increasing the number and size of corpora representing minoritized language varieties will not necessarily improve subsequent models if developers do not employ processes ready to address such variance appropriately (e.g., varying vocabularies, structures, and contexts). For example, Google's BERT relies on the Penn Treebank (Rogers et al., 2021), which limits grammaticality judgments used to evaluate BERT to only dialects represented in the tool. Researchers are beginning to recognize that we need better representation of L2 and nonstandard English patterns (e.g., Tan et al., 2020), but the development and testing of these tools has not yet become inclusive of the people whose language varieties are most stigmatized. This is an important target for HCI experts to contribute to.

Second, in pre-training stages, observed language patterns inform model parameters that can mimic general knowledge (e.g., Kauf et al., 2023). These parameters may include true and useful information, but they may also include known biases. The biases in training data are likely to remain problematic because the scale of this data is so large that no researcher can fully understand every bias that may be present (Biderman & Scheirer, 2020). Several responses to this problem are being explored, such as manually removing language patterns likely to contribute to these biases. Yu et al. (2023) propose a technique that optimizes weights contributing to specific types of bias, in this case, the gender-profession type, to counteract biases that are perpetuated from data. The proposed technique has shown success in identifying the sources of implicit bias in a large pretrained language model. Devlin et al. (2018) introduce BERT models, which can be fine-tuned for specific tasks and be able to counteract or neutralize biased patterns. While BERT still demonstrates biases, its models have room for de-biasing solutions (e.g., Bhardwaj et al., 2021; Mozafari et al., 2020) and are being widely employed.

Third, models undergo various task adaptations to improve their ability to make useful predictions (e.g., Diao et al., 2023; Li et al., 2023). Currently, these adaptations are mostly driven by improving model metrics that are unrelated to increasing fairness and equality for model outputs and end-user experiences. Relevant metrics are usually defined as matching human performance (Collins et al., 2022), a goal which could potentially lead to greater inequities in subsequent applications. Attending to outputs that mirror standard dialects and their evaluation as "better" is likely to perpetuate biases regarding other varieties. To improve equity in educational language technologies, the HCI community should work with developers to make sure that the task adaptation and fine-tuning processes are implemented in ways that (a) treat nonstandard language varieties as socially valid and (b) include ways of appropriately modeling the knowledge and contexts of relevant communities.

4.2 Improving Sampling Practices

Language models are often trained on a limited number of languages and dialects that either exclude "nonstandard" varieties or flag them as "incorrect." Moreover, the data may lack contextual information (e.g., about the language users, culture, region, and so on) that may contribute to understanding how language is used. Simply increasing sample sizes without context is unlikely to prevent bias. Curators of language corpora must intentionally collect datasets that are representative of relevant linguistic varieties, including engaging in authentic efforts to obtain data from underrepresented language users (e.g., Pham et al., 2024; Santiago et al., 2022). Of course, gathering data for uncommon or stigmatized language varieties may be difficult due to a scarcity of speakers or an unwillingness on their part to provide data. Thus, additional methods may be needed to overcome barriers to participation (e.g., time, travel, costs, and distrust) (Kuhlman et al., 2020). Despite those difficulties, the participation of individuals from varying backgrounds in data collection and the assessment of the resulting tools is crucial for genuine attempts at debiasing (Burgstahler, 2011; Hunt et al., 2015; Jackson et al., 2019; Lachney, 2017; Scott et al., 2015; Vakil et al., 2016) that are transparent and communicated to users (Patel, 2015).

Similarly, in datasets that include human ratings or annotations, such assessments must include evaluators representative of all relevant languages and communities (e.g., Larimore et al., 2021; Yin et al., 2023). If annotators from minoritized backgrounds are not sufficiently represented among other annotators, their relevant experiences and judgments will also be underrepresented in how the algorithm operates. Consistent group-level annotations from annotators of similar backgrounds should be considered in the algorithm development process to influence the eventual functionality. Research has begun to explore methods for preventing annotators' variance from being discounted as noise, particularly if it is consistent and related to demographic variance (e.g., Plank, 2022). Similarly, researchers are also exploring sources of annotator disagreement and their connections to identity (e.g., Goyal et al., 2022).

One way to include more diverse language varieties and perspectives in language technology development is through mindful participatory design research methods (Bang & Vossoughi, 2016). Participatory design practices have the potential to improve sampling practices, algorithm functionality, and tool interfaces by involving key audiences and stakeholders throughout the process. For example, Nekoto and colleagues (2020) describe a participatory design methodology that recruited participants without formal training to co-create a machine translation database for 30 African languages. Their recruitment sought partners through multiple channels, provided training tutorials, and enabled communication through online platforms (e.g., GitHub). Participants in the study represent populations who would not normally be recruited to take part in shaping machine translation datasets. This gave the researchers an even bigger benefit, in the form of diverse language datasets from 30 African languages.

In an example of participatory design research that involves educational technology, Hannon et al., (2012) worked with teachers to redesign a tool for collaborative, inquiry-based learning. In this study, the authors conducted a multi-year participatory design project with teachers who varied in their experience with inquiry-based learning. This collaboration was mutually beneficial, as teachers acquired important pedagogical skills as they provided the researchers with concrete suggestions on how best to improve the technology.

Notably, participatory methods must be employed in ways that are mutually beneficial rather than extractive (e.g., developers use participants as sources of inspiration and data) (Sloane et al., 2022), must authentically represent valid participants' choices (Pierre et al., 2021), and avoid introducing additional burdens (Delgado et al., 2023) such as travel and time costs (Pater et al., 2021).

4.3 Improving AI and Data Literacy

Other approaches for improving language technologies and reducing bias rely on changing human-computer interactions beyond technology development. Specifically, improving users' and teachers' AI literacy might encourage more critical use of language tools. Without a general understanding of how algorithms work and their limitations, it may be harder for users to critically consider outputs from language tools and use them most efficiently. For example, consider the polarizing "hype" surrounding artificial intelligence (e.g., Slota, 2020), wherein some users describe AI as nearly all-powerful whereas others report serious cases of algorithmic bias (Bender et al., 2021; Buolamwini & Gebru, 2018 Eubanks, 2018; O'Neil, 2017). AI literacy might support more balanced understanding and perspectives about AI capabilities and drawbacks.

One way to help students better understand AI-driven educational technologies and data could be a school requirement for AI and data literacy education (i.e., the ability to use and evaluate AI systems; Long & Magerko, 2020). Efforts are being made to develop and test programs and workshops meant to educate users of all ages about automated language technology, its abilities, limitations, and bias pitfalls (e.g., Hong & Kim, 2020; Lee et al., 2021a, 2021b, 2021c). These pilot programs have been shown to increase user AI literacy. However, there is insufficient data on what AI literacy interventions lead to student understanding of AI concepts (Casal-Otero et al., 2023), and there is a need for competency frameworks testing student uptake. In addition, without making technological literacy a mandatory part of education, it will be hard to ensure critical use of automated language tools.

Asset-based pedagogy can also help bolster users' critical approach to automated language technology. As language technologies become more prevalent and widespread, more concrete educational standards and assessments are needed to prioritize teaching and learning with AI-driven tools (Koh & Doroudi, 2023; Lee et al., 2020) and to prepare educators to use them effectively (Chang et al., 2023; Luckin et al., 2022). Teachers have also reported that professional standards of AI should include teaching students concepts of ethical issues in big data and media literacy (Chiu, 2023). The recently published educational policy guidelines on AI in education (e.g., Cardona et al., 2023; European Commission, 2022; Miao et al., 2021) represent an initial attempt to support teachers and students in using AI-tools effectively and safely. Still, the guidelines call for additional investment in teacher professional development (PD) to accomplish this goal (Cardona et al., 2023; European Commission, 2022; Miao et al., 2021).

A condition for successful uptake regarding AI literacy requires awareness of social ideological inequities contributing to algorithmic bias and its continuation. In other words, without awareness of standard language ideologies and their harm, students, teachers, and other language technology users are not likely to be critical of automated language technology (Lee, 2008). Even before widespread public access to generative-AI-driven language technology, existing language curriculum and assessment standards needed to be revised to integrate students' linguistic differences (Flores, 2020) and emphasize students' flexibility in using academic language skills (Uccelli, 2023). Increased access to AI-driven language technologies presents an opportunity for governments to develop and revise language and literacy curricula and assessments in a way that fosters the use of such technologies from an asset-based approach (Ocumpaugh et al., 2024).

5   Conclusions

In this paper, we considered contemporary language technologies in education with regards to potential language ideologies, biases, and solutions. Specifically, we briefly reviewed the concept of standard language ideologies and other linguistic biases that can affect language technologies (see Sect. 1). We argued that these language biases are intricately tied to social stereotypes and their embeddedness in language expression and processing. Language technologies, such as those that are being deployed in classrooms (see Sect. 2). For example, the "standardized" language varieties appearing in such technologies can reinforce and amplify biased ideologies, particularly if they are implemented in literacy instruction and feedback (e.g., automated writing evaluation). Finally, we described how problems related to demographic sampling and training data (e.g., the garbage in, garbage out problem) can contribute to biased language models. Moreover, the opacity of these complex models might exacerbate potential problems by making it harder to detect, test, or mitigate bias. Finally, we described concerns related to the use of LLMs in meeting the pedagogical needs of students.

In response to the above concerns, we began to outline ways to address these problems (see Sect. 3). We focused on areas that are well-suited for solutions from an HCI lens. For example, we described emerging research on machine learning techniques designed to retrain or filter biases. These techniques should be complimented by improved sampling across underrepresented language varieties, learning technologies that treat these varieties more equally, and further support for pedagogical development and instruction that recognizes that students' home languages are valuable assets. We also illustrated participatory design examples for achieving the goals outlined above. Attempts to mitigate the effects of standard language ideologies within language tools must involve users in a way that empowers and benefits them.

The various concerns and methods we considered in this paper are far from exhaustive; additional multidisciplinary actions will further aid in creating more equitable language technologies. For example, language technology developers and researchers may also need to consider *legal* and *regulatory* aspects of inclusive design and use, and how such concerns may influence corporate and school uptake. Legal protections already safeguard users' personal data, particularly in educational context where technology use may be mandated and when users are minors. Legal mandates may also be necessary for companies to be transparent about how their algorithms operate and the demographic composition of training datasets, and perhaps allowing users to provide feedback in cases of tool dysfunction or observed biases. The social consequences of biased language technologies are potentially far-reaching, and thus our prevention and responses to these threats will need to be equally expansive.

Acknowledgments. This work was funded in part by a grant from the Gates Foundation (INV-006213), by AERDF/EF+Math grant "Making learning visible: scalable, multisystem detection of self-regulation related to EF", and by the Institute of Education Sciences, U.S. Department of Education, through Grant R305A180261 to Arizona State University. Opinions, findings, conclusions, or recommendations expressed in this work are those of the author and do not necessarily reflect the reviews of funding sources.

Disclosure of Interests.   The authors have no competing interests to declare that are relevant to the content of this article.

References

Ajisoko, P.: The use of Duolingo apps to improve English vocabulary learning. Int. J. Emerging Technol. Learn. (iJET) **15**(7), 149–155 (2020). https://www.learntechlib.org/p/217084/. Accessed 15 Jan 2024

Alharbi, W.: AI in the Foreign language classroom: a pedagogical overview of automated writing assistance tools. Educ. Res. Int. 2023 (2023). https://doi.org/10.1155/2023/4253331

Ayres-Bennett, W.: Codification and prescription in linguistic standardisation. Constructing Lang. Norms, Myths Emotions **13**, 99 (2016)

Bang, M., Vossoughi, S.: Participatory design research and educational justice: Studying learning and relations within social change making. Cognition Inst. **34**(3), 173–193 (2016). https://doi.org/10.1080/07370008.2016.1181879

Baratta, A.: Accent and linguistic prejudice within British teacher training. J. Lang. Identity Educ. **16**(6), 416–423 (2017). https://doi.org/10.1080/15348458.2017.1359608

Barocas, S., Selbst, A.D.: Big data's disparate impact. California Law Rev., 671–732 (2016). https://doi.org/10.15779/Z38BG31

Bender, E.M., Gebru, T., McMillan-Major, A., Shmitchell, S.: On the dangers of stochastic parrots: Can language models be too big?. In: Proceedings of the 2021 ACM Conference on Fairness, Accountability, and Transparency, pp. 610–623 (2021). https://doi.org/10.1145/3442188.344 5922

Bender, E.M., Koller, A.: Climbing towards NLU: on meaning, form, and understanding in the age of data. In: Proceedings of the 58th annual meeting of the association for computational linguistics, pp. 5185–5198 (2020). https://doi.org/10.18653/v1/2020.acl-main.463

Ben-Simon, A., Bennett, R.E.: Towards more substantively meaningful automated essay scoring. J. Teach. Learn. Assessment **6**(1), 4–44 (2007). http://www.jtla.org

Bhardwaj, R., Majumder, N., Poria, S.: Investigating gender bias in bert. Cognitive Comput. **13**(4), 1008–1018. https://doi.org/10.1007/s12559-021-09881-2 (@021)

Blattner, L., Nelson, S., Spiess, J.: Unpacking the Black Box: Regulating Algorithmic Decisions (2021). https://doi.org/10.48550/arXiv.2110.03443

Blodgett, S.L., Barocas, S., Daumé III, H., Wallach, H.: Language (technology) is power: A critical survey of "bias" in nlp (2020). https://doi.org/10.48550/arXiv.2005.14050

Bødker, S., Dindler, C., Iversen, O.S., Smith, R.C.: Participatory design. Synthesis Lectures Hum.-Centered Inform. **14**(5), i–143 (2021)

Buolamwini, J., Gebru, T.: Gender shades: Intersectional accuracy disparities in commercial gender classification. In: Conference on Fairness, Accountability and Transparency, pp. 77–91. PMLR (2018)

Burgstahler, S.: Universal design: Implications for computing education. ACM Trans. Comput. Educ. (TOCE) **11**(3), 1–17 (2011)

Burner, T.: Formative assessment of writing in English as a foreign language. Scand. J. Educ. Res. **60**(6), 626–648 (2016)

Caliskan, A., Bryson, J.J., Narayanan, A.: Semantics derived automatically from language corpora contain human-like biases. Science **356**(6334), 183–186 (2017)

Cardona, M.A., Rodríguez, R.J., Ishmael, K.: Artificial intelligence and the future of teaching and learning. Office of Educational Technology (2023). https://tech.ed.gov/files/2023/05/ai-future-of-teaching-and-learning-report.pdf

Casal-Otero, L., Catala, A., Fernández-Morante, C., Taboada, M., Cebreiro, B., Barro, S.: AI literacy in K-12: a systematic literature review. Int. J. STEM Educ. **10**(1), 29 (2023). https://doi.org/10.1186/s40594-023-00418-7

Chan, M.P.Y., Choe, J., Li, A., Chen, Y., Gao, X., Holliday, N.: Training and typological bias in ASR performance for world Englishes. In: Proceedings of the 23rd Conference of the International Speech Communication Association (2022). https://doi.org/10.21437/Interspeech.2022-10869

Chang, D.H., Lin, M.P.C., Hajian, S., Wang, Q.Q.: Educational design principles of using AI chatbot that supports self-regulated learning in education: goal setting, feedback, and personalization. Sustainability **15**(17), 12921 (2023)

Chen, K.H.: Ideologies of Language Standardization. In: The Oxford Handbook of Language Policy and Planning. Oxford University Press (2018)

Chien, Y.H., Yao, C.K.: Development of an ai userbot for engineering design education using an intent and flow combined framework. Appl. Sci. **10**(22), 7970 (2020). https://doi.org/10.3390/app10227970

Chiu, T.K.: The impact of Generative AI (GenAI) on practices, policies and research direction in education: a case of ChatGPT and Midjourney. Interact. Learn. Environ., 1–17 (2023). https://doi.org/10.1080/10494820.2023.2253861

Choudhury, M. Generative AI has a language problem. Nat. Hum. Behav. **7**, 1802–1803. https://doi.org/10.1038/s41562-023-01716-4 (2023)

Curzan, A.: Fixing English: Prescriptivism and Language History. Cambridge University Press (2014)

Cushing, I.: 'Say it like the Queen': the standard language ideology and language policy making in English primary schools. Lang. Culture Curriculum **34**(3), 321–336 (2021). https://doi.org/10.1080/07908318.2020.1840578

Dalton, B., Proctor, C.P., Uccelli, P., Mo, E., Snow, C.E.: Designing for diversity: the role of reading strategies and interactive vocabulary in a digital reading environment for fifth-grade monolingual English and bilingual students. J. Literacy Res. **43**(1), 68–100 (2011). https://doi.org/10.1177/1086296X10397872

Deane, P.: On the relation between automated essay scoring and modern views of the writing construct. Assessing Writing **18**, 7–24 (2013). https://doi.org/10.1016/j.asw.2012.10.002

Delgado, F., Yang, S., Madaio, M., Yang, Q.: The participatory turn in ai design: Theoretical foundations and the current state of practice. In: Proceedings of the 3rd ACM Conference on Equity and Access in Algorithms, Mechanisms, and Optimization, pp. 1–23 (2023). https://doi.org/10.1145/3617694.3623261

Devlin, J., Chang, M. W., Lee, K., Toutanova, K.: Bert: Pre-training of deep bidirectional transformers for language understanding (2018). https://doi.org/10.48550/arXiv.1810.04805

DiChristofano, A., Shuster, H., Chandra, S., Patwari, N.: Performance disparities between accents in automatic speech recognition (2022). https://doi.org/10.48550/arXiv.2208.01157

Drake, G.: American Linguistic Prescriptivism: Its Decline and Revival in the 19th Century1. Lang. Soc. **6**(3), 323–340 (1977). https://doi.org/10.1017/S0047404500005042

Economidou-Kogetsidis, M.: Variation in evaluations of the (im) politeness of emails from L2 learners and perceptions of the personality of their senders. J. Pragmat. **106**, 1–19 (2016)

Eisenstein, J., Prabhakaran, V., Rivera, C., Demszky, D., & Sharma, D. MD3: The Multi-Dialect Dataset of Dialogues. https://doi.org/10.48550/arXiv.1904.05527 (2023)

Eubanks, V.: Automating inequality: How high-tech tools profile, police, and punish the poor. Martin's Press, St (2018)

European Commission, Directorate-General for Education, Youth, Sport and Culture, Ethical guidelines on the use of artificial intelligence (AI) and data in teaching and learning for educators, Publications Office of the European Union (2022). https://data.europa.eu/doi/https://doi.org/10.2766/153756

Fine, M., et al.: Participatory action research: From within and beyond prison bars (2003). https://doi.org/10.1037/10595-010

Flores, N.: From academic language to language architecture: Challenging raciolinguistic ideologies in research and practice. Theory Practice **59**(1), 22–31 (2020). https://doi.org/10.1080/00405841.2019.1665411

Gardner, J., O'Leary, M., Yuan, L.: Artificial intelligence in educational assessment: 'Breakthrough? Or buncombe and ballyhoo?' J. Comput. Assist. Learn. **37**(5), 1207–1216 (2021)

Goyal, N., Kivlichan, I.D., Rosen, R., Vasserman, L.: Is your toxicity my toxicity? exploring the impact of rater identity on toxicity annotation. In: Proceedings of the ACM on Human-Computer Interaction, 6(CSCW2), 1–28 (2022). https://doi.org/10.1145/3555088

Graham, S., Hebert, M., Harris, K.R.: Formative assessment and writing: a meta-analysis. Elem. Sch. J. **115**(4), 523–547 (2015)

Gupta, A.: African-American English: Teacher beliefs, teacher needs and teacher preparation programs. Reading Matrix Int. Online J. **10**(2) (2010). https://digitalcommons.odu.edu/cgi/viewcontent.cgi?article=1001&context=teachinglearning_fac_pubs

Gupta, A., Atef, Y., Mills, A., Bali, M.: Assistant, Parrot, or Colonizing Loudspeaker? ChatGPT Metaphors for Developing Critical AI Literacies (2024). https://doi.org/10.48550/arXiv.2401.08711

Gururangan, S., et al.: Whose language counts as high quality? measuring language ideologies in text data selection. In: Proceedings of the 2022 Conference on Empirical Methods in Natural Language Processing, pp. 2562–2580, Abu Dhabi, United Arab Emirates. Association for Computational Linguistics (2022). https://doi.org/10.48550/arXiv.2201.10474

Haig, Y., Oliver, R.: Language variation and education: Teachers' perceptions. Lang. Educ. 17(4), 266–280 (2003). https://doi.org/10.1080/09500780308666852

Hannon, D., Danahy, E., Schneider, L., Coopey, E., Garber, G.: Encouraging teachers to adopt inquiry-based learning by engaging in participatory design. In: IEEE 2nd Integrated STEM Education Conference, pp. 1–4. IEEE (2012). https://doi.org/10.1109/ISECon.2012.6204169

Heritage, M. Formative assessment: Making it happen in the classroom. Corwin Press (2021)

Hong, J. Y., Kim, Y.: Development of AI data science education program to foster data literacy of elementary school students. J. Korean Assoc. Inform. Educ. 24(6), 633–641 (2020). https://doi.org/10.14352/jkaie.2020.24.6.633

Horvath, B.M.: Australian English: Phonology. Varieties of English 3, 89–110 (2008)

Hovy, D., Yang, D.: The importance of modeling social factors of language: theory and practice. In: Proceedings of the 2021 Conference of the North American Chapter of the Association for Computational Linguistics: Human Language Technologies, pp. 588–602 (2021)

Hunt, V., Layton, D., Prince, S.: Diversity matters. McKinsey Company 1(1), 15–29 (2015)

Jackson, L., Kuhlman, C., Jackson, F., Fox, P.K.: Including vulnerable populations in the assessment of data from vulnerable populations. Front. Big Data 2, 19 (2019). https://doi.org/10.3389/fdata.2019.00019

Kauf, C., et al.: Event knowledge in large language models: the gap between the impossible and the unlikely. Cognitive Sci. 47(11), e13386 (2023). https://doi.org/10.1111/cogs.13386

Kendall, T., Farrington, C.: The corpus of regional African American language. Version 6, 1 (2018)

Kidd, M.A.: Archetypes, stereotypes and media representation in a multi-cultural society. Procedia-Soc. Behav. Sci. 236, 25–28 (2016). https://doi.org/10.1016/j.sbspro.2016.12.007

Knesek, G.E.: Why Focusing on Grades Is a Barrier to Learning. Harvard Business Publishing: Education. https://hbsp.harvard.edu/inspiring-minds/why-focusing-on-grades-is-a-barrier-to-learning, 24 Apr 2022

Koenecke, A., et al.: Racial disparities in automated speech recognition. Proc. Natl. Acad. Sci. 117(14), 7684–7689 (2020)

Koh, E., Doroudi, S.: Learning, teaching, and assessment with generative artificial intelligence: towards a plateau of productivity. Learn. Res. Practice 9(2), 109–116 (2023). https://doi.org/10.1080/23735082.2023.2264086

Kotek, H., Dockum, R., Sun, D.: Gender bias and stereotypes in Large Language Models. In: Proceedings of the ACM Collective Intelligence Conference, pp. 12–24 (2023). https://doi.org/10.1145/3582269.3615599

Krishnan, J., Black, R.W., Olson, C.B.: The power of context: exploring teachers' formative assessment for online collaborative writing. Read. Writ. Q. 37(3), 201–220 (2021)

Krishnamurthy, P. Understanding data bias. Towards data science. https://towardsdatascience.com/survey-d4f168791e57 (2019, September 11)

Kuhlman, C., Jackson, L., Chunara, R.: No computation without representation: avoiding data and algorithm biases through diversity (2020). https://doi.org/10.48550/arXiv.2002.11836

Kutlu, E., Tiv, M., Wulff, S., Titone, D.: The impact of race on speech perception and accentedness judgements in racially diverse and non-diverse groups. Appl. Linguis. 43(5), 867–890 (2022)

Kurinec, C.A., Weaver, C.A.: III Dialect on trial: use of African American Vernacular English influences juror appraisals. Psychol. Crime Law 25(8), 803–828. https://doi.org/10.1080/1068316X.2019.1597086 (2019)

Lachney, M.: Computational communities: African-American cultural capital in computer science education. Comput. Sci. Educ. 27(3–4), 175–196 (2017). https://doi.org/10.1080/08993408.2018.1429062

Larimore, S., Kennedy, I., Haskett, B., Arseniev-Koehler, A.: Reconsidering annotator disagreement about racist language: Noise or signal? In: Proceedings of the Ninth International Workshop on Natural Language Processing for Social Media, pp. 81–90 (2021). https://doi.org/10.18653/v1/2021.socialnlp-1.7

Lawton, R., de Kleine, C.: The need to dismantle "standard" language ideology at the community college: an analysis of writing and literacy instructor attitudes. J. College Reading Learn. **50**(4), 197–219 (2020). https://doi.org/10.1080/10790195.2020.1836938

Lee, I., Ali, S., Zhang, H., DiPaola, D., Breazeal, C.: Developing middle school students' AI literacy. In: Proceedings of the 52nd ACM Technical Symposium on Computer Science Education, pp. 191–197 (2021)

Lee, K.J., et al.: The show must go on: a conceptual model of conducting synchronous participatory design with children online. In: Proceedings of the 2021 CHI Conference on Human Factors in Computing Systems, pp. 1–16 (2021). https://doi.org/10.1145/3411764.3445715

Lee, I., Ali, S., Zhang, H., DiPaola, D., Breazeal, C.: Developing middle school students' AI literacy. In: Proceedings of the 52nd ACM Technical Symposium on Computer Science Education, pp. 191–197 (2021). https://dl.acm.org/doi/10.1145/3408877.3432513

Lee, H., Chung, H.Q., Zhang, Y., Abedi, J., Warschauer, M.: The effectiveness and features of formative assessment in US K-12 education: a systematic review. Appl. Measur. Educ. **33**(2), 124–140 (2020)

Lee, C.D.: The centrality of culture to the scientific study of learning and development: how an ecological framework in education research facilitates civic responsibility. Educ. Res. **37**(5), 267 (2008)

Liang, W., Yuksekgonul, M., Mao, Y., Wu, E., Zou, J.: GPT detectors are biased against non-native English writers (2023). https://doi.org/10.48550/arXiv.2304.02819

Lindquist, H., Levin, M.: Apples and oranges: on comparing data from different corpora. In Corpus Linguistics and Linguistic Theory, pp. 201–213. Brill (2000). https://doi.org/10.1163/978900 4490758_017

Lippi-Green, R.: English with an accent: Language, ideology, and discrimination in the United States. Routledge (2012)

Liu, C. C., Koto, F., Baldwin, T., Gurevych, I.: Are multilingual llms culturally-diverse reasoners? an investigation into multicultural proverbs and sayings (2023). https://doi.org/10.48550/arXiv. 2309.08591

Long, D., Magerko, B.: What is AI literacy? competencies and design considerations. In: Proceedings of the 2020 CHI Conference on Human Factors in Computing Systems, pp. 1–16 (2020). https://doi.org/10.1145/3313831.3376727

Luckin, R., Cukurova, M., Kent, C., du Boulay, B.: Empowering educators to be AI-ready. Comput. Educ. Artif. Intell. **3**, 100076 (2022). https://doi.org/10.1016/j.caeai.2022.100076

Maghbouleh, N., Schachter, A., Flores, R.D.: Middle Eastern and North African Americans may not be perceived, nor perceive themselves, to be White. In: Proceedings of the National Academy of Sciences **119**(7) https://doi.org/10.1073/pnas.2117940119 (2022)

Markl, N.: Language variation and algorithmic bias: understanding algorithmic bias in British English automatic speech recognition. In: Proceedings of the 2022 ACM Conference on Fairness, Accountability, and Transparency, pp. 521–534 (2022). https://doi.org/10.1145/3531146. 3533117

Martin, J.L., Tang, K.: Understanding racial disparities in automatic speech recognition: the case of habitual "be". In: Interspeech, pp. 626–630 (2020). https://doi.org/10.21437/Interspeech. 2020-2893

Martin, J.L., Wright, K.E.: Bias in automatic speech recognition: The case of African American language. Appl. Linguist. **44**(4), 613–630 (2023). https://doi.org/10.1093/applin/amac066

Mason, M., Carson-Berndsen, J.: Investigating phoneme similarity with artificially accented speech. In: Proceedings of the 20th SIGMORPHON Workshop on Computational Research in Phonetics, Phonology, and Morphology, pp. 49–57 (2023). https://doi.org/10.48550/arXiv.2305.07389

McNamara, D.S., et al.: The Writing-Pal: Natural language algorithms to support intelligent tutoring on writing strategies. In: K-12 Education: Concepts, Methodologies, Tools, and Applications, pp. 780–793. IGI Global (2014). https://doi.org/10.4018/978-1-4666-4502-8.ch045

Milios, A., BehnamGhader, P.: An analysis of social biases present in bert variants across multiple languages (2022). https://doi.org/10.48550/arXiv.2211.14402

Milroy, J.: Language ideologies and the consequences of standardization. J. Sociolinguistics 5(4), 530–555 (2001). https://doi.org/10.1111/1467-9481.00163

Milroy, L.: Standard English and language ideology in Britain and the United States. In: Standard English, pp. 173–206. Routledge (2002)

Milroy, J.: The ideology of the standard. The Routledge Companion to Sociolinguistics 133 (2007)

Miao, F., Holmes, W., Huang, R., Zhang, H.: AI and education: Guidance for policy-makers. United Nations Educational, Scientific and Cultural Organization (2021). https://unesdoc.unesco.org/ark:/48223/pf0000376709

Moore, B.: Speaking our language: the story of Australian English, pp. 97–8. Melbourne: Oxford University Press (2008)

Mozafari, M., Farahbakhsh, R., Crespi, N.: Hate speech detection and racial bias mitigation in social media based on BERT model. PloS one 15(8), e0237861 (2020). https://doi.org/10.1371/journal.pone.0237861

Munro, M.J.: Listening to the "noise" in the data: the critical importance of individual differences in second-language speech. J. Second Lang. Pronunciation (2023). https://doi.org/10.1075/jslp.23029.mun

Nekoto, W., et al.: Participatory research for low-resourced machine translation: a case study in african languages (2020). https://doi.org/10.48550/arXiv.2010.02353

Ocumpaugh, J., Roscoe, R.D., Baker, R.S., et al.: Toward asset-based instruction and assessment in artificial intelligence in education. Int. J. Artif. Intell. Educ. (2024). https://doi.org/10.1007/s40593-023-00382-x

O'Neil, C.: Weapons of math destruction: How big data increases inequality and threatens democracy. Crown (2017)

Paris, D., Winn, M.T. (eds.): Humanizing research: Decolonizing qualitative inquiry with youth and communities. Sage Publications (2013)

Parks, A.N.: Metaphors of hierarchy in mathematics education discourse: the narrow path. J. Curriculum Stud. 42(1), 79–97 (2010). https://doi.org/10.1080/00220270903167743

Patel, L.: Decolonizing Educational Research : From Ownership to Answerability. Routledge, NewYork (2015)

Pater, J., Coupe, A., Pfafman, R., Phelan, C., Toscos, T., Jacobs, M.: Standardizing reporting of participant compensation in HCI: a systematic literature review and recommendations for the field. In: Proceedings of the 2021 CHI Conference on Human Factors in Computing Systems, pp. 1–16 (2021). https://doi.org/10.1145/3411764.3445734

Peng, H., Ma, S., Spector, J.M.: Personalized adaptive learning: an emerging pedagogical approach enabled by a smart learning environment. Smart Learn. Environ. 6(1), 1–14 (2019)

Pham, N., Pham, L., Meyers, A.L.: Towards Better Inclusivity: A Diverse Tweet Corpus of English Varieties (2024). https://doi.org/10.48550/arXiv.2401.11487

Pierre, J., Crooks, R., Currie, M., Paris, B., Pasquetto, I.: Getting Ourselves Together: Data-centered participatory design research & epistemic burden. In: Proceedings of the 2021 CHI Conference on Human Factors in Computing Systems, pp. 1–11 (2021). https://doi.org/10.1145/3411764.3445103

Plank, B.: The 'Problem' of Human Label Variation: On Ground Truth in Data, Modeling and Evaluation (2022). https://doi.org/10.48550/arXiv.2211.02570

Preston, D.R.: The cognitive foundations of language regard. Poznan Stud. Contemporary Linguist. **53**(1), 17–42 (2017). https://doi.org/10.1515/psicl-2017-0002

Prinsloo, P.: Of 'black boxes' and algorithmic decision-making in (higher) education–a commentary. Big Data & Soc. **7**(1). https://doi.org/10.1177/2053951720933994 (2020)

Reyero Lobo, P., Daga, E., Alani, H., Fernandez, M.: Semantic Web technologies and bias in artificial intelligence: a systematic literature review. Semantic Web **14**(4), 745–770 (2023). https://doi.org/10.3233/SW-223041

Rose, H., Galloway, N.: Debating standard language ideology in the classroom: Using the 'Speak Good English Movement'to raise awareness of global Englishes. RELC J. **48**(3), 294–301 (2017). https://doi.org/10.1177/0033688216684281

Roscoe, R.D., McNamara, D.S.: Writing Pal: Feasibility of an intelligent writing strategy tutor in the high school classroom. J. Educ. Psychol. **105**(4), 1010–1025 (2013). https://doi.org/10.1037/a0032340

Santiago, H., Martin, J., Moeller, S., Tang, K.: Disambiguation of morpho-syntactic features of African American English--the case of habitual be (2022). https://doi.org/10.48550/arXiv.2204.1242

Scott, K.A., Sheridan, K.M., Clark, K.: Culturally responsive computing: a theory revisited. Learn. Media Technol. **40**(4), 412–436 (2015). https://doi.org/10.1080/17439884.2014.924966

Silaj, K.M., Frangiyyeh, A., Paquette-Smith, M.: The impact of multimedia design and the accent of the instructor on student learning and evaluations of teaching. Applied Cognitive Psychology (2023). https://doi.org/10.1002/acp.4143

Silber Mohamed, H., Farris, E.M.: 'Bad hombres'? an examination of identities in US media coverage of immigration. J. Ethnic Migration Stud. **46**(1), 158–176 (2020). https://doi.org/10.1080/1369183X.2019.1574221

Slota, S.C., et al.: Good systems, bad data? interpretations of AI hype and failures. Proc Assoc. Inf. Sci. Technol. **57**(1), e275 (2020). https://doi.org/10.1002/pra2.275

Snell, J.: Dialect, interaction and class positioning at school: From deficit to difference to repertoire. Lang. Educ. **27**(2), 110–128 (2013). https://doi.org/10.1080/09500782.2012.760584

Spence, J. L., Hornsey, M.J., Stephenson, E.M., Imuta, K.: Is Your Accent Right for the Job? A Meta-Analysis on Accent Bias in Hiring Decisions. Personality and Social Psychology Bulletin (2022). https://doi.org/10.1177/01461672221130595

Strickland, C.L., Young, S.: Dialect bias in questioning styles in the standard English classroom. In: Presented at Annual Research Forum (Winston-Salem, NC, December 1999), p. 121

Tan, S., Joty, S., Varshney, L.R., Kan, M.Y.: Mind your inflections! Improving NLP for non-standard Englishes with Base-Inflection Encoding (2020). https://doi.org/10.48550/arXiv.2004.14870

Teng, L.S.: Explicit strategy-based instruction in L2 writing contexts: a perspective of self-regulated learning and formative assessment. Assess. Writ. **53**, 100645 (2022)

Thompson, N.A., Weiss, D.A.: A framework for the development of computerized adaptive tests. Pract. Assess. Res. Eval. **16**(1), 1 (2019)

Trudgill, P., Hannah, J.: International English: A guide to the varieties of standard English. Routledge (2013)

Tuck, E., Yang, K.W.: Decolonization is not a metaphor. Tabula Rasa (38), 61–111 (2021). https://doi.org/10.25058/20112742.n38.04

Van der Linden, W.J., Glas, C.A. (eds.): Computerized adaptive testing: Theory and practice. Springer Science & Business Media. (2000)

Vakil, S., McKinney de Royston, M., Suad Nasir, N.I., Kirshner, B.: Rethinking race and power in design-based research: Reflections from the field. Cognition Instruction **34**(3), 194–209 (2016). https://doi.org/10.1080/07370008.2016.1169817

Walsh, J.A.: Natural language processing in educational contexts: opportunities and potential pitfalls (Doctoral dissertation) (2022)

Wassink, A.B., Gansen, C., Bartholomew, I.: Uneven success: automatic speech recognition and ethnicity-related dialects. Speech Commun. **140**, 50–70 (2022)

Wilson, J., Huang, Y., Palermo, C., Beard, G., MacArthur, C.A.: Automated feedback and automated scoring in the elementary grades: Usage, attitudes, and associations with writing outcomes in a districtwide implementation of MI Write. Int. J. Artif. Intell. Educ. **31**(2), 234–276 (2021). https://doi.org/10.1007/s40593-020-00236-w

Wingate, U.: The impact of formative feedback on the development of academic writing. In: Approaches to Assessment that Enhance Learning in Higher Education, pp. 29–43. Routledge (2014)

Wolf, M.J., Miller, K., Grodzinsky, F.S.: Why we should have seen that coming: comments on Microsoft's tay "experiment," and wider implications. ACM Sigcas Comput. Soc. **47**(3), 54–64 (2017). https://doi.org/10.1145/3144592.3144598

Yin, W., Agarwal, V., Jiang, A., Zubiaga, A., Sastry, N.: Annobert: effectively representing multiple annotators' label choices to improve hate speech detection. In: Proceedings of the International AAAI Conference on Web and Social Media, vol. 17, pp. 902–913 (2023)

Yu, C., Jeoung, S., Kasi, A., Yu, P., Ji, H.: Unlearning bias in language models by partitioning gradients. In: Findings of the Association for Computational Linguistics: ACL 2023, pp. 6032–6048 (2023). https://doi.org/10.18653/v1/2023.findings-acl.375

Zavala, M.: What do we mean by decolonizing research strategies? Lessons from decolonizing, Indigenous research projects in New Zealand and Latin America (2013)

Mutually Complementary HAR System Using IMU-Based Wearable Devices and Computer Vision

Woosoon Jung[1], KyoungOck Park[2], Jeong Tak Ryu[3], Kyuman Jeong[4], and Yoosoo Oh[4(✉)]

[1] Institute of Special Education and Rehabilitation Science, Daegu University, Gyeongsan-si, Republic of Korea
[2] Department of Elemantary Special Education, Daegu University, Gyeongsan-si, Republic of Korea
kopark@daegu.ac.kr
[3] Department of Electronic and Electrical Engineering, Daegu University, Gyeongsan-si, Republic of Korea
jryu@daegu.ac.kr
[4] School of AI, Daegu University, Gyeongsan-si, Republic of Korea
{kyuman.jeong,yoosoo.oh}@daegu.ac.kr

Abstract. Human Activity Recognition (HAR) is an effective approach to achieving intuitive Human-Computer Interaction (HCI). Pose estimation, which targets the entire body, is a major area of HAR, with a focus on skeleton estimation using computer vision. The primary advantage of estimating the skeleton using computer vision is the ability to reduce the dimensions of the data to be processed ultimately (advantage of skeleton extraction). However, there are physical limitations due to the nature of computer vision systems. Instances where the target is detected overlaps with other objects or the image is unclear due to ambient lighting serve as examples [1].

Furthermore, the skeleton estimation system represents the joints corresponding to the landmarks as 3-axis data. Given the nature of 2D data, the accuracy of the remaining axis is relatively low. To overcome these issues, we propose the application of wearable devices based on Inertial Measurement Units (IMUs) in conjunction with computer vision systems. IMUs are well-suited for measuring the movement of a target due to their lightweight and compact size. Although those are vulnerable to noise and require preprocessing [2], this drawback can be overcome with algorithms at the level of Kalman filters [3], and the required preprocessing level is lower when applied to AI (Artificial Intelligence).

In this study, we propose a system that mutually complements IMUs and computer vision systems. The most widely used Pose estimation framework is Google's MediaPipe, which defines 32 landmarks [4]. However, wearing 32 IMUs is not cost-effective or convenient. For this reason, this study proposes wearing 10 IMU sensors on the left and right shoulders, hips, knees, ankles, and wrists.

The contributions of the proposed hybrid system are as follows: In a 2D computer vision system, when the rest of one axis is incomplete, it can be complemented by IMU data. In the IMU system, when distance data between joints or position of joints is incomplete, it can be complemented by computer vision.

M. Antona and C. Stephanidis (Eds.): HCII 2024, LNCS 14696, pp. 291–299, 2024.
https://doi.org/10.1007/978-3-031-60875-9_19

When the target to be recognized is overlapped, IMU data can be used as ground truth. The performance of the proposed system is evaluated based on the skeleton extracted using both IMU data and images. A comparison and analysis are conduct-ed between cases where the skeleton is estimated based on the image and using IMU data.

Keywords: Skeleton Estimation · Vision-based system · IMU · Wearable Device

1   Introduction

In the field of Human Activity Recognition (HAR), most research is being conducted on pose estimation systems in computer vision. In particular, models such as MediaPipe and MoveNet are good at estimating even joints that are not visible due to the camera angle. However, the model's confidence is low if other objects overlay body parts completely. Due to the nature of HAR, there needs to be instantaneous estimation. However, if the application is applied in exceptional cases (e.g., the behavior of disabled people or the elderly), it should be fixed. Accordingly, we propose a complementary system combined with Inertial Measurement Units (IMU) to overcome the shortcomings of vision-based user pose estimation systems.

IMU-based HAR System. IMU systems have long been used for various self-measurements in automobiles, aircraft, and human bodies. The IMU is the most intuitive device to measure posture and has the advantage of being small in size. Disadvantages are that drift occurs, errors accumulate over time, and many complex preprocessing operations are required to handle noise. Overall, filtering and calibration processes are essential to deal with accumulated errors.

There are pros and cons to both vision-based and IMU-based systems, and they can complement each other. The most difficult thing when performing pose estimation with an IMU is that it is difficult to accurately determine the attached location. This can be easily solved with a vision-based system. In the opposite case, in a vision-based system, when the subject is obscured by other objects and is not visible, the angle information of the joint can be obtained using the IMU sensor. In this study, we propose a complementary system by combining the advantages of heterogeneous systems.

2   Skeleton Estimation

2.1   Vision-Based Skeleton Estimation

The vision-based approach used in this study is MediaPipe, the most popular pose estimation framework. MediaPipe provides both pose and face and hand detection and coordinates of the detected object, making it suitable for on-device Machine Learning (ML) applications. MediaPipe's pose estimation algorithm uses a total of 32 landmarks and estimates large joints and small body parts such as the eyes, nose, mouth, thumb, and index finger. MediaPipe is a well-validated and highly accurate framework. However, since it is a vision-based system, there are cases where estimation is physically impossible (e.g., when the target object is covered by the subject, when the image quality is insufficient, etc.). The MediaPipe's pose estimation model provides not only real-world 3D coordinates but also output defined as '*visibility*', which is the likelihood of the landmark being visible.

(a)   (b)

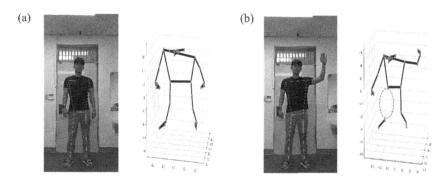

Fig. 1. Examples of joint estimation success (a) and failure (b) of the MediaPipe.

Figure 1 is an example of posture estimation using MediaPipe. In the Fig. 1(a), all joints are estimated normally. On the other hand, in the Fig. 1(b), the right leg is not observed. In the image, the '*visibility*' of the right knee joint is less than 0.3, which is a low value compared to other joints. As a result, the right thigh and calf are not drawn in the estimated skeleton.

2.2 IMU-Based Skeleton Estimation

IMUs have been used in HAR for decades. IMU-based systems have a variety of advantages, including non-invasiveness, portability, and cost. In particular, due to its low price and small size, it can be easily carried or embedded to be applied to applications such as sports activity recognition [5], indoor navigation [6], autonomous driving [7], and fall detection [8]. The trade-off between accuracy and preprocessing cost must be considered when applying IMU. IMU output is susceptible and requires much effort to preprocess. It is easily affected by interference from the external environment and even the body's natural vibration. Additionally, the drift problem occurring in IMU is the first problem to be solved in applications using IMUs [9, 10]. Drift in a gyroscope causes errors to accumulate over time, and magnetometers require periodic calibration because the surrounding magnetic field greatly influences them.

Most studies that have attempted pose estimation using IMU express them in 3D space by attaching an IMU to the location corresponding to each joint [11]. In the case of IMU Poser [12], posture is estimated using a smartphone, watch, and earbuds without implementing a custom device.

Figure 2 shows an example output from the IMU. In this example, a 6 Degrees of Freedom (6-DOF) IMU containing a 3-axis accelerometer and a 3-axis gyroscope is attached to the calf, and the user is walking. Even though it is a prolonged movement, much noise is generated.

Table 1 shows a comparison of each feature of the vision-based system and the IMU-based system.

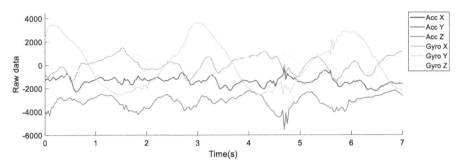

Fig. 2. Example of 6-DOF IMU output

Table 1. Comparison of features of vision-based and IMU-based systems.

	Vision-based System	IMU-based System
Landmarks	Includes face and fingers	Not suitable for small joints
Joint length	Estimable	Non-estimable
Joint angle	Estimable	Estimable
Computational complexity	Higher	Lower
System scalability	Very high (Infrastructure dependent)	Low (Requires custom implementation)

3   Proposed Method

The proposed method to ensure both the vision-based system's scalability and the IMU device's reliability is that if the MediaPipe outputs low '*visibility*', it is complemented with an IMU device. Choosing locations to attach the IMUs is essential. There are 32 landmarks used in MediaPipe's pose estimation, including the face, fingers, and feet. Since estimating small joints with an IMU sensor is inefficient, our scope is a large joint among MediaPipe's landmarks. The large joints defined in MediaPipe are shoulders, elbows, wrists, hips, knees, and ankles, but we excluded the elbow here. The elbow angle is estimated using the shoulder and wrist angle information. Since the IMU provides angle information, the attachment locations of each IMU are the end of each joint. The IMU for the shoulders is attached to the lateral deltoid muscles, and for the hips, it is attached to the thighs.

Figure 3 is a system diagram of the proposed system. Users attach 10 wearable devices designed in this study to large jointed body parts. The device consists of MCU, IMU, Zigbee, and 220mA battery. The system's connectivity is Zigbee and has a tree topology structure. A camera is connected to the PC that collects IMU data, so an IMU and vision-based system is built.

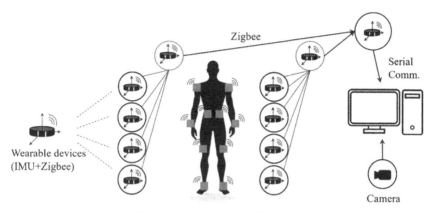

Fig. 3. Proposed system diagram.

4 Experimental Setup

4.1 Designing IMU-Based System

In MediaPipe, real-world coordinates of joints are extracted. The proposed wearable system designed to attach the IMU at the location corresponding to the joints is shown in the Fig. 4. The Printed Circuit Board (PCB) dimension smaller than 2 inches square. It comprises a 32-bit Cortex-M4 processor operating at 64 MHz, Zigbee, and IMU module. Since the IMU-based system is used together with the vision-based system, each wearable device must provide angle information of the attached joint. Therefore, a total of 10 wearable devices are attached per user. Since the number of nodes in the network is large, the Zigbee network was adopted. The wearable device is powered by a small-sized LiPo battery, both the processor and Zigbee module were adopted considering power consumption.

Fig. 4. Designed 10 IMU systems.

Complementary Filters are Mainly used to Estimate Posture by Combining Data from Accelerometers and Gyroscopes. The shortcomings of accelerometers, which are vulnerable to high-frequency noise, and gyroscopes, which are vulnerable to low-frequency noise, can be compensated for.

The Kalman Filter Assumes Gaussian Noise and Recursively Compares the System State and Predicted Values. It is very effective in removing noise and various expansion filters exist. In general, since matrix operations are performed, computational complexity is higher than that of complementary filters.

The Sensor Fusion Algorithm is a Method of Generating Reliable Information by Combining Multiple Sensors. When the sensor fusion algorithm is applied to an IMU system, it is suitable for estimating orientation and pose by integrating the accelerometer, gyroscope, and magnetometer of the 9-DOF IMU. The most widely used sensor fusion algorithms are the Madgwick algorithm and the Mahony algorithm [13], and both algorithms use the mathematical expression called Quaternium.

In this study, since the vision-based and IMU-based systems are used together, orientation can be inferred from the vision-based system. Therefore, 6-DOF IMU is adopted. Additionally, since wearable devices use limited computing resources and batteries, complementary filters are applied to reduce the amount of computation.

Simple complementary filter is shown below line.

$$\theta = \alpha \cdot (\theta + gyro\_rate \cdot \Delta t) + (1 - \alpha) \cdot accel\_angle \tag{1}$$

where θ represents the estimated orientation angle, $gyro\_rate$ is the angular velocity, t is the sampling time interval, $accel\_angle$ is the angle calculated from the accelerometer data and α is a filter coefficient.

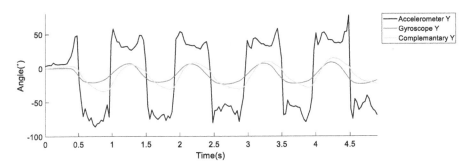

Fig. 5. Example of IMU output when rotating 90 degrees vertically.

Figure 5 shows the IMU output before and after preprocessing. The IMU data was not subjected to any filtering other than conversion to angular form. On the other hand, the red line in the figure is the result of applying a complementary filter with a coefficient of 0.96. Not only does it remove noise well, but the response delay due to filtering is also negligible. Since it is used together with MediaPipe, a short response delay from the complementary filter is tolerated.

Figure 6(a) is a 3D visualization experiment scene of the IMU-based system. It was confirmed that the rectangular 3D model implemented in the Pygame environment

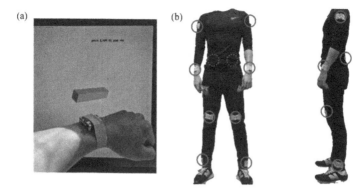

Fig. 6. Designed IMU-based System. (a): IMU Pose Estimation Test, (b): Example of Wearable System Attachment on Adolescents

reflects movement well in real time. As mentioned in the previous chapter, the biggest disadvantage of IMU is that it is vulnerable to ambient noise and has a drift phenomenon in which errors accumulate over time. Due to the applied complementary filter, the IMU output is more stable than before, but it was confirmed that drift phenomenon still occurs after a long period of time. Fortunately, this can be overcome in vision-based systems. Vision-based systems can know the direction more accurately than IMU applications. For this reason, since the user's direction can be determined, the computing resources of the wearable system can be saved by the corresponding task.

Figure 6(b) shows the wearing scene of the designed wearable system. A total of 10 systems were worn on the deltoids, wrists, hips (lower back), knees, and ankles, respectively. It communicates with Zigbee, which provides a low-power solution, and the IMU's output is ultimately transmitted to the PC.

4.2 Evaluations

In this study, we assumed cases where vision-based system is physically difficult to recognize. Even with well-verified systems, there are cases where the subject is not visible. For example, it is difficult for a vision AI (Artificial Intelligence) system to extract features if the subject is obscured by other objects or other body parts, or if the subject is wearing black clothes.

Figure 7(a), (b) shows examples where a desk obscures the subject's lower body. In both cases, MediaPipe was unable to detect the lower body. The '*visibility*' of the estimated lower body joints was low (below 0.1) which means MediaPipe did not detect objects. The second case is when the '*visibility*' recorded in MediaPipe is ignored and the skeleton estimated by MediaPipe is visualized (green skeleton). Even though the entire lower body was covered by the desk, it was confirmed that some inference was possible. The three figures on the right (red skeleton) are when MediaPipe and the designed IMU-based system are applied together. In the proposed system, if the '*visibility*' of MediaPipe is below the threshold, the physical limitation could be overcome using IMU. Figure 7(c) is an example where the right arm and right leg are invisible. As shown in the Fig. 7, MediaPipe could not detect subject since subject's right arm is held horizontally and

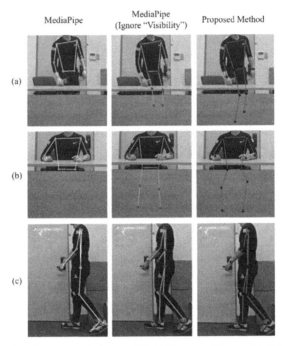

Fig. 7. Evaluation for the proposed system: MediaPipe considering '*visibility*', ignoring low '*visibility*' case in MediaPipe, and examples of skeleton estimation by the proposed system.

subject is wearing black clothes. As a result of estimating the pose while ignoring the low '*visibility*' of MediaPipe, the right leg was detected well, but the pose of the right arm was inferred from the left arm.

5   Conclusions

In this study, we proposed a mutually complementary HAR system combining vision-based and IMU-based systems. Despite the rapid development of AI-based computer vision technology, using IMU is still useful where estimation was impossible due to physical limitations. Furthermore, IMU can be applied efficiently in wearable devices with limited computing resources. The orientation problem that occurs when using the 6-DOF IMU was overcome by using a vision-based system. The contribution of this study is to introduce a complementary solution by combining the advantages of heterogeneous systems.

Acknowledgments. This work was supported by the Ministry of Education of the Republic of Korea and the National Research Foundation of Korea (NRF-2022S1A5C2A07091326).

Disclosure of Interests. The authors have no competing interests to declare that are relevant to the content of this article.

References

1. Dang, L.M., Min, K., Wang, H., Piran, J., Lee, C.H., Moon, H.: Sensor-based and vision-based human activity recognition: a comprehensive survey. Pattern Recogn. **108**, 107561 (2020)
2. Mendes, N., Ferrer, J., Vitorino, J., Safeea, M., Neto, P.: Human behavior and hand gesture classification for smart human-robot interaction. Procedia Manuf. **11**, 91–98 (2017)
3. Laput, G., Harrison, C.: Sensing fine-grained hand activity with smartwatches. In: Proceedings of the ACM Conference on Human Factors in Computing Systems (CHI'19), Glasgow, UK, 4–9 May 2019
4. Lugaresi, C., et al.: MediaPipe: a framework for building perception pipelines. arXiv:1906. 08172v1, pp.1–9, 14 June 2019
5. Rana, M., Mittal, V.: Wearable sensors for real-time kinematics analysis in sports: a review. IEEE Sensors J. **21**(2), 1187–1207. Springer, Heidelberg (2021). https://doi.org/10.1109/JSEN.2020.3019016
6. Jiménez, A.R., Seco, F., Prieto, J.C., Guevara, J.: Indoor pedestrian navigation using an INS/EKF framework for yaw drift reduction and a foot-mounted IMU. In: 7th Workshop on Positioning, Navigation and Communication, pp. 135–143. Springer, Dresden (2010). https://doi.org/10.1109/WPNC.2010.5649300
7. Wang, Z., Wu, Y., Niu, Q.: Multi-sensor fusion in automated driving: a survey. IEEE Access **8**, 2847–2868 (2020). https://doi.org/10.1109/ACCESS.2019.2962554
8. Lin, H.-C., Chen, M.-J., Lee, C.-H., Kung, L.-C., Huang, J.-T.: Fall recognition based on an IMU wearable device and fall verification through a smart speaker and the IoT. Sensors **23**, 5472 (2023). https://doi.org/10.3390/s23125472
9. Narasimhappa, M., Mahindrakar, A.D., Guizilini, V.C., Terra, M.H., Sabat, S.L.: MEMS-based IMU drift minimization: sage Husa adaptive robust Kalman filtering. IEEE Sensors J. **20**(1), 250–260 (2020). https://doi.org/10.1109/JSEN.2019.2941273
10. Kok, M., Hol, J.D., Schön, T.B.: Using inertial sensors for position and orientation estimation. Found. Trends Signal Process. **11**(1–2), 1–153 (2017). https://doi.org/10.1561/2000000094
11. Yi, X., Zhou, Y., Xu, F.: TransPose: real-time 3D human translation and pose estimation with six inertial sensors. ACM Trans. Graph. **40**(5), 1–13 (2021). https://doi.org/10.1145/3450626. 3459786
12. Mollyn, V., Arakawa, R., Goel, M., Harrison, C., Ahuja, K.: IMUPoser: full-body pose estimation using IMUs in phones, watches, and earbuds. In: Proceedings of the 2023 CHI Conference on Human Factors in Computing Systems, Hamburg, Germany, April 23–28, 2023, pp. 1–12. Springer, New York (2023). https://doi.org/10.1145/3544548.3581392
13. Mahony, R., Hamel, T., Pflimlin, J.M.: Nonlinear complementary filters on the special orthogonal group. IEEE Trans. Autom. Control **53**(5), 1203–1218 (2008). https://doi.org/10.1109/TAC.2008.923738

An Investigation of the Impact of Emotion in Image Classification Based on Deep Learning

Riccardo Emanuele Landi[1]([⊠]), Marta Chinnici[2], and Gerardo Iovane[3]

[1] Innoida S.r.l., Via Ex Aeroporto, 80038 Pomigliano d'Arco, Italy
riccardo.landi@innoida.it
[2] ENEA-R.C. Casaccia, Via Anguillarese 301, 00123 Rome, Italy
marta.chinnici@enea.it
[3] Department of Computer Science, University of Salerno, Via Giovanni Paolo II, 84084 Fisciano, Italy
giovane@unisa.it

Abstract. Emotion was found to improve memory and learning under certain conditions. In the context of deep learning, many neural models achieved competitive performances by considering the emotional factor in solving tasks of interest. Among them, investigations concerning the introduction of emotion for solving image classification tasks provided significant results. However, to our knowledge, a study on the impact of emotion on solving image classification through trainable encoders has never been conducted, yet. To perform experiments, the present study proposes the Emotional Regulation approach, which mainly consists of selecting non-emotional and emotionally-influenced representations according to a criterion. In particular, emotionally-influenced representations are learned by concatenating original embeddings with the representations obtained from a frozen emotional encoder. Experiments were performed by employing ResNet-50 and ViT-B/16 architectures, assuming CIFAR-10 and -100 as target datasets for training and evaluation. A set of emotional stimuli was employed to provide an emotional history, while the regulation process was conditioned on positive, neutral, and negative semantics. The results show that our approach improved the original backbones in classifying the considered target datasets, providing evidence for the effectiveness of emotion in supporting image classification based on deep learning.

Keywords: emotion · image classification · deep learning · emotional regulation · affective computing

1 Introduction

Emotion is a significant factor in human learning. Feeling specific affective states can increase the effectiveness of learning new concepts and stimuli. The influence of emotion on learning has been extensively investigated by Education, Psychology, and Neuroscience. Under certain conditions, emotion was proven to produce

M. Antona and C. Stephanidis (Eds.): HCII 2024, LNCS 14696, pp. 300–310, 2024.
https://doi.org/10.1007/978-3-031-60875-9_20

significant positive effects on memory and reasoning [1–3,5]. The introduction of emotional aspects into neural network training is of particular interest for improving state-of-the-art models for generic task resolution. Studying human cognition for designing artificial agents can contribute to the explainability of cognitive processes, as well as the design of superior-performing machine learning models. The main assumption is that an artificial agent, similar to a human being, should learn instances of the world more effectively through emotions. Therefore, introducing emotion in artificial learning could represent a consistent approach to improve neural networks in the resolution of generic tasks.

In the field of Affective Computing, specifically in the area of emotion-augmented machine learning, different approaches have been proposed to introduce emotions into the artificial learning process. The emotional factor has been deployed through the definition of specific back-propagation approaches, anatomy-inspired models, and reinforcement learning [6]. These studies have produced significant results, revealing emotions as an enhancing factor for improving learning models. Investigation of the effects of emotion on artificial learning has also led to the definition of neural networks that consider explicitly the emotional factor, i.e., the *Emotional Artificial Neural Networks* [8–10]; these types of models draw inspiration from the neurophysiological structure of the emotional brain. Other proposals introduce emotion using higher levels of abstraction; for instance, through the definition of an emotional history in which stimuli are associated with affective states. Recently, it has been proven that providing an emotional history to a frozen zero-shot encoder can enhance its accuracy in classifying images through supervised optimization [14]. However, to our knowledge, the effects of an emotional history applied directly to a trainable backbone architecture for image classification still require investigation. The present work is intended to investigate whether providing an emotional history to a learnable classifier could improve its performance.

The present study proposes an advancement in the study of artificial emotion effects in image classification by proposing the *Emotional Regulation* approach. The solution allows to study the impact of an emotional history on a learnable encoder, without neglecting the opportunity to exploit relevant non-emotional representations. Our solution consists of extending a backbone up to three classifiers, which represent *non-emotional, emotional,* and *emotionally-influenced* encoders. The first, i.e., the non-emotional encoder, is the original backbone; the second, i.e., the emotional encoder, is trained with an emotional history and outputs emotion probabilities; the third, i.e., the emotionally-influenced encoder, is trained by concatenating its resulting embeddings with the representations extracted from a frozen emotional encoder. The regulation process consists of selecting non-emotional representations in the case of significant emotion elicitation, while emotionally-influenced representations otherwise.

For conducting experiments, two famous and widely employed architectures, i.e., ResNet-50 [15] and ViT-B/16 [16], have been chosen to take the role of the considered encoders. Models have been trained and validated on CIFAR-10 and -100 [17] benchmarking datasets for accuracy comparison. Results show that our Emotional Regulation approach overcomes the accuracy of the original back-bones on the employed benchmarking datasets. Furthermore, it was found that coupling a classifier with an emotional encoder (i.e., introducing an emotional history) can improve its accuracy. Results enforce the effectiveness of employing emotion for improving image classification based on deep learning models.

In the first part of the paper, an introduction concerning the findings related to studies investigating the effects of emotion on human learning is provided. Subsequently, we discuss the state-of-the-art related to the introduction of emotion in the process of artificial neural networks' learning. For presenting our contribution, a description of the methods employed and the related experimental setup are highlighted. The work concludes by presenting the results and discussing future research directions.

2   Emotion as a Deep Learning Enhancer

Emotional activity in the human brain is significantly associated with the limbic system, especially with the amygdala. Emotion processing also involves sensory cortex (SC), prefrontal cortex (PFC), orbitofrontal cortex (OFC), hypothalamus, hippocampus, and thalamus, influencing memory, cognition, attention, and learning [3,6]. Congleton & Berntsen [2] investigated the influence of emotion on memory by proposing to participants a simulated event in the form of a first-person perspective video. They investigated the accuracy of memorizing central and peripheral details in scenes characterized by positive or negative emotional valence. The authors found that scene details were better memorized by participants involved in the negative emotional condition. In their meta-analysis, Yin et al. [3] recently found that emotion has significant effects on judgments of learning (JOLs) and memory. Emotional stimuli seem to produce higher JOLs and induce significant effects on memory, without finding significant differences between positive and negative valence. Images characterized by emotional content seem to provide a greater impact on JOLs than verbal content, revealing the importance of visual stimuli for eliciting emotions.

The aforementioned findings sufficiently motivate the investigation that was intended to be conducted in the present work, since affective reactions to stimuli, under certain conditions, can improve learning and memory. Artificial neural networks can be conceived as a suitable instance of artificial learning that takes inspiration from human cognition. Thus, the hypothesis that a neural network could improve its performance through emotion seems consistent. Several research studies considered emotion for improving deep learning models. Thenius, Zahadat & Schmickl [7] improved classical artificial neural networks by simulating the neuromodulatory hormonal system. Other models explicitly consider the amygdala, SC, OFC, and thalamus, together with their interaction paths. For instance, Shahid & Singh [10] proposed a hybrid model involving an emotional neural network and particle swarm optimization for coronary artery disease diagnosis. They found competitive classification performances compared with existing methods. Emotional neural networks were also employed for water quality index analysis [11] and flood forecasting [12]. Other investigations were performed in the context of reinforcement learning, where emotion was introduced as a factor related to reward [13].

Landi, Chinnici & Iovane [14] provided evidence for the effectiveness of emotion in improving image classification tasks. They employed a frozen zero-shot encoder for extracting significant image features. Representations were provided to several cognitive layers for learning an emotion classifier pre-trained on EMOd [18]. The results show an improvement in classifying target datasets, revealing the effectiveness of introducing an emotional history for improving classification. However, to our knowledge, an investigation of the impact of emotion on image classification by employing learnable backbones has never been conducted, yet. Therefore, in the present study, emotion was intended to be introduced actively in the learning process of a neural classification encoder.

3   Emotional Regulation

The proposed method for investigating the effects of emotion in image classification is described in Fig. 1. The approach is composed of three elements: i) *Non-emotional Encoder*, i.e., a backbone trained directly on a target classification dataset; ii) *Emotional Encoder*, i.e., an encoder trained on a dataset describing an emotional history; iii) *Emotionally-influenced Encoder*, i.e., an encoder characterized by the same architecture as the original backbone, trained on the same target dataset, considering features extracted from the Emotional Encoder; iv) *Emotional Regulation*, i.e., a process selecting emotionally-influenced or non-emotional features to perform the final classification.

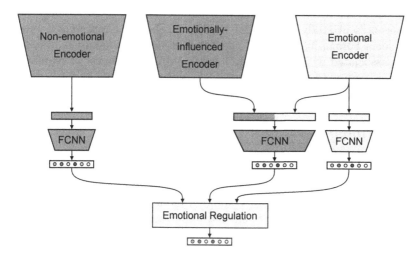

Fig. 1. The proposed Emotional Regulation approach.

The Non-emotional Encoder represents the part of the model that does not consider emotions; it acts as an "emotionally agnostic" model. This encoder receives an image and outputs an embedding describing non-emotional semantics. Probability scores related to the considered classes are predicted by learning a fully connected neural network (FCNN) at the end of the model. The Emotional Encoder represents a model of emotion; it learns to associate visual stimuli with the related emotional classes. This encoder is intended to be trained on a dataset representing an emotional history. It receives an image and outputs an embedding describing the related emotional content. The model employing this encoder provides probability scores associated with the considered emotional classes.

The Emotionally-influenced Encoder represents the part of the model considering emotion. It learns representations by concatenating features of the Emotional Encoder to the resulting embeddings. This encoder receives an image and outputs a representation that extends the knowledge of the original backbone. This new embedding describes the features of the input image from an emotional perspective. Even in this case, a fully connected neural network is learned for estimating probability scores associated with the considered classes.

Finally, the Emotional Regulation process acquires models' predictions and a reference criterion. The criterion consists of selecting non-emotional and emotionally-influenced predictions based on the emotional outcome. In the case of significant emotional occurrence, the Non-emotional Encoder is selected to perform the final classification; the Emotionally-influenced Encoder is selected otherwise. The above encoders are learnable and trained on a target classification dataset. The Emotional Encoder is frozen and pre-trained on a dataset describing an emotional history. It acts as a frozen encoder supporting the training of the Emotionally-influenced Encoder. The Emotional Regulation process is activated at inference time, when no training occurs.

In the present study, Emotional Regulation does not represent a model of emotion or a human-inspired computational model. The name *emotional regulation* is associated with the tendency of the proposed process to regulate classification according to predicted emotional categories. It should not be intended as a model inspired by theories or experiments in the field of Cognitive Science.

4   Experiments

4.1   Experimental Setup

Architectures employed for conducting experiments are ResNet-50 [15] and ViT-B/16 [16], as they represent widely adopted models in Computer Vision. Emotional and Non-emotional Encoders have the same architecture, with output representations in the $\mathbb{R}^{B \times F}$ domain, with B the batch size and F the number of dimensions describing the output embedding. For both the encoders, the FCNN layer consists of a linear layer projecting representations into the prediction space $[0, 1]^{B \times C}$, where the softmax is applied for computing probability scores related to the considered C classes. The Emotionally-Influenced Encoder has the same architecture as the above two encoders, producing output representations in the $\mathbb{R}^{B \times 2F}$ domain, where B represents the batch size and $2F$ denotes twice the number of dimensions defining the original output embedding. Similarly, it contributes to a model that projects representations into the prediction space $[0, 1]^{B \times C}$ through a linear FCNN layer. In the present experimental setup, the Emotional Encoder has the same architecture as the other two encoders. Its representations are in the $\mathbb{R}^{B \times F}$ domain, projected into the space $[0, 1]^{B \times E}$, with E the dimensions associated with the considered emotional classes, through a linear FCNN layer. Features extracted from the Emotional and Non-emotional Encoders are characterized by 2048 and 768 dimensions for the employed ResNet and ViT, respectively. For the same architectures, the representations of the Emotionally-influenced Encoder are characterized by 4096 and 1536 dimensions, respectively.

In the proposed experimental setup, the Emotional Regulation process considers positive and negative macro-classes of emotion. In particular, the regulation criterion is adopted for emotions associated with positive and/or negative semantics. Emotions of anger, disgust, fear, and sadness were considered as negative, while emotions of happiness and surprise as positive. The Emotional Encoder was trained on the EMOd dataset [18] concerning the six emotional classes of anger, disgust, fear, happiness, sadness, surprise, and the neutral state. The three considered encoders were pre-trained on ImageNet [19] and trained separately on the target datasets. The Emotional Encoder has been frozen and adopted for concatenating its features to the representations learned from the Emotionally-influenced Encoder.

For training the encoders, a batch size of 32 was imposed for 200 epochs. All the experiments have been performed with SGD (Stochastic Gradient Descent) as optimizer, with a learning rate of 0.001 and momentum of 0.9. Data was augmented during batch training with random rotation between -90 and 90 degrees, vertical flip, and horizontal flip with a probability of 0.5. Backpropagation was performed according to the cross-entropy loss. Experiments have been conducted by employing the CRESCO6 ENEA HPC infrastructure [20].

4.2   Results

The Emotional Encoder reached accuracy scores of 64.34% and 65.03% on the EMOd test set by employing ResNet and ViT, respectively. Tables 1 and 2 show the evaluation of the trained models on CIFAR-10 and -100. The results highlight that our Emotional Regulation approach overcomes the accuracy of the original backbones on the employed benchmarking datasets.

Improvements of 0.32% and 0.01% were found on CIFAR-10 by applying the proposed approach on ResNet-50 and ViT-B/16, respectively. Similarly, improvements of 0.64% and 0.19% were found by applying the regulation of ResNet-50 and ViT-B/16 on CIFAR-100, respectively. Furthermore, the evaluation of the Emotionally-influenced Encoder directly on the CIFAR-100 dataset provided an accuracy improvement of 0.68% compared with the original ResNet backbone.

Table 1. Accuracy results of the proposed approach on CIFAR-10.

Model	Regulation	Positive	Neutral	Negative	Total
ResNet-50 (backbone)	None	0.9353	0.9436	0.9154	0.9311
Emot-Inf-ResNet-50	None	0.9417	0.9447	0.9117	0.9329
Emot-Reg-ResNet-50	Positive	0.9353	0.9447	0.9117	0.9302
Emot-Reg-ResNet-50	Negative	0.9417	0.9447	0.9154	**0.9341**
Emot-Reg-ResNet-50	Positive, Negative	0.9353	0.9447	0.9154	0.9314
ViT-B/16 (backbone)	None	0.9684	0.9775	0.9686	0.9702
Emot-Inf-ViT-B/16	None	0.9643	0.9781	0.9681	0.9683
Emot-Reg-ViT-B/16	Positive	0.9684	0.9781	0.9681	0.9701
Emot-Reg-ViT-B/16	Negative	0.9643	0.9781	0.9686	0.9685
Emot-Reg-ViT-B/16	Positive, Negative	0.9684	0.9781	0.9686	**0.9703**

Table 2. Accuracy results of the proposed approach on CIFAR-100.

Model	Regulation	Positive	Neutral	Negative	Total
ResNet-50 (backbone)	None	0.7990	0.7635	0.7596	0.7768
Emot-Inf-ResNet-50	None	0.8094	0.7660	0.7606	**0.7821**
Emot-Reg-ResNet-50	Positive	0.7990	0.7660	0.7606	0.7779
Emot-Reg-ResNet-50	Negative	0.8094	0.7660	0.7596	0.7818
Emot-Reg-ResNet-50	Positive, Negative	0.7990	0.7660	0.7596	0.7776
ViT-B/16 (backbone)	None	0.8785	0.8454	0.8308	0.8543
Emot-Inf-ViT-B/16	None	0.8779	0.8500	0.8248	0.8541
Emot-Reg-ViT-B/16	Positive	0.8785	0.8500	0.8248	0.8543
Emot-Reg-ViT-B/16	Negative	0.8779	0.8500	0.8308	0.8557
Emot-Reg-ViT-B/16	Positive, Negative	0.8785	0.8500	0.8308	**0.8559**

In the case of ResNet-50, the introduction of an emotional history over-came the accuracy of the original backbone on both the target datasets. In the case of ViT-B/16, the above approach without regulation was not sufficient for improving classification performances. On CIFAR-100, the transformer architecture improved when introducing the Emotional Regulation, while, on CIFAR-10, the same model required the regulation concerning both positive and negative emotions to reach superior performances.

Figure 2 shows a t-SNE [21] visualization of representations learned through ViT and ResNet. For each model, the upper plot shows data points associated with the considered classes; the lower plot provides the emotions elicited concerning the same data points, according to the positive, negative, and neutral macro-classes.

As can be noticed from the plots, the Emotionally-influenced Encoder based on ResNet learned slightly better separation among classes, compared with the

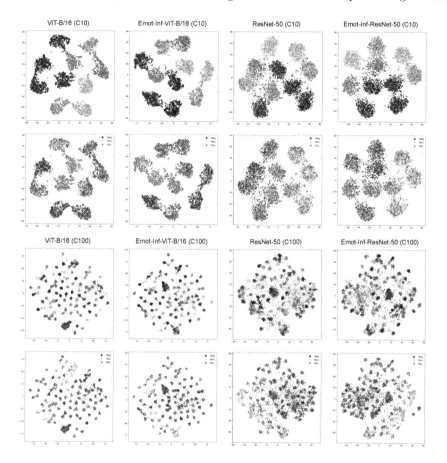

Fig. 2. Visualization based on t-SNE of the learned representations.

original backbone. The same result does not seem to hold for ViT. For both datasets, certain instances were better separated by the original Non-emotional Encoder, while other instances by the Emotionally-influenced model. The above characteristics were exploited by the Emotional Regulation process, which considers stimuli representations according to the predicted emotional state.

5   Discussion

The present study enforces evidence that emotion is a potential improving factor for image classification based on deep learning. The results encourage investigation of the impact of emotion in vision tasks. Image classification can be considered as a basic task through which more complex problems (e.g., detection, segmentation, etc.) can be faced. Further research could prove the effectiveness of an emotional history for improving other vision tasks.

In the considered experimental setup, the introduction of emotion in the learning process of a classifier based exclusively on feature concatenation was not always sufficient for obtaining better results. An increase in accuracy was found for all the considered target datasets and architectures by employing regulation. Emotion was found to be significant for achieving an improvement in classification when adopted as a criterion for selecting non-emotional and emotionally-influenced predictions. Future investigations could verify whether techniques different from feature concatenation can introduce further improvements.

Emotional Regulation is a process exploiting knowledge learned from a model to improve another model trained for solving a different task. In the context of the present study, emotional features were adopted for introducing further knowledge in the learning process, representing the criterion through which admissible (i.e., non-emotional and emotionally-influenced) representations were considered for classification. In the case of ResNet, experiments highlighted the improvement of a classifier by directly extending model features with emotional representations. In the case of ViT, the Emotional Regulation process was essential for obtaining an improvement with respect to a backbone. In both cases, emotion played a pivotal role in constructing a better semantic space. This result goes beyond the objectives of the present investigation, as our approach can potentially be extended to image classification tasks in general. An Emotional Encoder trained on emotional instances could be substituted with a model trained on a different dataset for improving a backbone through feature concatenation and regulation. Following the above approach, the training on CIFAR could be supported by an encoder trained on other benchmarking datasets.

A drawback of the proposed approach, as experimented in the present study, is related to computational complexity. Through our experimental setup, the Emotionally-influenced Encoder required two times the backbone parameters, while the Emotional Regulation required an increase of up to three times. The above limitation reduces the practical feasibility of Emotional Regulation in real-time scenarios. Future research could investigate an accuracy improvement by reducing the encoders' complexity. A suitable investigation may involve the distillation [22] of encoders, as well as the employment of architectures characterized by fewer parameters.

6   Conclusions

In the present study, an investigation of the impact of emotion in image classification based on deep learning was conducted by employing Emotional Regulation. The solution consists of training three encoders: the Non-emotional Encoder representing an original backbone; the Emotional Encoder adopted for producing artificial emotion through a history of affective stimuli; the Emotionally-influenced Encoder representing an emotional backbone. Non-emotional and Emotionally-influenced Encoders were trained on a target classification dataset, while the Emotional Encoder was optimized for estimating scores associated with emotional classes. The introduction of emotion in the learning process was imposed by concatenating frozen Emotional Encoder features with representations learned by the Emotionally-influenced Encoder. Emotional Regulation is a process evaluating emotionally-influenced representations in the case of a neutral state, while non-emotional representations in the case of significant emotion.

To conduct experiments, ResNet-50 and ViT-16/B architectures were employed for representing the above encoders in classifying CIFAR-10 and -100. Non-emotional and Emotionally-influenced Encoders have been trained on the above target datasets, while the Emotional Encoder on a collection of stimuli associated with emotional classes. The adopted criterion for regulation was experimented by imposing the association of the above emotional classes with positive, neutral, and negative semantics. The results show an increase in accuracy with respect to the original backbones on the considered target datasets, revealing Emotional Regulation as a promising approach for improving image classification.

The present study enforces evidence for the effectiveness of emotion in image classification based on deep learning. Improvements were found by considering emotion as a criterion for selecting non-emotional and emotionally-influenced representations through a process of regulation. Further investigation could verify whether the proposed approach can generalize the results across other datasets and vision tasks.

Acknowledgement. Marta Chinnici was supported for this research by Project ECS 0000024 Rome Technopole, - CUP B83C22002820006, National Recovery and Resilience Plan (NRRP), Mission 4, Component 2 Investment 1.5, funded by the European Union - NextGenerationEU.

References

1. Rodríguez-Gómez, P., et al.: Please be logical, I am in a bad mood: an electro-physiological study of mood effects on reasoning. Neuropsychologia **127**, 19–28 (2019)
2. Congleton, A.R., Berntsen, D.: The devil is in the details: investigating the influence of emotion on event memory using a simulated event. Psychol. Res. **84**, 2339–2353 (2020)
3. Yin, Y., et al.: The effects of emotion on judgments of learning and memory: a meta-analytic review. Metacogn. Learn. **18**, 1–23 (2023)
4. Kremer, T., et al.: Influence of negative emotions on residents learning of scientific information: an experimental study. Perspect. Med. Educ. **8**, 209–215 (2019)
5. Assunção, G., et al.: An overview of emotion in artificial intelligence. IEEE Trans. Artif. Intell. **3**(6), 867–886 (2022)
6. Strömfelt, H., et al.: Emotion-augmented machine learning: overview of an emerging domain. In: 2017 Seventh International Conference on Affective Computing and Intelligent Interaction (ACII). IEEE (2017)
7. Thenius, R., Zahadat, P., Schmickl, T.: EMANN-a model of emotions in an artificial neural network. In: Artificial Life Conference Proceedings. One Rogers Street, Cambridge, MA 02142-1209, USA journals-info@ mit.edu: MIT Press (2013)

8. Zamirpour, E., Mosleh, M.: A biological brain-inspired fuzzy neural network: fuzzy emotional neural network. Biologically Inspired Cognitive Architectures **26**, 80–90 (2018)

9. Roy, B., Singh, M.P.: A metaheuristic-based emotional ANN (EmNN) approach for rainfall-runoff modeling. In: 2019 International Conference on Communication and Electronics Systems (ICCES). IEEE (2019)

10. Shahid, A.H., Singh, M.P.: A novel approach for coronary artery disease diagnosis using hybrid particle swarm optimization based emotional neural network. Biocybern. Biomed. Eng. **40**(4), 1568–1585 (2020)

11. Abba, S.I., et al.: Integrating feature extraction approaches with hybrid emotional neural networks for water quality index modeling. Appl. Soft Comput. **114**, 108036 (2022)

12. Parvinizadeh, S., Zakermoshfegh, M., Shakiba, M.: A simple and efficient rainfall-runoff model based on supervised brain emotional learning. Neural Comput. Appl. **34**(2), 1509–1526 (2022)

13. Moerland, T.M., Broekens, J., Jonker, C.M.: Emotion in reinforcement learning agents and robots: a survey. Mach. Learn. **107**, 443–480 (2018)

14. Landi, R.E., et al.: CognitiveNet: enriching foundation models with emotions and awareness. In: Antona, M., Stephanidis, C. (eds.) International Conference on Human-Computer Interaction. Springer, Cham (2023). https://doi.org/10.1007/978-3-031-35681-0_7

15. He, K., et al.: Deep residual learning for image recognition. In: Proceedings of the IEEE Conference on Computer Vision and Pattern Recognition (2016)

16. Dosovitskiy, A., et al.: An image is worth 16 × 16 words: transformers for image recognition at scale. arXiv preprint arXiv:2010.11929 (2020)

17. Krizhevsky, A., Hinton, G.: Learning multiple layers of features from tiny images, p. 7 (2009)

18. Fan, S., et al.: Emotional attention: a study of image sentiment and visual attention. In: Proceedings of the IEEE Conference on Computer Vision and Pattern Recognition (2018)

19. Deng, J., et al.: ImageNet: a large-scale hierarchical image database. In: 2009 IEEE Conference on Computer Vision and Pattern Recognition. IEEE (2009)

20. Iannone, F., et al.: CRESCO ENEA HPC clusters: a working example of a multifabric GPFS Spectrum Scale layout. In: 2019 International Conference on High Performance Computing & Simulation (HPCS). IEEE (2019)

21. Van der Maaten, L., Hinton, G.: Visualizing data using t-SNE. J. Mach. Learn. Res. **9**(11), 2579–2605 (2008)

22. Gou, J., et al.: Knowledge distillation: a survey. Int. J. Comput. Vision **129**, 1789–1819 (2021)

HCI-Driven Machine Learning for Early Detection of Lung Cancer: An Ensemble Approach

Muhammad Sohaib[(✉)]

Department of Biomedical Engineering, University of Nevada, Reno, NV 89557, USA
msohaib@unr.edu

Abstract. Lung cancer is one of the deadliest cancers worldwide, resulting in millions of deaths annually. Early detection of lung nodules from the patient's case history and lifestyle is critical to treating this disease effectively. We proposed an innovative approach to predicting lung cancer diseases by utilizing a combination of four supervised classification machine learning algorithms and principal component analysis (PCA). The proposed model employs decision tree classifiers, random forest, KNN, and support vector machines (SVM) to classify patients into categories of having lung cancer or not. The study found that SVM and random forest had the highest accuracy of 94% among the algorithms used. PCA was employed to reduce the dimensionality of the data, and the model's performance was evaluated using precision, recall, and F1-Score. Beyond the technical aspects, our approach integrates Human-Computer Interaction (HCI) principles for a user-friendly web application seamlessly fitting into healthcare workflows. This tool not only assists healthcare practitioners but also contributes to predictive healthcare technology, with a focus on accessibility and an improved user experience. Its adaptability specifically extends to predicting lung cancer, promoting early detection, and enhancing overall healthcare outcomes.

Keywords: KNN · SVM · Random Forest · Lung Cancer · Decision Tree Classifiers · PCA · HCI

1 Introduction

Lung cancer is a highly deadly disease that results in a substantial annual mortality rate. Based on data provided by the World Health Organization (WHO 2020), this cancer will constitute 11.6% of all reported cancer cases, thereby establishing itself as the most diagnosed form of cancer on a global scale. According to the projections made by the American Cancer Society, it is estimated that there will be around 238,340 new instances of lung cancer in the United States in 2023. This figure is further divided into 117,550 cases among men and 120,790 cases among women. Additionally, it is anticipated that there will be approximately 127,070 deaths resulting from lung cancer, with 67,160 deaths occurring among men and 59,910 deaths occurring among women. The timely

M. Antona and C. Stephanidis (Eds.): HCII 2024, LNCS 14696, pp. 311–325, 2024.
https://doi.org/10.1007/978-3-031-60875-9_21

identification of lung cancer is imperative for effective intervention, and medical practitioners employ a variety of methodologies, such as physical assessments, hematological analyses, radiographic imaging, tissue sampling, and computed tomography, to ascertain its presence. Nevertheless, the analysis of the substantial volume of data produced by these diagnostic tools can present difficulties, particularly in cases where radiographs exhibit less distinctive features. For example, research indicates that the utilisation of CT scans for the purpose of lung cancer screening has the potential to decrease mortality rates associated with lung cancer by approximately 20%. This underscores the significance of precise and effective examination of medical imaging data, as referenced in scholarly sources [1, 2]. Lung cancer, being a highly prevalent form of cancer globally, is responsible for a significant number of annual deaths, reaching approximately 1.76 million [3, 4]. Consequently, the significance of timely screening and diagnosis cannot be emphasised enough. Several clinical trials have provided evidence of the effectiveness of low-dose CT screening in decreasing mortality rates among individuals who are at a heightened risk of developing lung cancer [5]. Additional recent research has also demonstrated the advantages of computed tomography (CT) screening in community environments, where timely identification and intervention can be especially crucial [6]. Nevertheless, the extensive implementation of lung cancer screening has led to a substantial influx of CT scans that necessitate interpretation by radiologists. The availability of trained radiologists is limited, and the process of reviewing each CT slice is labor-intensive, resulting in a demanding and fatiguing undertaking. The accurate evaluation of CT image data, which is available in a substantial quantity in the form of slices, poses a significant challenge and requires a considerable amount of time. Moreover, it has been observed that the diagnostic precision of human radiologists does not surpass 80%, resulting in potential jeopardy for the remaining 20% of cancer cases.

The situation imposes a substantial strain on healthcare resources and has the potential to give rise to interstate disputes, particularly in regions where resources are limited. For example, certain states may experience a scarcity of radiologists who are capable of interpreting medical scans, resulting in extended waiting periods for patients and subsequent disruptions in the timely administration of medical interventions. Furthermore, it is important to consider potential budgetary constraints that may arise from the expansion of the radiologist workforce, especially in regions where healthcare budgets are already strained. Resolving these conflicts presents a significant challenge due to the necessity of coordinating efforts among various stakeholders, such as healthcare providers, policymakers, and patients.

To tackle these challenges, researchers have developed computer-aided diagnostic systems with the purpose of assisting in the identification of pulmonary nodules on CT scans. The present research study offers a distinctive opportunity to examine the inflexibility of medical machine-learning models and assess the efficacy of different processing and classification approaches for chest CT images on a large scale [7]. In recent times, a multitude of techniques have been devised for the purpose of diagnosing lung cancer, with computed tomography (CT) scans and X-ray images emerging as the predominant modalities [8].

Our research encompasses a multifaceted approach to advance lung cancer prediction and application design. Firstly, the study aims to analyze and improve current lung cancer prediction methodologies using historical patient case records. Secondly, it seeks to investigate and evaluate multiple machine learning models, identifying the optimal model or combination for the highest accuracy in lung cancer prediction. Thirdly, the research focuses on assessing the performance and precision of various predictive models. Additionally, in tandem with machine learning objectives, a key research objective involves designing an optimal user interface. This includes implementing Human-Computer Interaction (HCI) principles to ensure user-friendly design, seamless healthcare workflow integration, and enhanced accessibility for practitioners. The ultimate goal is to develop an intuitive web application that efficiently interacts with users and contributes to the broader landscape of predictive healthcare technology.

The manuscript is divided into several sections. Section 1 introduces the topic and outlines our research goal. Section 2 covers the background of the study, while Sect. 3 analyzes the origin of the datasets used. In Sect. 4, we explain the research design and methodology. Section 5 presents the study's results and offers a detailed analysis. Moving on to Sect. 6, we address and discuss the limitations of the research. The paper concludes in Sect. 7 by summarizing the main findings and their implications. Additionally, recommendations for future research or policy actions based on the presented research are provided.

2 Background

Machine learning-based diagnostic models have been proposed by the author [9] to assist physicians in managing nonspecific pulmonary nodules. These models can reduce the variability in nodule classification, enhance decision-making, and decrease the number of unnecessary treatments given to patients, resulting in a more efficient use of clinical resources and time. The importance of early cancer detection in saving lives and improving patient outcomes has been highlighted by [10], who emphasises the significant role of technology in effective cancer detection. Lung cancer is a devastating disease that results from the uncontrolled growth of cells in the lungs, leading to high mortality rates for both men and women [11]. While it is not possible to prevent lung cancer, the risk of developing the disease can be reduced through measures such as quitting smoking. Early detection is crucial for improving the survival rate of patients. The term "chain smoker" typically refers to an individual who smokes cigarettes frequently throughout the day and has a high nicotine dependency. In their study, the authors [12] have proposed an automated lung cancer detection method that utilises CT imaging to identify autoimmune defects. This approach addresses the challenges associated with tumour differentiation and classification, which can be difficult due to the large amount of data and blurred boundaries in CT images. The proposed method offers the potential to increase diagnostic accuracy and efficiency while reducing the time required for diagnosis.

According to [13], cancer cells represent a complex and serious health challenge. While advancements in CT scan technology and novel approaches by various manufacturers offer computational insights that aid in medical decision-making, diagnosing lung cancer is particularly challenging. This is due to several factors, such as the difficulty in distinguishing between benign and malignant nodules, the variability in nodule shapes and sizes, and the potential for overlapping features with other pulmonary conditions.

Consequently, lung cancer is associated with a high fatality rate for both men and women. To improve patient outcomes, it is essential to detect nodules using a combination of imaging and diagnostic techniques promptly and accurately. Several approaches have been employed for early-stage diagnosis of lung cancer, including low-dose CT screening, machine learning-based models, and automated methods for nodule classification [14]. In their study, [15] highlighted the significance of using chest computed tomography (CT) for the identification of lung cancer and put forward several automated CT evaluation techniques. However, due to differences in the software dependencies of the methods described in various studies, it is uncommon for these methods to be compared or replicated. The aim of the research was to compare the approaches and performance of the winning algorithms that used machine learning modules for the detection of lung cancer, as part of the Cogley Data Science Bowl. Similarly, Timor Kadir and Fergus Gleeson [1] proposed machine learning-based models for the diagnosis of lung cancer, which can aid physicians in managing indeterminate pulmonary nodules that are detected through random screening. These models have the potential to enhance the accuracy of nodule classification, improve decision-making, and ultimately minimise the number of benign nodules that undergo unnecessary interventions.

According to [16], cancer is a global health issue with significant economic and societal costs, including increased mortality rates and healthcare expenditures. In recent years, however, advancements in high-output technology and emerging machine-learning methods have led to progress in cancer diagnosis based on symptoms, providing a more effective and accurate diagnosis. Machine learning methods have shown promise in effectively distinguishing lung cancer patients from healthy individuals, which is of great significance given that lung cancer is a leading cause of death in both men and women, with mortality rates continuing to rise. Similarly, [17] highlights that lung cancer is a common disease that affects the lungs and is difficult to diagnose at an early stage, with symptoms that are hard to detect. Thus, the use of machine learning algorithms, such as employing Chi-Square for feature selection, has been explored for lung cancer diagnosis, with various machine learning algorithms being developed to assist in the diagnosis process.

Medical professionals are increasingly utilising machine learning, a branch of artificial intelligence that allows computers to learn from existing data and quickly identify patterns in large and complex datasets. The authors in [18] emphasise that lung cancer is the primary cause of cancer-related deaths worldwide. Diagnostic tests such as X-rays, CT scans, sputum cytology, and biopsies are available, but they can be time-consuming and not always accurate. To improve early detection, machine learning data mining techniques are being used to analyse past patient case histories and identify cancer at an earlier stage.

3   Source of Dataset and Nature

The dataset, obtained from Kaggle, comprises case histories of 59 patients and includes six attributes for predicting lung cancer (Table 1).

In the field of machine learning, it is a widely adopted convention to partition a dataset into two distinct subsets, namely the training dataset and the testing dataset. This

Table 1. Features of Datasets

S. No	Features/Attributes	Quantitative	Data Type
1	Name	59	Object
2	Surname		Object
3	Age		Integer
4	AreaQ		
5	Alkhol		
6	Result		

facilitates a more precise evaluation of the efficacy of a model when the model is making predictions on previously unseen data. The researcher employed a conventional 80:20 ratio for partitioning the data into training and testing sets. Specifically, 47 patients were randomly allocated to the training dataset, while the remaining 12 patients were assigned to the testing set.

The datasets are represented as follows [19]:

1. Let the complete dataset be represented D = {D1, D2, D3, D4............D59},
2. Let the training dataset be presented as Train = {D1, D2, D3, D4....... D47},
3. Let the test dataset be represented as Test = {D48, D49, D50, D51....... D59}.

4   Research Methodology

This section outlines the different machine learning algorithms used to classify the data in the study. These algorithms include the decision tree classifier, the random forest classifier, the k-nearest neighbors' classifier, and the Support Vector Machine (SVM).

4.1   Decision Tree and Classifier

Decision trees use multiple algorithms to decide whether to split a node into two or more sub-nodes. The creation of sub-nodes increases the homogeneity of the resultant sub-nodes. The decision tree splits the nodes on all available variables and then selects the split that results in the most homogeneous sub-nodes.

$$E(T, X) = \Sigma_{c\varepsilon X} P(c) E(c) \tag{1}$$

T = Target Variables whereas, X = Independent Variable

Decision trees are a useful tool for effectively analyzing non-linear datasets. They can be classified into two types: categorical variable decision trees and continuous variable decision trees. The algorithm begins by comparing the attribute value of a node with those of other sub-nodes and then proceeds to the next node. This process is repeated until the leaf node of the tree is reached. The decision tree training process continues until completion. This algorithm provides a clear and concise explanation of the entire process.

Algorithm 1:

- **Step 1:** Begin the tree with the root node, S, which contains the complete dataset.
- **Step 2:** Find the best attribute in the dataset using the attribute selection measure (ASM).
- **Step 3:** Divide the S into subsets that contain possible values for the best attributes.
- **Step 4:** Generate the decision tree node that contains the best attribute.
- **Step 5:** Recursively make new decision trees using the subsets of the dataset created in Step 3. Continue this process until a stage is reached where you cannot further classify the nodes and call this final node a leaf node.

4.2 Random Forest Classifiers

Random forest is a popular supervised learning algorithm that is mainly used for classification tasks, although it can also be used for regression tasks. The algorithm consists of multiple decision trees, with the number of trees affecting the robustness of the forest. To create a random forest, the algorithm constructs decision trees using various subsets of the training data and different randomly selected features for each tree. The individual tree predictions are then combined using a voting mechanism to determine the final output of the model. This ensemble method is effective in reducing overfitting, a common issue in machine learning, by averaging the results across the trees. Compared to using a single decision tree, a random forest produces more accurate and stable results due to the combination of multiple trees. This makes it a popular choice in many applications, especially those with complex data or a large number of features.

Algorithm:

- **Step 1:** First, start the selection of random samples from a given dataset.
- **Step 2:** Next, this algorithm will construct a decision tree for every sample, and it will get the prediction result from every decision tree.
- **Step 3:** In this step, the predicted results from each individual tree are combined using a voting mechanism.
- **Step 4:** At last, select the most popular prediction result as the final prediction result.

4.3 K-NEAREST Neighbors Classifier

The K-Nearest Neighbors (KNN) algorithm is a classification method that assigns a label to an unknown data point based on its proximity to other data points. In other words, KNN determines the class of an unclassified data point by comparing its distance to known data points, where the distance is measured by well-known mathematical metrics such as Euclidean distance, Manhattan distance, Minkowski distance, Mahalanobis distance, tangential distance, cosine distance, and more. Generally, the shorter the distance between a new data point and an existing group, the higher the likelihood of the new data point getting classified into that group. For the data points X and Y with n features:

$$D(X, Y) = \left(\sum_{i=1}^{n} (|x_i - y_i|)P \right)^{1/P} \tag{2}$$

Hare $X = (x1, x2, x3, x4, \ldots\ldots\ldots x_n)$ and $Y = (y1, y2, y3, y4, \ldots\ldots\ldots y_n)$.

For data points X and Y with n features, it is possible to form a neighborhood comprising the n closest data points to the new data point. In order to determine the class of the new data point, the groups of classes having the maximum number of data points in the neighborhood and those that are closer to the new data point than other groups are considered. Based on these two factors, the class of the new data point is identified.

4.4 Support Vector Machine (SVM)

Support Vector Machine (SVM) is a classification algorithm used in machine learning that aims to find a hyperplane in the n-dimensional space that separates different classes while maximizing the margin. The decision function for SVM can be represented as

$$G(x) = w^T x + b \tag{3}$$

where x is the input vector, w is the weight vector, b is the bias term, and $G(x)$ is the decision function. To find the optimal hyperplane, we need to either keep $\|w\|=1$ and maximize k, or keep $k \geq 1$ and minimize $\|w\|$. The problem can be formulated as minimizing $\Phi(w) = 1/2\, w^T w$, subject to $d_i(w^T x + b) \geq 1$ for every training data point x_i, where d_i represents the class label. To solve this optimization problem, we can use Lagrange multipliers and represent the problem as

$$\text{Minimize}: \ J(w, \ b, \ a) = 1/2\, wTw - \sum_{i=1}^{n} a_i d_i \left(|wTxi + b|\right) + \sum_{i=1}^{n} a_i \tag{4}$$

such that $a_i[d_i(w^T x_i + b) - 1] = 0$, where $i = 1, 2, \ldots, n$. Here, a_i is the Lagrange multiplier for the ith data point, and d_i is its corresponding class label. The quantity $\sum_{i=1}^{n} a_i$ is known as the duality gap, and a_i is non-zero only for the support vector data points. By using Lagrange duality, we can reformulate $J(w, b, a)$ as $J(w, b, a) = -\sum_{i=1}^{n} a_i + 1/2 \sum_{i=1}^{n} \sum_{j=1}^{n} a_i\, a_j\, d_i\, d_j\, x_i^T x_j$, subject to $a_i \geq 0$ for $i = 1, 2, \ldots, n$ and $\sum_{i=1}^{n} a_i d_i = 0$. The dual form J represents the SVM problem in terms of a set of Lagrange multipliers (a) and known scalars (x_i, d_i). The SVM model uses classification algorithms for two-group classification problems. After training the SVM model with a labeled training dataset for each category, it can categorize new data points, making it useful in text classification problems.

5   Results and Discussion

In this section, we present the outcomes of our machine learning models and delve into the tools and technologies employed in constructing the web application for predicting lung cancer. The discussion will encompass the performance metrics, insights gained from model results, and the technological framework that underpins the functionality of our predictive web application.

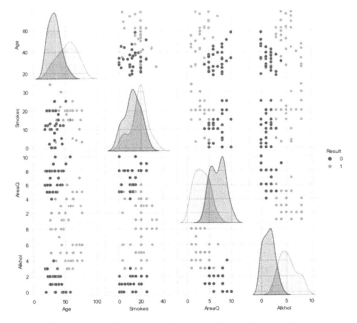

Fig. 1. Data Distribution Diagram. (Color figure online)

5.1 Machine Learning Model Results:

We train multiple machine learning models that utilize age (numerical), smoking status (binary 0 or 1), AreaQ (data type?), and Alkhol (data type?) as input features to predict the presence of lung cancer cells (binary 0 or 1).

The Fig. 1 illustrates a data analysis report that investigates various factors associated with lung cancer, such as age, smoking, area Q, and alcohol consumption. These factors are examined in relation to the dependent variable, Result, which indicates the presence or absence of cancer cells, represented by binary values of 0s and 1s. The blue dots in the visual representation denote individuals who do not possess a prior medical record of lung cancer, whereas the red dots signify individuals who have a documented history of the ailment. The findings of the analysis indicate that age plays a significant role in the prediction of lung cancer, particularly among individuals aged 60 years or older, who exhibit a heightened vulnerability to the disease.

The prevalence of lung cancer among patients is attributed to a number of factors, including their smoking habits, alcohol consumption, and the level of pollution in the areas where they live (as shown in Fig. 1).

The correlation matrix depicted in the heat diagram above shows the strength of the relationship between dependent and independent variables used in the analysis of lung cancer. The features analyzed in the study are age, smoking habits, AreaQ, and alcohol consumption. The matrix is represented by r-scores, where a higher value indicates a stronger correlation between two variables. The data analysis report shows that AreaQ has a negative impact on lung cancer, whereas Smokes and Age have a moderate value and show very little impact on lung cancer patients (Fig. 2).

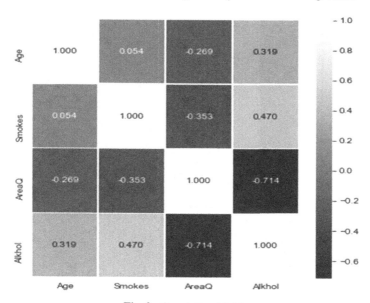

Fig. 2. Correlation Matrix

Table 2. Machine Learning Algorithms and Accuracy Level

Machine Learning Algorithms	Accuracy Score
Random forest	0.944444
SVM	0.944444
Decision tree	0.833333
KNN	0.277778

The study utilised four distinct machine learning (ML) algorithms, specifically Decision Tree Classifiers, Random Forest, K-Nearest Neighbours (KNN), and Support Vector Machine (SVM), to categorise patients based on their lung cancer status. The results of the analysis indicate that the Support Vector Machine (SVM) and Random Forest algorithms demonstrated a noteworthy accuracy rate of 94%, whereas the Decision Tree Classifier exhibited a commendable accuracy rate of 83%. On the other hand, the K-nearest neighbours (KNN) algorithm exhibited suboptimal performance, attaining a mere 27% accuracy rate. Table 2 provides a comprehensive overview of the performance exhibited by each algorithm. Moreover, the assessment of the Support Vector Machine (SVM) algorithm demonstrated a precision rate of 0.94, a recall rate of 0.83, and an F1 score of 0.909. Conversely, the K-Nearest Neighbours (KNN) algorithm exhibited an accuracy of 0.27, a recall rate of 0.27, and an F1 score of 0.43, as depicted in Fig. 3. The findings of this study underscore the superior performance of Support Vector Machine (SVM) and Random Forest algorithms in accurately classifying patients with lung cancer. However,

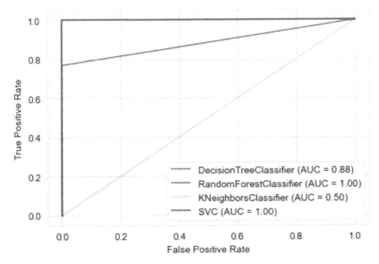

Fig. 3. Accuracy Analysis of Different Predictive Models

it also highlights the limitations of the K-Nearest Neighbours (KNN) algorithm in this task.

Evaluation of SVC-Most Significant Predictive Model

The accuracy of the SVC model is: 0.9444444444444444
  The precision of this SVC model is: 1.0
    The recall score of the SVC model is: 0.8333333333333334
    The f1-score for this dataset is: 0.9090909090909091

Evaluation of KNN-Least Significant Predictive Model

The accuracy of the KNN model is 0.2777777777777778.
  The precision of this KNN model is: 1.0
  The recall score of KNN model is: 0.2777777777777778
  The f1-score for this dataset is:0.4347826086956522

The graph depicted in Fig. 4 offers valuable insights into the application of principal component analysis (PCA) on the dataset pertaining to lung cancer. The graph illustrates the proportion of variability in the dataset that is accounted for by individual principal components. The horizontal axis of the graph represents the quantity of principal components utilised in the analysis, whereas the vertical axis represents the proportion of variance accounted for by each component. The curve depicted in the plot illustrates the cumulative sum of the explained variance as each subsequent principal component is added. The plot aids in the determination of the optimal number of principal components to be retained in the analysis. In general, it is customary to choose the number of principal components that account for a substantial proportion of the variance observed in the dataset. Additionally, the utilisation of the plot can serve as a valuable tool in discerning the fundamental framework of the data and detecting any possible anomalies or influential data points. In general, the principal component analysis (PCA) analysis

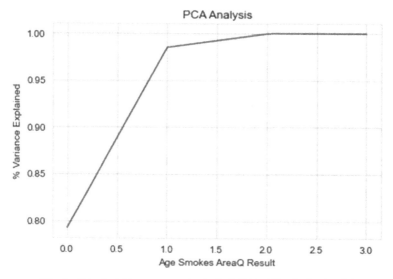

Fig. 4. Principal Components Analysis (PCA) of Predictive Model

and its associated plot contribute to the reduction of dimensionality and the selection of features for subsequent machine learning models.

The analysis of data encompassed variables such as patients' age, smoking habits, AreaQ, and results. The evaluation results of the Support Vector Machine (SVM) model indicate an accuracy of 0.94, a recall score of 0.83, and an F1 score of 0.909. Conversely, the evaluation of the K-Nearest Neighbours (KNN) model yielded an accuracy of 0.27, a recall score of 0.27, and an F1 score of 0.43. The research revealed that variables such as age, smoking habits, and AreaQ exerted a substantial influence on the outcome of the dependent variable, particularly in the context of individuals diagnosed with lung cancer.

5.2   Real-Time Cancer Prediction Web Application Using SVM

In addition to developing a robust cancer prediction model based on Support Vector Machine (SVM), we have extended our efforts to enhance user interaction by constructing a web application. This application empowers users to make real-time predictions by inputting specific cancer-related factors.

Key Features of the Web Application. Our web application offers an intuitive interface for seamless interaction with the SVM model, enhancing user experience and effectiveness. The user-friendly design is a standout feature, enabling individuals of varying technical backgrounds to effortlessly navigate the application and input pertinent cancer-related factors. Real-time predictions further amplify the application's utility, allowing users to receive instant insights by entering specific cancer-related data. The SVM model efficiently processes this input, ensuring swift and accurate predictions. Accessibility is a paramount consideration, as the application is thoughtfully designed to be compatible with various devices and platforms. Users can conveniently access the predictive capabilities whether on desktops, laptops, or mobile devices, contributing to the application's versatility and widespread usability.

Integration with SVM Model. The core predictive engine of our web application is built on the SVM model discussed in Sect. 5.1. This model, with its ability to identify cancer instances accurately, forms the backbone of our real-time prediction system.

Tools and Technology. Our client-side application is built using the Quasar framework, Vue.js, and Node.js. The server-side infrastructure is developed in Python. Communication between the server and client is facilitated through WebSocket technology. The PostgreSQL database is employed to store comprehensive patient records and the outcomes of cancer prediction analyses. This technology stack ensures a robust and efficient system for managing and processing health-related data.

Design Explanation. In Fig. 5, the user interface allows anyone to input data and predict the likelihood of Lung Cancer. The input fields are described as follows:

Name: These fields capture the patient's first and last names but are excluded from the analysis as they are deemed irrelevant for the study. **Age:** This field represents the patient's age, providing demographic insights into the dataset. **Smokes:** Indicates the patient's smoking level, potentially denoting the daily number of cigarettes smoked or another metric related to smoking habits. **AreaQ:** Reflects the air quality of the patient's residential area, offering a quantitative measure of environmental conditions. **Alkhol:** Represents the patient's alcohol intake level, providing information on the frequency, quantity, or other aspects of alcohol consumption. **Result:** A binary variable indicating the patient's lung cancer diagnosis. "1" indicates a positive diagnosis, while "0" signifies no detection of lung cancer. This intuitive interface simplifies the prediction process by allowing users to input relevant data and obtain a prediction based on the specified parameters.

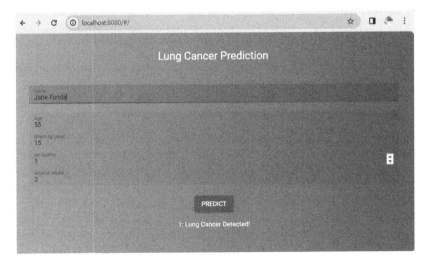

Fig. 5. Real-Time Lung Cancer Predictions Using the Web Application

6 Limitations

In developing an ensemble of classification machine learning algorithms for the detection of lung cancer, our study has yielded a proficient and precise predictive model. However, certain limitations warrant consideration. The utilization of a dataset exclusively obtained from a single hospital may restrict the generalizability of our findings to diverse contexts or demographics. Furthermore, the relatively limited quantity of training data points in our dataset could potentially impact the overall reliability and effectiveness of our model's predictive capabilities. Despite successfully identifying age, smoking habits, and AreaQ as significant predictors of lung cancer, there exists a possibility that additional pertinent features or factors were not accounted for. It is essential to recognize that the efficacy of machine learning models hinges on the quality of training data; thus, future studies must prioritize rigorous data validation and consider acquiring larger, more diverse datasets. Although our study makes a significant contribution to the efficient detection of lung cancer using machine learning, addressing these limitations is paramount. Subsequent research endeavors will focus on mitigating these challenges through advanced methodologies and continual refinement of our predictive model. Looking ahead, our commitment to advancing cancer prediction involves strategic enhancements to our model and research methodology. Ongoing efforts will focus on the collection and integration of diverse and larger datasets to bolster the accuracy and generalization capabilities of our model. Implementation of a user feedback system is planned, enabling continuous learning and refinement based on real-world user interactions. Additionally, we aim to enhance user understanding by introducing graphical representations of SVM decision boundaries and feature importance. These visualization tools will provide users with deeper insights into the model's decision-making process, fostering transparency and trust in its predictions. As our research evolves, we recognize the importance of addressing limitations and embracing continuous improvement to ensure the resilience and applicability of our predictive model in real-world scenarios.

7 Conclusion

In conclusion, our research represents a significant stride in utilizing ensemble techniques of classification machine learning algorithms to develop a potent predictive model for lung cancer identification. The findings, particularly the outstanding efficacy of the support vector machine (SVM) and random forest algorithms, underscore the potential of machine learning in advancing healthcare diagnostics. With a remarkable accuracy score of 94%, surpassing alternative models, the SVM and random forest algorithms exhibit promise for precise patient classification. Looking ahead, our research doesn't solely focus on the algorithmic aspects but extends to the user interface domain through the development of a frontend web application. This application follows Human-Computer Interaction (HCI) principles, emphasizing user-friendly design and accessibility. The HCI-driven frontend not only facilitates user interaction but also aligns with the broader objective of improving healthcare outcomes. As we chart a course for future research, we advocate for further investigations that validate the accuracy and reliability of our predictive model within clinical contexts. Utilizing more extensive datasets encompassing diverse demographic and clinical attributes will fortify the model's robustness. Additionally, extending the study to assess the model's efficacy across various forms of lung cancer holds the potential to broaden its applicability. Importantly, the incorporation of HCI principles into our frontend application contributes to its user-centric design, ensuring that healthcare practitioners can seamlessly leverage the predictive model in their workflows. This synergy between HCI and machine learning has the power to streamline the identification of individuals at higher risk, allowing for proactive medical interventions and ultimately improving patient outcomes. In summary, our research not only showcases the prowess of machine learning methodologies in constructing a prognostic framework for lung cancer but also highlights the transformative potential of HCI in the development of user-friendly applications. Future investigations will continue to refine and extend our approach, ensuring its effectiveness in diverse clinical settings and reinforcing the positive impact on patient care.

Availability of Data and Materials. The datasets supporting the conclusions of this article are included within the article and its additional files.

References

1. Rubin, G.D., Leo, J.K., Pack, D.S., Sherbondy, A.J., Chou, L.C., Leung, A.N.: Pulmonary nodules on a multi-detector series CT scan: functional comparison of radiologist and computer-aided detection. Radiology **234**(1), 274–283 (2005)
2. Singh, S.P., Girada, D.S., Pinsky, P., Sanders, C., Fineberg, N., Sun, Y.: Reader variability in detecting pulmonary nodules on chest radiograph from National Lung Screening Trial. J. Thorac. Imaging **27**(4), 249–254 (2012)
3. Bray, F., Furley, J., Sorzomatram, I., Siegel, R.L., Tore, L.A., Jemal, A.: Global cancer statistics. GLOBOCAN estimates the worldwide incidence and mortality of 185 cancers in 36 countries. CA Cancer J. Clin. **68**(6), 394–424 (2018)
4. Torre, L.A., Bray, F., Siegel, R.L., Furley, J., Lort-Tuilent, J., Jemal, A.: Global cancer statistics (2012). CA Cancer J. Clin. **65**(2), 87–108 (2015)
5. Doi, K.: Computer aided diagnosis in medical imaging: historical review, current status and future probability. Comput. Med. Imaging Graph. **31**(4–5), 198–211 (2007)
6. Yu, K., Beam, A.L., Kohane, I.S.: Artificial intelligence in healthcare. Nat. Biomed. Eng. **2**(10), 719–731 (2018)
7. Awai, K., Murao, K., Ojawa, A., Komi, M., Hayakawa, H., Hori, S.: Pulmonary nodules in chest CT: the effect of computer-assisted diagnosis on the radiologist's identification function. Radiology **230**(2), 347–352 (2004)
8. Lam, V.K., Miller, M., Dowling, L., Singhal, S., Young, R.P., Kabebe, E.C.: Community low-dose CT lung cancer screening: a prospective integrative study. Lung **193**(1), 135–139 (2015)
9. Qadir, T., Gleason, F.: Lung cancer prediction using machine learning and advanced imaging techniques. Transl. Lung Cancer Res. **7**(3), 304–312 (2018). PMCID: PMC6037965, https://doi.org/10.21037/tlcr.2018.05.15
10. Chaturvedi, M.P., Jumb, A., Nemade, V.V.: International Conference on Applied Scientific Computational Intelligence Using Lung Cancer Diagnosis and Classification, Data Science (ASCI 2020) Using Machine Learning Techniques, 22–23 December 2020, Jaipur, India (2020)

11. Radhika, P.R., Rakhi, A.S., Nair, V.G.: A comparative study of detecting lung cancer using machine learning algorithms. In: 2019 IEEE International Conference on Electrical, Computer and Communication Technologies (ICECCT), INSPEC Access No: 19127616 (2019). https://doi.org/10.1109/ICECCT.201988

12. Vaishnavism, D., Arya, K.S., Devi Abhirami, T., Poetry, M.N.: Lung cancer diagnosis using machine learning. Int. J. Eng. Res. Technol. (IJERT) RTICCT - 2019 **7**(01) (2019). Published (1st Online): 5 April 2019, ISSN (Online): 2278-0181

13. Stephen, E., Bhattacharya, D., Janarthan, M.C.: A comprehensive review of the detection of lung cancer using machine learning techniques. J. Crit. Rev. **7**(14) (2020). https://doi.org/10.31838/jcr.07.14.68

14. Abdullah, D.M., Ahmad, N.S.: A review of the most recent lung cancer detectives using machine learning. Int. J. Sci. Bus. **5**(3), 159–173 (2021)

15. Yu, K.-H., Lee, T.-L.M., Yen, H.: Reproductive machine learning methods for the detection of lung cancer using computed tomography images: algorithm development and validation. J. Med. Internet Res. **22**, e16709 (2020)

16. Obulesu, O., et al.: Machine learning and blockchain technology for smart healthcare and human health. J. Healthc. Eng. **2021**, Article ID 5912051 (2021). https://doi.org/10.1155/2021/5912051

17. Vikas, P.K.: Lung cancer detection using chi-square feature selection and support vector machine algorithms. Int. J. Adv. Trends Comput. Sci. Eng. **10**(3), 2050–2060 (2021). ISSN 2278-3091

18. Sajjad, F., Vignesh, V., Flashing, C., Jishnu, V., Anoop, P.S.: Effect of principal component analysis on lung cancer detection using machine learning techniques. Int. Res. J. Eng. Technol. (IRJET) **6**(05) (2019). E-ISSN: 2395-0056. www.irjet.net p-ISSN: 2395-0072

19. Lung Cancer Dataset. https://www.kaggle.com/datasets/yusufdede/lung-cancer-dataset. Accessed 25 Mar 2023

Investigating OpenAI's ChatGPT Capabilities to Improve Accessibility of Textual Information: An Explorative Study

Tiberio Uricchio, Silvia Ceccacci[(✉)], Ilaria D'Angelo, Noemi Del Bianco, and Catia Giaconi

University of Macerata, Via Crescimbeni 30/32, Macerata, Italy
silvia.ceccacci@unimc.it

Abstract. With the expansion of the Internet and mobile services, digital exclusion due to accessibility barriers remains a concern, particularly in understanding complex web content. This study investigates the application of Large Language Models (LLMs) like OpenAI's ChatGPT for simplifying sentences in line with easy-to-read (E2R) guidelines. Through two exploratory studies, we assess LLMs' awareness of E2R guidelines and their capability to simplify sentences to enhance cognitive accessibility in an archaeological museum context. The first one aims to assess LLMs' general knowledge about E2R guidelines. The second one evaluates their ability to perform SS conforming to E2R guidelines in order to generate accessible textual information for an archaeological museum. To this end, results of SS provided by LLMs are compared with text made by students who attended training on the E2R guidelines and those made through a co-design process with people with cognitive disabilities. Our findings support the discussion of the current potential and limitations of using LLMs as tools to improve the cognitive accessibility of text, providing insights into their potential role in making information more accessible.

Keywords: Large Language Models · Cognitive accessibility · Easy to Read · Sentence Simplification

1 Introduction

The rapid expansion of services provided through the Internet and mobile devices increasingly carries the risk of excluding segments of the population from essential services, both in private and public settings [1]. Over the years, thanks to the W3C's Web Accessibility Initiative (WAI), many steps have been made towards Web content accessibility, so much so that today, the technical aspects of Web content accessibility are addressed by international guidelines and legal regulations in many countries. However, many barriers still exist when it comes to understanding complex Web content. In particular, a considerable number of people remain currently excluded from digital services because of cognitive accessibility issues.

M. Antona and C. Stephanidis (Eds.): HCII 2024, LNCS 14696, pp. 326–336, 2024.
https://doi.org/10.1007/978-3-031-60875-9_22

Our understanding is that the creation of cognitively accessible web content involves a dual challenge: ensuring that the language of information text is clear and easy to understand and that the web page's content, structure and layout help the user to find, understand and use the information. Both aspects are equally important in ensuring a good Web experience for users with intellectual disabilities and other groups (e.g., the elderly, people with learning disabilities, individuals with limited reading and language skills) who face problems with "standard" information on the Web.

On the other hand, large language models (LLMs) surfaced as a new tool that is able to solve a wide variety of natural language processing tasks [2, 3]. However, their use in the SS task is limited so far to a few investigations like [4, 5], with no accurate studies on the specific capability of the SS task for such models. Moreover, considering that such models are generally trained with text crawled from the web, they are reported to be more proficient in languages that are frequently used, with limited understanding of infrequent ones [6]. For instance, Italian is identified as one of the languages with limited representation on the web, constituting only 2.4%[1] of online content. This scarcity poses even more challenges for using such models in the SS task that involve local languages.

In this context, this paper reports the results of an exploratory study that aims at understanding whether a state-of-the-art LLM system (i.e., OpenAI's ChatGPT), is capable of performing SS in a way that conforms to easy-to-read italian guidelines, so that it can provide support to an E2R guidelines expert in order to streamline the process of designing an alternative text.

2   Research Background

The Web Content Accessibility Guidelines 2.0 (WCAG 2.0) [7], recognized as the predominant framework for web accessibility, offer directives for crafting accessible web content. However, they provide only a limited set of recommendations for mitigating the complexity of information [8, 9].

On the one hand, there are international organizations' ease-to-read (E2R) guidelines and recommendations that aim at presenting documents that are clear and easily understandable, such as the International Federation of Library Associations and Institutions (IFLA) [10], the International League of Societies for Persons with Mental Handicap (ILSMH) [11], and Inclusion Europe [12]. Such guidelines comprise the writing of texts, the supporting images, the design and layout of documents, and the final editing format.

They are used in the manual processes of (a) adapting existing documents and (b) creating new materials. The process of adapting existing documents is cyclical and involves three activities: analysis, transformation and validation. Due to the need to involve people with intellectual disabilities as well as E2R experts, all these activities are human resource intensive.

Over the years, to streamline this process, various semi-automatic systems based on artificial intelligence have been proposed to support the analysis of texts in order to verify their compliance to E2R guidelines, such as that proposed in [13, 14], and to provide some suggestions useful for their transformation (e.g. [13]).

---

[1] https://w3techs.com/technologies/overview/content_language.

Regarding the idea of transforming reading materials based on E2R guidelines in an automatic way, a relevant approach that can be applied is the so-called sentence simplification. Sentence simplification (SS) is the "task of modifying the content and structure of a text in order to make it easier to read and understand while retaining its main idea and approximating its original meaning" [15]. Over the years, several automatic sentence simplification methods have been proposed based on supervised and unsupervised machine learning techniques (e.g., [16–20]). In recent years, large language models (LLMs) emerged as promising new tools that outperform the ability to solve a range of natural language processing tasks [2, 3]. However, only a few studies so far have investigated the performance of LLMs in generic SS tasks (e.g. [4, 5]) but they are limited on evaluating sentence structures for a generic adult audience, use older models and do not consider expert guidelines for accessibility of sentences. No study has focused on the actual capability of these tools to perform sentence simplification to improve cognitive accessibility of textual information.

Among recent notable LLMs, ChatGPT, launched by OpenAI in November 2022, has swiftly garnered attention across various sectors, notably in education and academic writing [21], for its capability to process natural language in a manner akin to human communication, further improved with the recent release of ChatGPT 4. Despite concerns regarding academic integrity and students' dependency on such tools, there is a growing consensus on the use of ChatGPT as an educational resource to develop critical and digital literacy skills [22]. Moreover, it is becoming a hot topic in various other fields, as demonstrated by the significant increase in the number of publications on ChatGPT [21].

3 Explorative Study

Among the current availability of LLMs, we considered for the analysis LLM models that are currently reported as the best in class in a general crowd tested benchmark[2]. At the moment of writing, ChatGPT 4 is reported as the best in terms of user evaluations. Considering its popularity, together with the 3.5 version, we make the decision to use these two models for our experiments. We consider both the web version (i.e. ChatGPT) and the GPT models available through the API, considering the current best models suggested by OpenAI. Specifically, we used versions tagged "gpt-4-0125" and "gpt-3.5-turbo-0125", suggested as the best general model by OpenAI at time of writing.

To determine whether the considered LLMs possess adequate knowledge and skills to properly perform SS based on the E2R guidelines, we designed two experiments, the first one to assess the knowledge of the guidelines and a second one to evaluate the performance in assisting a user on the SS task.

3.1 Experiment 1 - Evaluation of ChatGPT Knowledge Level

In this experiment, we manually evaluated the knowledge level of the LLMs with experts on the E2R guidelines and in writing accessible textual information.

---

[2] https://huggingface.co/spaces/lmsys/chatbot-arena-leaderboard.

We followed previous work on LLMs evaluation [2] and prepared a test made of open questions, to be answered freely without any purported structure, by the model. We asked three Italian experts on text accessibility and E2R to prepare 10 questions that covered the most practical aspects of the E2R guidelines. The considered questions are reported in Table 1.

The questions were submitted to ChatGPT by using OpenAI's API with a Python script, directly as they are, ensuring each tested version receives exactly the same question text. Each question was submitted in a thread by themselves without any additional text and without other textual context. The answers were recorded as they are given by the models without additional post-processing.

Three independent experts were asked to independently rate the responses given by the two versions of chatGPT, using a 1–5 Likert scale, where 1 means "Completely incorrect", 2 means "Non-sufficiently correct", 3 means "Sufficiently correct", 4 means "More than sufficiently correct" and 5 means "Completely Correct".

3.2 Experiment 2 - Using ChatGPT to Assist in Sentence Simplification

To evaluate the performance in assisting a user on the SS task, a comparative study has been carried out. A total of 7 informative texts have been adapted to make them compliant to E2R, in the context of an archeological Museum (i.e., Museo Archeologico Gentiloni Silverj of Tolentino). Each text was rephrased through 3 simplification process were carried out in parallel:

- Text adaptation using sentence simplification performed by ChatGPT. We utilized a Python script to submit queries individually, crafting a specialized prompt to steer ChatGPT towards producing text that not only aligns with the SS task but also adheres closely to easy-to-read (E2R) guidelines. This prompt was designed to embody a GPT "personality" expert in SS, fully versed in E2R guidelines, aiming to assist users in text simplification. Users could input text needing simplification directly, to which the model, equipped with this "personality," would respond with a simplified version. The prompt included a) a contextual backdrop prompting the model to act as an accessibility expert, b) a detailed presentation of the E2R guidelines, and c) explicit instructions to apply these guidelines meticulously in simplifications, considering the needs of users, including those with intellectual disabilities (thus, consider the guidelines in any answer given).
- Text adaptation performed by a group of students in pedagogy, trained on E2R guidelines. A group of 5 students were involved in text simplification activities. They worked in team and performed text adaptation following these procedural phases:
    1. reading the entire text;
    2. identification of difficult periods and terms;
    3. rephrase of difficult periods and terms into Easy-to-Read language;
    4. reorganization of information;
    5. rereading of the revised text.
- Creation of an Easy-to-Read text through a co-design process, involving both E2R experts and people with intellectual disability. Co-design activities have been carried

Table 1. Considered prompts and questions.

	Prompt: **Rispondi alla domanda molto brevemente in 3 frasi** *(Answer the question very briefly in 3 sentences)*
Q1	Nell'ambito della scrittura di testi facili da capire, perché è consigliato utilizzare parole di uso comune? *(In order to write easy-to-understand texts, why is it recommended to use common words?)*
Q2	Nell'ambito della scrittura di testi facili da capire, perché è importante coinvolgere le persone con disabilità intellettiva nella creazione di informazioni? *(In order to write easy-to-understand texts, why is it important to involve people with intellectual disabilities in information creation?)*
Q3	Nell'ambito della scrittura di testi facili da capire, perché è preferibile evitare l'uso di concetti complessi come le metafore? *(In order to write easy-to-understand texts, why is it preferable to avoid the use of complex concepts such as metaphors?)*
Q4	Nell'ambito della scrittura di testi facili da capire, qual è il ruolo degli esempi nella spiegazione di concetti complessi? *(In order to write easy-to-understand texts, what is the role of examples in explaining complex concepts?)*
Q5	Nell'ambito della scrittura di testi facili da capire, perché è importante evitare l'uso eccessivo di sottotitoli ed elenchi puntati? *(In order to write easy-to-understand texts, why is it important to avoid overuse of subtitles and bulleted lists?)*
Q6	Nell'ambito della scrittura di testi facili da capire, qual è il beneficio di utilizzare frasi con costrutto positivo invece che negativo? *(In order to write easy-to-understand texts, what is the benefit of using positive sentence construction instead of negative ones?)*
Q7	Nell'ambito della scrittura di testi facili da capire, perché è importante fare attenzione con i numeri e le percentuali nei testi comprensibili? *(In order to write easy-to-understand texts, why is it important to be careful with the use of numbers and percentages?)*
Q8	Nell'ambito della scrittura di testi facili da capire, qual è il vantaggio dell'organizzazione delle informazioni in modo chiaro e coerente? *(In order to write easy-to-understand texts, how information must be organized to make it as clear and consistent as possible?)*

(continued)

Table 1. (*continued*)

	Prompt: **Rispondi alla domanda molto brevemente in 3 frasi** *(Answer the question very briefly in 3 sentences)*
Q9	Nell'ambito della scrittura di testi facili da capire, perché è importante mantenere un linguaggio diretto quando si scrivono testi comprensibili? *(In order to write easy-to-understand texts, why is it important to maintain direct language when writing understandable texts?)*
Q10	Nell'ambito della scrittura di testi facili da capire, in che modo va utilizzata la punteggiatura per rendere i testi facilmente comprensibili? *(In order to write easy-to-understand texts, how should punctuation be used to make texts easily understandable?)*

out within the TIncTec Research Center of the University of Macerata, following the procedural phases proposed in [23].

A selected panel comprising three independent experts, each possessing extensive experience in the field of cognitive accessibility and Easy-to-Read (E2R) guidelines, undertook the task of evaluating the resulting texts. To ensure an unbiased assessment, the panel operated under a blind review protocol, meaning they were unaware of the source of each text, be it ChatGPT, students, or co-design efforts. This approach aimed to eliminate any potential bias that could influence the evaluations based on the text's origin. Each expert was asked to rate each text on a 1–5 Likert scale to rate each text's adherence to E2R guidelines, where:

- 1: Absolutely non-compliant – indicates a text significantly deviates from E2R guidelines, failing to meet basic standards of cognitive accessibility.
- 2: Non-sufficiently compliant – denotes texts that show an attempt to align with E2R guidelines but fall short in several major aspects.
- 3: Sufficiently compliant – signifies texts that meet the E2R guidelines adequately, ensuring a basic level of cognitive accessibility.
- 4: More than sufficiently compliant – represents texts that exceed the basic requirements of E2R guidelines, but still could be improved in minor aspects.
- 5: Completely compliant – reserved for texts that perfectly adhere to E2R guidelines, offering optimal cognitive accessibility.

In addition to numerical ratings, experts were asked to provide qualitative feedback on each text, highlighting strengths and areas for improvement. This dual approach allowed for a comprehensive understanding of how each text aligned with E2R principles and identified specific elements that contributed to or detracted from cognitive accessibility.

Following expert evaluation, the texts underwent a second assessment from individuals with intellectual disabilities. This group consisted of nine participants, selected to represent a broad spectrum of cognitive abilities within the context of intellectual disabilities. Participants were asked to rate the ease of understanding of each text, again employing a blind review format to ensure impartiality. They were asked to identify the five easiest to understand and the five most difficult to understand out of all 28 proposed text adaptations.

4 Results

Table 2 shows the median ratings expressed from the independent experts on the correctness of responses by the two versions of ChatGPT for each question. ChatGPT 4 achieved a score of at least 3 (indicating sufficient correctness) for 9 out of 10 questions, surpassing ChatGPT 3.5, which did so for only 7 questions. Specifically, ChatGPT 4 provided perfectly accurate answers to question Q3, while its responses to questions Q2, Q7, Q8, Q9, and Q10 were merely sufficient. Conversely, ChatGPT 3.5 outperformed ChatGPT 4 on five questions (Q1, Q2, Q4, Q8, and Q10), delivering completely accurate answers for four of them (Q1, Q2, Q4 and Q10). Notably, both versions failed to answer question Q6 correctly.

Table 2. ChatGPT knowledge level.

	Q1	Q2	Q3	Q4	Q5	Q6	Q7	Q8	Q9	Q10
Chat GPT 3.5 0125 turbo	5	5	3	5	1	1	2	4	3	5
Chat GPT 4 0125 preview	4	3	5	4	4	1	3	3	3	3

The correct answer to that question Q6 is:

"Positive sentences are preferable to negative ones because their greater brevity and simpler structure, combined to the direct and unequivocal expression of the content, make them both easier to understand and more incisive."

Instead, both the systems considered provided responses such as:

"The use of positive language can create a more optimistic and encouraging atmosphere for the reader."

"Using a positive language can foster greater motivation and involvement of the reader in the subject matter."

Regarding the experiment 2, Table 3 reports the median of judgments expressed by the independent experts about the level of compliance of adapted versions for each text, respectively resulting from:

- SS task performed using ChatGPT 3.5 and ChatGPT 4;
- simplification process carried out by the students;
- co-design process involving people with intellectual disability.

As observed, only 1 out of 7 texts provided by ChatGPT 3.5 was judged to be sufficiently compliant with the easy-to-read guidelines (i.e., T3), while 4 out 7 texts simplified using ChatGPT resulted sufficiently, or more than sufficiently, compliant with E2R.

Table 3. Effectiveness of ChatGPT in SS task compared to students and co-design process.

	T1	T2	T3	T4	T5	T6	T7
Chat GPT 3.5 0125 turbo	2	1	3	2	1	2	2
Chat GPT 4 0125 preview	2	1	1	3	3	4	3
Students	5	5	4	4	4	3	4
Co-design process	4	4	5	5	5	5	5

In general, based on experts' judgements, the texts provided by ChatGPT 4 do not seem to be comparable to those produced by students, let alone those resulting from the co-design process, in terms of compliance with E2R guidelines.

As noted by experts, the provided texts reworked by ChatGPT are characterized by:

- complex semantic structure (e.g., T2, T3, T4, T5);
- inadequate exemplification of complex terms (e.g., T1, T3);
- too long sentences (e.g., T1, T2, T3, T7).

Only in the case of text T6 the SS performed by ChatGPT 4 resulted better than that proposed by the students.

Surprisingly, however, these results are not entirely consistent with the judgments of the individuals with intellectual disabilities who participated in the evaluation.

As reported in Table 4, while people with disabilities rated many of the texts provided by ChatGPT 3.5 as the worst, they preferred most of the texts provided by ChatGPT 4, because they found them easier to understand.

Table 4. The Five best (B) and the five worst (W) texts as judged by people with intellectual disabilities

	T1	T2	T3	T4	T5	T6	T7
Chat GPT 3.5 0125 turbo	W	W	W		W		
Chat GPT 4 0125 preview		B	B		B		B
Students							
Co-design process	B						W

5 Discussion and Conclusions

This exploratory study aimed to assess the capabilities of Large Language Models (LLMs), specifically OpenAI's ChatGPT, in enhancing the cognitive accessibility of textual information via SS in line with E2R guidelines. The outcomes revealed mixed effectiveness. Experiment 1 demonstrated that ChatGPT 4 possesses a generally sufficient understanding of E2R guidelines, outperforming its predecessor, ChatGPT 3.5, in answering related queries. However, both versions struggled with certain aspects, notably in providing a fully correct response to the importance of using positive over negative sentence constructions.

Experiment 2's comparative analysis of SS tasks underscored that while ChatGPT can generate texts that are somewhat compliant with E2R guidelines, its outputs in the case of Italian language do not always consistently match the quality of those produced by human experts or co-design processes involving people with intellectual disabilities.

Notably, based on the experts' judgements, texts simplified using ChatGPT often retained complex semantic structures and exhibited inadequate exemplification and lengthy sentences, detracting from their accessibility. Nevertheless, based on the experience of people with intellectual disabilities, the texts provided by ChatGPT 4 can result in an excellent level of cognitive accessibility. Such results may seem incoherent. However, while it may seem strange that experts' judgements seem to disagree with those of people with disabilities, we must remember that perfect compliance with the guidelines per se may not be entirely necessary or sufficient to ensure that texts are understandable for people with intellectual disabilities. In fact, as stated by the Inclusion Europe Association the brochure titled "Do not write for us without us" [24] only "people with intellectual disabilities know best what is good for them. They know best what they need to understand information. No easy-to-read text should ever be written without people with intellectual disabilities taking part at some point."

While LLMs like ChatGPT can serve as auxiliary tools for simplifying text, human oversight remains crucial to ensure compliance with heterogeneous needs of target audiences. We highlight the importance of integrating LLMs within broader co-design frameworks that include stakeholders from diverse backgrounds, including people with cognitive disabilities. Such inclusive approaches can enhance the relevance and accessibility of simplified texts, leveraging the strengths of both AI and human expertise. Future studies should aim to optimize the prompt to be used to perform SS using ChatGPT through co-design processes, involving people with intellectual disabilities, and to the definition of new approaches aimed at optimizing SS tasks by taking advantage of LLMs' learning ability based on user feedback.

Acknowledgements. Thanks to ANFASS of Macerata for participating in this research.

References

1. European Commission. Web accessibility. Shaping Europe's digital future (2023). https://digital-strategy.cc.europa.eu/en/policies/web-accessibility

2. Min, B., et al.: Recent advances in natural language processing via large pre-trained language models: a survey. ACM Comput. Surv. **56**(2), 1–40 (2023). https://doi.org/10.1145/3605943

3. Liu, Y., et al.: Summary of ChatGPT-related research and perspective towards the future of large language models. Meta-Radiology **1**, 100017 (2023). https://doi.org/10.1016/j.metrad. 2023.100017

4. Feng, Y., Qiang, J., Li, Y., Yuan, Y., Zhu, Y.: Sentence simplification via large language models. arXiv preprint arXiv:2302.11957 (2023). https://arxiv.org/pdf/2302.11957.pdf

5. Bertin, S.: Scientific simplification, the limits of ChatGPT. In: CEUR Workshop Proceedings: CLEF 2023: Conference and Labs of the Evaluation Forum, 18–21 September 2023, Thessaloniki, Greece (2023). https://ceur-ws.org/Vol-3497/paper-244.pdf

6. Basile, P., Musacchio, E., Polignano, M., Siciliani, L., Fiameni, G., Semeraro, G.: LLaMAntino: LLaMA 2 models for effective text generation in Italian language. arXiv preprint arXiv:2312.09993 (2023)

7. Web content accessibility guidelines (WCAG) 2.0. https://www.w3.org/TR/WCAG20/

8. Schmutz, S., Sonderegger, A., Sauer, J.: Easy-to-read language in disability-friendly web sites: effects on nondisabled users. Appl. Ergon. **74**, 97–106 (2019). https://doi.org/10.1016/j.apergo.2018.08.013

9. Nietzio, A., Naber, D., Bühler, C.: Towards techniques for easy-to-read web content. Procedia Comput. Sci. **27**, 343–349 (2014). https://doi.org/10.1016/j.procs.2014.02.038

10. International Federation of Library Association and Institutions. IFLA Professional Reports, No. 120. Guidelines for easy-to-read materials. https://www.ifla.org/wp-content/uploads/2019/05/assets/hq/publications/professional-report/120.pdf

11. ILSMH European Association. Make it Simple. European Guidelines for the Production of Easy-to-Read Information for People with Learning Disability for authors, editors, information providers, translators and other interested persons. https://core.ac.uk/download/pdf/512 4495.pdf

12. Inclusion Europe. Information for All. European standards for making information easy to read and understand. German. OCLC: 838005460. Inclusion Europe, Brüssel (2009). ISBN: 9782874601101. https://short.upm.es/yuh77

13. Suárez-Figueroa, M.C., Diab, I., Ruckhaus, E., et al.: First steps in the development of a support application for easy-to-read adaptation. Univ. Access Inf. Soc. (2022). https://doi.org/10.1007/s10209-022-00946-z

14. Suárez-Figueroa, M.C., Ruckhaus, E., López-Guerrero, J., Cano, I., Cervera, Á.: Towards the assessment of easy-to-read guidelines using artificial intelligence techniques. In: Miesenberger, K., Manduchi, R., Covarrubias Rodriguez, M., Peňáz, P. (eds.) Computers Helping People with Special Needs, ICCHP 2020. LNCS, vol. 12376, pp. 74–82. Springer, Cham (2020). https://doi.org/10.1007/978-3-030-58796-3_10

15. Alva-Manchego, F., Scarton, C., Specia, L.: Data-driven sentence simplification: survey and benchmark. Comput. Linguist. **46**(1), 135–187 (2020). https://doi.org/10.1162/coli_a_00370

16. Nisioi, S., Štajner, S., Ponzetto, S.P., Dinu, L.P.: Exploring neural text simplification models. In: Proceedings of the 55th Annual Meeting of the Association for Computational Linguistics, vol. 2: Short Papers, pp. 85–91, July 2017. https://doi.org/10.18653/v1/P17-2014

17. Surya, S., Mishra, A., Laha, A., Jain, P., Sankaranarayanan, K.: Unsupervised neural text simplification. arXiv preprint arXiv:1810.07931 (2018). https://arxiv.org/pdf/1810.07931.pdf

18. Dong, Y., Li, Z., Rezagholizadeh, M., Cheung, J.C.K.: EditNTS: an neural programmer-interpreter model for sentence simplification through explicit editing. arXiv preprint arXiv: 1906.08104 (2019). https://arxiv.org/pdf/1906.08104.pdf

19. Martin, L., Fan, A., De La Clergerie, É., Bordes, A., Sagot, B.: MUSS: multilingual unsupervised sentence simplification by mining paraphrases. arXiv preprint arXiv:2005.00352 (2020). https://arxiv.org/pdf/2005.00352.pdf

20. Kumar, D., Mou, L., Golab, L., Vechtomova, O.: Iterative edit-based unsupervised sentence simplification. arXiv preprint arXiv:2006.09639 (2020). https://arxiv.org/pdf/2006.09639.pdf
21. Aydin, Ö., Karaarslan, E.: Is ChatGPT leading generative AI? What is beyond expectations? Acad. Platform J. Eng. Smart Syst. **11**(3), 118–134 (2023)
22. Araújo, S., Aguiar, M.: Simplifying specialized texts with AI: a ChatGPT-based learning scenario. In: Mesquita, A., Abreu, A., Carvalho, J.V., Santana, C., de Mello, C.H.P. (eds.) International Conference in Information Technology and Education, vol. 366, pp. 599–609. Springer, Cham (2023). https://doi.org/10.1007/978-981-99-5414-8_55
23. Shogren, K.A., Caldarelli, A., Giaconi, C., D'Angelo, I., Del Bianco, N.: Co designing inclusive museum itineraries with people with disabilities: a case study from self-determination. Educ. Sci. Soc. **2**(2022), 214–226 (2022)
24. Inclusion Europe. Do not write for us without us. http://sid.usal.es/idocs/F8/FDO23139/write_for_us.pdf

Tax and Welfare Chatbots Used by Young Adults with Dyslexia: A Usability Study

Guri Verne[1] , Gerd Berget[2]([envelope]) , Anton Lilleby[1]([envelope]) , and Steffen Marstein[1]([envelope])

[1] University of Oslo, Blindern, 0316 Oslo, Norway
guribv@ifi.uio.no
[2] Oslo Metropolitan University, Postboks 4 St. Olavs Plass, 0130 Oslo, Norway
gerdb.berget@oslomet.no

Abstract. Information regarding tax and welfare is now increasingly disseminated online, where web pages and chatbots in many contexts have replaced direct contact with case workers. The shift in interaction forms, from verbal to written communication, may be troublesome for certain users, such as people with impaired reading or spelling. People with dyslexia comprise a cohort who often have challenges with textual input and reading and comprehending long texts containing complex words. This paper reports the findings from a study of how young adults with dyslexia experience chatbots from the Norwegian tax and welfare agencies. A qualitative usability test was conducted to explore how the chatbots functioned in practice. The participants reported challenges related to both reading and writing when communicating with chatbots, which may hamper the understanding of and access to public information. The result might be a less inclusive society. Some implications for improved chatbot design focusing on ameliorating challenges with reading and writing are suggested.

Keywords: Chatbots · Dyslexia · Usability

1 Introduction

Information regarding tax and welfare is now increasingly disseminated online, where web pages and chatbots often replace direct contact with case workers. Chatbots are increasingly introduced into the public sector to give the citizens general answers to questions about family, unemployment benefits, tax rules and regulations [1]. Chatbots are expected to replace some of the human contact with a public administration and reduce the load on staffed services. A benefit for the users is to receive quality assured answers without needing to assess search results from a general Web search engine.

The Norwegian welfare administration expects that contact between citizens and staffed services over telephone or over the counter in service offices will be reduced considerably by 2025 [2]. According to a governmental action plan, Norway has a goal to become universally designed by 2025 [3]. Moreover, universally designed ICT-systems are required by law [4]. To comply with action plan and jurisdiction and ensure equal accesses to information for everyone, however, a better understanding of the accessibility of chatbots for a diversity of users is required.

A chatbot is an automatic system that can chat with a user online [5]. Development in machine learning technology have resulted in better chatbot responses [6–8]. Nevertheless, using a public chatbot can still provide challenges for all types of users [1]. Where a human call advisor will actively help a caller with little previous knowledge about tax, the chatbot will present the rules that apply on the topic [9]. A chatbot is based upon textual communication and may therefore be particularly challenging to use for people with impaired or reduced reading and/or writing skills.

People with dyslexia is an example of a cohort who frequently produce spelling errors and experience challenges with reading comprehension [10]. Further, users with dyslexia experience challenges related to searching, reading, and writing online [11, 12]. When having to rely on information retrieval through chatbots or textual information on web pages, many people with dyslexia may lose access to important public information.

This paper reports the findings from a study of how young adults with dyslexia experience using chatbots from the tax and welfare agencies in Norway. Young adults encounter many tax issues for the first time when they enter adult life and is therefore a user group that often contact the tax call center by telephone [13]. Young adults with dyslexia may also need to apply for benefits or support from the welfare agency to get access to e.g., expensive assistive technology. This study addresses how the chatbots responded to the questions inputted by the participants, how the participants interpreted the responses from the chatbots as well as their overall experience using the chatbots.

The contribution of this paper is to provide knowledge about how two important public sector chatbots function in practice and how dyslexia can affect the interaction between chatbots and end users. Moreover, some implications for design are suggested which may improve the chatbot experience of people with dyslexia. Users with dyslexia often produce misspellings, misread or struggle with the long and complicated terminology applied by the tax and welfare agencies, which may also be problematic for other types of user groups. The findings may therefore have implications for many other users.

The paper is structured as follow: First, a background is provided regarding research on chatbots, the two chatbots applied in this study and dyslexia. This is followed by the methodology. Then, the findings from the usability test are presented before some implications for design of chatbots are suggested. The findings are discussed, followed by a conclusion.

2 Background

2.1 Chatbots

A chatbot presents an alternative way for users to ask questions and receive answers instead of searching web pages or making a phone call. Chatbots are used for many different purposes, such as customer service, public information, entertainment, socializing or from curiosity of a new phenomenon [5, 6]. Research on chatbots is often carried out from the perspective of the provider with a focus on profit and customer satisfaction [14]. For use in customer service, a chatbot will need to be trusted by its users [5]. In a literature review of educational chatbots in various learning domains, Kuhail et al. [15]

found that design guidelines and usability heuristics for special learner groups were not part of the design rationale for the chatbots.

A chatbot can also be used to give social support, which is important for health and well-being for young people [14]. A chatbot often mimics human communication but has in addition endless patience [16]. However, creating successful non-trivial chatbots within specific topics has proved more difficult than anticipated [17]. A chatbot can give confusing answers where background knowledge will be beneficial in producing a well-formed request and to assess the quality of the response [1]. Users can also be reluctant to ask a chatbot for more complex and sensitive tasks [7].

Chatbots that provide public information about citizens' rights and duties will need to give correct and relevant responses to citizens' requests. Verne et al. [8] showed that the LWA chatbot gave correct but not always complete answers to the requests received. The match with the citizen's request was not always correct. Hence the citizen easily will misunderstand the response, believing it would be relevant for them. A misleading response can occur in a chat session where a keyword from the opening request is lost. When this keyword is not part of forming the answer, the chatbot response will not be complete [1].

2.2 The Two Chatbots Applied in This Study

The two public sector chatbots applied in this study are the chatbots of the Norwegian tax administration and the labor and welfare administration LWA (see Fig. 1). The LWA chatbot was introduced to the public in the spring of 2018, is called Frida and is visually depicted as a young woman. This chatbot was originally designed to only be able to answer general questions about family and children benefits but is later developed to cover more topics within labor and welfare.

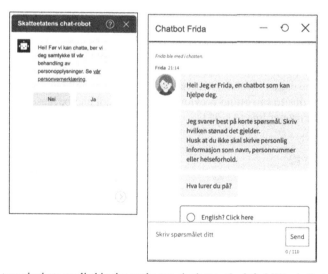

Fig. 1. The two chatbots applied in the study, tax chatbot to the left, LWA chatbot to the right.

The tax chatbot was introduced to the public in 2019 and did not have a human-like name. The text in the chatbot window says "chat-robot", and it is depicted as a small robot. For both chatbots, machine learning technology is used to interpret the query from the chatbot user, identify "intention" of the query and select the best response. In both public administrations, the response texts are articulated by experienced advisors as answers to example questions and are quality assured from the administrations.

2.3 Dyslexia

Dyslexia is prevalent in 5 to 20% of the population [18], depending among others on the definition applied and the first language, since dyslexia manifest differently in dissimilar languages. This specific learning disorder typically causes impaired reading and writing skills [19] but can also affect information processing skills, working memory [20], rapid naming skills [21], and concentration [22]. Although most of these characteristics are found in all individuals with dyslexia, they occur differently and in varying degrees. For example, some people read slowly, but have a good understanding of the content, while others are fast readers, but make more errors.

Comorbidity is often found among individuals with dyslexia, where the most common combination is dyslexia and ADHD [23]. Other conditions are also commonly co-occurring, such as dyscalculia or dyspraxia [24]. Although reading and writing skills are affected throughout life, many people with dyslexia develop life experience and coping strategies that will reduce the impact of dyslexia and improve quality of life [25]. Nevertheless, reduced self-esteem and anxiety are frequently reported, among others due to negative experiences in school, academic or work-related contexts [26, 27]. Consequently, many people rely on support from family members or others [28].

Most research on dyslexia addresses children, with a particular emphasis on learning how to read at school. There are, however, many tasks that may be challenging later in life, such as information retrieval [12, 29, 30], filling out forms and understanding official documents [28]. Researchers have also addressed layout and implications for reading speed and reading flow, including purposeful font types, sizes, and line lengths [31, 32]. It is reported that the eye movements of people with dyslexia can follow different patterns than with people without dyslexia [33]. Moreover, it is suggested that short line lengths, where the reader must move between lines in the middle of sentences can cause challenges, both due to forgetting previously read content and because of difficulties in navigating to the proper line [31, 32].

3   Methodology

3.1 Procedure

The study took place during the fall of 2019 and the spring of 2020. The aim was to explore how using a chatbot is experienced by young adults with dyslexia and how the two chatbots can be improved for this user group. The study was interpretive with an aim to understand the experience of the participants [34]. Two methods were applied; interviews and a usability test comprising five young adults with dyslexia who tested two chatbots.

The usability test was developed with the aim to increase the usability of the chatbot interface for young adults with dyslexia. The test followed the criteria by Dumas and Redish [35] where the participants are users of the interface, and the assignments reflect real issues. The tasks were designed to be relevant for young adults getting their first job and finding out if they apply for special benefits.

Before the usability test, each participant was interviewed about the use of assistive technology and previous experiences with chatbots. The usability test consisted of four assignments for each public sector areas tax and labor/welfare to be solved using the chatbots. (The assignments are presented in the next section together with the findings.) What the participants said during the usability test was recorded and transcribed, and the data was analyzed to find problematic issues and suggest improvements. The participants were interviewed after the usability test about suggestions for improvements of the chatbots. For both the tax and welfare chatbots, the participants were asked about their overall experiences with and impressions of the chatbots.

3.2 Participants

Three participants were recruited through Dyslexia Norway and two people through an extended network. The participants were 18–30 years old, three women and two men. All participants had some degree of dyslexia. They all stated that activities such as reading and writing were time-consuming, and they frequently produced spelling errors. Moreover, all the participants preferred conversations over written communication. Following this study's ambition of giving the young participants with dyslexia a voice, they are also given fictional names in this paper, the pseudonyms Rick, Mary, Ruth, Annie, and Paul.

3.3 Analysis

According to the interpretive research paradigm [34], analysis is a continuing process where analytical themes emerge during the whole research process. Some themes were identified in the initial interviews. After all usability tests were carried out, the results were given an inductive analysis aimed at identifying new themes and topics [36], where elements were categorized and organized into broader topics.

The analysis was carried out by two of the authors and consisted of four steps: a) Sticky notes were used to note findings and descriptions from each usability test. b) The notes were categorized and organized into groups (see Fig. 2). c) Notes with findings and descriptions were collected in themes. If a note did not match, new themes were identified. d) All notes within a theme were inspected and checked by these two researchers.

3.4 Ethical Concerns

The study had received privacy clearance from the Norwegian center for research data. All participants were given information about the study, which was described as a web experiment focusing on universal design of a "chat-robot". The term "web experiment"

Fig. 2. The analysis of issues and topics from a single usability test. White: findings from interviews, blue: tax, pink: welfare, and yellow: needs and wishes expressed by the participant. (Color figure online)

was used to avoid the ambiguous term "test". The recruitment letter explicitly stated that the participant's skills were not the focus of the "web experiment" but rather the chat-robot solution. All participants signed consent forms where they agreed to take part in a pre-interview, the actual experiment, and a post-interview.

4 Findings

In the next subsections, general findings from the pre-interviews are presented first. Then, the assignments of the usability test and a description of the main findings are presented together with the participants' experiences. For both chatbots, the first assignment was designed to investigate whether the participants could locate the chatbot online. The next three assignments asked the participants to use the chatbot to find some topic-related information, and finally they were asked about their overall impressions.

4.1 Pre-interviews

In the pre-interviews all participants described activities which included reading and writing as time-consuming due to reading and spelling errors. They preferred talking over writing and listening rather than reading. Over the years, reading and writing had become less problematic due to the development of coping skills. Nevertheless, the participants reported experiencing stigmatization when engaging in activities requiring reading or writing. All participants had used technical reading and writing support software or acquired better reading and writing skills. Such tools were still used actively by two of the participants.

All participants mentioned that they did not like chatting or messaging in social media or with e.g., a customer service because chatting was regarded as time-consuming, and they were easily exhausted. All the participants had experience from using chatbots before this study. Ruth reported that she always immediately asked for a human advisor. Mary mentioned that she missed the emotional aspect when chatting with a chatbot and that time limits connected to such services made the conversation stressful. However, she added that the quality with a chatbot is that it cannot criticize or condemn her for spelling errors. The participants did not use reading or writing support software for activities such as chatting.

4.2 The Tax Agency Chatbot

Locating the Chatbot. The first task was to navigate to the tax agency's chat about personal tax. All the participants found the chatbot web site, but three people took much time. Rick produced a spelling error when looking up the web site so that he did not find the right web page without help from the test leader. Annie and Paul did not easily find the link to the chatbot from the contact page. Mary and Annie remarked that the chatbot box was small compared to the available space on the web page, while Paul used a zoom-function to read the text. When the chatbot opened, all the participants got the first impression that they were communicating with a machine, not a person. Annie, however, pointed out that it seemed like the chat-bot tried to appear as a human, which might be misinterpreted by some people.

Availability of Tax Forms. The second task was: "You want to know when the tax report form for 2019 will be available. How will you proceed to retrieve this information by using the chatbot?". Two participants found an answer, while three people (Rick, Mary, and Ruth) found it difficult to formulate a request.

Several queries were misspelled when solving this task. Mary wrote a question containing a spelling error. She got a reply that the chatbot did not understand the question, but it responded adequately with a relevant link. Ruth misspelled the same word, but with two errors related to both spelling and word-division. In this case, the response was that the chatbot did not understand the question. Ruth was unsure whether she had conducted a spelling error or if the chatbot did not analyze the question correctly: "*is it because I am spelling incorrectly now?*". The links provided by the chatbot contained links to writing tips or other ways to contact the tax office, but no links related to the actual topic searched for. Ruth then entered the query into Google's search field, which suggested corrections, and the corrected query was inputted into the chatbot. When Ruth still did not get a relevant reply, she gave up.

The participants were positive to response alternatives from the chatbot because they gave an overview of possible alternatives to follow up and did not demand textual input. According to Rick: "*The advantage with response alternatives is that one doesn't have to write*". Moreover, if the participants could refrain from inputting text, they avoided misunderstandings. It was, however, sometimes difficult to choose the correct alternative. Uncertainty and confusion could arise when the options were perceived as too similar. In some cases, however, none of the suggestions seemed purposeful, and the request had to be reformulated.

Advance Tax Forms. The third task was: "Imagine that you have got a new job and your employer tells you to update the income figure in the advance tax form. How will you use the chatbot to figure out how to do this?". All the participants received an adequate reply with several response alternatives. Although the chatbot did understand some of the spelling errors, it did not understand all. Several alternatives were presented, but Mary and Annie did not perceive them as relevant because they did not provide an actual answer to the question. The responses were too general, and the participants had to reformulate their queries. Mary found the answer but said she *"would have called them now, this gets too complicated"*. Annie decided to end the chat and start over again to avoid the previous context of tax report, saying *"one has to find these keywords"*.

Ruth and Mary found it problematic that the chatbot produced much text in response to their question. To read all the text they needed to navigate upwards by scrolling in the chat window. If they started to read the text before the chatbot had finished writing, their reading flow was interrupted. While experiencing this, Ruth elaborated: *"it abrupts the reading and that is annoying"* and Mary exclaimed: *"this is horrible"*.

Ordering a New Advance Tax Card. The fourth task was: "You have updated your income as requested in the previous task and want the new advance tax card sent through the mail. How will you investigate if this is possible by using the chatbot?". Two issues were revealed during this task, namely a low tolerance for spelling errors and the chatbot not preserving the context from previous input during the chat.

Several spelling errors occurred in this assignment. For example, Rick asked for the advance tax card in the mail, inputting the word 'posten' in Norwegian, but produced a spelling error and wrote 'poten'. The chatbot responded with a general reply: *"I do not quite understand what you were asking"* and gave the response alternative *"request a tax card"*, which was not what the participant requested. Rick could locate the spelling error but was frustrated that the chatbot did not overcome this small error: *"That wasn't a big spelling error, so I don't understand why it didn't comprehend that"*. He corrected the error but gave up when he still did not receive a relevant reply: *"I have written everything correctly. Here I would have asked someone for help because it is impossible for me to get any further"*.

Mary wanted to discover whether the chatbot could answer her regarding how to order an electronic advance tax card. She formulated her question with a small spelling error, writing 'bestille elektroniks skattekort' inputting 'elektroniks' instead of 'elektronisk'. She got the following response from the chatbot: *"I think I understood what you wrote, but I did not understand 'elektroniks'"*, followed by a general response alternative for ordering a tax card. When this participant reformulated the word "electronic" spelled correctly, believing that the context of the request was preserved, the chatbot gave an unspecific *"I do not understand your question"*. The participant found this frustrating and she *"would rather google to find the answer"*.

Overall Impressions of the Chatbot. Paul found the chatbot surprisingly efficient, but thought it was confusing when many messages came after each other. He would rather prefer one longer message and wanted an option to talk to a person more easily available. Annie reported that the chatbot was successful at retrieving answers for simple questions, but wished it was easier to find on the webpage and a response for "none of the answers", to avoid dead ends. Rick found the chatbot ok to use, but somewhat stressful. Mary emphasized the difficult terminology applied, and that it was advantageous that the chatbot to some degree helped with misspelled words. However, she also perceived the chatbot as very stressful to use and would have preferred talking to a person. Ruth considered this chatbot to be better than other chatbots she had experienced, but wanted clearer instructions that the best way to input queries was through keywords.

4.3   The Welfare Agency Chatbot

Locating the Chatbot. The first task was to navigate to the welfare agency's chat for job seeking. Two participants, Mary and Ruth immediately googled "LWA chatbot" and were taken directly to the chatbot web page. It was, however, a more cumbersome process to locate the chatbot from the LWA landing page. Annie and Rick took so much time on this task that they gave up and had to get help from the test leader. Rick commented: *"It should be easier accessible. For example, an icon visible in a corner"*.

When asked directly, all participants believed that they met a chatbot. There was, however, some uncertainty whether the chat was controlled by humans or a machine in the beginning. Mary asked when she found it: *"What does 'chat with us' mean, does it mean chatting with a person?"*. Annie found it strange that the chatbot had a female name and a female avatar (see Fig. 3). She was unsure if she would have understood that the conversation would be with a chatbot and not a real person.

Work Assessment Benefits. The second task was: "You want to clarify what 'work assessment benefits' means (abbreviated AAP in Norwegian). How will you go about finding this out by using their chatbot?". All participants solved this task, including two participants who despite spelling errors received relevant response from the chatbot. For this task the chatbot produced the most text (see Fig. 3), which all participants found overwhelming. Rick found it hard to read repetitive text, so he often skipped words and whole sentences. Ruth ignored huge parts of the text and pushed the link on the last response from the chatbot. Annie said that the language was difficult and more comprehensive than necessary: *"It is a very long sentence, and it doesn't need to respond with this because it was not what I asked for "*.

The answer from the chatbot was split into several messages. The first part of the text disappeared on top of the chat window as more text was produced, and scrolling was necessary to read it all. There was no conventional scroll bar available, and Mary and Ruth needed help to navigate back in the chatlog to see the entire text.

Work Assessment Benefits. The third task was: "Imagine that you have 'reduced working capacity' and you want to investigate whether you have a right to work assessment benefits. How will you use the chatbot to find this information?". All participants succeeded in solving the task, three of them with some effort, and were provided with several response alternatives from the chatbot. Two participants received a reply that the chatbot had already answered the question, which it had not. This issue was solved by inputting a reformulated query. Rick stated: *"this makes no sense, it was only a small spelling error, a person would have understood this immediately"*. When he reformulated the question, he received a correct response.

Very different answers were provided to the participants on this task, and the large amounts of text seemed irrelevant. For example, Paul referred to the first answer as sufficient to answer his question. Ruth found the information overwhelming and would have preferred talking to a person if she had reduced work capacity. She tried correcting her query when she found a spelling error, but more text was produced by the chatbot while she was inputting her query. Both Mary and Annie commented that their reading was interrupted. Annie elaborated on this issue: *"One starts to read and then the chatbot interrupts you"*.

Fig. 3. The LWA chatbot

Paul, Mary, and Annie found it useful to receive response alternatives. According to Annie, this feature could be applied more often. However, as with the tax chatbot, the participants found it difficult to understand what the response alternatives entailed.

Personal Communication. The fourth task was: "Let us assume that you did not get sufficient information about the work assessment benefits and you want to know more by chatting with a human advisor. How will you go about starting a chat with a person?". All the participants queried the chatbot to get in contact with an actual person. Annie had read before she started that the chatbot could redirect her to a chat with a person, but you had to go through the chatbot to achieve this contact. Some users inputted simple queries, such as Ruth who inputted 'advisor'. A few simple spelling errors occurred inputted by Mary and Ruth, but the chatbot gave adequate responses. In this assignment it was probably helpful that, as a fallback question, the chatbot was designed to ask if the user wanted to be redirected to chat with a human if it could not interpret the request. Mary was wondering about the answer from the chatbot using the word 'chat': "*does that mean talking to a real person?*". When Paul inputted the query 'contact advisor', the chatbot did not understand. It still provided a response on how to get in touch with a person. Paul commented: "*one has to be specific but not too specific simultaneously*".

Overall Impressions of the Chatbot. Paul found the chatbot somewhat messy and with much unnecessary information. He was expecting the chatbot to be dumb but had hoped it would be smarter. Annie wished the chatbot had been "*more precise*" and felt that much of the text felt like "*copy paste*" from law texts. Rick expected the chatbot to become better at spelling errors and to have an autocomplete function. Mary liked that the chatbot had a larger display. She was, however, not interested in writing to it and would rather talk to a person or search Google. Ruth found the chatbot clear but thought a person would be able to explain laws and regulations better.

4.4 Summing up and Post-interviews

Table 1 illustrates the participants performance during the different tasks. There were experiences discussed by all the participants. Both chatbots showed some tolerance for spelling errors and interpreted many requests correctly even when they contained some spelling errors, particularly if the spelling error occurred in the keywords related to special topic areas. Nevertheless, the participants expected a higher tolerance for spelling errors than the chatbot had implemented. Moreover, they found that the chatbots disturbed their reading flow by providing too much text so that they had to scroll backwards to read the full reply, which they found annoying.

Table 1. Summing up how the participants succeeded with the assignments. Green/1: found an answer, yellow/0.5: found an answer after some trial and error, red/0: no answer found.

Task	Rick	Mary	Ruth	Annie	Paul
Tax1	0.5	1	1	0.5	0.5
Tax2	0.5	0.5	0	0.5	0.5
Tax3	0.5	0.5	0.5	0.5	0.5
Tax4	0	0.5	0.5	1	1
Lwa1	0	1	1	0	0.5
Lwa2	0.5	1	1	1	1
Lwa3	0.5	1	0.5	0.5	1
Lwa4	1	1	1	1	0.5

5   Implications for Chatbot Design for Young Adults with Dyslexia

The results from this study indicate that some of the problems that the participants experienced related to reading, writing and comprehension probably was accentuated by the dyslexia:

- Sometimes, the chatbot produced too much text, often over several messages. This interrupted the reading flow, because participants had to scroll backwards to pick up where they were, which can affect the reading flow [31, 32]. This behavior may also potentially be related to impaired short-term memory or reading errors, resulting in a need to revisit previous text.
- The terminology was unfamiliar and difficult and often with too long explanations. This will be problematic for all citizens but will probably be accentuated by the dyslexia.
- A low tolerance for some of these users' spelling errors was shown by the chatbot.

To better support reading and writing experiences for people with dyslexia when using a chatbot we suggest some improvements to the design:

- Avoid interrupting the reading process. The chatbot could freeze the text that is produced and signal that more text is added, or messages are written further down in the chat window. A larger chat window will also provide sufficient space for longer texts without the need for scrolling. Increased line lengths may potentially also make the text easier to read [31, 32]. The window frame can be larger and does not need to be conform with the restrictions of a mobile phone screen for all users.
- To keep the reading context, special terminology can be explained in a short pop-up message within the chat window. These explanations can also have a reading aloud option, to reduce the need to read long texts.
- Higher tolerance for spelling errors will benefit both people with dyslexia and people without dyslexia, but the systems need to have tolerance towards some of the spelling errors produced by people with dyslexia, which may differ from other users [11, 12].
- Some people with dyslexia may prefer listening to the response over reading. As the chatbot messages are predefined they can easily be converted into human voice messages activated by a click from the user.
- The text inputted by the user can be read aloud when clicking a button as a help to locate spelling errors. Since this text is written by the user, it will need to be read by a synthetic voice.
- The format of the chatbot can be extended with images and video explanations that are shown outside the chatbot frame.

These implications for design barely scratch the surface of the possibilities for improving conditions for better reading, writing and comprehension for people doing inquiries for public information. Nevertheless, they may accommodate several of the issues experienced by the participants in this study and may also benefit other users, since spelling errors may be produced by all types of users.

6 Discussion

The chatbots in this study provide information about tax and welfare benefits which may be crucial for citizens and impact their economic situation and well-being. These chatbots are therefore different from chatbots made available for sales or service, socializing, engagement, and transformation [37]. The consequences for users who give up using the chatbot or do not understand its responses can be much more severe than in other contexts, where the user for example has the option of choosing another online store or service provider. In the cases of tax and welfare, the users have few quality-assured alternative information sources other than the official communication channels.

Formulating effective queries to a chatbot and understanding the responses correctly can be challenging for all types of people [1]. Some of the comments from the participants in this study appear to address general issues not related to having dyslexia. Reactions to the female avatar, information overload or irritation about a lacking tolerance for spelling errors are probably experienced by everyone. An additional challenge for young people may be a lack of domain knowledge and little experience with tax, labor and welfare compared to older users, who have previous experience and may be familiar with key terms for these topics.

During a chat session, citizens can ask to be set over to chat with a person. It has been suggested that small talk as time-fillers from the chatbot will ameliorate the waiting time [38]. Smalltalk that produces more text from the chatbot, possibly not even related to the question, will increase the textual output. Consequently, the cognitive load will be increased, and the irrelevant content may also be perceived as confusing. An alternative could be offering users the option to view small instruction videos on topics related to the queries they have recently inputted.

An increasing number of public services are transformed into online self-services. Finding relevant information online can be demanding for everyone but may be more difficult for young adults with dyslexia due to the heavy reliance on textual communication.

Reading and writing are activities that all people find challenging from time to time. The ability to read and write can be affected by not only having a reading or writing impairment, but also by being ill, stressed, tired or worn out. Permanent or temporary motor impairments can also impact the ability to use a keyboard for textual input, for example if a person has a broken wrist. Findings from this study suggest that some people with dyslexia might prefer using speech recognition. However, since the chatbots seem to work better when searching for keywords than longer sentences, speech recognition will probably result in less precise results.

Issues related to writing, reading, and comprehending text will be more pronounced for the young adults with dyslexia [19], making the overall experience with the chatbot more demanding and frustrating than for other users. Moreover, much of the bureaucratic language contains long and complicated words, which makes reading even more challenging. A lack of self-esteem and reliance on help from others, may also negatively affect the experiences with chatbots [26–28]. Consequently, people with dyslexia more easily may lose courage and give up, resulting in negative experiences with chatbots. Often the participants could not understand whether their question was answered satisfactorily by the chatbot. This was stressful, and on some occasions the participants expressed that they would have made a phone call to make sure that they understood the response. This finding may also be related to the lack of self-esteem found among many people with dyslexia [26–28].

Research on chatbots for all is an important topic [39]. For chatbots that are applied by users to inquire and learn about tax or welfare it is obviously very important that all citizens are included. One way to strive for this is through studies like this, where the needs of specific groups are considered. In line with Paddison and Englefield [40], usability tests will give more precise knowledge about the different user groups´ unique requirements. Moreover, previous research has emphasized people with dyslexia as a purposeful cohort to include in user tests, because design improvements for this user group will also increase the usability for others [22]. A more thorough discussion of design implications can be found in Lilleby and Marstein [41].

This study has a few limitations. It is a small exploratory study with only five participants. Moreover, chatbots are under continuous development and both the web pages and the chatbot responses may have changed since the study was carried out. Some of the design suggestions presented here may conflict with the needs for other groups. For example, reading the chatbot responses aloud, will conflict with usability for people with impaired hearing. More tolerance for spelling errors can give wrong interpretations of words, leading to irrelevant chatbot responses which can be misunderstood. It is therefore important to consider using several modalities to accommodate a broad diversity of users.

7 Conclusion

Reading and comprehending (long) texts and complex words are particularly challenging for people with dyslexia. This study explored how two important public sector chatbots, which are based upon textual input and output, function in practice and are experienced by young adults with dyslexia. The usability test revealed that both chatbots in many cases had problems understanding misspelled queries, produced too much and fragmentary text, and that special terms were difficult to comprehend. It seems like the combination of impaired reading and writing skills and self-esteem heavily resulted in many users preferring to talk to an advisor rather than communicating with the chatbots.

Understanding public information and services is important for the democratic rights and responsibilities for all citizens. Some of the challenges for people with dyslexia are shared with the general public, but their problems with reading and comprehension are more severe. The design suggestions provided here may help people with dyslexia, while improving the accessibility for other types of users.

Some results from this study are contradictory. People with dyslexia seem to prefer to talk with a person. However, writing to a chatbot can be more comfortable because nobody will pay attention to spelling errors and there will be no stigma. There is a need for more research on how chatbots function in practice for this cohort, but also for various other user groups, such as non-native speakers, people with impaired vision, other neurodiverse citizens, or elderly people.

Acknowledgments. The authors wish to thank the participants for their time and effort and Dyslexia Norway for helping with recruitment.

Disclosure of Interests.   The authors have no competing interests to declare that are relevant to the content of this article.

References

1. Simonsen, L., et al.: "I'm disabled and married to a foreign single mother": public service chatbot's advice on citizens' complex lives. In: Hofman, S., et al. (eds.) Electronic Participation 2020, pp. 133–146. Springer, Cham (2020). https://doi.org/10.1007/978-3-030-58141-1_11

2. Simonsen, T.: Digitalisering i NAV [Digitization in NAV]. https://slidetodoc.com/digitalisering-i-nav-21-05-19-terese-simonsen/. Accessed 4 Dec 2023

3. Ministry of Children and Equality: Norge universelt utformet 2025: Regjeringens handlingsplan for universell utforming og økt tilgjengelighet 2009–2013 (Norway universally designed 2025: The government's action plan for universal design increased accessibility 2009–2013). Barne-og likestillingsdepartementet, Oslo (2009)

4. Ministry of Culture: Act relating to equality and a prohibition against discrimination (Equality and Anti-Discrimination Act). https://lovdata.no/dokument/NLE/lov/2017-06-16-51. Accessed 10 Dec 2023
5. Brandtzaeg, P., Følstad, A.: Chatbots: changing user needs and motivations. Interactions **25**(5), 38–43 (2018)
6. Brandtzaeg, P.B., Følstad, A.: Why people use chatbots. In: Kompatsiaris, I., et al. (eds.) Internet Science 2017, pp. 377–392. Springer, Cham (2017). https://doi.org/10.1007/978-3-319-70284-1_30
7. Luger, E., Sellen, A.: "Like having a really bad PA": the gulf between user expectation and experience of conversational agents. In: Kaye, J., et al. (eds.) CHI Conference on Human Factors in Computing Systems 2016, pp. 5286–5297. ACM, San Jose (2016)
8. Verne, G.B., Steinstø, T., Simonsen, L., Bratteteig, T.: How can I help you? A chatbot's answers to citizens' information needs. Scand. J. Inf. Syst. **34**(22), Article 7 (2022)
9. Verne, G.: Giving help or information?: A human advisor and a chatbot answers requests from citizens. In: 21st European Conference on Computer-Supported Cooperative Work 2023, pp. 1–16. European Society for Socially Embedded Technologies (EUSSET), [s.l.] (2023)
10. Snowling, M.J., Hulme, C., Nation, K.: Defining and understanding dyslexia: past, present and future. Oxf. Rev. Educ. **46**(4), 501–513 (2020)
11. Berget, G., Sandnes, F.E.: Searching databases without query-building aids: Implications for dyslexic users. Inf. Res. **20**(4), paper 689 (2015)
12. Berget, G., Sandnes, F.E.: Do autocomplete functions reduce the impact of dyslexia on information-searching behavior?: The case of Google. J. Am. Soc. Inf. Sci. **67**(10), 2320–2328 (2016)
13. Verne, G.: The winners are those who have used the old paper form: on citizens and automated public services. University of Oslo, Oslo (2015)
14. Adam, M., Wessel, M., Benlian, A.: AI-based chatbots in customer service and their effects on user compliance. Electron. Mark. **31**(2), 427–445 (2021)
15. Kuhail, M.A., Alturki, N., Alramlawi, S., Alhejori, K.: Interacting with educational chatbots: a systematic review. Educ. Inf. Technol. **28**(1), 973–1018 (2023)
16. Brandtzæg, P.B.B., et al.: When the social becomes non-human: young people's perception of social support in chatbots. In: Kitamura, Y., et al. (eds.) CHI Conference on Human Factors in Computing Systems 2021, pp. Article 257. ACM, Yokohama (2021)
17. Laschke, M., et al.: Otherware needs otherness: understanding and designing artificial counterparts. In: Lamas, D., et al. (eds.) Nordic Conference on Human-Computer Interaction: Shaping Experiences, Shaping Society 2020, pp. Article 131. ACM, Tallinn (2020)
18. Wagner, R.K., et al.: The prevalence of dyslexia: a new approach to its estimation. J. Learn. Disabil. **53**(5), 354–365 (2020)
19. Brante, E.W.: 'I don't know what it is to be able to read': how students with dyslexia experience their reading impairment. Support Learn. **28**(2), 79–86 (2013)
20. Fostick, L., Revah, H.: Dyslexia as a multi-deficit disorder: working memory and auditory temporal processing. Acta Physiol. **183**, 19–28 (2018)
21. Nergård-Nilssen, T., Hulme, C.: Developmental dyslexia in adults: behavioural manifestations and cognitive correlates. Dyslexia **20**(3), 191–207 (2014)
22. McCarthy, J.E., Swierenga, S.J.: What we know about dyslexia and Web accessibility: a research review. Univ. Access Inf. Soc. **9**(2), 147–152 (2010)
23. Germanò, E., Gagliano, A., Curatolo, P.: Comorbidity of ADHD and dyslexia. Dev. Neuropsychol. **35**(5), 475–493 (2010)
24. Willcutt, E.G., et al.: Understanding the complex etiologies of developmental disorders: behavioral and molecular genetic approaches. J. Dev. Behav. Pediatr. **31**(7), 533–544 (2010)
25. Swanson, H.L., Hsieh, C.-J.: Reading disabilities in adults: a selective meta-analysis of the literature. Rev. Educ. Res. **79**(4), 1362–1390 (2009)

26. Lithari, E.: Fractured academic identities: dyslexia, secondary education, self-esteem and school experiences. Int. J. Incl. Educ. **23**(3), 280–296 (2019)
27. Novita, S.: Secondary symptoms of dyslexia: a comparison of self-esteem and anxiety profiles of children with and without dyslexia. Eur. J. Spec. Needs Educ. **31**(2), 279–288 (2016)
28. Carawan, L.W., Nalavany, B.A., Jenkins, C.: Emotional experience with dyslexia and self-esteem: the protective role of perceived family support in late adulthood. Aging Ment. Health **20**(3), 284–294 (2016)
29. Berget, G., Sandnes, F.E.: Why textual search interfaces fail: a study of cognitive skills needed to conduct successful queries. Inf. Res. **24**(1), paper 812 (2019)
30. Morris, M.R., et al.: Understanding the needs of searchers with dyslexia. In: Mandryk, R., Hancock, M. (eds.) CHI Conference on Human Factors in Computing Systems 2018, pp. 1–12. ACM, Montreal (2018)
31. Berget, G., Fagernes, S.: "I'm not stupid": attitudes towards adaptation among people with dyslexia. In: Kurosu, M. (eds.) HCI International 2018: Human-Computer Interaction. Theories, Methods and Human Issues 2018. LNCS, vol. 10901, pp. 237–247. Springer, Cham (2018). https://doi.org/10.1007/978-3-319-91238-7_20
32. Berget, G., Fagernes, S.: Reading experiences and reading efficiency among adults with dyslexia: an accessibility study. In: Antona, M., Stephanidis, C. (eds.) HCI International 2021: Universal Access in Human-Computer Interaction. Access to Media, Learning and Assistive Environments 2021, vol. 12769, pp. 221–240. Springer, Cham (2021). https://doi.org/10.1007/978-3-030-78095-1_17
33. Starr, M.S., Rayner, K.: Eye movements during reading: some current controversies. Trends Cogn. Sci. **5**(4), 156–163 (2001)
34. Schwartz-Shea, P., Yanow, D.: Interpretive Research Design: Concepts and Processes. Routledge, New York (2012)
35. Dumas, J.S., Redish, J.C.: A Practical Guide to Usability Testing. Intellect Books, Exeter (1999)
36. Sharp, H., Preece, J., Rogers, Y.: Interaction Design: Beyond Human-Computer Interaction. Wiley, Indianapolis (2019)
37. Roussou, M., et al.: Transformation through provocation? In: Brewster, S., et al. (eds.) CHI Conference on Human Factors in Computing Systems 2019, pp. Paper 627. ACM, Glasgow (2019)
38. Wintersberger, P., Klotz, T., Riener, A.: Tell me more: transparency and time-fillers to optimize chatbots' waiting time experience. In: Lamas, D., et al. (eds.) Nordic Conference on Human-Computer Interaction: Shaping Experiences, Shaping Society 2020, pp. Article 76. ACM, Tallinn (2020)
39. Følstad, A., et al.: Future directions for chatbot research: an interdisciplinary research agenda. Computing **103**(12), 2915–2942 (2021)
40. Paddison, C., Englefield, P.: Applying heuristics to perform a rigorous accessibility inspection in a commercial context. ACM SIGCAPH Comput. Phys. Handicapped **73–74**, 126–133 (2002)
41. Lilleby, A., Marstein, S.: "Chatbot for alle?»: En kvalitativ studie av dyslektikeres opplevelser med chatbot [«Chatbot for all?»: a qualitative study of people with dyslexia and their experiences with chatbot]. University of Oslo, Oslo (2020)

Author Index